Diplomacy and Capitalism

POWER, POLITICS, AND THE WORLD

Series editors: Christopher R. W. Dietrich,
Jennifer Mittelstadt, and Russell Rickford

Power, Politics, and the World showcases new stories in the fields of the history of U.S. foreign relations, international history, and transnational history. The series is motivated by a desire to pose innovative questions of power and hierarchy to the history of the United States and the world. Books published in the series examine a wide range of actors on local, national, and global scales, exploring how they imagined, enacted, or resisted political, cultural, social, economic, legal, and military authority.

A complete list of books in the series
is available from the publisher.

DIPLOMACY AND CAPITALISM

The Political Economy of U.S. Foreign Relations

EDITED BY
Christopher R. W. Dietrich

PENN

UNIVERSITY OF PENNSYLVANIA PRESS

PHILADELPHIA

Published by
University of Pennsylvania Press
Philadelphia, Pennsylvania 19104-4112
www.upenn.edu/pennpress

Printed in the United States of America on acid-free paper
10 9 8 7 6 5 4 3 2 1

Hardcover ISBN 9780812253955
Paperback ISBN 9780812225310
Ebook ISBN 9780812298567

A catalogue record for this book is available from the Library of Congress.

For Vero and Emil

CONTENTS

INTRODUCTION

On Value and Values: Power, Progress, and Inequality in the American Century

Christopher R. W. Dietrich

The U.S. government granted Raytheon Corporation a $50 million munitions control export license for sales to Saudi Arabia in February 1967. The license covered vehicles and weapons, including, most importantly for the company and its client, state-of-the-art surface-to-air Hawk missiles. When the license expired in August, only the missiles had not been delivered. The State Department concluded then that it was in the national interest to approve an extension and thus "not interfere with the orderly implementation of this private American contract with a friendly Arab Government." The rationale connected free enterprise to regional stability, more specifically through the linked provision of military and psychological support for a critical ally. Hawk missiles would be an effective deterrent against United Arab Republic president Gamal Abdel Nasser's "external aggression," Secretary of State Dean Rusk wrote. Given the context of intensified attacks from Yemen, supported by the pan-Arabist government in Cairo—"the hostile UAR presence on Saudi borders"—the State Department believed that to extend the license was to act in the nation's deep interest in Saudi territorial integrity. The sale was equally crucial to reassuring the Saudi government that it had the steadfast support of the United States. "We are interested in doing all we can to maintain close relations with Arab moderates," Rusk told his ambassador in Jeddah.[1]

Rusk made a similar argument to U.S. President Lyndon Baines Johnson a year later. The United States needed to relax the arms sales restrictions it had put into place after the Six-Day War, especially those "affecting the moderate Arab states." Above all, Rusk said, arms sales demonstrated to "Western-oriented

Arab leaders" like King Faisal of Saudi Arabia that they derived "tangible benefit from a policy of close relations with the United States."[2] Again, commerce and diplomacy were intertwined in his analysis. American companies faced stiff competition from British and French arms manufacturers for the growing caches of Saudi oil money. To lose arms sales, one official wrote, would be "a significant set-back for our long-term position of primacy in Saudi Arabia and would have adverse repercussions on our gold-flow difficulties."[3]

The questions of oil diplomacy shaped other domestic political-economic considerations, too. The June 1967 Arab-Israeli War and subsequent Arab oil embargo revealed for many the economic vulnerability of the United States. The threat of oil shortages, higher prices, and what came to be called "the energy crisis" would soon become subjects of intense public scrutiny. Already they were topics of importance among high-placed politicians and officials. The nation faced "the very great need to stimulate the exploration for new petroleum reserves" at home, the governor of Mississippi wrote the president in August 1967.[4] Substantial evidence exists that the United States did just that, as the Department of the Interior approved a number of new programs, including the fast-tracking of leases for offshore oil and even Project Gasbuggy, a $4.7 million joint project of the Atomic Energy Commission, the Bureau of Mines, and the El Paso Natural Gas Company that sought to employ "the first industrial use of a nuclear explosion"—at 4,240 feet below the earth's surface.[5] Such projects revealed that "the petroleum industry was responding both to the need for keeping capital investments at home and to the lessons of the Middle East War," Secretary of the Interior Stewart Udall told Johnson in 1968.[6]

These interlocking discussions occurred in a specific time and place. The late 1960s and early 1970s were a period of transformational change in the global economy, in U.S. relations with the world, and in the regional politics of the Middle East. As in all such moments, the nature of change was deeply contested. The decisions to increase arms sales to Saudi Arabia and reinvigorate American domestic oil production came despite fear of a regional arms race and vigorously posed environmental concerns. The policies warrant close inspection for their particular dynamics, and for the broader context too. The moment was shaped by disenchantment with the Vietnam War, a yawning trade deficit, the threats of dollar depreciation and high inflation, the beginning of deindustrialization, and the familiar fear of dependence on foreign oil.[7] The problems at that particular intersection of political economy and national security took place at a time that seemed to be characterized by the end of the vitality that had driven the United States' ideological and geopolitical Cold War for the previous quarter century.

But the Hawk missile sales are also interesting for their place in a longer narrative of U.S. foreign relations, as revealed by both the secretary of state's and the secretary of the interior's historically charged claims of national interest, national security, and national vulnerability. Even the bare-bones sketch above offers a window into a deeper and longer dimension of U.S. diplomacy in the twentieth century: the history that U.S. foreign relations shares with global capitalism.[8] The points of contact between capitalism and diplomacy, between political economy and national security, have shaped important facets of the development of U.S. foreign relations since independence, and indeed even before. Historians and other scholars have long recognized this. Diplomacy and the forces of capitalism have never been fully separate in the histories of war, territorial and economic expansion, policy planning and implementation, employment and unemployment, modernization and development, production and consumption, transportation and infrastructure, or rights and sovereignty—even if they are sometimes treated as such.[9] Capitalism and diplomacy continually evolved together at different levels of global, national, and local transformations. Wealth and power structured each other and helped create important policies, institutions, and laws in and out of the United States.

The essays in this volume begin by assuming the basic importance of looking at events through the overlapping lenses of political economy and diplomacy, noting that those terms themselves are necessary shorthand for the many complex policies formed at the intersection of profit and power. In their critical focus on U.S. economic statecraft in the twentieth century, each chapter examines important tensions and motivations within the national and international landscapes of diplomacy and capitalism. Individual stories ask and answer broader questions: As the United States became more powerful and processes of trade, investment, and development intensified in the twentieth century, how did the relationship between capitalism and diplomacy change over time? What were the causes and consequences of the different state and corporate associations? Who set, shaped, limited, and dissented to policy? What were their ideologies and rationales? How did outcomes line up with expectations?

* * *

Several broad themes emerge from the authors' investigations into these questions. This introduction focuses on three: power, progress, and inequality.

The interplay of the three themes, in turn, captures some of the importance of this book's new narratives in the overlapping histories of capitalism and U.S. foreign relations.

The first theme, power, builds from a basic premise shared by U.S. decision makers throughout the twentieth century, namely that the growth of American-led business was a crucial component of the nation's rise to greatness. Diplomats worked to claim a degree of private economic control over foreign resources, land, and people for businesses owned by U.S. citizens. Economic and business expansion, from their perspective, was not only or even principally about the pursuit of profits for those specific companies. It was about creating a world—through trade, law, or commodity exploitation—in which the United States could thrive, first as a great power and then as a superpower.[10] Wealth and power were mutually constitutive according to this perspective. The most obvious examples of this may be the well-studied link drawn between foreign markets and domestic economic growth and political stability, from Open Door diplomacy at the turn of the twentieth century to globalization at the turn of the twenty-first.[11] But power took many shapes and forms at the nexus of capitalism and diplomacy. Like the naked use of military force or its threat, capital in the form of aid and investment was also an arm of national power that responded to dynamic political and ideological motivations.[12] American policymakers used economic diplomacy to court allies and exploit weaknesses of adversaries, even as many argued that tighter global economic integration along capitalist lines lessened the likelihood of interstate conflict.[13]

Historians who write about power also emphasize the fact that U.S. diplomats and business leaders shared cultural attitudes premised on a celebration of individualism, nation-building, and the free market as neutral or universal values.[14] Indeed, arguments for the protection of private capital consistently defeated or marginalized those about the expansion of self-determination in the international politics of the twentieth century.[15] To recognize this influence is also to understand that the ideology of capitalism formed part of the base from which national power grew. Debates about the benefits of capitalism as a means to order U.S. and international society reveal the influence of the assumption that capitalism—not fascism, socialism, or other grand doctrines—was the superior means to organize the economic affairs of states and their people.[16] Policymakers and business executives often made that point through depoliticized arguments about expertise or justifications for free enterprise.[17] Such use of language and ideology to shore up the power of the United States occurred at home and abroad.[18] Capitalist ideology developed in support of the further expansion of U.S. power in the world.

To take up the second theme, progress, U.S. leaders understood the expansion of national power in the world as means to human development. For many, there was no insoluble tension between power and progress. Rather, although it was accepted that capitalist pursuits might sometimes be cynically self-serving, most U.S. leaders in business and government held faith in the virtues of spreading their brands and their beliefs. As business historians and historians of development have long argued, erstwhile profit makers and modernizers were true believers in the righteousness of their different projects, much in the same way many economists and lawyers believed that the sanctity of private property and the protection of investments made for a more equitable and better world.[19] The expansion of American power was crucial, accordingly, to the material *and* moral well-being of the United States *and* its allies. From this perspective, capitalist connections not only sustained democratic values but established important alliances that protected others in a threatening world.[20] Those alliances extended to themes well beyond the discussions of national security that dominated foreign policy at its highest levels. In U.S. foreign relations, then, the emphasis on progress reveals that the bond between state and market—between the public and private—was less one of opposition and more one of perceived common interest.[21] Experts in agriculture, finance, industry, and economic planning were politically committed to alleviating poverty and designed projects with the benevolent ends of economic growth and human security in mind.[22]

Power and progress thus overlapped in many ways at the international, regional, national, and local levels. One shared sensibility became folded into American minds throughout the twentieth century: a pursuit for political-economic success narratives characterized U.S. relations with industrialized Europe and Asia, as well as with the so-called less developed nations. This pursuit was also a historical interpretation that framed different problems and anticipated their resolutions. Capitalism and diplomacy drew deeply from a script of market-driven mass industrialization and market-sanctioned security that was often totalizing in its attempt to transform other societies.[23] In preaching the virtues of privately led commerce and investment, government officials often found political and intellectual allies among large corporations, foundations, and other transnational organizations.[24] As models that could be deployed at later dates in other settings, development projects were a form of soft power meant to underscore the fruits of an alliance with the United States, before and after but especially during the Cold War.[25] This again reflected the fundamental ideological assumption that capitalism was the superior means with which to organize the United States' and the world's economy. Such a view often led U.S. policymakers to tout their own expertise and dismiss local actors and their knowledge.[26]

Third and relatedly, even as many Americans and others believed the advancement of U.S. power was beneficial to the global order, the problems of inequality and the abuse of power stand out in histories of capitalism and diplomacy. Americans employed a language of capitalism throughout the twentieth century that linked it to the provision of social welfare and the protection of freedom and democracy.[27] But quite often the infrastructures of capitalism and practice of diplomacy revealed contradictions to this line of reasoning. The drive to project capitalism abroad and promote economic growth at home resulted in disparities that were formal and informal, small-scale and large-scale. (U.S. diplomacy also resulted in many cases in the suppression of self-determination or the hollowing of sovereignty.)[28]

An emphasis on inequality returns to the assumption that private capital was useful as leverage for official diplomacy, and vice versa. That focus also reminds historians that the development of modern industrialism and an energy-intensive world of capitalism and diplomacy led to systems in which some actors benefitted greatly while others, often at the source of raw material or agricultural production, faced economic destabilization and environmental degradation.[29] In a number of cases, the infusion of private investment, aid, or development expertise further enriched the haves, impoverished the have-nots, and hardened long-running inequalities. In such processes, the will of an elite minority was often forced on a recalcitrant majority; capitalism and diplomacy together brought not opportunity but dispossession. Historians have written lucidly about how capitalist expansion informed and rationalized policies meant to help assert or shore up U.S. control and, in many cases, have noted how diplomacy broke the declared bond between the free market and self-determination.[30]

The United States' diplomatic and capitalist expansion meant coercion in many cases—as historians of race, labor, gender, immigration, and globalization have shown—and often framed coercion as imposing necessary discipline on irrational or disorderly actors.[31] Inequality was just as often seen as an unfortunate by-product. But as a number of the essays here argue, inequality was not entirely unintended. Instead it was inherent to many instances of diplomacy in the twentieth century.[32] In this sense, the United States was heir to the imperial mantle of European colonialism, even if it consistently emphasized its status as a postcolonial power.[33] The joint expansion of U.S. power and capitalist exploitation became linked in many peoples' minds, and that link fueled local, national, and international dissent.[34] In the same way that modernizers sought out success stories, then, other U.S. leaders looked at economic nationalism as a dangerous threat to capital investment and national security.[35]

In examining specific cases in which inequality, progress, and power intersected, the essays that follow take in hand some of the immensity of the twentieth-century history of U.S. capitalism and diplomacy. They seek to explain the effects of ideas, interests, and policies at distinct moments in the history of U.S. foreign relations. In doing so, they reveal that capitalism and diplomacy never followed single or simple agendas. Yet the themes of power, progress, and inequality remain important throughout, in the same way that none of these histories can be divorced from the broader context of the global rise of liberal capitalism, mass production and consumption, and the division of labor that has taken place since early in the twentieth century. In many cases, influential actors in the United States and the world understood capitalist growth as beneficial to their own and the national interest. In others, they sought the humanitarian goals of material and social welfare. In other cases, the technical language of international law and economic expertise echoed the oppressive hierarchies of colonialism. In still others, the assumptions of American superiority and the inequalities of capitalist relationships made critiques of capitalism and power compelling to a wide variety of actors inside and outside the United States.

* * *

In each case, individuals charted their own courses as they dealt in and with diplomacy and capitalism. The careful reconstruction of specific histories of power, progress, and inequality reveals the difficulties people faced in making coherent or unified policies. In describing their challenges and choices, the analyses that follow provide insight into the nature and form of the crucial historical links between capitalism and diplomacy. These scholars' discussions, briefly summarized here, thus perform the vital public service of preserving past relationships of American wealth and power.

Max Paul Friedman excavates the central debates about the potential of U.S. capitalism for the creation of Latin American wealth in Chapter 1. Latin American governments and their U.S. counterparts consistently discussed the roles and rights of creditors and borrowers in the early twentieth century. For many Latin Americans, foreign investment promised development that, on closer scrutiny, seemed hollow. Worse, capital investment held the danger of stealing away sovereignty. It led to the extraction of resources and profits and, in some cases, resulted in political-economic and military intervention. The most important U.S. policymakers showed a surface sympathy for Latin American sovereignty, Friedman says, but ultimately defended intervention on the grounds that the United States needed to protect the "rights" of its citizens who invested abroad. Investment begat invasion in a recurrence that mirrored European colonialism. Latin American presidents, diplomats, and lawyers all pushed back against the economic and legal principles of intervention. Mexico and Argentina, in particular, created what the Nicaraguan poet Rubén Darío called in 1911 "the counterweight to Yankee power." In forging transnational intellectual links and elaborating international to protect their nations from the more predatory powers of capital, they created new terms for investment. For reasons that were as self-interested as they were idealistic, the U.S. government concluded that coercion hurt investments in the long run.

The fact that the Latin American nations eventually forced the United States to voice its adherence to a basic standard of nonintervention points to changing norms in international diplomacy. But respect for sovereignty was often rhetorical. Joseph Fronczak examines the "dirty work" that occurred behind the scenes of economic expansion in Chapter 2. Just as the needs of capitalists during the Second Industrial Revolution impelled formal imperialism, he argues, the United States remade capitalism as a global infrastructure of extraction, production, finance, and loans. The nation undertook this global coordination through specific steps, many of which required blunt force, and Fronczak traces that force through the life itinerary of U.S. marine Smedley Butler and his exploits in Cuba, the Philippines, China, Panama, and Nicaragua. Expansion and violence—markets and marines—are best appreciated in the same intellectual framework. The looting of Peking, the Boxer Protocol of 1901, and the establishment of corvée labor and U.S.-managed customs houses in the Caribbean should be understood as parts of a larger "financial appropriation" of the global economy. Cold and technical terms like "market expansion" or "the first wave of globalization" should not mask the coercion that was the means of their attainment.

One of Smedley Butler's outposts of coercive capitalism was Haiti, where Alec Hickmott sets Chapter 3. He examines the relationship between Haiti's race-conscious political populism and the United States' rural development efforts through the experience of the African American economist and U.S. government official Giles Hubert. Although the U.S. occupation of Haiti ended seven years before the first U.S.-Haiti agricultural initiative, a rubber plantation to aid the Allied war effort founded in 1941, Hubert's life reveals how the occupation shaped ongoing U.S. political and economic influence. But Hickmott also notes an important difference: Hubert and others sought to use development initiatives to reinforce Haitian sovereignty, democracy, and prosperity. Interestingly, the means by which they sought rural progress emerged out of both historically black colleges and universities and the New Deal state, in particular the Farm Security Administration. While Hubert believed in the potential of an empowered government to transform economic life, he was also viscerally aware of the ways that racism and economic inequality walked hand in hand. Moreover, he identified farm tenancy and rural poverty as problems faced not only in Haiti but also in the rural south of the United States. Hubert's state-sponsored development projects revealed a sensitivity to those dualisms as he moved from the Jim Crow South to postoccupation Haiti.

In Chapter 4, Jason Scott Smith places state-driven development into the broader context of the United States' project to generate economic growth by forging a global economy that was friendly to American corporations. In a close study of multinational firms in Venezuela and Brazil in the 1950s, he examines the forms by which Washington exported capitalism through infrastructure projects. Most importantly, the spread of American-style capitalism drew on a belief in the mutually beneficial relationship between private profits and public well-being, as embodied by Nelson Rockefeller's International Basic Economy Corporation. Smith argues that this group and others expanded the New Deal framework of government-led capitalist growth by linking public credit for infrastructure to private investment opportunities. Rockefeller—like Hubert, Butler, and Rubén Darío—was thus concerned with the moral character of capitalism. Unlike the others, he consistently argued that corporations improved peoples' lives. At the same time, the problems with tunnels in Brazil and Venezuela revealed limits to the good intentions of his "technocratic liberalism."

In Chapter 5, Erum Khalid Sattar also focuses on the questions of infrastructure in the postwar era. She shifts our gaze from Latin America to South Asia, from roads and farms to water, and from investment to international law. The case of the Indus River valley reveals that the problem of development and law was also a problem of territorial control. A close reading of the famous modernizer David Lilienthal's analyses of South Asia and the disputed

Kashmir region for *Collier's* magazine reveals the severe obstacles independence posed for irrigation systems built in the colonial era. Lilienthal and others hoped that American-led cooperation on water management could create "harmony and increased prosperity" in a region in which Partition had torn apart the "natural" link between the Indus River's headwaters and its basin. Managed by engineers, the productive wealth drawn out of fertile land would in turn foment greater trust and closer relations between Indian and Pakistan. What Lilienthal described as "a feasible engineering and business problem" could thus overcome the postcolonial and religious schism on the subcontinent. His hopes did not come to pass, as Sattar writes, and the Indus Waters Treaty of 1960, which the World Bank helped negotiate, led to greater dependence in both states on foreign investment.

The history of Cold War diplomacy is in part the history of ideological promotion of capitalism by the U.S. government, as alluded to in the cases of the Indus River and Latin American tunnel building. In Chapter 6, Giulia Crisanti examines U.S. information and propaganda strategies in Italy during the early Cold War. In a close reading of films from the remarkable audiovisual library of the U.S. Information Service found in the Trieste State Archive, she analyzes how arguments about productivity served as an instrument of foreign policy. Productivity and democracy were presented as parallel and mutually constitutive values of American-led postwar capitalism. They were not only economic principles but also indicators of proper social behavior. Short films produced in the late 1940s and early 1950s, like *Worker in Detroit* and *Antioch College*, worked to convince Italians that the social, cultural, and political-economic model offered by the United States was a means to prosperity far superior to the Communist alternative.

What exactly did the United States have to offer its allies? As Nicole Sackley explains in Chapter 7, Hubert Humphrey, Murray Lincoln, and others inserted cooperatives into the 1961 Foreign Assistance Act as a practical means to support the "vital role of free enterprise" in ordering global affairs. Cooperatives were useful as diplomacy in many ways. They helped keep down the cost of foreign aid and, according to boosters like the Cooperative League of the United States of America or the National Rural Electric Cooperative Association, they taught democratic and capitalist principles to groups in the Third World that were especially susceptible to communism. Supporters of the cooperative movement in the United States argued that cooperatives promoted a "superior face of American capitalism," because they avoided the pitfall of bigness and overweening power that defined both corporate capitalism and state control. Sackley's analysis of Indian economic planning reveals the potential role envisioned for Nationwide Insurance, credit unions, and other U.S. cooperatives, in particular in confronting that nation's ongoing food crisis.

American policymakers claimed that economic diplomacy in the form of U.S. assistance would lead to greater productivity, which would in turn bring about not only lower production costs and higher profits, but also better wages and more social and political stability. In Chapter 8, Jennifer Miller analyzes productivity programming conducted by U.S. policymakers and organizations like the Ford Foundation in Japan. For them and their Japanese counterparts, the purpose was nothing short of the "mental and psychological transformation" of postwar Japan. The U.S.-supported Japan Productivity Center meant to teach labor unions—the more political of which were depicted as deviant, selfish, or irrational—that economic health relied on their apolitical acquiescence to the capitalist hierarchy. Supported by American management consultants like Peter Drucker and W. S. Landes, the psychological emphasis on capitalist cooperation over class confrontation became a crucial tool of U.S. diplomacy in Japan. As the Japanese "miracle" became a model in the 1960s, the transformation of its entrepreneurial vision itself became a regional export.

If films, cooperatives, consultants, and foreign government organizations held considerable influence in diplomacy, so too did private corporations. As Alanna O'Malley writes in Chapter 9, the influence of corporations became one of the more controversial aspects of diplomacy in the decolonizing international community. Private finance played an active role in shaping U.S. policy toward decolonization and economic development in Central Africa. In so doing it also preserved vestiges of colonial power. American and other Western companies even strengthened the preexisting colonial financial architecture, in this case through their support of the Anglo-American Corporation of South Africa and its director, the South African tycoon Harry Oppenheimer. A number of U.S. officials and institutions—including from the Export-Import Bank and the Eisenhower and Kennedy administrations, as well as U.S.-based foundations and diamond companies—shared a stake in maintaining the profitability of Oppenheimer's networks of finance and mining. In great part because of reliance on South African gold to preserve the dollar-based international financial system, they worked to enlarge the role of private finance in Central Africa. The Global South nations sought to regulate these activities through the United Nations, focusing on the need to limit the power of industrial and business elites. In the process, groups like the UN Department of Economic Affairs and regional economic commissions used the politically charged question of private investment and resource control to assert new claims about the meaning of decolonization and economic sovereignty.

Even as it was often connected to the problems of inequality amid decolonization, American capital investment was seen by some as liberating. Abou Bamba focuses on the life of Ivorian statesman Félix Houphouët-Boigny in Chapter 10. The diplomat mobilized Cold War sentiment in the United States to advance his agenda of courting American capital and converting Ivory Coast into the "economic miracle" of West Africa. Here the link between decolonization and capitalism is different from that of O'Malley or Sattar. Not only did Houphouët-Boigny and others seek to reduce Ivorian dependence on their former French rulers, they also spearheaded a public relations campaign in the United States to attract foreign investment. The nation would be a good investment for Americans for many reasons. French colonial rulers had already created an economic infrastructure through commercial farming and agronomic research that inserted the territory into the world capitalist economy before independence. Ivory Coast also marketed its mobilization of science for productivity as an example of successful modernization. In targeting U.S. investment from the 1960s to the 1980s, Ivorians worked closely with American public relations experts to lobby for increased official aid and private investment in agriculture and, increasingly, in the growing energy and industrial sectors. Other African nations did the same, evidence that they collectively believed in the benefits offered by a closer association with the United States.

That vision subscribed to a market ideology that became prevalent in the late Cold War. In Chapter 11, Jayita Sarkar examines the role of "the boys from Bechtel" in the making of U.S. foreign relations in the early 1980s. She notes in particular how the U.S. nuclear energy industry sought to rehabilitate itself as a viable energy alternative in the wake of the energy crisis, high energy prices, and the 1979 Three Mile Island accident. It did so by working to reduce government oversight of the industry as part of Ronald Reagan's energy policy task force. That intense lobbying began in the 1950s with a partnership between the firms that built nuclear reactors and the Export-Import Bank, which points to the historical dependence of the industry on federal patronage. Economic statecraft, Sarkar says, is a crucial lens by which to add to questions of deterrence and arms control if we wish to understand the politics and policies of nuclear nonproliferation. At the same time that social movements criticized nuclear power and nuclear weapons, the U.S. government supported the nation's business leaders as they looked abroad for markets.

* * *

What is at stake for historians of capitalism and of U.S. foreign relations in these essays? In 1902, John Hobson criticized the growth of economic nationalism in Europe for assuming "the antagonism of nations as an all-important and final fact." For him, nationalism was the most dangerous factor of modern politics and the "chief motive for war." At the root of this malfeasance were "economic driving forces" that halted the evolution of social consciousness at national borders, caused ever greater antagonism, and ultimately acted to the detriment of national and international interest. For Hobson, such a cut-rate understanding of life was too limiting. And it was these very limits, occurring as they did amid the transformative global interconnections of the late Industrial Revolution, that would most perplex "the future historian."[36]

The historians in this volume would likely find much with which to disagree when reading Hobson. But they would concur that the shared history of U.S. diplomacy and capitalism is about much more than a balance sheet. Understanding the events that follow can be perplexing because they are about understanding value—and values—in twentieth-century U.S. foreign relations. Historians have argued and will continue to argue over diplomacy and its relation to political economy. Yet one important quality emerges from the essays as a whole, which is related to another of Hobson's insights: to understand the interrelated dimensions of capitalism and diplomacy in a period marked by American expansion and hegemony, to describe the features of particular episodes, it is necessary for historians to work on multiple scales. The stories recounted here move among national actors, to be sure, but also global and local ones. Such a multifarious perspective allows for a closer understanding of different strategies. In turn, it draws scholars' attention not only to the reach and grasp of American diplomacy but also to its limits. Historians who focus on different levels of analysis can learn a great deal from each other.

In the same way, histories of American diplomacy and American capitalism enrich each other. A great terrain of possibilities—those traveled and those foreclosed—existed in the past. The yoked histories of capitalism and diplomacy, like all history, evade easy labels and are marked as much by contingency and chaos as by intention. Yet even as the chapters in this book emphasize individual human agency and specific political-economic struggle, a number of patterns and themes emerge: growth, trade, investment, development, productivity, public relations, and infrastructure, to name a few. Most crucially, the book helps us begin to chart the parallel growth of global capitalism and American power in the twentieth century. These expansionary forces coexisted and interacted in different ways. To explore their origins, formation, and consequences—to examine power, progress, and inequality in that shared history—is well worth our time today.

CHAPTER 1

Investment and Invasion: The Clash Between Capitalism and State Sovereignty in Latin America, 1903–1936

Max Paul Friedman

One way to understand U.S. relations with Latin America in the first third of the twentieth century is as a series of clashes over the relationship between international capitalism and state sovereignty, at a time when there was a close link between investment and invasion. Ever since the arrival of the Spanish and Portuguese colonizers, foreigners have engaged in the extraction of wealth and resources from what Eduardo Galeano called the open veins of Latin America.[1] From independence until today, the arteries infusing capital from the world's major industrial powers into Latin America were an equally vital element of the same circulatory system: investment poured in, profits and commodities poured out. Political and military intervention followed the pathways of those same capital flows. Where investment capital pooled, sites of conflict erupted, resulting in the literal spilling of blood. From the Pastry War of 1838, when a French squadron blockaded Mexican ports, to the shelling of Venezuelan port cities by a joint Anglo-Italo-German naval force in 1902 to the Marine landings on Caribbean beaches in the 1910s and 1920s, gunboat diplomacy to force the repayment of debts was a norm for Europeans and North Americans. "Between 1870 and 1913," a team of scholars calculated, "defaulting governments ran a forty-percent chance of facing foreign intervention via blockades or, more commonly, via the imposition of foreign control over their domestic finances under the *threat* of blockade."[2]

Escalating U.S. intervention in the Caribbean in this era was driven by a combination of financial interest, geopolitical rivalry, and an ideology that combined faith in progress with a pronounced racial hierarchy. Sometimes this took the form of direct protection of U.S. investments from peril or diminished profit when nationalists came to power and renegotiated the sweetheart concessions made by their positivist predecessors, or threatened to do so. Other times, the Marines landed to ensure repayment of massive loans made by J.P. Morgan, National City Bank, Brown Brothers, and other major banking houses, especially through the innovation of customs receiverships that redirected national income from taxes on imports and exports, the principal source of revenue for most small countries, from national development and patronage networks to foreign investors. A strategic element entered into Washington's calculations when European lenders were prominent, because their similar conduct was deemed intolerable under the Roosevelt corollary to the Monroe Doctrine. The Monroe Doctrine, an early assertion of U.S. primacy in the Western Hemisphere, held that Europeans should not extend their political systems to independent countries in the Americas. Theodore Roosevelt's corollary was the claim that in order to forestall European gunboat diplomacy—the use of force to collect debts—the United States would unilaterally intervene in Latin American countries at will. Latin American complaints and proposed alternatives were discounted in part because they came from "beneath the United States," from people deemed inherently inferior.[3]

This essay focuses on the clashing visions of international capitalism in the first third of the twentieth century by U.S. and Latin American officials, who, conferring in the shadow of the gunboats, diverged in their understanding of the role of foreign capital, the rights of creditors and borrowers, and the appropriate relationship between foreign investment and the state. Their debates and the changes to policy and practice they wrought reflect this volume's theme that, as Christopher Dietrich writes in the introduction, "diplomacy and the forces of capitalism . . . have continually evolved together and shaped each other at different levels of global, national, and local transformations."[4] Theodore Roosevelt, Woodrow Wilson, Elihu Root, and other U.S. officials with deep understanding of economics and international affairs spoke simultaneously of the need to protect U.S. investments and of the need for a better approach to Latin America. Regardless of their sensitivity to Latin American sovereign rights, these officials defended intervention in the region on the articulated principle that investor and creditor rights demanded it. The United States was not a monolith, and the two leading political parties differed somewhat in their approach to capitalism. The laissez-faire era of the late nineteenth century gave way under early-twentieth-century Republican presidents Roosevelt and Taft to modest Progressive regulation of the market and some restrictions on powerful corporations. The parties and their standard-bearers expressed differences on foreign investment and military intervention, at least rhetorically, but in practice, the distinction weakened at the water's edge. Woodrow Wilson, a Democrat, denounced his Republican predecessors for intervening militarily in Latin America—and then outdid them in the number of interventions he ordered. Republican presidential candidate Warren G. Harding then attacked Wilson's Democratic administration for its "rape of Haiti," where, he claimed, he would not write "a constitution for helpless neighbors in the West Indies and jam it down their throats at the point of bayonets borne by U.S. Marines."[5] Once in office, he did not end the occupation. Leading U.S. officials in this era were united in heeding the principle that investment may call for invasion when the national interest demanded it. As Dietrich writes, "U.S. decision makers understood the growth of American-led business as a crucial component of its national power in the twentieth century. American diplomacy often worked to claim a degree of private economic control over foreign resources, land, and people for businesses owned by citizens. Capitalist expansion, from this perspective, was not only or even principally about the pursuit of profits. It was about creating a world—often through trade, law, or commodity exploitation—in which the United States could thrive, first as a great power and then as a superpower."[6]

Against this trend, Latin American leaders such as Argentine president Hipólito Yrigoyen and Mexican president Venustiano Carranza and influential diplomats such as Carlos Calvo and Luis María Drago of Argentina and Isidro Fabela and José Manuel Puig Casauranc of Mexico, promoted new rules of the road for international capitalism designed to change the terms under which foreign capital was linked to foreign state power. They aimed to protect debtor nations from the hazards to their sovereignty posed by their reliance on foreign investment—capital that was simultaneously essential to their development and the chief menace to their independence. It would take decades of effort and a sea change in international economic conditions—the global crisis of the Great Depression—for them to achieve most of their goals.

The surprising degree to which their ideas acquired purchase in the inter-American system is significant for debates over a diffusionist model that emphasize North-South transmission of ideas, as well as for understanding how a disproportionately powerful state can be hemmed in by the concerted efforts of weaker states that find effective venues and circumstances in which to advance their claims.

* * *

Argentine thinkers had been wrestling for some time with the need to preserve inflows of foreign capital while protecting weaker Latin American states from the power of the investors' home governments when disputes arose. Long dependent on British capital, Argentina seemed vulnerable, even as its export-led growth made it seem on the cusp of acquiring the status of a great power in the early twentieth century. This paradoxical condition—an acute sense of vulnerability combined with ambition to be treated as the equal of the world's leading states—provided the context in which Argentines would assert their standing to create or interpret international norms and to challenge those coming from the global North and increasingly the United States. Two of Argentina's best-known diplomats, Carlos Calvo (1824–1906) and Luis María Drago (1859–1921), would come to promote formal doctrines forbidding gunboat diplomacy. As early as the 1860s, Calvo began to campaign for an absolute prohibition on diplomatic or military intervention for debt collection. His *Le droit international théorique et pratique* (Theoretical and Practical International Law, 1868) challenged extraterritoriality, the principle by which European powers and the United States held that their nationals living in "backward" countries were subject to their own laws. This claim that "national law" (i.e., the law in one's country of citizenship) superseded "domicile law" (i.e., the law in one's country of residence) was a "juridical fiction" for Calvo. Instead, he insisted, disputes must be resolved through the courts of the country in which the business took place.[7]

Although the Calvo doctrine did not find formal acceptance in international law, and D. R. Shea's major study went so far as to claim that Calvo's ideas had no impact and were effectively "dead," Argentine diplomats pressed for the adoption of new norms to constrain the great powers in international venues.[8] In 1889, U.S. secretary of state James Blaine launched the First Pan-American Conference to try to create a customs union and system of arbitration in Latin America, both under U.S. leadership. This was the first of many meetings that would create the formal machinery of the inter-American system, what eventually became the Organization of American States in 1948. At the first meeting, held in Washington in 1889–1890, the Argentine delegation was successful in rallying Latin American opposition to block the U.S. projects.[9] At the Second Pan-American Conference in 1902–1903, Argentina submitted a version of the Calvo doctrine, prohibiting extraterritorial intervention (diplomatic or military) to resolve pecuniary disputes and holding that natives and foreigners were equal before the law.

During the Venezuela crisis of 1902–1903, Foreign Minister Drago wrote a message to the Roosevelt administration calling for an absolute prohibition on military intervention in "the territory of American nations."[10] Roosevelt ignored him. While belatedly objecting to European intervention, President Roosevelt claimed a special U.S. right to intervene. The United States, he declared, must exercise "international police power" in the hemisphere, in what came to be known as the Roosevelt corollary to the Monroe Doctrine. The enduring image was of the hemispheric policeman, but it should have been of an armed debt collector. Roosevelt explained the need for intervention with a countercase: "If a nation shows that it knows how to act with reasonable efficiency and decency in social and political matters, if it keeps order *and pays its obligations*, it need fear no interference from the United States."[11] The converse was the unspoken but unmistakable warning: Falling into arrears was good reason for fear.

Drago made the opposite argument in the note he asked his minister in Washington, Martín García Mérou, to deliver to Roosevelt. Debt default led to such grave consequences in loss of prestige and denial of access to future credit that there was no need for foreign intervention to aggravate "the transitory calamities of insolvency," he said. Public debts and the obligations to repay them "are in no way divested of value because the collection cannot be carried out in practice by way of force." He offered the case of Argentina's payments to European creditors, twice suspended when lengthy nineteenth-century crises made it impossible to stay on schedule, and resumed once circumstances permitted. "Now we have the most cordial relations with all of them," Drago concluded.[12] He could have added that the investors continued to profit handsomely from Argentina's growth.

The State Department's solicitor, William L. Penfield, wrote a stern defense of gunboat diplomacy in response. Drago's "ingenious" paper showed "much art and skill in persuasive and insinuating appeals," he admitted. But if adopted, it would "result in the sacrifice of the interests and of the right to justice, of those enterprising Americans who have invested large sums in the development of the resources of Central and South America." Even worse, it "would forever stop the United States from resorting to armed intervention for the protection of its vast and growing interests in the Latin-American States."[13] Investment required reserving the right to invade.

Latin American opposition to gunboat diplomacy was increasingly focused on the United States, because after 1903 the United States was increasingly responsible for gunboat diplomacy in the circum-Caribbean. The Roosevelt corollary followed the taking of Panama and then was made flesh by interventions in Cuba (1906) and the Dominican Republic (1905), where the United States set up a customs receivership to ensure the House of Morgan would be first in line for any government revenues. William Howard Taft continued the practice, extending customs receiverships to Haiti and Honduras, and gave rise to the term "dollar diplomacy" by telling Congress he was "substituting dollars for bullets." But he soon sent bullets after the dollars, dispatching troops to Nicaragua in 1909 and 1912 to thwart rebels opposed to U.S. loans and to enforce a customs receivership. This was "an assault on the sovereignty of an independent republic," the influential Mexican foreign affairs expert and advisor to Mexican presidents Isidro Fabela would later explain, because dollar diplomacy "consisted of lending money to poor and weak countries by diplomatic force, in order later to collect by force of arms."[14] U.S. officials claimed that the interventions were necessary for the sake of preserving stability. The U.S. military governor of Cuba, General Leonard Wood, summed up the underlying policy in a sentence: "When people ask me what I mean by stable government, I tell them, 'money at six percent.'"[15]

These policies drew fire from across the region.[16] To try to improve the U.S. image, Secretary Root in 1906 undertook a tour to reassure Latin Americans. "We neither claim nor desire any rights or privileges or powers that we do not freely concede to every American Republic," Root declared, overlooking the right of "international police power" Roosevelt had arrogated exclusively to the United States.[17] (At a speech for U.S. and British expatriates at Prince George's Hall in Buenos Aires, Root was more direct about his broader purposes: "I should like to see the great surplus capital which we are accumulating in the United States turn southwards."[18] He was already doing his part; on his previous stop he signed a contract in Brazil that replaced Argentine flour imports with U.S. flour imports.[19]) Former foreign minister Drago tried to pin Root down at a banquet for six hundred guests at the Teatro Colón: could the prohibition against "the forcible collection of public debts by European nations" become as much a "principle of American diplomacy" as was the Monroe Doctrine? Root's reply contained key weasel words: "the United States of America has never deemed it to be suitable that she should use her army and navy for the collection of *ordinary contract debts* of foreign governments to her citizens."[20] This only nodded toward the Drago doctrine, because the specification of "ordinary contract debts" excluded the major category of public debt, that is, loans to governments in the form of bonds, which had been the issue at stake in both the Venezuelan and Dominican crises. Soon Root acknowledged more clearly that nothing had changed. In response to a Panamanian request for a clarification of U.S. policy, Root stated that "the United States possesses the inherent right to protect its property and enforce its rights wherever located and wherever imperiled."[21]

Argentina's efforts continued. At the Third Pan-American Conference in 1906, Argentina sought the adoption of the Drago doctrine but was blocked by the United States.[22] At the Second Peace Conference at The Hague in 1907, the Argentine delegation was able to get a modified Drago doctrine accepted, albeit with a major loophole forced through by the U.S. and UK delegations. Drago made his case on principle tied to practice. Public debts were issued to investors "who acquire the bonds at their actual value on the market . . . [with] the origin, their risks, and their certainties perfectly indicated by the interest rate." In the event the foreign government were to suspend payments on its debt, "foreign bondholders suffer the same kind of loss that one who has invested his money in a private enterprise would when it goes bankrupt," he said. "The only difference is the holder of government bonds is in a more advantageous position than the shareholder, because the State does not disappear and, sooner or later, becomes solvent again, whereas a failed company sinks into oblivion forever with no hope of rehabilitation." How, he asked, could any of this justify a war? Moreover, the bonds were traded on world markets, going from hand to hand with the "risks voluntarily accepted by the creditor expecting to realize considerable gains." This was not an attack on international finance but a reflection of its principles. Drago quoted Prime Minister Sir Henry Campbell-Bannerman, a free trader, on the relationship between risk and reward: "if all the power of the British Empire were placed behind the capitalist, the risk would disappear for the latter and the dividends should diminish by the same proportion."[23] His position was in line with other prominent free traders, such as the giant of nineteenth-century British foreign affairs, Lord Palmerston, who instructed British diplomats in 1848 that "British subjects who buy foreign bonds do so at their own risk and must abide the consequences."[24]

The U.S. and UK delegations nevertheless pressed amendments that weakened Drago's doctrine. Where Drago had spoken of public debt and urged an absolute prohibition on military force, the amended version pushed through by U.S. delegate Colonel Horace Porter referred only to "contractual debts" and called for compulsory arbitration enforced by military action. The "Porter doctrine" inserted international arbitration as an intermediate step between complaint and armed intervention, hardly a shining victory. Nonetheless, the Calvo and Drago doctrines had ripple effects of some significance. Without a strong collective resolution at The Hague, Latin American governments began writing new norms on investment and intervention into national law. Calvo's principles appeared in the language of corporate contracts, legal statutes, and constitutions in the form of the so-called Calvo clause, requiring parties doing business under those laws or contracts to agree to host country jurisdiction rather than extraterritoriality. The law of domicile, not the law of nation, would apply. Argentina, Bolivia, Colombia, Ecuador, Mexico, Peru, and Venezuela all adopted a version of the Calvo clause.[25] This Argentine contribution to the international system could be considered an act of "peripheral precedence," an innovation brought from South to North that altered a system of international law originally designed to uphold the privileges of northern great powers.[26]

Latin Americans likely to be in the direct path of intervention drew hope. In 1911, Nicaraguan nationalist poet Rubén Darío wrote optimistically, "On the balance scales of the American continent, it is the Argentine Republic that gives us the counterweight to Yankee power, that will save the spirit of our race and put a stop to imperialist projects undoubtedly already approved."[27] Within a year, U.S. Marines landed in his country, making the last words of his prediction more prescient than the first. The Argentines would need to gather more weight. It would come from the opposite end of Latin America.

* * *

During the long Porfirio Díaz regime (1877–1911), U.S. officials generally considered Mexico a stable and compliant ally. Mexico welcomed U.S. investments and seemed unlikely to lead opposition to U.S. foreign policy. Theodore Roosevelt was so pleased he went as far as to propose to Díaz's ambassador in Washington that reliable Mexico should annex Cuba and the Dominican Republic and also "run" Central America, because "if all the other Latin American republics would stand as Mexico did, and would have such a government as Mexico has, there would be no necessity for any interference in any way, shape, or form on the part of the United States." Satisfying investors was the best protection from invasion. The Mexican ambassador replied that his country had never had the intention of expanding its territory at the expense of a neighbor—a sharp riposte when uttered by a Mexican to a U.S. president.[28]

Mexicans caught up in the revolution that engulfed their country from 1910 to 1917 might initially have had reason to hope that the United States had gotten the message. Woodrow Wilson, after all, campaigned against the dollar diplomacy of the previous occupants of the White House. In the first year of his presidency, he expressed more understanding of the connection between finance capital and the risk to sovereignty than had yet been uttered by a high-ranking U.S. official:

> You hear of "concessions" to foreign capitalists in Latin America. You do not hear of concessions to foreign capitalists in the United States. They are not granted concessions. They are invited to make investments. . . . foreign interests are apt to dominate their domestic affairs, a condition of affairs always dangerous and apt to become intolerable. . . . They [the Latin Americans] have had harder bargains driven with them in the matter of loans than any other peoples in the world. Interest has been exacted of them that was not exacted of anybody else, because the risk was said to be greater; and then securities were taken that destroyed the risk—an admirable arrangement for those who were forcing the terms![29]

The "securities" that "destroyed the risk" were of course the customs receiverships that guaranteed payment, backed by the U.S. military. He continued in his Fourth of July oration in 1914 to question the wisdom of sending U.S. diplomats or troops "to support every man who wanted to earn anything anywhere if he was an American. . . . there ought to be a limit to that," Wilson intoned.[30] But by then, Wilson had begun to set the record for ordering the most armed interventions in Latin America of any U.S. president. He ordered the five-month occupation of Veracruz (1914) and the year-long campaign by General John J. "Black Jack" Pershing's army, which repeatedly violated Mexican sovereignty to try to stop border incursions by Mexican rebels (1916). It was a hard fall from the lofty promises made at Mobile. Instead, he seemed to be carrying out the vow he made privately to a British diplomat: "I am going to teach the South American republics to elect good men."[31]

These acts reinvigorated Mexico's interest in constraining military intervention by changing international norms. Once the revolution was consolidated, Mexico asserted control over its own mineral resources in Article 27 of the new constitution, incorporated the Calvo clause in Article 103, and then nationalized foreign petroleum enterprises in 1938. Mexico's domestic norm-setting through legislation and policy accompanied an ambitious foreign policy agenda aimed at spreading the revolution's conceptions of international behavior to other states in the Americas. President Venustiano Carranza (1917–1920) issued what came to be known as the Carranza doctrine in 1918, embodying Mexico's vision of how international affairs should be conducted: "All nations are equal; they must mutually and scrupulously respect their institutions, their laws, and their sovereignty; no country may intervene in any form and for any motive in the internal affairs of another. . . . Nationals and foreigners must be equal before the sovereignty of the country in which they find themselves."[32] Not only did the Carranza doctrine thus assert a prohibition on military intervention, but it rejected the basic principle of extraterritoriality that led to special protections for foreign investors.[33]

There was by this time only one obvious target for anti-interventionism in the region, and Latin American countries were beginning to coalesce against the leading practitioner of gunboat diplomacy. No European power had intervened militarily since the 1902 blockade of Venezuela, but Taft and Wilson had ordered long-term occupations of the Dominican Republic (1916–1924), Haiti (1915–1934), and Nicaragua (1912–1933), during which these were largely governed by U.S. naval officers, their finances administered by U.S. bankers and economists.

One reason for the endurance of the U.S. model of gunboat diplomacy was that, taken on its own terms, it was successful. In the era of dollar diplomacy marking the roughly twenty-five years of informal empire following the Roosevelt corollary, intervention "generated a large and sustained fall in the perceived default risk of the bonds of circum-Caribbean countries."[34] The bankers did not have to price into their own costs the risk-reducing cost of military occupations, because those expenses were socialized via the federal budget. But attenuating investment risk through the threat and practice of invasion brought other costs to the United States, beginning with reputational costs that fostered diplomatic isolation.

* * *

Foreign, and increasingly U.S., capital was essential to Latin American governments for infrastructure and debt service. But this growing dependence in the 1920s, in the context of increased U.S. military action, especially the counterinsurgency campaign against rebels led by Nicaragua's Augusto Sandino, who held off a force of five thousand Marines, led to demands to codify what was and was not permitted. In spring 1927 the International Commission of Jurists, made up of leading experts on international law from across the Americas, came together at Rio de Janeiro. The State Department made clear to the U.S. delegation that as far as the U.S. was concerned, this was to be nothing but a purposeless gabfest: "You will, of course, take no position on any question which might be construed as committing the Government of the United States in any way whatsoever."[35] That command was made in part to avoid the elephant in the room. "The case of Nicaragua dominated our spirits," recalled one of Cuba's delegates at Rio, Orestes Ferrara.[36]

The main point of dispute at Rio was over Article 3 of the commission's draft report, which held that "No state may intervene in the internal affairs of another." Ferrara wrote that "this occupied all attention" at the conference.[37] Nicaragua's minister in Mexico, Pedro José Cepeda, sent a telegram that the president of the commission read aloud: "I beg you, in the name of my countrymen sacrificed in ten months of a titanic struggle, to make an express declaration which will condemn the unlawful policy of the Department of State of the United States of North America. . . . Nobody is more authorized than this honorable assembly to make such a vindication of international law, trampled under foot by force." The commission declined because, as an assembly of jurists without political authority, it was not empowered to make such a declaration.[38] Mexico and the Dominican Republic jointly introduced a proposition that "No State may in the future directly or indirectly, nor by reason of any motive, occupy even temporarily any portion of the territory of another State." Haiti proposed that any treaty procured by pressure or menace of armed force shall constitute intervention, and Argentina added "external" to the principle that no state may intervene "in the internal or external affairs" of another. The U.S. delegates prevented unanimous adoption, so the commission forwarded the proposals without a recommendation to a body empowered to take a stand.[39]

At the 1928 Pan-American Conference held in Havana, the stage was thus set for confrontation. President Calvin Coolidge arrived for the opening on board a huge battleship escorted by a flotilla of destroyers. When he left the conference in the hands of U.S. chief delegate Charles Evans Hughes, the Argentine delegation led broad Latin American demands for a general agreement against intervention in light of three decades of U.S. Marine landings in Central America and the Caribbean. The head of the Argentine delegation to the conference, Honorio Pueyrredón, denounced U.S. intervention in Nicaragua and quit the conference when Hughes refused to consider the issue. Argentina received the support of the Mexican delegation and those from El Salvador, the Dominican Republic, Ecuador, Haiti, Guatemala, and Colombia.[40] The decision of whether to challenge the United States was not reducible to structural factors. To be sure, Argentina's production of exports that mirrored exports from the U.S. heartland, and the sheer distance between the two countries, made it more reliant on European markets and capital and therefore at lower risk of retaliation. The leaders of other countries made complex calculations involving their assessments of the issues at stake in the context of their economic and political relations with the United States. An experience of U.S. intervention could sharpen the desire to challenge U.S. unilateralism, but it could also foster caution.

As president-elect in late 1928, Herbert Hoover went on a ten-week goodwill tour of Latin America. President Hipólito Yrigoyen of Argentina confronted him directly in public: U.S. power should not be "a shadow projected upon the sovereignty of the other states." In a private meeting, the Argentine president went further. Argentina, like all South American countries, closely observed the U.S. policy of intervening and disregarding the sovereignty of those states where it felt the interests of its citizens were insufficiently respected. This practice seemed to have turned into "a real danger the incorporation of private American capital into the internal economy of other nations" because doing so had made intervention "a norm of US foreign policy." By stating that U.S. investment capital was now literally hazardous, Yrigoyen shocked Hoover and left him arguing ineffectively that the U.S. landed troops only to "save the lives of his fellow citizens and avoid the bloodshed of which they had been constant victims."[41] After an anarchist tried to assassinate Hoover, Yrigoyen spent the rest of the visit at the president-elect's side to guarantee his safety, giving them plenty of opportunity to talk. In a parting message delivered to Hoover as he sailed out of Buenos Aires harbor, Yrigoyen emphasized that the American nations should respect the "equality of their free sovereignties."[42]

The message sank in. Shortly after taking office, Hoover announced that "it never has been and ought not to be the policy of the United States to intervene by force to secure or maintain contracts between our citizens and foreign States or their citizens." This statement made Hoover the first U.S. president to largely accept the Argentine and Mexican doctrines, even if the distinction between contracts and public debt remained. He then withdrew the Marines from Nicaragua, where their war against Sandino's rebels, Secretary of State

Henry Stimson acknowledged, had "damaged our good name, our credit, and our trade far beyond the apprehension of our own people."[43] Invasions had ultimately hurt investments, and ending the former was now thought essential to protecting the latter. Armed insurgencies in the Dominican Republic, Haiti, and Nicaragua against the Marines had also inflicted pain that contributed importantly to the U.S. withdrawal.[44]

By 1933, Mexico's foreign secretary, José Manuel Puig Casauranc, sensed that the international correlation of forces had changed. The collapse of international trade during the Great Depression and the failure of the London Economic Conference aimed at currency stabilization left the United States more reliant on Latin American markets than ever before, giving Latin Americans a rare moment of leverage "to obtain definitive advantages of a higher order than the amendments of tariffs with the United States or general improvement of commerce that result from bilateral or multilateral pacts . . . the moment has arrived in which cooperation from Latin America has become vitally necessary for the United States."[45] He wrote to his Argentine counterpart, Carlos Saavedra Lamas, that as a result they could now achieve at the upcoming Seventh Pan-American Conference in Montevideo what had long been on their respective agendas. "My ambition is that in Montevideo we completely destroy the thesis of Colonel Porter," Puig wrote, "and bring to discussion at the VII Conference, in all of its pristine purity, the Drago Doctrine. If we achieve the acceptance of this Doctrine and its juridical translation into a Pan-American convention, the threat that has always hovered over almost all of the countries of Latin America will disappear."[46]

To clinch the support of Chile's Foreign Minister Juan Guzmán Cruchaga and Argentina's Saavedra Lamas, Puig relied on the Mexican essayist and diplomat Alfonso Reyes.[47] It was a challenging assignment. Reyes, who as Mexico's ambassador in Buenos Aires in the late 1920s went into personal debt renovating the embassy and throwing lavish parties to try to convince high society that all Mexicans were not peasants, regretted that "between Mexico and Argentina, Nature placed distances and accumulated mountains."[48] Still, he did his best to flatter and persuade. Puig told Reyes to push two interlinked and "transcendental themes of vital interest to Latin America": a moratorium on debt service for the whole continent and "a joint declaration on nonintervention of any kind in states to obtain payments or obligations resulting from the debt of countries with banks or other nations."[49] After Reyes won over both Cruchaga and Saavedra Lamas, Puig parlayed their assent into unanimous Latin American support for a nonintervention resolution.[50]

Puig did not have Reyes's literary gifts—a critic once remarked that his writing was "as monotonous as a donkey ride across the Mesa Central"—but the content of what he said was compelling.[51] In his opening speech in Montevideo, he expressed sympathy with North Americans who had suffered losses at the hands of the same forces that Mexico now sought to constrain. "I lived for several years in the United States as a young man," Puig recalled. He had worked there as a medical doctor, and witnessed his patients working hard and striving to get ahead. But today, in 1933, "an enormous majority of all the middle classes and lower classes and skilled workers; nearly all men who had been able, at the cost of work, the efforts of intelligence, the fatigue of their muscles or weariness of their minds, to prepare themselves for a better future for themselves or their children, almost all of these men have been robbed of their efforts, of their noble savings, of the past 25 years—the savings of a whole generation!—by the organizations of international super-bankers." He was not making an attack on ordinary bankers as a profession, or on capitalism itself, Puig assured his audience. But he opposed the "perverted legal formulas" of "orthodox economic science" that causes great suffering. He then proposed a moratorium of six to ten years on the "religious" repayment of the "depredations" of the bankers, "who have already collected their commission and gained healthy differences in the prices of shares and bonds."[52]

Puig had come, in short, not to bury capitalism but to save it. As Christy Thornton has explained, this was part of a broader Mexican effort to go beyond defensive nationalism and economic nationalization projects in order to develop a new, fairer model of international economic cooperation.[53] Indeed, Puig's proposal was not merely a self-interested strategy: debt relief was less crucial to Mexico than to the majority of Latin American countries that had already defaulted during the Depression.[54]

Puig did not persuade the conference to go along with his moratorium. It was a bridge too far for countries that, like Brazil, did not want to offend the United States or, like Uruguay, were negotiating trade deals with Great Britain and did not want to scare off their customers who were also their creditors.[55] Latin American success in getting a more progressive economic order onto the international agenda was still nearly a decade off.[56] But every Latin American country lined up behind a resolution that brought together the Drago doctrine and the Carranza doctrine, since Carranza in 1918 had asserted that "no country may intervene in any form and for any motive in the internal affairs of another."[57] At Montevideo, conferees resolved that "no state has the right to intervene in the internal or external affairs of another." Secretary of State Cordell Hull signed the resolution but presented reservations.

The elusive quest for a definitive standard was finally achieved in 1936. By then, the rise of the fascist powers in Europe and a German trade offensive in Latin America, along with the increasing dependence on Latin American trade that Puig had observed and Hull sought to manage through bilateral tariff reductions, motivated the United States to improve cooperation with Latin American countries. At another Pan-American Conference at Buenos Aires, with President Roosevelt himself in attendance, the Latin American diplomats were successful, gaining unanimous agreement to an unqualified resolution prohibiting intervention "directly or indirectly, and for whatever reason, in the internal or external affairs of the parties."[58] The Argentine author Manuel Ugarte had once predicted that a pan-American system with the United States at its head would be "a congress of mice presided over by a cat."[59] It had taken them a while, but if the Mexicans and Argentines had not ceased being mice and the United States a cat, at Buenos Aires they managed to hang a bell around its neck.

* * *

FDR displayed far more tolerance for Mexican economic nationalism than his cousin Theodore likely would have, influenced in part by the desire to avoid pushing Mexico toward Nazi Germany and in part by counsel from advisors such as Sumner Welles and Josephus Daniels, whose enlightened approach to Mexican affairs was leavened with a dose of paternalism. "Be patient with these children of our younger sister Republic," Daniels advised FDR. "Let them grow up."[60] Roosevelt was not immune to such condescension. "They think they are just as good as we are," he told reporters about Latin Americans, "and many of them are."[61]

Nonetheless, through his actions more than his words, Roosevelt impressed even lifelong critics. The ever-vigilant Isidro Fabela warned on the one hand that U.S. capital posed a special danger "that should never be forgotten: the peseta, the franc, the pound sterling, the mark, do not arrive in these lands escorted by their flags and their warships, whereas the dollar arrives in our haciendas, our petroleum wells, our factories wrapped in the flag of the stars and stripes."[62] Nonetheless, he told his ministry, "None of the recent presidents of the United States has so completely rectified the imperialist policy of the White House as the present leader Franklin D. Roosevelt; none has shown himself to be as humanitarian as he, practicing the principles of the equality of sovereignties and respect for weaker states."[63]

Ironically, it had taken the worst crisis in the history of international capitalism to demonstrate to U.S. leaders that Latin Americans had a point when they criticized the practice of backing investment with invasion. Although, as Dietrich writes, "the protection of private capital trumped arguments about the expansion of self-determination again and again in the twentieth century," this exception that proves the rule is an indication that initiatives coming from the South were not inconsequential, especially when circumstances were propitious.[64] The restoration of state sovereignty in Latin America was in some ways ephemeral, as post-Rooseveltian interventions would increasingly take the form of covert operations. But the very fact of Washington's need for plausible deniability showed how much norms had changed. Today it is inconceivable to imagine that a Latin American country falling into arrears on its debt service would face the shelling of its ports or the military occupation of its cities—even though debates over the less dramatic, yet far-reaching mechanisms of structural adjustment programs show that the proper relationship between sovereignty and international capitalism remains the subject of bitter dispute.

CHAPTER 2

Gangster for Capitalism: Smedley Butler Abroad in the Age of Empire

Joseph Fronczak

"I spent 33 years and 4 months in active service as a member of our country's most agile military force—the Marine Corps," recounted Smedley Butler in retirement. "And during that period I spent most of my time being a high-class muscle man for Big Business, for Wall Street and for the bankers." This explosive claim Butler backed up with a roll call of his exploits: "I helped make Mexico . . . safe for American oil interests in 1914. I helped make Haiti and Cuba a decent place for the National City Bank boys to collect revenues in. I helped in the raping of half a dozen Central American republics for the benefits of Wall Street. The record of racketeering is long. I helped purify Nicaragua for the international banking house of Brown Brothers in 1909–12. I brought light to the Dominican Republic for American sugar interests in 1916. I helped make Honduras 'right' for American fruit companies in 1903. In China in 1927 I helped to see to it that Standard Oil went its way unmolested."[1] When his confession appeared in print in 1935, it startled readers with its sensationalistic tone. It seemed to smack of hyperbole and exaggeration. And Butler certainly had written the essay in an immoderate and hard-boiled style. Yet read today in light of the past few decades' worth of scholarship on the history of U.S. empire and its effect on global capitalism, what's more striking about the passage is just how precise, and accurate, Butler was in identifying primary players (National City Bank, Brown Brothers, Standard Oil) in the United States' early assertions of global economic power. And what's more striking still is the extent to which Butler himself took part in so many of the specific initiatives that historians of U.S. foreign relations now point to in attempting to explain the United States' contributions to the construction of a new world economy at the dawn of the twentieth century.

Given how precisely and accurately Butler assigned responsibility in his confessional essay, it is ironic that the line ostensibly drawn from it that historians have invoked the most is apocryphal. Butler is often thought to have called himself "a gangster for capitalism."[2] But what he actually suggested was that, because of the manipulations of the likes of Brown Brothers, Standard Oil, and National City Bank, "in short, I was a racketeer for capitalism"—*racketeer*, not *gangster*.[3] Similar words, to be sure, but each with its own subtly different connotations. To call Butler a racketeer, as he called himself, is to recognize that he enlisted in a coercive scheme, an exploitative swindle. To think of him as a gangster, as he's been remembered, does much of the same but puts a bit more emphasis on the violence that made the racket work.

Regardless of how one phrases it, the line is fitting because, as Butler suggested in his essay, during his marine career from 1898 to 1931 he had been called on time and time again to do unsavory work of the sort that readily lends itself to comparison with a gangster's or a racketeer's trade. And the line is instructive, too, because as brief a comment as it is, it nonetheless effectively situates his marine career within the bounds of the history of capitalism. Indeed, in this chapter I'll lay out the case for thinking of the sort of tasks that Smedley Butler and his fellow marines performed as essential work in the making of the distinctive global system of political economy that ended up prevailing in the twentieth century.

And yet marines don't figure very prominently in most histories of twentieth-century capitalism. When looking at the period of Butler's career, historians of capitalism, it is fair to say, have paid more attention to the professional class of the era: managers, economists, "money doctors" and "dollar diplomats," financial experts, policymakers, investment bankers, and the like. It would certainly be a mistake to lose sight of such figures, all of which played significant roles in shaping twentieth-century capitalism, but nonetheless in this chapter I'd like to make two arguments about the system's enforcers—the system's "muscle," to use Butler's word. First is simply that the enforcers had a role to play in making twentieth-century capitalism. At the century's onset, they worked to impose the new economic regime and to make it function as an integrated global system. And so just as "money doctors" and investment bankers have a secure place in the history of twentieth-century capitalism, so too should marines. The second argument, though, goes beyond simply asking you to consider the marines' inclusion in the history of capitalism. It asks you to consider that the role that the marines and other enforcers of their sort played was exceptional and that as such their actions, when looked back on today, are exceptionally useful for understanding the nature of twentieth-century capitalism in its formative era. The simple fact that the marines took part at all in setting up the new economic system undermines its most fundamental ideological justifications, the framing of it as "liberal capitalism."[4] With someone like Smedley Butler front and center, the making of liberal capitalism looks very little like any of the normative stories told about liberalism and the sort of economy it cultivates.[5] Beneath the more familiar economic history of laissez-faire liberalism, the gold standard, international trade and finance, specialization and the division of labor, expertise and the managerial class, and mass production and consumption, there lies another history of twentieth-century capitalism's making in which the marines can be seen laboring away from dawn to setting sun, performing the "dirty work" that was needed to bring about the economic integration and market expansion that yielded the world economy's golden age. The marines' work was so crucial at the time and is so exceptionally revealing in retrospect because it so squarely concerned coercion; it consisted of imposing globalization on those who resisted it, those whose economic interests, moral beliefs, and political welfare pointed them away from world economy—away from liberal capitalism.

The decades on either side of the turn from the nineteenth century to the twentieth brought about an intense globalization of capitalism.[6] And they also marked the definitive age of empire.[7] The story usually told of capitalism and imperialism's correlation has it that capitalism's globalizing hunger for new markets and more resources, brought on by the Second Industrial Revolution, led to the voracious imperialism of the age.[8] Contemporaries otherwise as different as Cecil Rhodes and Vladimir Lenin agreed that industrial capitalism necessitated imperialism.[9] As historians have taken pains to show, however, imperialism also worked to restructure capitalism—it was imperialism that demanded the construction of long-distance commodity transit infrastructure to connect the world's farthest corners; it was imperialism that imposed specialization on entire national and colonial economies and that designated vast countries as extraction and export zones; it was imperialism that financialized the world economy with innovations such as the international loan regime; and it was imperialism that established both the new markets of the era and the rules of those markets' exploitation.[10] Such extravagant transformation ran into no small number of obstacles and caused no shortage of social and political problems. The stories of how those obstacles were overcome, of how those problems were sidestepped or squashed, dictate much of the larger story of how liberal capitalism swept across the world in the twentieth century.

Since U.S. Marines appear in so few studies that take capitalism as their principal subject of analysis, it is fortunate that there is an excellent literature on the part that soldiers have played in creating and policing the U.S. empire.[11] If you even just take note of the insights to be found in scholarship on soldiering in the U.S. empire and apply them to the very much related question of the establishment of twentieth-century global capitalism, you can quickly see a prominent place for enforcers in the history of twentieth-century capitalism. And to look at the history of twentieth-century capitalism from where such enforcers stood—out in the field, feet on the ground—many of the pieties expressed by the economic order's advocates lose their force. My aim, then, is to clarify the role of blunt, physical force in the making of twentieth-century global capitalism, and to show just how different the system's making looks as seen from the vantage point of its enforcers. Examined from there, conceptions of hegemony give way to those of domination; consent of the governed yields to the coercion of the ruled; questions of subjecthood are overshadowed by those of subjection; and laissez-faire transmogrifies into faites-faire, as the invisible hand of the market gives way to fisted force. The role of the marines serves as a reminder that fabulistic meta-abstractions of macroeconomic theory, like "the market," deflate without corporeal imposition and enforcement, despite the remarkable powers of world-changing agency scholars often invest in such concepts. Indeed, it is striking how frequently, reading the historiography of capitalism, one might read "the marines" for "the market" and gain insight from the substitution. In short, my method is to trace the formation of the new economic world order in the age of empire by way of Smedley Butler's brush-clearing, earth-scorching, market-making path, and my point is that Butler's trajectory makes evident the centrality of violence—and of coercion—in the construction of twentieth-century global capitalism.[12]

Marines and Market Making

Smedley Butler's boots were on the ground for each of the three major steps toward global power that the United States took at the nineteenth century's end. The steps were also moves in the remaking of global capitalism for the twentieth century: by seizing the lands, making the markets, and enacting the strategic principles that generated its global power, the United States, with each step, also worked to reconfigure the world economy. Cuba to the Philippines to China, 1898 to 1900: Butler's first itinerary abroad makes sense only when one understands how the world economy that was being constructed at the moment relied on coordinating distant space into a single, integrated structure. Commodity chains linked together the new structure, so it's unsurprising that Butler's tour would trace the stages of commodity formation, from point of extraction all the way to market: Butler began his trip in Cuba, where capitalists imagined vast plantations producing enough sugar to dominate the world market, and he finished it two years later in China, where capitalists imagined making the world's ultimate market.[13]

Butler did not know of the economic forces that threw him out into the world. They lurked under the surface: sixteen-year old Smedley Darlington Butler in small-town Pennsylvania could only think of the *Maine* sinking in Havana harbor. Raised as a Quaker in Chester County—where the Smedleys, the Darlingtons, and the Butlers were all prominent Quaker families—he and his family spoke plainly to each other: *thou*, *thee*, *thy*, and *ye*. He was taught pacifism, though his family had a reputation as fighting Quakers, going back to the U.S. Civil War, and his father, who entered Congress in 1897, made his name as one of the principal builders of the modern navy during his three-decade career in Washington.[14] In young Smedley's mind, what put him in motion in 1898 was the savage despotism of the Spanish Empire. School, Butler recalled in his autobiography, suddenly "seemed stupid and unnecessary" and "Cuba now seemed more important than all the Latin and history in the world": he was among the schoolboys chanting "Remember the Maine, to Hell with Spain." Enraged by the thought of "those poor Cuban devils being starved and murdered by the beastly Spanish tyrants," determined to "help free little Cuba," also yearning to avenge "the death of our gallant American sailors," he signed up for the Marine Corps. He may well have spoken for his generation of white American men when he exhaled, "here was the war at last."[15]

The war, the one Butler set out to fight, was over in less than four months. Butler arrived when most of the action had just finished—he described anchoring within view of a still-burning beached Spanish cruiser—and he reported for duty along "the beautiful hill-circled waters of Guantanamo Bay."[16] He did not take part in even one prolonged engagement at Guantánamo (he did once come under sniper fire) before he was en route to the Philippines, "sailing for the Orient," as he put it in his autobiography, "to take part in the Philippine Insurrection."

It was an odd way to think of it. The insurrection was that of Filipino nationalists *against* U.S. military rule.[17] Filipino nationalists had fought alongside U.S. forces against the Spanish Empire, but on victory, rather than recognize the nationalists' revolutionary government, the United States cut a deal with Spain and claimed the 7,100 islands as so many colonial possessions.[18] As in Cuba, sugar contributed to U.S. calculations, but more central to President William McKinley's thinking than the sugar productivity of the islands themselves was the geoeconomically strategic position of the Philippines. The Philippines, the place-itself, mattered less than the much larger, proximate opportunity afforded by naval power around the Philippines: the China market. American speculation of China's commercial and capital possibilities was feverish enough at the time that it produced hallucinatory visions of China as a place beyond political sovereignty, a radically economic, even antipolitical, realm where concepts such as sovereignty and nation were estranged, where capital was king. The scholars Eleanor and Owen Lattimore aphorized these illusions with the phrase "China as a market," and the historian of China Rebecca E. Karl has warned of the power of such illusions by invoking what she calls "the magic of concepts."[19]

McKinley—who had wanted to annex all of Cuba but was boxed in by beet sugar interests to accept only naval bases and "acquisition without annexation"—would have been happy with only a naval base aimed at China in Luzon's Manila Bay, but he concluded that to hold Manila he had to hold all of Luzon, and to hold Luzon he had to hold all the Philippine islands.[20] There was also the matter, even were Luzon to be held without the entire archipelago, of other imperial powers, in particular the German Empire, establishing rival bases to stare down U.S. forces on Luzon.[21] It was for McKinley, having lost out on Cuban annexation, a happy coincidence of interest that the Philippines were the world's third-largest sugar producer.[22] McKinley's choices followed a chain of logic, and it was the age of imperialism that had laid the chain.

From their naval station at Cavite, on Manila Bay, the marines regularly set out into the interior to take out the revolutionary forces, known, like the Cuban revolutionaries, as *insurrectos*. In a deadly assault on the nearby insurrecto town Noveleta, young Butler found himself thrust into leadership of his company after his superior officers were wounded; he led his company's charge on insurrecto forces, wading waist deep through rice paddies, and took the town. Afterward, the marines retraced their steps, burning huts along the way.[23]

When the insurrection appeared knocked on its heels, Butler received orders in June 1900 to sail for Tientsin, China, to take part in quelling the Boxer Rising.[24] Comprising impoverished peasants, the Boxers most notoriously targeted missionaries and Christian converts, but what catalyzed their insurgency was not religious strife but rather a series of interrelated economic incursions by foreign empires: Germany, Russia, France, and Britain all had recently grabbed new lands, charting out railroad lines to drain resources from mines and fields.[25] China's resilient nineteenth-century economic order, which had relied on profitable regional exchange to fend off British and U.S. attempts to mold the country into a market of the world economy, collapsed with China's 1895 defeat in the Sino-Japanese War.[26] Japan then forced China to accept the financially punitive Treaty of Shimonoseki. With an onerous indemnity due, China reluctantly sought loans from foreign financiers.[27] Former U.S. secretary of state John W. Foster, leading a surreptitious New York syndicate, even encouraged China to fight off Japanese territorial demands by agreeing to an even larger indemnity—which his group could finance up to $400 million.[28] With the treaty having wounded China, a new scramble was underway, the logic of it playing out remarkably similarly to the partitioning of Africa. Eric Hobsbawm aptly described the preying imperial powers—Japan, Britain, France, Russia, Italy, Germany, Austria-Hungary, and the United States—as "wolves" sensing China's vulnerability, hungrily racing each other on the hunt.

Butler arrived as part of a multi-imperial military force twenty thousand strong marching under a convoluted, makeshift joint command of the eight imperialist powers. In his 1935 confessional essay, part of Butler's indictment was how the international dimensions of capitalism troubled ideas of national interest, security, and independence of action. Once the Boxers rose, the imperial powers stopped racing each other and instead, as Hobsbawm put it, "the wolves were ready to form a pack against the prey." There remained, however, Hobsbawm added, the problem that "they could not agree on the division of the immense carcass."[29]

Butler arrived at Taku Bar in the Yellow Sea and boarded a German freighter to Tangku, downriver from Tientsin. He was shot in the leg during hellacious combat, some of it hand to hand, at Tientsin, where the marines, along with Russian, British, German, and French soldiers, laid siege to the city's forty-foot-high wall. After taking Tientsin, his wound somewhat healed, Butler marched south with the interimperial army to Peking, taking out Boxer strongholds along the way. In his autobiography, he described seeing a series of "villages surrounded by mud walls. The houses were smouldering, the walls riddled with bullets, the dead Chinese piled in the courtyards."[30] Butler left unstated how this had come to be; another American, an army general, was more explicit: "The villages had been burned and looted by the allied columns, the people had fled from their homes . . . the sedgy banks of the Peiho were reeking with the stench from the floating bodies of dead Chinamen."[31]

On August 14, 1900, the imperial powers hit Peking. Butler always depicted the occupation of Peking as a Hobbesian war of all against all, no order, no discipline, not even factions, nothing but human greed and worse. Most who saw and commented on it described something similar. The looting of Peking, as it became known, gained worldwide notoriety as a vast collective crime, one that could be seen either as the perfect symbolic act defining its age or as a dodge from reckoning with the greater act of plunder, the imperialist powers' exploitation of China that followed. This enveloped the appropriation of much vaster sums of riches—though it lacked the visual theater of open looting in city streets and palaces. One soldier observed at the Palace of the Eighth Prince, where Butler stayed, that officers' quarters there contained ever larger "piles of loot" stuffed into Chinese trunks.[32] Though it was the pettiness of the cupidity that made the scene so unseemly, the petty scale of such theft clarifies how different in kind the actions of these soldiers were from the imperialist mission itself. That is to say, none of the looting compared to the Boxer Protocol of 1901. Few acts of financial appropriation, legal or illegal, could. The text of the protocol authorized foreign powers to maintain their military presence in China, without regard to Chinese authorities, in perpetuity, and it indemnified China for damages of 450 million taels, equivalent to $333 million, to be paid in gold at 4 percent interest; China's actual payments would eventually amount to more than double the original penalty.[33]

With the subjugation of the Boxers, and the subjection of China to the Boxer Protocol, the sweeping overture to Butler's marine life ended. From Quaker Pennsylvania, he had cut a path to Guantánamo Bay to Luzon to Tientsin to Peking in three years. The labor he performed was the spadework of both empire building and market making. On the ground, where Butler stood, the making of a market for twentieth-century global capitalism appeared a sanguinary, coercive affair, and only a considerable amount of abstraction could subsume such a pattern into the category "free market."[34] In the new century, Smedley Butler had more markets to make; more doors to crack open; more diverse economic cultures to homogenize; more community-based, and even autarkical, local economies to overhaul into outlets of a world system; more governments and revolutions to break. But the form of what followed was established by the time he left Peking. Present at the creation of twentieth-century capitalism, his course was set.

Making Capitalism Work

His course was set for Central America, where Butler spent much of the next dozen years. His choice of metaphor in his confession, of sexual violence, to describe his role there—"I helped in the raping of half a dozen Central American republics for the benefits of Wall Street"—was ubiquitous among his generation of imperialist American men. When Theodore Roosevelt explained to his cabinet how deeply involved he had been in dislodging from Colombia its Panamanian department so that a canal could be built under U.S. control, Secretary of War Elihu Root retorted, "you were accused of seduction, and you have conclusively proved that you were guilty of rape."[35] Butler's use, however, was not rote; his confessional context, and the aptness of the application, gave vivid meaning to the metaphor: marine action as rape intimated assault, asymmetry of strength, infliction of lasting trauma, and conquest driven by a perpetrator's own impulses, desires, and self-indulgences. It posed the matter as one of coercion, compulsion, consentlessness.[36]

Generally speaking, Root and Butler were speaking of the same violation. Butler and his battalion went to Central America in September 1902, before Panama was split from Colombia, to be in position to sweep in and secure Panama should the occasion arise. Fourteen months later, an unseemly plot separated Panama from Colombia, the United States seized canal rights, and Roosevelt broke the news to Root. When Butler had arrived, the Central American canal had remained the great unfinished infrastructural project for globalizing capitalism: the third and final piece, along with the Suez Canal and the North American transcontinental railroad, needed to connect a new world-spanning commodity circuit. But while the Suez Canal and the railroad were both completed in 1869, ready to catapult commodities across the globe and to connect remote markets just as the Second Industrial Revolution hit, the isthmian project languished. To build the canal would be to finish the physical fusion of the new world economy, and to do so perfectly according to its place-stripping, time-saving, space-splicing, globe-stitching logic: rip up Panama to pull closer together Pittsburgh and Peking. Strategically positioned naval bases—Guantánamo, Manila Bay—were to protect the path.

That it was a marine who was present for each mutually necessary step of this dizzying choreography of production, transit, and market conveys the extent to which this was a work of imposition, always requiring "muscle."

After several other labors in the region, such as making "Honduras 'right' for American fruit companies in 1903," Butler arrived in Panama proper at the end of 1909 as commander of a battalion. He remained stationed there until the canal was completed in 1914, witnessing up close the herculean task of carving the land. Butler remembered the site as "a spasm of engineering convulsions. Locks and dams were being built, steamhammers were pounding, dredges snorting, and a ceaseless activity was going on." But his marines "had hardly planted our feet on Panama soil when we were packed off on the railroad crossing the Isthmus," destined for Nicaragua.[37]

Nicaraguan dictator José Santos Zelaya had done much to draw the ire of U.S. Secretary of State Philander Knox, including securing a £1.25 million loan from European creditors that Knox had sought to circumvent.[38] He likely had already crossed the point of no return with his ongoing bold attempt to construct an isthmian canal—to be financed by Japanese or British or French capital—to rival the U.S.-controlled one being built in Panama.[39] Just as locking down all the Philippines had meant both naval power at the gateway to East Asia *and* assurance that Imperial Germany could not establish its own foothold there, taking out Zelaya meant that the United States could establish a monopoly on what promised to become the pivotal turnstile of the world economy. In terms of economic power, it was undoubtedly in Nicaragua's interest to build a rival route across the isthmus; Knox had to figure out how to make Nicaragua fail to act according to its national interest, and his only instrument to do so was the U.S. Marine Corps.

But there was more to the intervention than that—and Smedley Butler could smell it. A Pittsburgh-based mining concession connected to Knox, the Compañia Minera La Luz y Los Angeles, was, as the U.S. consul later testified, "the cause of the desire to eliminate Zelaya."[40] How much interest Knox personally had in La Luz y Los Angeles has never been established. Later, at least, Horacio Blanco Fombona, the fearless publisher of a Dominican weekly, accused Knox of being its principal shareholder, and Butler knew by 1933 that Knox "was reported to own stock."[41]

The Knox nexus matters because the man orchestrating the regime change that drew Butler and the marines to Nicaragua was Adolfo Díaz, a lowly Costa Rican secretary at La Luz y Los Angeles who, despite drawing a salary of about $1,000 per year, was able to supply revolutionaries with perhaps

$600,000 capital (a point Nicaraguan nationalist revolutionary Augusto Sandino would later take to noting in his criticisms of U.S. imperialism).[42] Díaz eventually took power as president of Nicaragua (one of his first acts was to "reimburse" himself the $600,000 "loan"). Whatever the truth of Knox's relation to La Luz, word of it was not only an after-the-fact invention. Rumors abounded at the time. In June 1910, Butler wrote to his father from Bluefields, along the so-called Mosquito Coast, "will thee please find out . . . about Secretary Knox's mining interests here?"[43]

Butler suspected that he was making capitalism work when it ought to have failed—when, without the force of the marines, it would have failed. Butler wrote his father to explain, "This is not, by any means, my first experience wielding the 'Big Stick' in shady diplomacy [. . .], but it is the most sickening." Referring to the U.S. capitalists in Nicaragua as "<u>renegade swine</u>," Butler accused them of having placed "a 100 to 1 shot on a horse race" before calling in muscle "to hold all the other horses."

It followed that Butler suspected that the marines were propping up the revolution that Díaz was funding. At this point, Zelaya had fled but the revolutionary forces, bankrolled (even aside from Díaz's contributions) by U.S. capitalists and working in consultation with the U.S. State Department, could not dislodge from Managua Zelaya's handpicked successor. The leader of the revolutionary forces himself, Bluefields governor Juan José Estrada, suggested that U.S. capitalists had provided him with $1 million for the revolution.[44] What was called the revolution, Butler decided in July 1910, "really consists of an American Consul, two U.S. Gunboats and 200 American Marines." He fumed, "The whole attitude of our State Department is beyond me, but of course I am simply a hired policeman and am not supposed to understand affairs of state. I <u>can</u> see, with my untrained eyes, however, that were we not living in this town the revolution would be over in a few minutes."[45]

Butler could also see the brutality of the capitalists' revolution. Even if the revolution was a sham, its consequences were real, and they wore away at him. He came to find the situation "pitiable," and he wrote his father, "I have made up my mind not to permit any more fighting around this town, for it would mean untold suffering to both sides." After a battle in which "fully 700 were killed," Butler counted that "fully 3000 have been killed during the revolution." Butler explained that he had decided to tell combatants "that I have stopped their engagement for the sake of humanity. I have carefully thought this over, Father, and have firmly resolved, if I lose my commission, to stop this butchery of people too weak to help themselves." Butler's plan was a sort of small-scale doomsday machine, with his marines acting as the deterrence device: were the combatants to refuse his demand, "I now have 400 fine soldiers and can lick both sides if necessary with the automatic guns we have. I am in absolute command on shore."[46] If the claim of absolute command was overstated, the U.S. consul nonetheless understated the situation when he later commented, "Major Butler asserted his militarism a little bit sometimes, but I had told him that would not work; that he was there to protect American property and lives and that was all."[47]

That, of course, was not all: the month after Butler pointed out the revolution's flimsiness, the central government nonetheless fell. Estrada became president, then within months ceded to Díaz. Force had made fiction into reality. More to the point, the new reality possessed a force of its own, with ramifications for global capitalism. Butler's short trip from Panama to Nicaragua shadowed capital's final transformation in the making of twentieth-century capitalism: the financialization of a world economy that had been launched at Shimonoseki. In moving from Panama, where the canal was a colossal infrastructural edifice, to Nicaragua, where matters of political economy quickly fell subject to the quicksilver-slippery abstractions of finance capital, credit, interest, and market price, Butler watched as international finance took command.[48]

More than any of his previous exploits, his time in Nicaragua stirred Butler's political-economic consciousness. When, in his confession, he explained, "I suspected I was just part of a racket at the time" (whereas "now I am sure of it") he meant Nicaragua.[49] Within a week of Díaz's rise, Knox secured from his administration the Knox-Castrillo Convention, handing over financial control of Nicaragua to Wall Street firms Brown Brothers and J. & W. Seligman & Co.[50] The convention provided that "should the circumstances require," the United States "will in turn afford such protection as it"—the United States—"may find requisite."[51] Brown Brothers and Seligman acted as creditors, providing $15 million. The splash of millions meant something other than the everyday meaning of the word *loan*. As the socialist muckraker John Kenneth Turner commented, close examination of the terms reveals "that the bankers were never to pay out any such sum as $15,000,000; that such sums as they paid out were to be paid chiefly *to themselves*."[52]

The marines had played no small part in setting the table for the Knox-Castrillo Convention. And enforcing it also required the marines. Díaz's position remained tenuous, in need of legitimization. Speaking years later, to an audience of industrialists in Pittsburgh, Butler spoke unguardedly of his final act as capital's bodyguard in Nicaragua, his role manipulating the election of Díaz in 1912. In retrospect Butler freely admitted "the fellow we had in there nobody liked. But he was a useful fellow—to us—so we had to keep him in." He added, "How to keep him in was the problem." After studying Nicaraguan election law, Butler simply opened polls with five minutes' notice—with handpicked voters preassembled—and then closed the polls "in about two hours."[53]

Leaving Nicaragua after the fixed election, Butler was fêted in Managua with a victory ball hosted by Brown Brothers, where he was hailed by one British attendee as the "Kitchener of Nicaragua."[54] Butler had not scorched the earth, actually, in Nicaragua, as Lord Kitchener had in South Africa. Butler would do that in Haiti.

Customhouse Capitalism and Corvée Labor

Speaking in Brooklyn in 1933, Butler declared that he had been "canned" in Haiti because, as the *New York Herald Tribune* reported his words, "'I didn't want to make the Haytians raise sugar' for a New York bank."[55] Butler's claims are somewhat puzzling because he actually had done much to make Haitians raise sugar during his time there, and he was not "canned," but rather he asked to be reassigned to fight the Great War in Europe. Closer to capturing his role in Haiti were Butler's words in his confession two years after the Brooklyn speech, that he had indeed helped to make Haiti "a decent place for the National City Bank boys to collect revenues in."

The National City Bank (today morphed into Citibank) had boomed during the Second Industrial Revolution, with wealthy clients including Standard Oil. And as the United States asserted its global power, the bank began looking to operate abroad, first in Cuba, Mexico, and Panama and then, beginning with 1909 negotiations arranged by Knox, in Haiti.[56] Those negotiations yielded the Banque Nationale de la République d'Haïti, which, its name notwithstanding, was ruled by a City Bank–led consortium of international capital; in turn, the bank quickly came to rule Haiti—as the historian Suzy Castor put it, as "a state within a state."[57] The City Bank's interests were the most sizable of foreign firms' in Haiti when the marines stormed Port-au-Prince on July 28, 1915, and established a military occupation in the name of protecting "American and foreign lives and property."[58] Butler arrived within two weeks of the invasion, commanding a battalion. Before Butler even arrived in Haiti, new secretary of state Robert Lansing wrote to President

Woodrow Wilson to "confess that I am a little suspicious as to the City Bank's attitude toward the Republic of Haiti." He put it diplomatically that "certain actions taken by them [City Bank] are at least criticizable."[59]

Lansing had good reason to be suspicious. The previous year, City Bank's consortium had decided that it was "very urgent" that the Banque Nationale "transfer to New York $110,000 in gold," as the matter had been put by the bank's vice president in his wire to Lansing's predecessor at State, William Jennings Bryan. Within days, the bank more than quadrupled the amount to be "transferred"—a word choice that obscured the fact that the gold to be moved was not bank revenues but the Haitian republic's reserves. And with that, a bank heist of extraordinary proportions was plotted out. Banking officials in Port-au-Prince pointed out that the most dangerous part of the heist would be the getaway, warning, "Must advise you that transportation from the bank to the wharf presents serious danger owing to the state of mind of the population." Bryan's solution was simple: "Request Commanding Officer *Hancock* to land as many marines as necessary to furnish safe escort for gold from bank to *Machias*."[60] The marines hauled the gold out of the bank, through Port-au-Prince by wagon to the wharf, and aboard the *Machias*, which promptly left harbor for New York, the gold destined for a Wall Street vault. The scene of marines, white foreigners carrying canes and guns, on a wagon sagging from seventeen crates of gold, making their way through the streets of revolutionary Port-au-Prince must have been a pedagogical spectacle for all.[61]

The military occupation of Haiti by the marines began seven months later. However symptomatic of the City Bank's activity in Haiti the seizure of gold was, U.S. intervention was not directly about the Banque Nationale. Even the heist had not been about the gold itself: the principal reason the U.S. State Department and City Bank plotted the removal had been to hold the gold hostage to coerce Haiti into handing over control of its customhouses.[62]

To understand how Butler came to make Haiti a decent place for City Bank to collect revenues—and to understand how the world market came to rule the countries it exploited in the early twentieth century—go to the customhouse by the wharf. That was where a country's worth of export commodities converged on its exit point to the outside world. That was where the capital created by imperial incursion accumulated. That was where the social power to be had from export commodity production concentrated. That was where, ultimately, consortia of international banking firms consolidated their power to bundle capital and take away the lion's share before the host country's government even touched the revenues collected. In short, City Bank grabbed hold of the wealth Haiti produced by holding sway over one location: the Cap-Haïtien customhouse.

This made the marine with a gun in his hand at the customhouse door, once again, the necessary man. Such outsize importance being funneled into one spot derived directly from the transformative, and homogenizing, force of global capitalism: in hacking away at Haiti's diverse, sprawling, and intertwined local, regional, and national economic bonds, in revamping the intricate Haitian economy for specialized, simplified plantation production of an export commodity, the capitalist revolution created a choke point of concentrated power to control the entire Haitian economy—at the precise point of export, the customhouse. It was this way the world over, from Honduras and Nicaragua to Egypt and China. In China, it had been the customhouses that represented the guarantee for the loans taken out to pay the Japanese Empire the indemnity imposed at Shimonoseki, and then it had been the customhouses that served to guarantee the indemnity to the eight imperialist powers imposed by the Boxer Protocol.[63]

The classic case showing customhouses' centrality to a global political economy had unfolded right across Haiti's border, in the Dominican Republic, where the catalysis for the Roosevelt Corollary to the Monroe Doctrine had been the seizure—first by Dominican nationalist "mobs" and then by marines—of the Puerta Plata and Monte Cristi customhouses.[64] The Roosevelt Corollary provided a mechanism to subdue homegrown nationalist revolutionaries—in that case, nationalist revolutionaries who understood only too well that a successful revolution meant seizing the customhouse just as surely as it meant storming the palace. As a 1904 report on the Dominican Republic coauthored by Admiral George Dewey promised, "If the United States controlled the custom-houses there would be nothing for the revolutionists to fight for."[65] Actually controlling the customhouses, though, was the rub. And where the marines entered.

It is crucial to understand how profoundly transformative of political economy such control was. A properly functioning customhouse in port meant changes in the land across the entire countryside. Under eighteenth-century French colonial rule, specialization in sugar had meant homogenizing the Haitian landscape into a vast plantation machine, run on slave labor. Since winning independence in 1804, Haiti, tellingly, had pivoted to diversify economy with coffee, cotton, and cocoa.[66] Even more telling than the independent nation's export-commodity diversification was the work of nineteenth-century Haitian producers themselves to turn away from the world market entirely, to make local marketplaces and to practice small-scale subsistence agriculture, strategically establishing themselves on an economic terrain favorable to cultivating autonomy—freedom from the plantation and its overseer, and freedom from the market, debt, assessment and taxation, surveillance, wage dependence, dispossession, and proletarianization.[67]

The age of empire paved over this rediversified postemancipation landscape.[68] Globally, this sort of work was mostly done via railroad.[69] Railroad lines worked to strip the surrounding landscape of its thickets and to bridge its chasms, sand away its frictions and polish its peculiarities, and straighten its switchbacks, so as to make the steam engine's charge no different from the crow's flight. In Haiti, it was largely roadworks that achieved the reclamation of the land for global capitalism. Overseeing road construction was Smedley Butler. Butler described himself as "chief of police in Haiti," which he was, but the broader purpose of his presence was to superimpose a world economy infrastructure on the local landscape.[70]

Butler had to impose labor on locals to do so: he initiated and oversaw the infamous corvée system of unwaged, unfree labor that came to symbolize the marines' occupation of Haiti. Labor historians of the U.S. empire have expertly excavated the forgotten toil of "making the empire work" at sites like the Canal Zone and Guantánamo.[71] However, there necessarily was an additional logic at work beyond imperialism. Always, making the U.S. empire work was also making global capitalism work. Which leads to the insights gained from placing Smedley Butler and the marines in the history of capitalism. Much of the historical problem that the labor historians of U.S. empire unpack is the puzzle of neocolonial subjects performing imperial labor. The answer often hinges on coercion, which, again, leads to the marines' dirtier work: making the empire, and capitalism, work—by making people work.[72] Butler had employed coerced labor in Nicaragua as well: from there Butler had written home with stories about supervising political prisoners, "about 150 of them" as they dug out works—"Of course we are not coercing these poor devils," Butler had written, "but are simply making them help themselves, without their feeling the pressure."[73]

Butler's theorization of not-coercing/simply-making was far from a liberal free labor ideology, but it underpinned the production of liberal capitalism's critical labors nonetheless.[74] Corvée labor similarly had cut away the earth at Suez; coerced labor built much of global capitalism's infrastructure—much of the economy itself. It is not far from acknowledging the role of coerced labor to acknowledging the role of coercion—all the expressions of liberal freedoms like free trade, free markets, free labor, and free choice notwithstanding. The world economy was bludgeoned into being, and it was to enforcers like the marines that fell the task of coercing, of producing, labor—the task, as Butler had put it in Nicaragua, of *making* labor happen. Butler even imagined his corvée system in liberal terms, believing it would pave a road away from revolution. It was through corvée labor, he explained, that "we hope to absolutely do away with the desire on the part of any Haitian to revolt against his government."[75] In this way, Butler's choice to coerce labor was rooted in the central concern of Wilsonian liberalism: how to make a world without revolutions.

To the Pennsylvania Quaker, the corvée scheme seemed "somewhat like a barn raising"; to others it looked like the reintroduction of racial slavery to the land of Toussaint L'Ouverture.[76] James Weldon Johnson personally blamed Butler for the corvée régime, suggesting that it had been Butler who "discovered the obsolete Haitian *corvée* and decided to enforce it with the most modern Marine efficiency."[77] Predictably, the corvée exacerbated the problem Butler meant it to solve, providing the fuel for the Caco peasant insurgency that spread across the Haitian countryside.[78] The Caco resistance recognized the roads, railroads, customhouses, and wharves as a sort of weaponization of the land, instruments destroying the postemancipation Haitian economy. Accordingly, they struck these points. It had been the same among the Boxers, who destroyed rails along the Beijing–Baoding line one day in May 1900 and then burned a station along the Beijing–Tianjin line the next day.[79] Resistance movements like the Cacos and the Boxers, however, did not represent the entireties of their societies. Not even close. Haiti, like China, and like Nicaragua, was an endlessly complex country in the age of empire; not all who crossed paths with the marines and other agents of the world economy were at odds with the project of global capitalism. Local liberals, emergent bourgeoisies, and opportunistic officials all saw great opportunity to collaborate. I've emphasized resistance because it is the confrontation between implementation and resistance that reveals the nature of the whole, and as such it was between those who forcibly imposed the world economy and those who actively resisted it that one sees clearly the chasm between actually existing liberal capitalism and the thing in theory.

Butler, tasked with overseeing corvée roadwork, was also tasked with crushing the Cacos. He did so with scorched-earth tactics. After an incident in which his men "killed and wounded about 40" Cacos, "we burned every house within a mile and just laid the country bare."[80] This was part of a widespread campaign.[81] Butler despised the Cacos and resented the attempts of naval officers to negotiate a peace with them. In the letters he wrote at the time, he used repugnant, racist language to depict the Cacos, and he seethed with anger that his superiors would attempt to negotiate with such "an ignorant, treacherous crowd."[82] Only total war of the sort that he and his men were waging, Butler insisted, would end the resistance.

The marines' labors could accomplish more than that. Wherever the marines' violence strengthened U.S. imperial rule, it also made the host country more fit for global capitalism. By fighting their way across the Haitian countryside and by scorching the earth in search of Cacos, Butler's marines were also breaking down peasant economy-ecologies and liberalizing the Haitian economic landscape, paving roads for commodities to roll frictionlessly down to sea level, to the customhouse at the wharf.[83] In a way, they worked hand in hand with "the National City Bank boys." But the marines undoubtedly did the dirtier work. They were the ones who cracked open the doors, burned down the homes, manned the gunboats, and guarded the vault doors. They executed people and inflicted what one investigation at the time termed "bodily tortures." They administered "the 'water cure'" and in at least one case burned a man's body, as documented by the same inquiry, "with a red-hot iron."[84] The bankers, for their part, took the loot.

Why did Smedley Butler look back on all this and bitterly confess he had been made a racketeer for capitalism? He did not claim to have been innocent or ignorant of capitalism's iniquities or its destructive force. He sorrowfully admitted that he himself "had, as the boys in the back room would say, a swell racket. I was rewarded with honors, medals, promotions."[85] In retirement, perhaps returning to his Quaker roots, he sought peace, and he felt that capitalism was too invested in war not to make the next one inevitable. He charged that the U.S. government "is at the mercy of the rulers of industry and finance." Once the ultimate militarist, he now inveighed against militarization, against armament, and, above all else, against empire. He lugubriously warned of war if the United States kept the Panama Canal and the Philippines, if it kept protecting "American lives and property" in China. At home in Quaker country, Pennsylvania, he prophesied, regarding the Philippines, "War is in the air in the Eastern world, and sooner or later, if we hold on to them, America will be jerked into a war before we know what it's all about."[86]

The year that his "racketeer for capitalism" confession appeared in print Butler delivered his polemical pamphlet *War Is a Racket* to a Christian publisher. He dolefully condemned militarism, empire, debt, financial capitalism, and the capitalist class. He wished the *Maine* had never gone to Havana harbor. He prescribed that no U.S. naval ship ever leave the continental coastline, "to make certain that our military forces are truly forces for defense only." Leave Guantánamo Bay and the Canal Zone; leave Standard Oil to its own devices in China; leave Nicaragua and Haiti alone; liberate the Philippines, Puerto Rico, and Guam. He called for declarations of war to depend on referenda rather than senate votes—moreover, plebiscites limited to "those who would be called upon to do the fighting and the dying." Butler charged that there "wouldn't be much sense in having the 76-year-old president of a munitions factory or the flat-footed head of an international banking firm" vote on questions of war. Such men, Butler wrote, "see visions of tremendous profits in the event of war." And such men, of course, "would never be called upon to shoulder arms—to sleep in a trench and to be shot." Beyond his call to anchor naval ships forevermore along the continental shore and to choose war only by means of direct democracy, Butler also called for the conscription of capital in the event of war: let the munitions manufacturers, the oil barons, the profiteers, "the bankers and the speculators" all be conscripted, "to get $30 a month, the same wage as the lads in the trenches get."[87] Take the profit out of war, he said, surrender the empire, go home, and war would be no more.

CHAPTER 3

From Nashville to Port-au-Prince: Giles A. Hubert and the Agrarian New Deal in Postoccupation Haiti

Alec Fazackerley Hickmott

Seated at the head of the table in his home in Pétion-Ville, an affluent suburb on the outskirts of Port-au-Prince, Giles Hubert was in his element. Hubert, an African American economist who worked as an agricultural attaché at the American embassy between 1948 and 1951, had often used his residence to play host to visiting black intellectuals from the United States, including the novelist Richard Wright and the sociologist E. Franklin Frazier, both of whom had enjoyed long evenings of conversation on the house's veranda overlooking Port-au-Prince Bay.[1] But on this occasion, Hubert's guests represented the past and future of Haitian governance (Figure 3.1). Attendees were drawn from the ranks of both embassy officials and Haiti's new political elite, two groups whose relationship, in the aftermath of the occupation and the 1946 overthrow of the U.S.-supported presidency of Emile Lescot, was far from ensured.

The dinner seemed, on its face, a harmonious occasion. Seated opposite Hubert was the embassy's chargé d'affaires. Listening attentively to the conversation was Clément Jumelle, a Haitian Labor Department official and future candidate for president.[2] To Hubert's right sat Alain Turnier, a former student of Hubert's at Fisk University in Nashville, Tennessee, who—like a number of other Haitian students at Fisk, including Jumelle—had returned home to serve in the administration of the newly elected president Dumarsais Estimé. On the wall of the dining room framing the festivities hung a poster advertising one of the Estimé government's most notable initiatives—the Exposition

Fig. 3.1. Giles Hubert, Alain Turnier, and Clément Jumelle in Pétion-Ville, Haiti. Source: Giles Hubert Papers, Box 15, Folder 1, Amistad Research Center, New Orleans, LA.

Internationale, which opened in December 1949 as a celebration of Port-au-Prince's bicentennial and the possibilities of Haitian modernity.

Having assumed power as a result of the 1946 revolution, Estimé's presidency promised both greater national sovereignty and popular empowerment. Estimé, as the future president François Duvalier wrote in 1948 in *Le Problème des Classes à Travers l'Histoire d'Haïti*, was an "authentic son of the peasant masses," and his newly black-dominated administration signaled his commitment to a new race-conscious populism.[3] The ambitions of this project, however, would be structured by the fact that the United States retained a number of methods of economic coercion in the country, including veto power over Haitian budgetary and taxation policy. In addition, American private capital remained an influential actor in the agricultural sector. As such, the popular overthrow of the U.S.-sponsored Lescot regime had only begun a process of restoring national self-determination, and the dinner at Hubert's residence was thus an occasion on which the terms of future Haitian-American relations were an inescapable subtext.[4]

Hubert's presence in Port-au-Prince, at the very least, suggested the possibility of constructive collaboration on a project of rural reform. But the precise problems of the Haitian countryside were by no means unambiguously clear. Writing in 1915, the African American intellectual W. E. B. Du Bois, himself the son of a Haitian immigrant to the United States, extolled the country's virtues, particularly because it had "succeeded in placing on their own little farms the happiest and most contented peasantry in the world."[5] Though the countryside remained largely poor and dominated by subsistence farming in the early decades of the twentieth century, Du Bois viewed Haitians' widespread access to land—something increasingly denied to African Americans in the United States—as something to be celebrated. And it was certainly true that, in contrast to other parts of the region, plantation agriculture was a relatively minor feature of the Haitian economic life. Resistance to peasant dispossession was a recurring phenomenon in the countryside, suggesting the durability of what scholars have identified as a "counter-plantation" tradition in the Caribbean.[6]

Paradoxically, however, the possibilities of postoccupation Haiti were also rooted in the era of occupation which, as Chantalle Francesca Verna has shown, produced a tentative tradition of inter-American collaboration on rural issues.[7] In 1924, the École Centrale d'Agriculture was established with the intent of training agricultural technicians, following a model of agricultural extension work that had been developed in the United States.[8] As Suzy Castor argues, however, such development efforts represented only a "veneer" of modernization.[9] The occupation had fundamentally altered the possibilities for rural reform in Haiti by strengthening the central power of the Haitian state, but it had not entailed a carte blanche for American financial and agricultural interests.[10] As one scholar estimates, as few as 28,000 hectares were turned over to American foreign-owned enterprises.[11] Rather, it was during the postoccupation years that Haitian and U.S. rural development initiatives intensified. Created in 1941, the Société Haïtiano-Américaine de Développement Agricole (SHADA) combined Haitian and American technical expertise with a $5 million loan from the Export-Import Bank in Washington, D.C., toward the goal of establishing rubber production in Haiti to aid the U.S. war effort. Then-president Elie Lescot proclaimed in 1942 that "collaboration with the USA is for the best of the country because it is America that we must look to in our search for the secret of democracy."[12]

Hubert's time in Haiti between 1948 and 1951 as an employee of the U.S. State Department in part advanced America's postwar foreign policy goals in the Caribbean, which were first and foremost concerned with promoting political stability and American economic interests.[13] But Hubert was also one of the few African Americans employed in the foreign service, and he arrived in Haiti with sympathy for the Estimé regime's efforts to build a more democratic, modern, and prosperous economic order in the Caribbean's first black republic. Haiti had long held a central place in the black political imaginary, and at least since the 1930s the nation had been envisioned by many as a potential site of a pan-African black capitalism.[14] These transnational dialogues were part of a period, as Millery Polyné notes, in which a range of African American organizations, intellectuals, and bureaucrats sought "to realize the promise of modern industrial and technical development in the black world, and, second, to demonstrate they were active supporters of and participants in U.S. foreign policy."[15] By the early 1950s, the African American journalist and committed pan-Africanist Claude Barnett could write confidently in the pages of *News of Haiti* that "Not only in Haiti is this spirit of development arising. . . . Darker peoples all over the world from Liberia and Ethiopia and Africa in general . . . are feeling a new sense of self-determination."[16] Hubert was very much a part of a political and intellectual milieu that thought about conditions of unfreedom in consistently transnational terms, and as such this essay contributes to a broader literature on African Americans' globally oriented visions.[17]

This essay, however, focuses attention on another aspect of Hubert's biography: his work as an exponent of what scholars of rural America have termed the "agrarian New Deal." An agricultural economist by training, Hubert worked extensively for the USDA's Farm Security Administration (FSA) in the 1930s and 1940s. Hubert's career, this essay contends, offers a new way trace both the global reverberations of New Deal agricultural reform as well as the Jim Crow origins of development thought and practice and its transmission to the Global South. While there is an emerging literature tracing the history of the "global New Deal," little has been said about Haiti or the racial politics of development discourses and ideology.[18] In fact, there was a receptive audience for this project in Haiti. Dumarsais Estimé, in particular, was effusive in his praise for the work of the USDA; in an early meeting with Orme Wilson, the U.S. ambassador, Estimé "referred to the immense productivity of the American soil" and said that he "had read with interest some of the works of former Vice President [and former USDA Secretary] Henry Wallace."[19] Hubert was thus uniquely situated to link agricultural reform efforts in the rural South to those in the Global South. As an FSA administrator who himself hailed from a landowning family in rural Georgia, Hubert was first and foremost an exponent of a version of New Deal agricultural policy that favored the aspirations of small farmers and recognized the importance of land security, education, and rural justice issues more broadly. In Haiti, however, Hubert found himself at the crosscurrents of both Haitian politics and a version of rural development that increasingly tended to emphasize—as the early New Deal did—questions of productivity, efficiency, and scale that would be eventually expanded into a broader global development paradigm: the Green Revolution.[20]

Focusing on Hubert's work as a social scientist, this essay makes the case for African Americans' contributions to the theory and practice of development and for the importance of adding the Jim Crow South to an increasingly transnationally oriented literature tracing the roots and evolution of development knowledge.[21] On the hand, Hubert's work as a scholar and teacher in Fisk University's Department of Social Sciences reveals the largely unacknowledged role of historically black colleges and universities (HBCUs) to postwar diplomatic history.[22] Most famously, Howard University's Division of Social Sciences hosted a major conference on "The Economic Future of the Caribbean" in 1943.[23] But southern HBCUs such as Fisk—often viewed as more parochial institutions—also played an important role. Hubert, alongside a number of other Fisk social scientists, built a body of knowledge about the rural South that came to significantly inform policy deliberations in the FSA during the 1930s and 1940s. And as USDA officials such as Hubert—a group that Sarah Phillips terms "resource technicians"—became part of America's Cold War statecraft, they remained bearers of a development paradigm shaped by its initial articulation in a Jim Crow world.[24] The career of Giles Hubert makes the case for the dialectical, transnational origins of development knowledge.[25] This, I argue, was a synthesis, combining Hubert's rootedness in the communities and culture of the black rural South, his faith in the transformative potential of state power, and his recognition that what white practitioners imagined as a universal mode of human uplift could also disguise ongoing forms of racial exclusion and imperial coercion, as was the case in Haiti.

* * *

Giles Hubert's commitment to rural progress sprang from roots planted deep in both the southern soil and the southern past. His father, Zachary Taylor

Hubert, was born in 1877, the son of former slaves in Warren County, Georgia. Zachary was raised amid a family of landowners who built their community's first postemancipation institutions, including a school and a church. He attended preparatory and collegiate classes at Atlanta Baptist College (now Morehouse University) before he moved north in 1902 to attend Massachusetts Agricultural College (now the University of Massachusetts). Hubert was one of the first African American graduates of that school, in 1904. Thereafter, his working life would take him on a tour of historically black colleges and universities, as a professor of science and agricultural at Florida A&M and an administrator at Spelman College, before serving as president of both Jackson College in Mississippi and Langston College in Oklahoma. In 1930, Zachary returned to Georgia to serve as an extension service agent at the USDA.[26]

One of three brothers, Giles Hubert followed in his father's footsteps for a time. Having attended Jackson College while his father was president of the institution, Hubert went on to earn a master's degree at the University of Iowa, before enrolling in a Ph.D. program at the University of Minnesota with the assistance of a Julius Rosenwald Fund fellowship.[27] Having met Muriel Patillo, his future wife, while teaching for a period at Arkansas State University, Hubert joined the faculty of Tennessee Agricultural and Industrial College. Shocked that he was expected to manage the college farm rather than teach agricultural economics, Hubert soon retreated to his father's home in rural Georgia, where he spent a year working on cooperative agriculture and rural credit union development.[28] By the beginning of the 1934 academic year, however, he received the call he had been waiting for: an opportunity to join the faculty of Fisk University's Department of Social Sciences in Nashville, Tennessee.[29]

Established in 1928 to study "the Negro and race relations in the United States" with a special emphasis on sociology and economics, the department's head and intellectual driving force was Charles S. Johnson, an African American sociologist and expert on rural life.[30] It was his intention, Johnson wrote in an early memorandum to Fisk's president, that the department would "establish in the South, which is the matrix of the Negro and race relations problems, a center or research into the very immediate questions of Negro life and status." As such, he continued, it would "provide a definite service to communities . . . particularly in the South through Special Surveys, investigations and researches."[31] Hubert was appointed as an assistant professor of economics, joining an ever-expanding faculty that was both interracial and, increasingly, international. A globally oriented approach characterized both the research being produced by the faculty and their work in the classroom.

As Edgar T. Thompson, a sociologist who evaluated the department's significance in 1945, observed, Fisk scholars were "much more interested in the comparative use of non-southern experience in the analysis of southern society," seeking "to wrench analysis clear of the particularistic assumptions of a single culture and to put the phenomena of southern life in a wider context of relationship and meaning."[32]

Hubert's career trajectory also fulfilled the department's commitment to engage the world beyond the university. In the mid-1930s, Hubert took time away from Fisk to work as an economic analyst for the Resettlement Administration (RA), a New Deal agency that struggled, against a growing tide of poverty and displacement, to manage the reorganization of American agriculture at the height of the Great Depression. The RA, as historian Jess Gilbert has argued, was animated by the idea that "poor land caused poor people, and vice-versa." Hubert would return to work for the agency at various times during the late 1930s and early 1940s, as it evolved into "one of the largest, most radical, and least racist of federal entities . . . [functioning] effectively as a 'poor man's department of agriculture.'"[33] Hubert also found time to take leave from Fisk in September of 1937 to travel to Denmark (again, courtesy of a Julius Rosenwald Fund scholarship) to study low-income rural cooperatives and farm ownership issues under the mentorship of O. H. Larsen, the head of the Danish Bureau of Farm Economics.[34] It was intended, as newspaper coverage reported, to "throw light on planning for treatment of the problem of farm tenancy in [the] southern United States."[35]

In 1939, Hubert would rejoin the FSA (the now-renamed RA) as a community management specialist. Beginning work in June, Hubert joined an agency whose radical potential had been dulled by a series of reforms sidelining earlier efforts to give poor farmers access to better land through centrally planned cooperatives and collectives. Exponents of this "agrarian" New Deal had argued consistently that land insecurity was a major factor in the South's economic woes, a position that recently evicted African American sharecroppers would likely have been sympathetic to.[36] More radical solutions to the problem of land tenancy and rural poverty, however, were undermined by the 1937 Bankhead–Jones Farm Tenant Act, which pushed the FSA toward establishing private ownership initiatives and away from Rexford Tugwell's favored communitarian land-planning programs. Nonetheless, under the guidance of Will W. Alexander, a collaborator of Charles Johnson and a leading southern liberal, the FSA battled to sustain its commitment to the concerns of the rural poor. Through supervised credit programs, the agency assisted more than eight hundred thousand low-income farmers and remained a consistent target for conservative opponents of the New Deal.[37]

Hubert's work during this period, as he recalled, was focused on the plight of black farming communities, particularly with regard to land tenure issues and local leadership development. As southern agriculture moved from labor-intensive to capital-intensive production, Hubert observed that "Many black farming communities did not have the capital or technical know-how or leadership to make the change."[38] In an effort to address this problem as a USDA official, Hubert relied extensively on his connections to Fisk. Hubert worked with both Johnson and Lewis Wade Jones, another rural sociologist based in the Department of Social Sciences, to give students enrolled in the university's seminar in rural problems direct, hands-on experience with FSA managed farming communities in the South. The program also placed Fisk students in more than thirty communities, including the Log Cabin Community in Hancock County, Georgia, where Hubert's family had been raised.

Like his father, Giles was committed to a project of community development in the rural South. While with the FSA he authored a number of memos specifically related to the transformation of what he termed "natural Negro neighborhoods," an effort that eventually became institutionalized in the agency's Negro Community Program.[39] The first memorandum, entitled "Community Organization among Negro Farmers," was premised on the idea that effective rural development could not start from scratch but instead had to facilitate collaboration between existing black farming families. Hubert inherited a skepticism of putting theory before grassroots practice from his father, who had wryly commented in a letter to his son that the "ideas of the 'Brain Trusters'" had been given too much credence. "Theorists, pure and simple," the elder Hubert complained. "When they make a mess of things, as they most often do, the men of action must come forward to cover their errors."[40] Giles reported to his father that his ideas had received considerable support within the FSA, with the report having caused "quite a bit of excitement," particularly among higher-level administrators in Washington, D.C.[41] The head of the tenant purchase division, for instance, agreed that it would be best "to concentrate Negro loans in certain areas where somewhat cohesive Negro communities are already established."[42]

In this period, Hubert was also finding his feet as an important scholar of the rural South. Toward the end of his time with the FSA, he would publish an essay in the *Journal of Negro Education* on the future of southern agriculture. Like many African Americans during the early 1940s, Hubert fused black interests with wartime imperatives, arguing in "The Negro on the Agricultural Front" that surplus agriculture labor in the rural South could be put—with state assistance—to more valuable purposes. He proposed a range of programs, including the redirection of black rural labor to industrial jobs, agricultural production in other parts of the country, and farming initiatives in the South that better reflected wartime needs, particularly food production rather than long-standing southern commodities such as cotton and tobacco.[43] Helping black farmers in the South to transition to food production reflected both the work of the USDA, particularly identified in the agency's 1942 publication *Food for Freedom*, and the general drift in farm policy more generally toward economies of scale in production.[44] Black farmers in particular, Hubert contended, were in dire need of larger landholdings if they were to join the ongoing agricultural revolution. With great pride, Hubert's essay cited the work of the FSA in this regard, noting the relative success of black FSA-assisted farmers in raising their productivity levels.[45]

While Hubert's essay revealed his deepening engagement with emerging theories of economic transformation, it was also rooted in forms of Jim Crow knowledge. Though the labor reserves in the rural South were in one sense "inefficient," Hubert argued that it was a political "status quo"—the racial hierarchy of the segregationist South—that worked to thwart the empowerment of black farmers. "The negative reaction of southern planters to the migration of Negro workers," he wrote, "is based on the desire . . . to keep for the cotton and tobacco plantations a large and under-employed labor force which is cheap."[46] The process of modernizing southern agriculture, Hubert contended, need not be predicated on the dispossession of black farmers, but could potentially augur a new, more prosperous era. Looking to the future of the rural South, Hubert predicted that "General reorganization in Southern agriculture may take either or both of two trends. . . . It might lead to the setting up of adequate sized family units. . . . Such an organization could support the maximum possible population at satisfactory living standards. It would thus provide the foundation . . . for a democratic agricultural society on a secure and enterprising rural yeomanry—a yeomanry which would take advantage of all scientific knowledge in the operation of the individual farm and through cooperation secure most of the benefits of mechanized and scientific progress in agriculture."[47] Elsewhere, Hubert regularly offered vigorous defenses of the democratizing potential of FSA agricultural policy.

Cooperatives, Hubert argued, were critical democratic institutions in a profoundly undemocratic Jim Crow South, as well as institutions that inculcated egalitarian sensibilities in their participants. In an unpublished essay, Hubert wrote that cooperatives had led to the creation of "Free and friendly relation[s]" and had made "a decided contribution to racial understanding and racial relationships in the community."[48]

Hubert would spend five years working for the FSA. By 1942, when the agency was moved to a new headquarters in Cincinnati, Ohio, Hubert had ascended to a position as assistant to the director of the Rural Rehabilitation division. The so-called decentralization program, however, was in fact the beginning of a final—and fatal—attack on the more progressive policy impulses of the agency. Led by conservative southern Democrats and a number of large-farm organizations, most notably the Farm Bureau, the FSA was defunded by Congress in 1943, and many of the agency's projects were brought to a halt. Seeing the writing on the wall, Hubert resigned his position in September 1943 to return to Fisk, where he assumed the rank of full professor of economics.[49]

Hubert's eventual journey from Nashville to Port-au-Prince, however, was inseparable from the Department of Social Sciences' growing commitment to an international and comparative approach to the study of race relations. In 1943, the year of Hubert's return to Fisk, the department initiated a program in African and Caribbean studies.[50] Charles Johnson envisioned both a theoretical and a pragmatic role for the curriculum, particularly with the prospect of decolonization on the horizon. "The vocational aspect of these studies," Johnson wrote in a program prospectus, "must be emphasized. Opportunities will be increasingly offered for American Negroes to share with Africans in Africa these advantages which they have gained in the United States."[51] Furthering this global agenda, Fisk hosted a conference on African studies in November 1943, which brought together a range of scholars, including Melville Herskovits, W. E. B. Du Bois, Ira De A. Reid, and Rayford Logan.[52] In 1945, Fisk received funding for a Creole language project and soon thereafter established an exchange program that allowed a number of faculty to undertake research in Haiti, at the same time as students from the island, now freed from American occupation, made their way to Fisk.

Various other figures also played a role in drawing Hubert toward the study of the Caribbean. The arrival of Haitian students at Fisk was an important contingency, particularly as a number educated in the Department would eventually return to their home country to assume government positions.[53]

The flow of students in the late 1940s kept Fisk faculty abreast of political developments in Haiti as they sought to strengthen their institutional connections to the nation in a time of political upheaval. For instance, Hubert corresponded with Clovis Charlot, who had developed close contacts with the Comité Exécutif Militaire that had assumed power following the removal of Élie Lescot. Charlot informed Hubert that Franck Lavaud, the acting head of state, had been informed of Fisk's interest in creating a "Caribbean Institute" to "study all of the problems arisen in the life of the people of the Caribbean area."[54] Charlot also reported on the wish of various Haitian statesmen—particularly Emile Saint-Lôt, a sitting Senator—to deepen the country's connection to the expertise and institutions of black America. Hubert worked behind the scenes to fund Saint-Lôt's visit to Nashville as part of a tour of the United States organized by J. Max Bond, Sr., an African American scholar and educator who was at that time head of the Inter-American Educational Foundation.[55]

Another important connection between African American public life and Haiti was Claude Barnett, the head of the Associated Negro Press and a man one contemporary referred to as the "unofficial Secretary of State" of black America.[56] In the mid-1940s, Barnett had assumed a role as a consultant to the USDA, where among other initiatives he was involved in arranging for the importation of Caribbean labor to farms in Florida. Barnett and Hubert corresponded in the mid-1940s about their shared concern over the impact of agricultural mechanization on African American farmers. Relaying a conversation with an executive of International Harvester, Barnett informed Hubert that "The [mechanical] cotton picker . . . is really here."[57] In addition, Barnett held a significant interest in the fate of the Caribbean, particularly Haiti. Hubert's eventual appointment to the American embassy was a partial fulfillment of Barnett's belief that pan-American relations would be drastically improved by the presence of more African Americans in the U.S. diplomatic core in Haiti.[58]

Hubert's move beyond the boundaries of the United States was also a reflection of his growing interest in the spatial nature of economic processes, one that was to a significant degree a product of discipline's postwar structuralist movement. As Joseph Love has argued, proponents and theorists of structuralism concerned themselves first and foremost with identifying and then reforming the factors that made "underdeveloped" parts of the world immune from the prescriptions and rules of neoclassical economic theory.[59]

Notably, Hubert was writing and thinking as the Argentine economist Raúl Prebisch and the Economic Commission on Latin America were developing a body of economic theory that explained underdevelopment in terms of the relationship between an economic "center" and a "periphery."[60] As a part of this movement, Hubert produced a 1946 essay, "A Framework for the Study of Peripheral Economic Areas," which he published in the *Journal of Farm Economics*. In the essay, Hubert identified the Caribbean's predominately agricultural economy as located on the periphery of an economic orbit articulated toward an industrial core in the northeast of the United States.[61] Here, Hubert was indebted to the work of the German economist J. H. von Thunen and the American business historian N. S. B. Gras, the latter of whom would later review Hubert's work favorably.[62] But if this agglomerate was in fact a "natural [trade] community," Hubert observed, then any close attention to the Caribbean would identify some limitations to this model. One would expect, Hubert noted, that population densities would decline the further one was removed from the center. In fact, Hubert noted, the Caribbean—characterized broadly by an agricultural export economy—had relatively high population densities. This was the result, Hubert argued, of the legacy of slavery and colonialism where "a premium was placed on a plentiful supply of cheap labor to be exploited," and as a reflection of island agricultural communities where there was less opportunity "for rural-urban migration." Drawing a comparison to the United States, Hubert noted the Caribbean might have been more profitably transformed if population "had flowed . . . in toward the urban concentrations . . . just the same as it had flowed inward from Alabama, Mississippi or Georgia."[63] For Hubert, the "marginal" nature of the Caribbean presented its biggest obstacle to development, of "being partially within the orbit and yet partially without." This would "remain a severe problem until proper orientation occurs."[64]

These were not just idle speculations or abstract theorizations on the part of Hubert. In fact, Hubert had visited Haiti in the summer of 1945 as part of an FSA-sponsored visit that also included stops in Puerto Rico and the Virgin Islands. While in Haiti, Hubert spent time at the Haitian American Damien Agricultural School, the site of a student strike in 1929 that had done much to escalate what would become widespread protests against the U.S. occupation.[65] Hubert wrote to Louis Decatrel, an instructor at the school, to thank him for his role in organizing a number of trips into Haiti's rural interior and to advise on the possibility of Damien students applying for admission to Fisk.[66] With a wealth of experience in hand, Hubert had also returned to Nashville intent on developing "a course on the economics of West Indian (or Caribbean) nations," requesting the help of Lloyd Hughes, who worked as an officer at the Inter-American Educational Foundation, in supplying "statistical materials on the commerce and trade of Latin American nations."[67]

In August 1947, Hubert passed the foreign service manpower examination, making him eligible for employment overseas.[68] His appointment to the embassy in Port-au-Prince, however, relied on some behind-the-scenes influence on the part of Mary McLeod Bethune, whose work as head of the National Youth Administration's Division of Negro Affairs during the New Deal had accorded her sizeable clout in Washington, D.C. Indeed, Hubert had first contacted Bethune in 1946 in an effort to protect African American officials in the FSA on the verge of unemployment, a result of the Truman administration's plans to shutter the agency. In an impassioned plea, Hubert wrote Bethune that it was imperative to maintain "continued liberality in this important bureau [the USDA] of our government—the best way to do this is to keep good Negro personnel in strategic positions. . . . These fellows in FSA have worked too hard, suffered too much and have done too good a job to be abandoned now."[69] Bethune was no match for the conservative war on the progressive enclaves still remaining in the USDA, but she did repay Hubert in short order by working to fulfill his "desire for a diplomatic post in Haiti."[70] Years later, Bethune would use her nationally syndicated column to praise Hubert's work in the foreign service as evidence that "the influence of our people in foreign lands continues to broaden."[71]

When he arrived in Port-au-Prince in February 1948, much of Hubert's work involved improving ties between the United States and the Haitian state, particularly as recent collaboration on rural development initiatives had not gone well. The SHADA experiment, for one, had ended in disaster. Much like the modernization of the rural South, SHADA policies had promoted widespread displacement and dispossession in the Haitian countryside. Almost 50,000 acres of land were expropriated by the Haitian state, while SHADA directives—despite the increasing protestations of Maurice Dartigue, its deputy director and the Haitian agricultural minister—led to the razing over a million fruit trees. A simultaneous reduction in rice production had also led food prices to rise across the country. When harvests in 1943 and 1944 were underwhelming and rubber demand dropped following the conclusion of World War II and the wider use of synthetic rubber, there was little to show for the effort.[72]

Hubert characterized his work as the embassy's agricultural attaché as combining the responsibilities of "a diplomat, a technician, a reporter and an adventurer."[73] Indeed, much of his time in the early days of his appointment was spent on the ground in the interior of Haiti, where he traveled frequently from his villa in Pétion-Ville. The American embassy had been without an agricultural attaché since November 1947, so much of Hubert's early work entailed catching up on a significant backlog of reports on productivity in the Haitian countryside. Over the summer of 1948, Hubert visited sisal (agave) plantations in northern Haiti, rice cultivators in the Artibonite Valley, and peasant farmers in the lowlands of the Plaine du Cul-de-Sac and the Plaine Agricole de Léogâne, among others. In a letter to Edward Tanner, his predecessor in Haiti who had moved on to a similar position in Costa Rica, Hubert reported on the uneven efforts at agricultural development—pyrethreum plantations abandoned by American investors because of inadequate plot sizes; plantation owners' belief that "the wage level has to be kept very low"; coffee production plans that had been undermined by the Haitian legislature; and the aborted nationalization of banana cultivation, which Hubert referred to as the "banana mess."[74]

Hubert thus arrived in Port-au-Prince in a period when skepticism about American intentions, expertise, and authority was high. Lescot's successor, Dumarsais Estimé, had come to power on a platform of both progressive reform and anti-imperial politics, which included efforts to create a social security system, establish new proworker labor legislation, and expand educational access to a greater proportion of the population. In the realm of rural development, the government sought to improve agricultural productivity through a range of initiatives including irrigation and reforestation, as well as UNESCO-sponsored rural development initiatives in 1949 and 1950.[75] Hubert's ability to navigate this political environment was presumably eased by his racial status, which was compatible with the ascendant race-conscious populism at the heart of the Estimé's *noiriste* government. The Estimé government represented what historian Matthew J. Smith terms the "nationalization of Black Power," a moment in which black Haitians assumed widespread and unprecedented control of the state apparatus. Self-described "*authentiques*," this generation of functionaries, including a number of Fisk students, claimed themselves as the true heirs to the legacy of the revolutionary leader Jean-Jacques Dessalines. Equally, as Smith notes, they represented "the intellectual pinnacle of the black middle class. Black power was for them a national mission."[76] Hubert's efforts to carve out a role in

Port-au-Prince cannot also have been harmed by a concurrent effort on the part of the NAACP, and Walter White in particular, to rehabilitate Haiti in the eyes of the American public.[77]

Much of Hubert's work in this period revolved around his participation in a seminar organized by the Haitian-American Institute, which operated as a subsidiary of the Institute of Inter-American Affairs and quickly became an important venue of collaboration on a range of policy issues. Because of Hubert's presence and influence, the Haitian-American Institute functioned as a node in a circuit of developmental knowledge that connected Nashville, the rural South, and Fisk's Department of Social Sciences to the project of Haitian nation-building. Almost immediately on arrival in Port-au-Prince, Hubert wrote to Fisk to request a copy of a former student's master's thesis, entitled "The Position of Haiti on the American Market." The thesis, which Hubert wanted for discussion at the seminar, was written by Clement Jumelle, a man who would eventually run for president of Haiti in 1957 and who, following political exile thereafter, became a fierce critic of the Duvalier dictatorship.[78] Recounting the successes of the effort in a letter to Charles Johnson, Hubert reported that early meetings at the institute had attracted participants of "high calibre," including directors of the Haitian Bureau of Rural Economics and the Bureau of Labor and representatives from the Banque Nationale d'Haiti (BNH). "Many people have written to me or have come to me to say how much they appreciate this effort to stimulate economic thinking, discussion and research," Hubert wrote, while expressing optimism that the work of the institute "may be the foundation for something very substantial in the future."[79] Hubert's work with the institute in turn cemented his position as an informal advisor to the Estimé government. In a long letter sent in 1949, the undersecretary of labor (and future president) François Duvalier wrote to Hubert to request the American's participation in a national labor conference. Duvalier wrote to Hubert to express his hope that the interests of both business and labor "can be reconciled to the field of social justice and [that] the forces of labor can develop their relations in the best interest of the community . . . to establish social peace on solid foundations." Hubert's presence, Duvalier continued, would be a "precious contribution to the study of these problems."[80] Hubert replied in the affirmative, promising a presentation that would discuss "The Training of Industrial Workers in the United States."[81]

While abroad, Hubert worked to maintain his ties to both Fisk University and the USDA. Hubert remained in close contact during this period with

Charles Johnson about the potential for developing an exchange program. In response to a series of questions posed by Hubert, Johnson was unequivocal in his support for the program, noting his conviction that "Haiti could provide an educational and social scientific laboratory for research."[82] Only two year earlier, Johnson had made a similar argument in the pages of *Phylon*, where he dwelled at length on the Haitian peasantry. While anthropologists, particularly Melville Herskovits, had asked important questions, Johnson contended, "The sociologist in Haiti can begin almost from scratch." "New policies of enlightenment, economic development and dependency on foreign trade," Johnson wrote, promised to bring Haiti into closer contact with the United States. But he also warned of the potential for peasant dispossession by foreign capital. "It will take wise direction and intelligent economic policies, perhaps along cooperative lines," he said, "for the present ruling group in Haiti to combat this tendency."[83]

Though he would not stay in Haiti to see its completion, Hubert was at the heart of early discussions of a development effort that embodied the perils of rural reform in Haiti: the Artibonite Valley project. Tracking the 320-km-long Artibonite River, the Valley had long occupied a place in the imaginary of pan-African black capitalists. In 1934, the Haitian Afro-American Chamber of Commerce's head, Willis N. Huggins, had identified the region as a "vast underdeveloped area which awaits settlers from America who with patience, money and brains can make that valley blossom like a rose."[84] As Haiti became a "nation of projects" in the 1940s and 1950s, development experts returned to the valley as a potential site of national transformation. As was the case in many corners of the global South, planners took inspiration from the Tennessee Valley Authority.[85] It was hoped constructing a dam on the Artibonite River would irrigate more than 120,000 acres of surrounding land while providing rural electrification, education, and technical assistance to the region's farmers. In the early stages of planning, Hubert worked to secure the participation as consultants of former colleagues in the USDA, including Marshall Harris, who at that moment headed the land tenure section of the USDA's Division of Land Economics.[86]

The immediate fate of the valley's peasant farmers and the question of land tenure quickly became a critical issue for the project's planners. Hubert was initially clear that the project necessarily would entail "revision of the settlement land tenure and agricultural pattern of the area."[87] Later documents, however, suggested officials tended to take a more communitarian approach to development that reflected the grassroots imperatives of early New Deal agricultural policy. In 1952, a report prepared by the Inter-American Institute of Agricultural Sciences argued that "involving the people of the Valley in the development and operation of the Project transcends all other recommendations" and that the project would advance a "dual policy of maintaining the family operation and small ownership pattern of land tenure existing in the valley, while working the area in large units for certain mechanical operations."[88] UN advisors to the project, however, were adamant that land use "must be centrally controlled."[89] The project remained under consideration for a number of years, amassing a wealth of data, surveys, and studies, before the Péligre Dam was finally completed in 1953.

Hubert's extensive work in the field did not mean he completely abandoned his scholarly pursuits, however. While serving in Haiti, Hubert would publish perhaps his most important contribution to the nascent field of economic development. Appearing in 1950 in the journal *Inter-American Economic Affairs*, "Some Problems of a Colonial Economy: A Study of Economic Dualism in Haiti" reflected Hubert's training, the work of the Haiti-American Institute seminar, and his observations on the ground over the previous two years.[90] The immediate impetus for the writing of the essay, however, had come from an invitation extended by David McCord Wright to participate in the 1949 meeting of the Southern Economic Association; Wright hoped Hubert might contribute to a session on "comparative economic systems."[91] Hubert did so—although he could not attend the meeting, held in Nashville, in person. Encouraged by the responses he received in writing from attendees, he revised the manuscript in short order.

Building on his earlier work, Hubert identified Haiti as part of a group of "economic semi-colonies" whose developmental potential had been circumscribed by its historically subordinate relationship to a more "industrially and commercially advanced region."[92] Thus defined, Hubert's paper probed what occurred when so-called capitalistic modes of production, investment, and culture "encountered a pre-capitalistic or-non capitalistic economy." Hubert thus sought to define Haiti as a "dual economy," a characterization that built on scholarship rooted in an assessment of other colonial contexts.[93] Hubert's use of the concept of economic dualism marks the essay and his work as an economic thinker more as part of a broader process in which black intellectuals in both the United States and other parts of the diaspora began to wrestle with the relationship between development, decolonization, and nation building. Emblematic—and most well known—in this regard is the work of the Saint Lucian economist W. Arthur Lewis, whose 1954 essay "Economic

Development with Unlimited Supplies of Labor" was a foundational contribution to the field. In a number of ways, Hubert's essay anticipated Lewis's "dual sector model" that scholars commonly understand as pioneering a theory of economic transformation and a broader body of scholarship that, as Robert Tignor notes, was "suffused with the optimism that marked this era of political decolonization."[94] Premised on existing conceptions of economic dualism, Lewis argued that the principal challenge in colonial economic contexts was the existence of a subsistence sector that disincentivized investment in the modern, "capitalist" sector. As Lewis argued,

> The fact that the wage level in the capitalist sector depends upon earnings in the subsistence sector is sometimes of immense political importance, since its effect is that capitalists have a direct interest in holding down the productivity of the subsistence workers. Thus, the owners of the plantations have no interest in seeing knowledge of new techniques conveyed to the peasants, and if they are influential in government, they will not be found using their influence to expand the facilities for agricultural extension. They will not support proposals for land settlement, and are often instead to be found engaged in turning the peasants off their lands. . . . This is one of the worst features of imperialism, for instance.[95]

Hubert's essay anticipated the later concerns of Lewis's work in a number of ways. Neither scholar, for instance, understood the challenge of growth as dependent on industrialization exclusively. Both men also shared concerns about questions of population, specifically the challenges to prosperity and development represented in "overpopulated" locales such as Haiti, which had high population densities relative to natural resource endowments, including land.[96] Perhaps most importantly, both scholars also shared a reluctance to identify agriculture as an exclusively "traditional" economic sector. Rather, as Hubert noted in his essay's conclusion, the challenge was at least in part "to find some mechanism to take the place of the colonial plantation in bridging the gap between non-capitalistic economy and modern capitalism (principally along agricultural lines with whatever supplemental industry that may be possible) and thus to reduce the dualism in the economic structure of the country."[97]

Hubert would leave Haiti in 1951 just as a new, ambitious approach to rural development was being articulated by Paul Magloire, the new president.

Magloire, in contrast to his predecessor, actively courted both American and international aid and investment. In an effort to revive the fortunes of the Haitian peasantry, his administration announced a five-year plan that was supported by assistance from the United Nations, the World Health Organization, and the United States' Point IV Program.[98] This effort was well received in the United States, where *Time* ran a cover story celebrating Magloire's "modern Black Magic," which readers learned would include a new infrastructure of rural reconstruction: "agricultural schools, a county-agent system, cooperative use of tractors, a farmers' bank, reforestation and grain storage."[99] Certainly, these initiatives were reminiscent of various elements of the agrarian New Deal. Little of this would come to fruition, however. Despite these progressive aspirations and the eventual completion of the Artibonite Valley Dam, the 1950s were a catastrophic decade for Haitian agriculture in general. Magloire hoped to diversify the country's export sector, but this effort foundered on the shoals of soil depletion and deforestation, two factors that intensified migration from the countryside to Port-au-Prince. Combined with a global collapse in coffee prices and the devastating effects of Hurricane Hazel in October 1954, agricultural productivity (which accounted for 86 percent of Haiti's GNP) sank to levels that resembled the worst years of the nineteenth century.[100] Writing in the early 1980s, one social scientist and scholar of Haiti's rural political economy found that the ambitions and expertise of the age of development had largely not found its way into the rural interior, where the "technology of the peasant is still dominated by a few simple tools—the hoe and the machete—by unimproved seed varieties, by a lack of manure and fertilizers, by lack of crop rotation, and by a general lack of knowledge."[101] At least in the case of Haiti, the agrarian New Deal had failed to take root.

* * *

Haiti was not the end of Hubert's sojourn through the global South. In 1951, he was reassigned to India to work as an executive assistant to the American consul in Bombay, Clare Timberlake.[102] While India has often been viewed in scholarship on American diplomatic history as a foundational arena for the elaboration of America's modernizing pretensions in the postwar era, the career of Giles Hubert suggests that scholars also take Haiti seriously as a critical space for analyzing the strange, paradoxical career of the agrarian New Deal. Evaluating this history requires coming to terms with the broader contradictions of the "age of development," as well as the specificities of Haiti and the role of American power and influence that endured long after the end of the occupation. As Daniel Immerwahr has argued, when this communitarian, grassroots versions of the New Deal went abroad, it often sidestepped many of the "structural issues most obviously responsible for the depressed conditions of the lower orders: debt, unequal land tenure, caste and patriarchy."[103] Hubert's aspirations as an exponent of the agrarian New Deal were clear: he believed he could establish new lines of subaltern development expertise that connected grassroots knowledge generated by the black experience in the United States and the vibrant world of social scientific inquiry at HBCUs with the project of rural empowerment and nation-building in Haiti. This flow of ideas and personnel was to a significant degree successfully cultivated in the years around the turn of the century, adding a new layer to the long-standing relationship between Haiti and black America. But Hubert's racial status went only so far; he was also an American, a New Deal technocrat, and an agricultural economist trained broadly in a field that was largely unprepared to recognize "irrational" economic behaviors, indigenous rural institutions in Haiti such as the *coumbite* and *lakou*, and forms of land tenure that did not lend themselves to quick and easy reform. Other black intellectuals of his generation would come to the same modernizing conclusion. As he imagined the future of the region in 1942, the great Caribbean radical and economic historian Eric Williams wrote that "We must not harbor the mistaken notion that the alternative to the plantation with its army of landless blacks is a system of peasant proprietorship, the division of the large estate into small farms."[104]

Constrained by the larger context of American foreign policy ambitions in the era of the Cold War, Hubert could certainly be viewed a conduit for new forms of postwar American power that arrived in Haiti under the guise of newly available development aid. To be sure, the era of the Good Neighbor policy retained elements of the United States' earlier, imperial ambitions in Latin America and the Caribbean.[105] But centering Giles Hubert and his work with a Haitian state grappling with the possibilities of postoccupation world suggests the degree to which American power coexisted with new, inter-American forms of exchange, collaboration, and cosmopolitanism. Ultimately, Hubert's journey suggests the possibility of drawing new connections between the histories of race in the United States, transformations in American foreign policy, and changes in the organization of global history of agriculture. As one social scientist wrote in 1945, "it may be suggested that the area we now call "the South" was originally not South at all . . . [but rather] the northern subregion of the Caribbean-Gulf plantation region.[106] In this regard, Hubert's effort to turn his experience with the chronically poor communities of the black rural South to emancipatory ends outside the borders of the United States ultimately suggests some of the unrealized potential of the agrarian New Deal.

CHAPTER 4

Weapons of the Strong: The Multinational Firm, Infrastructure, and the Neoliberal Legacies of the New Deal

Jason Scott Smith

The intersection of private capitalism, public authority, and American hegemony has a long history. This essay explores how a range of actors mobilized and transformed ideas about government-sponsored economic development after World War II, and it argues that this moment reflects a consolidation and transformation in how American liberals viewed capitalism. The ability of New Deal liberalism to generate economic growth and regulate the creative destruction of capitalism did not disappear after World War II. In fact, this reform ideology and a number of associated public policies played vital roles, creating the institutions that expanded the reach of American business abroad. After 1945, American government and business aimed to enact a New Deal for only part of the world, one that often focused less on advancing human rights abroad and more on providing America firms with unfettered access to foreign markets. This project, to be sure, was often met with skepticism and outright resistance from foreign actors, who often sought to assert their own claims to sovereignty as they welcomed selected aspects of American investment. In the face of these reactions, American liberalism, infused by a renewed anticommunism, tried to build a postwar global economy that was decidedly friendly to multinational corporations based in the United States. Although New Deal conceptions about the proper place of big business in society faded from prominence within the United States after World War II—what Alan Brinkley has called the "end of reform"—during this period liberal ideas about regulating capitalism gained traction despite provoking suspicion among elites throughout Europe, Japan, and Latin America.[1]

During the postwar years, many elements of the New Deal traveled overseas. These reform impulses were carried abroad by New Dealers such as Adolf Berle (coauthor of the 1932 classic *The Modern Corporation and Private Property*), who served as ambassador to Brazil at the close of World War II. They were transmitted by multinational corporations, who took their experience working for the federal government during the Great Depression and applied it in foreign markets. They were also present in Bretton Woods, New Hampshire, as New Dealers, scarred by the economic collapse of the 1930s and the devastation of World War II, worked with colleagues from other nations to create postwar institutions like the International Monetary Fund, the International Bank for Reconstruction and Development (the World Bank), and the General Agreement on Tariffs and Trade, injecting stability into the global economy. As these ideas and institutions shaped the economies and societies of other nations, they were often subsequently imported back into the United States, usually with little knowledge of their real origins.[2]

Historians have, in different ways, noticed this circular trajectory. Daniel Immerwahr, for example, has observed that the community strategies of the New Deal "didn't disappear; they moved abroad." The subsequent use of these strategies in Lyndon Johnson's War on Poverty "did not appear from thin air but rather were based, in large part, on overseas community development—the boomerang returning home."[3] This essay seeks to contribute to this growing conversation by focusing directly on the governmental and nongovernmental organizations, specifically the multinational firm. In shifting our focus to how elements of American capitalism were exported abroad after World War II to Venezuela and Brazil, I draw on the work of Frederick Cooper to underscore the impact and ability of these institutions and organizations to cross national borders in a robust fashion. As Cooper has argued, power in developing and colonial societies "was more arterial than capillary," in the Foucauldian sense of the term, and was "concentrated spatially and socially, not very nourishing beyond such domains, and in need of a pump to push it from place to place." Nonstate actors such as the multinational firm functioned as Cooper's pump, representing an example of what I call "weapons of the strong." Recovering their histories reminds us of the ability of these companies to project their power across multiple sovereignties.[4] In doing so, the actions of these firms anticipate our neoliberal moment.

* * *

By the middle of the twentieth century, American-style capitalism unfolded across the planet, a missionary-like undertaking led by entrepreneurs and multinational firms, many of whom wanted to make money while raising the standard of living for people around the world.[5] As investment banker and vice chairman of the War Production Board Ferdinand Eberstadt recognized, the end of World War II left the United States positioned as a global hegemon. "Of course, we want first to give generously to relieve the afflicted" in other nations, Eberstadt declared at a conference on "The Role of American Industry in the Postwar Era." "But beyond charity lie the postwar world's great business needs for almost all items in the catalogue of our products and productive skills," he said. "America, alone among the great nations, will end the war with its industry intact—yes, even strengthened and enlarged. Within our borders will be almost half the world's industrial plant. Through war's relentless drive our managerial skills and our techniques in design, in engineering, in production and construction have reached their highest peak. Our working force is larger and more skillful than ever in our history. Our financial strength is the greatest of all nations. And, most important of all, our faith in our own productive powers has been confirmed."[6] Other nations, Eberstadt argued, would look to the United States not simply for products. "They seek our industrial skills—our 'know-how'—even more," he declared. "Our neighbors to the north and south . . . as well as Central America, South America, China, India and Russia, are all eager customers in this field. They want to build new railroads, highways, bridges, airfields, communications systems, power plants and transmission lines. In the art of their construction, our engineering and construction firms excel."[7] Eberstadt was by no means a lone voice in recognizing the opportunities available to American businesses.

Others, of course, noted the threats that a postwar economy could pose to firms based in the United States. One journalist worried that American business was overlooking the competitive threat posed by growing firms in South America. "Busy searching for evidence of what the Germans, Italians, Japanese and Stalinists have been doing to create friction in the American hemisphere," during the war, "observers have entirely overlooked what the South Americans themselves have been doing," argued William LaVarre. "Sherlock Holmes, when he wanted to hide something, placed it on plain view on the mantelpiece—and nobody saw it." LaVarre urged American industrialists to "migrate" their operations directly to South America, following the examples of Elizabeth Arden (beauty products), DuPont (rayon; gun powder and dynamite), Johnson & Johnson (surgical and medical products), Ford (rubber, cotton, and auto assembly), and others. If the American business community did not follow the examples of these "pioneers," as LaVarre called them, they could fall victim to a growing South American economy and its business community. "South America is probably the last New Frontier for industrial and commercial expansion. Ten years from today will it record you as one of the pioneers—or will your company be among the frantic also-rans?"[8]

LaVarre's point about the robust activities of foreign firms signals the broader context of the postwar years (1945–1973): U.S.-based multinational firms did not operate in a vacuum—far from it. During this period a variety of approaches to economic development and international assistance contested this moment, presenting compelling options to the model of capitalism presented by the United States and its companies. The Soviet Union, for example, sought to modernize the poorest regions of the USSR, successfully building the Nurek Dam in Tajikistan and signaling to the world the potential for Soviet communism to counter the legacies of colonialism. In Latin America, nations such as Chile would experiment with different levels of state involvement with the economy after World War II. Salvador Allende, for example, helped create Chile's national health service and made nationalization of his nation's copper industry a key element of his presidential campaigns from 1952 to 1970, successfully placing it under government ownership during his short term as president (1970–1973). Elsewhere, the rise of political movements, such as the Front de Libération Nationale in Algeria, gave definition to the term "Third World." The FLN inspired a bold attempt to remake a political and economic order imposed by European colonialism, adopting an aggressive practice of nonalignment to exploit international tensions with the Soviet Union and the United States. Elites in nations such as India, for their part, used development aid from the two superpowers to gain political advantage and power at home, even if the "price of aid," as David Engerman has argued, ultimately was an erosion of sovereignty. Indeed, over the past two decades a range of works in the field of international history have broadened our perspective: while the postwar United States and American companies held great power, these public and private actors were far from uncontested or unopposed in the global political economy.[9]

As American business contemplated the political terrain of the international economy after World War II, organizations like the Council on Foreign Relations set up seminars for executives, raising awareness of the advantages of foreign investment and such initiatives as Harry Truman's "Point Four" program. One such seminar series brought together midlevel executives from twenty firms in fields like law, banking, transportation, and export businesses to focus on such topics as U.S.-Soviet relations, U.S.-British relations, Western Europe's political and economic situation, American policies in the Middle East, relations with Asia, overseas investment and Point Four, and the place of the United States within the United Nations. As one staff member of the council described the initiative, "we should put emphasis on the educational value of the seminar in increasing understanding of American policy in critical areas of the world," adding, "We hope to make it possible for the young men who participate to get the benefits indirectly of the most important research work now being done at the Council."[10]

Perhaps no firm better epitomized the combination of public spirit and private profits than did the International Basic Economy Corporation (IBEC), founded in 1947 by Nelson A. Rockefeller, heir to the Standard Oil fortune. Rockefeller was, in many respects, Franklin Roosevelt's favorite kind of Republican: one who was deeply sympathetic to the New Deal's project of using public authority to extend credit and state-sponsored infrastructure into the economic periphery, with the goal of stimulating private economic growth. Rockefeller had served FDR's administration during World War II; Roosevelt appointed him head of the Office of Inter-American Affairs in 1940 (in part as an effort to keep the Rockefellers from backing Wendell Willkie in 1940) and then assistant secretary of state for American Republic Affairs in 1944. In these positions, Rockefeller built on his deep interest in Latin America, looking to strengthen U.S. ties with the region and promote American values and institutions.[11]

Long fascinated with Latin America (Rockefeller had served on the board of Creole Petroleum, the Venezuelan division of Standard Oil of New Jersey, from 1935 to 1940), with IBEC Rockefeller aimed to create a private corporation that would complement another of his organizations, the American International Association for Economic and Social Development (AIA), which Rockefeller set up to do good in the world. As Rockefeller adviser John Lockwood told his boss, "You have to realize . . . that in our Christian world, during the week you make money, and on the weekend you go to church and you give it away. But it's two different processes."[12] AIA would thus be Rockefeller's "Sunday" foundation and IBEC would function "during the week" to pay AIA's bills, doing good in the world, to be sure, but also making money and turning a profit. IBEC, the company's certificate of incorporation declared, would "promote the economic development of various parts of the world . . . increase the production and availability of goods, things and services useful to the lives or livelihood of their peoples . . . [and] better their standards of living."[13]

Focused initially on Brazil and Venezuela, IBEC's many activities signaled an approach to development modeled in many respects on that of the New Deal, one that exported the methods and philosophies that the New Deal had first road tested with the Tennessee Valley Authority in the 1930s.[14] In these two South American nations, Rockefeller and his employees learned a lesson that had been taught to many American businessmen, that U.S. corporations could never simply project American-style capitalism abroad. Henry Ford, for example, may have been able to give his name to a rubber-producing industrial town in Brazil, but he and his employees were not able to make it a successful venture in the face of a range of local obstacles. While some members of the business community resented U.S. practices, others looked at them as an opportunity. For example, some industrialists in Brazil and in other nations had long borrowed from corporate practices that had originated in the North Atlantic, at the same time transforming them. In São Paulo, for example, industrialists adapted the tools of applied psychology, scientific management, and organizational theory in order to increase productivity while maintaining social stability within the working class. In short, in exploring opportunities abroad IBEC's executives confronted a complicated set of social relations and business environments that were difficult to navigate.[15] In setting up a for-profit corporation to promote economic development, Rockefeller's IBEC was functioning—as Inderjeet Parmar has noted of foundations generally—as "*effectively* extensions of the state" and not somehow "above the fray of politics and business."[16] Indeed, as we shall see, while rooted in the techniques of the New Deal, the activities of the Rockefeller Foundation were also firmly embedded in the fray of politics and business.

* * *

The Rockefeller Foundation undertook a number of important projects in Venezuela, looking to intervene in its economy to address food shortages and studying the possibility of participating in the funding and construction of the Caracas-La Guaira Highway in Venezuela. One of the most expensive roads ever constructed, this highway would link Venezuela's capital with its major port city via a set of tunnels carved through mountainous terrain. For Rockefeller, this project and a range of other IBEC programs represented a chance to demonstrate to the new center-left government of Venezuela that American-style capitalism could bring about greater social good. Indeed, the end of World War II marked an inflection point in the history of democracy across Central and South America. As Leslie Bethel and Ian Roxborough have noted, the years 1944 to 1946 witnessed "a sudden and dramatic advance of democracy throughout Latin America," with anti-Nazi and pro–United States propaganda making the case "in favor of U.S. political institutions, the U.S. economic model, and the American way of (and standard of) life."[17] This short period of a democratic spring, then, contextualized the moment of IBEC's creation.

Writing to Veneuzeulan president Rómulo Betancourt, Rockefeller declared "it is my firm belief that peace, individual liberty, and respect for human dignity cannot be attained in the world until standards of living are raised and peoples enjoy good health, education and well-being," and, as Rockefeller believed, "efficient cooperation between the government and private enterprise" was crucial in order to harness this "dynamic force of private enterprise." Private enterprise, Rockefeller continued, "acting within the framework of a democracy, has the necessary creative energy to stimulate the production of such items as food and other products of prime necessity required by the Venezuelan economy."[18] While Rockefeller's capitalism drew on a similar mix of public-private activity in the economy that had been pioneered by the New Deal, exporting it abroad exposed a new tension, one that New Dealers (for the most part) did not have to deal with during the 1930s: that of national sovereignty.

Betancourt, the head of the center-left Acción Democrática (AD), had come to power via a coup d'état that overthrew the presidency of Isaías Medina Angarita in 1945. The AD was determined to put into place reforms that would reduce the profits of foreign oil companies, challenge the authority of the church, and promote labor unionization as well as state-funded welfare, education, and development programs. Popularly elected three times, the AD drew on support from the rural and urban working class but its reform program did not directly challenge capitalism or threaten foreign investments in Venezuela. Betancourt's government did impose new tax rates on foreign oil companies, though, forcing them to split oil revenues fifty-fifty with Venezuela. (Venezuela's oil exports had increased dramatically thanks to World War II, doubling between 1943 and 1945.) This seemingly novel shift in policy actually originated, however, in a 1943 law adopted under the previous president, Medina Angarita. In this political context, foreign oil companies embraced Rockefeller's plans to channel foreign investment in Venezuela to raise the nation's standard of living (for example, lowering the prices of food by creating networks of supermarkets and a program that would lower the cost of fish). Rockefeller, observed biographer Cary Reich, was "evangelical" about the ability of capitalism (via IBEC) to forge "new business trails in the underdeveloped world so that less daring investors might follow." IBEC, Rockefeller believed, had to function "on a sound paying basis which will attract other private capital and management to undertake similar activities."[19]

Rockefeller thus had to navigate a middle ground between his colleagues in the oil industry on the one hand, who viewed his investments in Venezuela as a kind of ideological smoke screen to hide their desire to exploit Venezuela's oil wealth, and the Venezuelan government and public, which viewed Rockefeller's IBEC corporation skeptically. For example, one left-wing newspaper wrote of Rockefeller's subsequent investments in farming, "Who is silly enough to believe for one minute that the great Rockefeller is interested in raising pigs?" continuing, "This whole farm business.... It is just a scheme to get hold of future oil lands."[20] Rockefeller, following several days of face-to-face negotiating with Betancourt, came to an agreement: no restrictions would be placed on IBEC's Venezuelan subsidiary (the Venezuelan Basic Economic Corporation, or VBEC) with respect to capital gains or dividends; in return, Venezuela's economic development corporation, the Corporación de Venezolano Fomento, would hold a 50 percent stake in each company VBEC created, with the understanding from Rockefeller that Venezuelan investors would have a majority stake within ten years.[21]

While the AD, under Betancourt and his successor Rómulo Gallegos, charted a pragmatic path in governing, explicitly reassuring foreign firms and the U.S. State Department of their support of capitalism and private property, as well as their opposition to communism, in 1948 Gallegos was deposed in a coup as the military took control of the government. While foreign oil companies were more concerned with the strength of Federpetrol, the Venezuelan union of oil company workers, than they were with the political positions of the AD and its leadership, the instability of Venezuela's government underscored a concern for Rockefeller and IBEC. The key difficulties regarding the construction of the Caracas-La Guaira Highway, from the perspective of Rockefeller and his advisers, revolved around the issue of national sovereignty as it applied to financing the highway's construction and to the question of contracting with private firms to build the road. An undertaking of the magnitude of the proposed highway would require access to capital on a grand scale. As Rockefeller and his advisers viewed the matter, the logical borrower for such capital ought to be the Venezuelan government itself, but as one of Rockefeller's employees put it, the "constitutional difficulties of the present revolutionary government" could make it difficult to borrow on the international market. If VBEC had to arrange for borrowing, however, Rockefeller's advisers feared that they would face the prospect of borrowing at higher interest rates than what a stable Venezuelan government could command. That said, John Lockwood, one of VBEC's officers in Venezuela, proposed that VBEC ask that Venezuela's Corporación de Fomento finance the project costs that would occur in bolivars and that project costs incurred in dollars be financed by the United States' Export-Import Bank. If VBEC then offered Fomento preferred stock in a new entity representing the Venezuelan-VBEC partnership, it would give the government an explicit stake in the potential profits of the enterprise. "It would mean," Lockwood cautioned, "that the Venezuelan Government's position was junior to the Export-Import Bank, but I do not believe it could object to this, since the whole enterprise is for its benefit."[22]

Robert Moses, the powerful New York planner, responded with caution to a request from IBEC officials for input, on the basis of his experience with public works construction in the United States. Moses warned that the Venezuelan government's engineering data "is inadequate" and urged that IBEC's technical services division be up-front about this fact in its proposals. Moses added that "There is one additional piece of highly technical consulting work which should be done immediately, and this has to do with tunnel ventilation. For this work I would suggest that IBEC Technical Services arrange through Madigan-Hyland for the employment of Ralph Smillie, Chief Engineer in charge of the Brooklyn-Battery Tunnel." As to the question of financing, Moses recommended that Rockefeller attempt to discuss issuing bonds that were backed by the World Bank.[23] The World Bank, for its part, hedged on the question of whether it could do business with Venezuela's revolutionary regime, with its president, Eugene Black, telling Rockefeller officials that it was unclear what the World Bank could do.[24]

Ultimately, VBEC concentrated its Venezuelan enterprises in other sectors of the economy, creating subsidiaries that worked to ease the shortage of food in the country. VBEC's farming company PACA (Productora Agropecuaria Compañía Anónima) promoted the growth of commercial agriculture, its fishing company PESCA (Pesquerias Caribe Compañía Anónima) promoted the growth of commercial fishing, and its wholesale division CADA (Compañía Anónima Distribuidora de Alimentos) built and improved networks of warehouses and supermarkets throughout Venezuela. Undertaking direct participation in the construction of the Caracas-La Guaira Highway proved, for Rockefeller and his colleagues, too risky a proposition. Morrison-Knudsen undertook the $20 million task of building the two tunnels for the highway, implementing the designs of Ralph Smillie, the engineer that Moses recommended to Rockefeller.

* * *

In comparison to Venezuela, Rockefeller's advisors were more pessimistic about the prospect of succeeding in Brazil. As William Alton wrote to Rockefeller, while "the problem in Venezuela is one of making adjustments here and there, in Brazil one feels the need of a fresh outlook, and orientation." Alton found IBEC's Brazilian outpost to be "a mixture of great discouragement and tremendous hope." IBEC needed better management, Alton believed, one with a grasp of business practices and leadership qualities. On the staff front, however, Alton found IBEC in Brazil to be "splendid." He recommended that Rockefeller's ventures in both Brazil and Venezuela prepare a capital budget and an expense budget, in order to refine budgetary controls.[25]

As was the case in Venezuela, Rockefeller and his advisors believed in strengthening Brazil's infrastructure as a way to support increased economic activity. Much in the same way that the Brazilian-style corporatism of the 1930s and 1940s was, as Melissa Teixeira has argued, "influenced by a global circulation of ideas and institutions concerning the transformation of law into an effective tool in state-building and social policy," roadbuilding, and state-funded infrastructure more generally, formed a parallel arena of global circulation. Ideas and methods about producing public works projects that had been developed during the New Deal and deployed within the United States were, with Rockefeller's IBEC, exported abroad.[26] In studying how to promote the building of roads in Brazil, Rockefeller's advisors viewed the issue of finance as crucial. One approach, advisor Charles Pineo argued, could be to fund such a program through selling bonds, subject to a set of arrangements to guarantee the bonds's marketability. The arrangements that

Pineo suggested were fairly conventional: the bonds should be issued in an amount at least equal to the projected construction costs, in order to protect bondholders and to offer assurance that contractors will be paid on schedule. Bonds should be issued serially over a period of years not too much longer than the time it would take to complete the highway they are to fund, so that credit could also be made available to finance the construction of additional highways. Finally, Pineo proposed, "The saleability of the bonds could be greatly increased if funds awaiting transfer into foreign currencies could be invested in them under a guaranty of the availability of the foreign currency at a fixed rate of exchange to permit prompt transfer of the interest and principal of the bonds when paid."[27] To accomplish this, Pineo recommended that a legal entity be created, with "ultimate control over the issue and sale of bonds," adding, "The bonds could be either issued by the entity itself with payment guaranteed by the Brazilian government, or bonds issued directly by the Brazilian Government."[28] In addition to providing for financing, the proposed entity might also be used to review the plans and specifications for highways, review the contracts for construction, and suggest financing options for the maintenance of highways after they are completed.[29]

Nelson Rockefeller countered this plan with a number of concerns. First, he commented that Pineo's proposal, as conveyed by Rockefeller's advisor John Lockwood, was "patterned very largely on the 'authority' pattern used so successfully in the United States, which frankly I don't think will work in Brazil in connection with the objectives which are sought in this program." Authorities, Rockefeller continued, are better suited for roads "which are not a part of the ordinary state or federal highway system," adding, "Were the authority set up to be used along the lines outlined in your memorandum, it would mean that ultimately this authority would maintain, operate, and control roads all over Brazil in competition with the Federal State and Highway Departments."[30] Rockefeller preferred that a quasi-public corporate entity be in charge of financing, engineering, and supervising the construction of highways, after which they would be handed over to the relevant agency of Brazil's government. "I'm very much against the instrumentality acquiring property rights or rights of way in their own name. Were this to be done, I fear that the people would begin to think of it as some form of superstate."[31]

Rockefeller tried to consult beyond the Americans on IBEC's staff, writing to Brazilian Teodoro Quartim Barbosa for his opinion of IBEC's plan, once Pineo had revised it. From a wealthy family, Barbosa was described in U.S. State Department communications as a prominent banker, a conservative with links to the Social Democratic Party.[32] Educated as an agricultural engineer, Barbosa had technical expertise as well as a knowledge of the Brazilian political and business elite, and he served as IBEC's representative in Brazil. Rockefeller was particularly interested in Barbosa's opinion of two elements of Pineo's proposal. First, he was interested in the structuring of a bond series so that it offered buyers protection against the cruzeiro's possible depreciation against the dollar. Second, Rockefeller wanted Barbosa's opinion of IBEC's idea to propose placing tolls on the completed highway, in order to use the collected funds to finance the building of additional highways, as well as a further safeguard for bondholders in case the bonds went into default. If Barbosa approved, Rockefeller was anxious to dispatch Robert Moses to Brazil, in order to "acquaint him with conditions and problems in Brazil so that he can more effectively advise us in our thinking and plans later in the operation."[33]

Barbosa was direct in his response. "Since you asked me for my 'frank and confidential' comments and reactions," he wrote, "I think Charlie's suggestions are rather imperialistic." He continued, "It all boils down to wanting to put the highway department under the corporation's control. We must organize our company within the existing legislation and not expect to modify laws and organizations to agree with our desires or to suit our convenience." In sum, Barbosa concluded, "Charlie's proposal is among those classic models of capitalistic government loans for debtors in default." He proposed instead that IBEC present itself "as a purely private enterprise," one that "avoid[s] any idea of privilege and special concessions." Rockefeller underlined the phrase "rather imperialistic" and put four question marks in the margin next to Barbosa's text, conveying his incredulity.[34] If IBEC were to proceed, however, it was clear that it would have to incorporate Barbosa's advice.

* * *

In its activities abroad, IBEC's history illustrates how the multinational firm could become idealized, mobilized, and extended as an instrument of economic development during the postwar era. By 1972, the twenty-fifth anniversary of IBEC's founding, Nelson Rockefeller was finishing his thirteenth of fourteen years as governor of New York. His son Rodman traveled on his behalf in response to an invitation from Brazil's minister of foreign relations to mark the occasion, taking with him the former head of the TVA, David Lilienthal. Lilienthal, who himself had founded his own multinational development firm, Development and Resources Corporation, in 1955, also served on IBEC's board of directors. For Rodman, the trip served as confirmation of "Rockefeller capitalism," underscoring that IBEC "has a great opportunity to be among the leaders . . . in the participation of private enterprise in the national planning process." Lilienthal, Rodman wrote, traveled as "the spiritual father of regional development planning," adding, "It was touching to see young economists and planners come up to him with a look of awe and almost worship on their faces. One middle-aged planner actually bowed when he met David Lilienthal. Yet, Mr. Lilienthal did not act the part of demi-God, but rather the part of an enthusiastic, youthful thinker, being exposed for the first time to one of the largest arenas of development left to be accomplished in the free world. When you show a river to Mr. Lilienthal, he gets excited. When you show him the largest river system in the world, untapped and undeveloped, he gets so excited he can hardly contain himself." This seeming golden age of technocratic expertise and international development, of successfully exporting the New Deal, was short-lived, and never as triumphant as its evangelists supposed. By the end of the decade both Nelson Rockefeller and David Lilienthal had died; Rodman Rockefeller presided over the liquidation of Lilienthal's company, as well as the end of IBEC and VBEC.

While this essay has focused on particular interactions between the United States, Venezuela, and Brazil, it indicates some broader conclusions. First, the postwar activities of IBEC signal the importance of attending to the historical specifics of how, exactly, American technical knowledge and expertise has been applied across the world. These applications were not limited to just Venezuela or Brazil, of course, but also included such undertakings as the Rockefeller Foundation's efforts to improve agriculture in Africa, which then cross-pollinated back to Mexico, Colombia, and India, as well as many others. The result of these policy innovations—a technocratic liberalism—was an uneasy product of good intentions and unexpected outcomes. Liberal statecraft could indeed successfully regulate the activities of private firms and stimulate economic growth, but the pursuit of these goals at many points served to enhance the hegemony of the United States (and the profits of American firms) at the expense of broader concerns about social justice and the global distribution of wealth.

Second, viewed as a whole, the actions of governments and private firms spread a vision of capitalist development overseas, one that had strong roots in the New Deal. While this vision had clear limits, these concrete activities did reshape the global economy in important ways while also providing a kind of evidence for a range of contemporary midcentury social theorists who were occupied with formulating deeper understandings of capitalism. Karl Polanyi was of course a key player in this intellectual project; others who provided their own critique of capitalism during this period were Harvard sociologist Talcott Parsons, radical-turned-conservative James Burnham (author of *The Managerial Revolution*), New Dealers such as Adolf Berle, and management theorist Peter Drucker, among others.[35]

Finally, while the multinational firm served as a crucial vehicle for transmitting midcentury ideas about capitalism abroad, in demonstrating the potential of infrastructure to shape different markets and society it also functioned to remake these ideas. The writings of historian Arthur Schlesinger, Jr., are reflective of this process. A player in the transformation of liberal ideas advanced by the Democratic party in the years following World War II, Schlesinger viewed the New Deal's project of state capitalism and economic development—so powerful and effective in lifting the Tennessee Valley out of poverty—as a weapon that could be deployed overseas to demonstrate the power of liberal capitalism. As he put it, in his classic statement of liberal anticommunist ideology, *The Vital Center*, "Our engineers can transform arid plains or poverty-stricken river valleys into wonderlands of vegetation and power," arguing that "the Tennessee Valley Authority is a weapon which, if properly employed, might outbid all the social ruthlessness of the Communists for support of the people of Asia." These weapons of the strong, as we might term these New Deal–inspired economic development projects, ultimately failed in remaking the developing world in the image of the United States.[36] However, when viewed through the lens of international development and within a broader historical perspective, we can see that this ideology profoundly shaped how the United States interacted with other nations. The power and limits of this ideology reveal an affection for the power of market capitalism, something that midcentury developmentalism and its advocates shared, ironically, with the architects of neoliberalism.[37]

CHAPTER 5

Rivers of Money: American Expert Influence on Pakistan and the Indus' Water Economy

Erum Khalid Sattar

Rudyard Kipling's novel *Kim* was originally published in 1889, when Kipling was based in Lahore, British India. In his 1955 address to the U.S. National Commission for UNESCO in Ohio, Sir Zafarullah Khan, Pakistan's stellar foreign minister, evoked Kipling's famous verse:

> East is East and West is West,
> And never the twain shall meet.

As we know, the geographical refrain is famous. As Sir Zafarullah pointed out, less well known is the next stanza:

> But there is neither East nor West,
> Nor border, nor breed, nor birth,
> When two strong men stand face to face,
> Though they come from the ends of the earth.[1]

This chapter explains the spread of American technocratic expertise deployed in the Indus River Basin in modern-day Pakistan after Partition from united India as a political tool used by the United States to advance its perceived Cold War strategic interests. Treating water as a "resource" meant that American engineers and policymakers could work with Pakistani bureaucrats to undertake a massive program of construction and put in place conduits for the sharing of what we understand as technical assistance. The buildup to this water-as-political-power Cold War strategy was long in the making, harking back to policy choices and theories about the relation between water management and economic development at the start of the postcolonial moment, the period in which the inheritor bureaucracies of the new nations, Pakistan and India, which replaced the vacating empire of the British Raj in 1947, embraced wholeheartedly. Broadly, as part of its power politics strategy, the United States through its involvement with water sharing and governance in the region, extended its influence in South Asia. Worried that India might fall into the communist sphere of influence, the United States sought to bring its technocratic water expertise to solve the water dispute that emerged from the contested territorial control of Kashmir—that dreaded "K" word—between the new nations. The U.S. concern was that if the broader Muslim world came to the aid of the Kashmiris and Pakistan's claim on the region to challenge Indian territorial control, then India might be led closer to communist forces to help bolster its claim to the region. Thus, the United States stepped in to reduce tensions and stave off any such outcome—and focused most immediately over control of water, that eternal conduit.

In this climate, it was the newly minted World Bank, seeking credibility, that became the vehicle for a large-scale, infrastructure-heavy, technocratic vision of water management and the development of dams and canals to bring water from the west to the east, to lands previously fed by the eastern tributaries of the Indus River that India now claimed for its use. A fledgling nation with limited resources, Pakistan didn't have anything close to the myriad resources it would need to build new infrastructure. Into this situation, the United States, with its ascendant postwar global role, led friendly western governments under the rubric of the World Bank to finance a massive construction project. This project privileged and further reinforced the prime role of the engineering profession in the Indus (building on British history of canal development), a basin that the British had in fact created as part of their rule of the Indian subcontinent. The United States and the World Bank thus built on the foundation of British rule during the heyday of colonial rule, always with the enthusiastic support of local elites. Tying new nations to itself during the Cold War was critical to the United States. Through the massive infrastructure funding of dams and link canals for irrigation in Pakistan, its development model focused on strengthening and expanding the reach of agricultural commodity markets in the largest contiguous irrigation network in the world, a system that, with the drawing of the boundary line, had been ripped apart by a Partition award made by a British civil servant.[2]

To understand the history of the United States and the Indus River Basin, it is important to briefly examine the international and local contexts that shaped it. At the end of World War II, the worldwide struggle for influence between competing American and communist camps drew the United States into the most important unfinished business from the Partition of the Indian subcontinent. The pivotal struggle between the new nations of India and Pakistan centered on the disputed Himalayan region of Kashmir and the life-giving waters of the Indus River and its tributaries, which in the plains nourished a vast civilization. For Pakistan—the younger, smaller downstream nation—the waters of the Indus were an existential requirement. At the same time, the United States worried that India might join the communist camp to protect itself from Pakistan's claims and the potential support from Muslim-majority nations. Into these powerfully churning geopolitical and local forces stepped David Lilienthal, the famed ex-chairman of the New Deal's Tennessee Valley Authority (TVA). As historian David Ekbladh has written, the TVA "was seen as a means to achieve development democratically," and Lilienthal "was the major reason for the institution's allure."[3] How did Lilienthal, in 1951, recently retired at the age of 49 from a distinguished nineteen-year career in public service, insert himself into the ongoing struggle for water in the Indian subcontinent in 1951? How did the World Bank follow his lead for a "resolution" of the conflict? How did his actions open the way for the United States' and international organizations' near-permanent involvement in the region's continuing struggles to create water security?

This chapter poses answers to those questions, even as it asks others. In places of hydrological challenge and without adequate annual rainfall, available water resources must be managed carefully to create social stability and lay the foundations for growth.[4] The crucial link to stability and growth is what makes water and the pathways of engagement it opens up uniquely important as a subject of study, and U.S. diplomats and officials have long been and continue to be concerned about global water security[5] and its implications for U.S. national security.[6] At the same time, water security has been depicted as a success story in the U.S.-led postwar order. According to the World Bank, the Indus Waters Treaty of 1960 between Pakistan and India, with the World Bank as guarantor, is "seen as one of the most successful international treaties" of the twentieth century. Not only did it survive "frequent tensions, including conflict," it also provided the necessary "framework for irrigation and hydropower development for more than half a century." Former U.S. president Dwight Eisenhower described it as "one bright spot . . . in a very depressing world picture that we see so often."[7] Eugene R. Black, who was the World Bank's president from the start of treaty negotiations through to its signing, recounted its significance thus: "It took us seven years to do it. That was the beginning of it. It was very discouraging. It cost us a lot of money, a lot of time. . .over that period of years, we prevented any bad situation from developing. I think we stopped the war. It's the most important thing the Bank has ever done, by far."[8] That was recognition of the high stakes involved, and this chapter analyzes both the origins and the validity of these self-assessments.

As Black alluded, many feared that India and Pakistan had reached a point at which war might break out in 1951, when the World Bank entered the dispute and began to work on the water-sharing problem based on Lilienthal's proposal. It was perhaps but natural that international institutions would turn to the respected American administrator. The TVA was understood as a remarkable success, and people around the world, especially in the newly decolonized countries, looked to that project as an emblem of what the United States had to offer as a development model for their newly independent populations. Lilienthal's evocative phrase in his 1953 book—"Democracy on the March"—pointed toward U.S. infrastructure development as something to be learned and emulated.[9] "It was an attraction that carried over into international affairs during the Cold War, where the sort of modernization with which the TVA was associated emerged as a key part of U.S. strategy in the 'Third World,'" Ekbladh writes. "The attention the TVA received during the Depression and World War II made it an easily recognizable symbol for the U.S. government as well as for nongovernmental groups carrying out modernization programs postwar."[10] It is telling, as Lilienthal's biographer Steven Neuse writes, that the book *Democracy on the March* itself became a basic source document for modernization.[11] A fuller account of the TVA's shortcomings did not come for another generation.[12]

In the global struggle with communism, Lilienthal's uniquely American model of development became a potent symbol unlike any other. Lilienthal himself insisted on the transferability of the TVA model abroad. In *Democracy on the March*, for example, he recounted the experience the respected Supreme Court associate justice William O. Douglas culled from his many summers of travels on horseback. Douglas traveled the "villages of Asia through what he describes as 'the vast underbelly of Russia that extends from Lebanon and Syria on the west through India on the east.'" In that massive region, teeming with tens of millions of people of many cultural and economic patterns of life, Douglas allegedly encountered a uniform question. "Everywhere I went, people asked, 'Why can't we have a TVA?'" But the Supreme Court justice reiterated that it was more than security from hunger and deprivation and the protection from floods that had caught people's imagination—the TVA was "a symbol of a new order, a new way of life—security and independence for themselves and their children." Douglas went on to argue for the centrality of industrial development to American success in the Cold War: "If we are bold enough to make this device an instrument of our Asiatic foreign policy, we can take the political initiative away from Soviet Russia, turn the tide and win country after country for the democratic cause. . . . TVA represents an idea that can be utilized as one of the major influences to turn back the tide of Communism which today threatens to engulf Asia."[13] The message was clear. If the United States could only do in postcolonial Asia what it had done in the American South, it could bring those new nations into the capitalist and democratic bloc.

We can see echoes of that call in the 1951 Lilienthal proposal for peace between Pakistan and India. As was true for many others, World War II internationalized Lilienthal's perspective such that a global war created a global footprint. As Neuse writes, Lilienthal did not exhibit an interest in international affairs until 1942, when he concluded that another war could be avoided only if the United States took a more active role in the "problems of the world."[14] At the same time, American industrial development also became an object of international interest. The TVA became "a mecca for foreigners anxious to see if the authority could provide an example for their countries."[15] Asian voices echoed the potency of the TVA in the early postwar era. Writing in *Foreign Affairs* in 1952, former mayor of Bombay M. R. Masini wrote, "The United States has no better ambassador-at-large in Asia than the one which bears the initials T.V.A."[16]

The TVA and the United States in the Postcolonial World

It was in this context that Lilienthal became the "originator" of the Indus River Basin plan.[17] And while the constitutional status of the erstwhile state of Jammu and Kashmir is beyond the scope of this chapter,[18] it is crucial to note that Lilienthal's personal involvement took place in another context too: the end of British rule in the subcontinent.[19] Lilienthal's insertion of the United States and the World Bank into the waters dispute raised important questions about the nature of international power in the new postcolonial moment in the Indian subcontinent: How does a new power step into the shoes of an old? How does it use its newly acquired power?

Most important for our purposes, what of the old does the new adopt and adapt? In 1947, following soon on the end of World War II, Britain as a colonial power lost its hold on the Indian subcontinent. An India that had been politically unified, or at least controlled, under Britain gave way to the traumatic emergence on the world stage of the two new nations of Pakistan and India. The end of empire and the rise of national sovereignty also shaped the debate over the Indus River Basin. Many Americans, including Lilienthal, believed the United States was well situated to step into global power without taking on the imperial mantle. He recorded a meeting with General Douglas MacArthur in 1951 in Japan, in which MacArthur told him, "The British way of colonizing has hurt us Americans in this part of the world. The way is wrong and it won't work anymore. We are witnessing right now the end of the white man in Asia as a dominant force. The white man is through in Asia in the British sense, and will never come back again."[20]

That quote reveals something important about Lilienthal's assumptions regarding the nature of American power. To American eyes, the task of stepping into what appeared to be a power vacuum, at least as far as sharing of their valued expertise was concerned, seemed a relatively simple undertaking. Both Pakistan and India needed capital and expertise to make good the hopes of their populations. Their people wanted better lives in their newly independent countries—they believed that being citizens instead of colonial subjects would improve their lot, and that concrete benefits would flow from independence after their long struggles against the British colonial raj. To complement these aspirations, America emerged as the world's strongest nation, ready to step into its leading role on the world stage: a role of influence without direct rule.

To put these two strands together, postcolonial aspirations and the leading role of the United States on the world stage, it is helpful to think of the American power as Lilienthal and others did: as a bridge that connected separate parts of the world in new ways. But American involvement did more than that: it strengthened preexisting forces. As Lilienthal and others knew, this was not a one-way street of influence flowing outward from America as a primary provider of development finance to meet the aspirational needs of the new countries. As the historian David Engerman has shown, American aid was used by the Indians to strengthen preexisting power structures.[21] And as this chapter shows, through Lilienthal's intervention and the involvement of the World Bank, Pakistan used international financing to strengthen the preexisting irrigation networks, themselves a colonial construct.

The Lilienthal Trip

Lilienthal threw himself into that complex situation in 1951. As he knew, the canal waters dispute between Pakistan and India had raged for three years. Most recently, Pakistan "had seriously contemplated taking the matter to the UN Security Council."[22] Lilienthal, in what turned out to be a momentous turning point in the dispute, arrived on the subcontinent at the invitation of Indian prime minister Jawaharlal Nehru. The two had met in 1949, when Nehru had visited the TVA as a model for potential replication through the Damodar Valley Corporation in India.[23] Lilienthal's visit was undertaken as a private citizen on behalf of *Collier's*, the famed American magazine that paid for the cost of his trip. But before he left Washington, D.C., he had offered his services as a private "unofficial" ambassador to Secretary of State Dean Acheson, and Assistant Secretary of State George McGhee had written him that "at this particular time you can render a service no one else can, going as a private citizen."[24] India's chief engineer for the Treaty talks, N. D. Gulhati, later noted that Indian officials assumed that Lilienthal spoke for the U.S. government. It was only years later that he learned that Lilienthal's trip was on a private basis.[25] The endeavor of course raises broader questions about the proverbial revolving door and the roles and influence of former officials as entrepreneurial private citizens.

For our present purposes, leaders of both India and Pakistan were on safe ground in assuming that Lilienthal had the ears of the highest echelons of American power, such that the trip was treated as an official one on the subcontinent. Saiyid Ali Naqvi reported that Lilienthal had been invited by both India and Pakistan "to study the irrigation systems in the Indus Basin."[26] Even before the trip, Lilienthal met Pakistan's representatives in New York at Pakistan House. There, Foreign Minister Zafarullah Khan—"a distinguished-looking man with a gray rough beard, an American manner and idiom, quite a philosopher"—and Secretary-General of the Pakistani delegation to the United Nations Mohammed Ali took out "a wonderful map of Pakistan." They spoke to Lilienthal passionately of the rivers of the Punjab. The supreme importance of the question became clear to Lilienthal when Khan explained that Punjab meant "five rivers" as he "quite dramatically" spread out the fingers of his hand across the map.

At the time of Lilienthal's trip, the global Cold War was only getting hotter on the Asian continent. Both the rise of "Red China" and the Korean War stood at the forefront of his mind, and on his return to the United States, he wrote two articles for *Collier's* magazine (his trip's sponsor): "Are We Losing India?" and "Another Korea in the Making?"[27] Both articles were of seminal importance for U.S. Cold War policy in South Asia, and the latter may arguably be the most influential piece ever written for a magazine. Briefly and as detailed below, it influenced the making of an international treaty to control the sharing of water resources across political boundaries, as well as the operation of a continuing dispute settlement mechanism, that involved the World Bank, the United Nations, the president of MIT, the rector of Imperial College, London, the chief justice of the Supreme Court of the United States, the lord chief justice of England, and the International Court of Arbitration.[28]

"Another Korea?" revealed how, in Lilienthal's view, decisions by the British Empire made the control of water a Cold War concern. For him, the famous Radcliffe boundary line, which divided the massive province of Punjab between the two nations, was an example of a basic planning flaw: action without adequate administrative preparation.[29] To date, in the realm of water, the successor nations continue to deal with the fallout.[30] Radcliffe's partition award gave the headworks of colonial-era irrigation canals to India while giving the lands that the canals irrigated downstream to Pakistan, resulting in the disintegration of what had been constructed to be an integrated system. This severing of the integrated pre-Partition canal irrigation network meant that control of territory became crucial to the control of water and that the two new countries' interests were in stark opposition.

Lilienthal's interpretation of the colonial roots of the Cold War problem of water management emerged from his discussions with the leaders of both nations. In Karachi, he met with Pakistan's first prime minister, Liaquat Ali Khan. When asked about the issue of the canal waters dispute, Lilienthal wrote in his journal, the prime minister "snapped this answer: Unless the Kashmir issue is settled it is unreal to try to settle the issues about water."[31] Through further interactions, he came to see the broader resonance of the conflict—for instance, when he met with a delegation from Syria in Karachi. "In the valleys of Kashmir," one Syrian official said and Lilienthal reported, "it is not Pakistan alone which has her honor at stake, but the whole Moslem world."[32] In India, Lilienthal wrote that Nehru was grappling with the future direction of his country. The stakes for the United States could not be higher. Lilienthal argued to *Collier's* readers and through the magazine to American policy makers that the direction that India took in the Cold War would fundamentally affect the rest of Asia. As it did for other influential Americans, the "loss" of China weighed heavily on his mind. "If we lose out in India, as we have in China, all hope for us on the continent of Asia is gone," he wrote. "The world balance of population will be overwhelmingly against us." But if the prospect of losing India was a shocking possibility, Lilienthal also believed "that there are things that can be done with a reasonable prospect of turning this tide."[33] The optimistic note at the end, the possibility of American success, was of critical importance to its author.

Lilienthal made explicit what those things were that the United States could do to intervene in the postcolonial split and, perhaps unsurprisingly given his TVA experience, arrived at the idea that water management could be one solution to the Cold War problem. If water could be managed in such a way that would ensure that the interests of the two nations aligned, perhaps cooperation regarding the Indus River could lead to a greater alleviation of broader tensions. He even hoped that if the two nations could learn to cooperate around water management, thereby building trust in the vital domain and making Partition meaningless in significant ways, then perhaps they could learn to cooperate in other ways—perhaps even, he dared further to hope, "solving" Kashmir. Such optimism reflected his deeply held belief that engineers and technocrats had a role to play in the Cold War. At the same time, it points to a related belief: that engineers could rise above politics because they could neutrally talk professional sense to each other. Eugene Black thought engineers "were different from other people" and were "interested in combating nature."[34] For Lilienthal, the balance of the Cold War in Asia hung on this vision, on this technocratic understanding of the world. As the piece in *Collier's* summarized it, "A dispute between India and Pakistan over possession of Kashmir threatens to erupt into a war which could involve the U.S."[35] But Lilienthal believed such a war could be prevented.

He advocated for the United States to help solve the water dispute Partition had led to. He stated his public determination to prevent the India-Pakistan Kashmir dispute from spilling over in ways that would tempt India into the communist camp. His working assumptions also drew directly from his experience during the Great Depression. Among them was the belief that the Radcliffe boundary had torn apart the "natural" character of an integrated river basin that engineers on both sides of the Punjab province had previously managed collectively. There is little evidence that he grappled with the fact that it was British policy and irrigation engineers that had in the first place created an integrated water management system, one that over time became the largest contiguous irrigation network in the world. To speak of the Indus River Basin as "natural" thus glossed over a long history of colonial pacification through irrigation, land settlement, the creation of primary commodity production, the link of that production to global trade, and even the supply of horses to the British war effort in Australia.[36] The Indus River Basin was a man-made imperial invention, the foundations of which had been laid in the nineteenth century. But Lilienthal undoubtedly adhered to a simpler and more understandable logic of thinking of the Indus River the same way he thought of other rivers: as a hydrological unit. "A thousand valleys over the globe and our valley here are in this way the same: everywhere what happens to the land, the forests, and the water determines what happens to the people," he wrote about the Tennessee River. That river had always been "an idle giant and a destructive one." But with American skill and innovation, its "boundless energy" now worked for the people that lived near its waters. This could be true, too, for "thousands of rivers the world over."[37]

Or as *Collier's* put it in introducing his article, the harmony and prosperity he offered to the Indian Subcontinent dealt with a project similar to but "vaster than the Tennessee Valley Authority." According to this logic, American-driven technocratic expertise could overcome the failures of imperialism and decolonization and in doing so protect the U.S. national interest in the Cold War.

Deploying American Power: Capital and Expertise

Lilienthal believed that, given the right circumstances, India would be amenable to an alliance with the United States. But he vocally worried that India would seek other allies if "the Moslem world arrayed against her." If Pakistan widened the conflict in this way, he believed it was likely that "Red Russia and Red China would cultivate the opportunity for Communism all this added turmoil in Asia would provide."[38] He sought a local solution to the potential geopolitical problem. If the United States was interested in preventing India from joining the communist camp, it should help the two countries create a joint cooperation mechanism for water flowing through Kashmir.

This in turn could avert the potential flaring up of the dispute and the widening of the conflict to draw in those actors who waited for the opportunity to take advantage of any opening. What had been managed by engineers as professionals, surmounting their religious affiliations during the colonial era, could come to be again. Although he expressed concern that it might not be possible for the United States and the United Nations to fashion a political settlement that could avoid war in Kashmir, he did believe the only way it was possible was to make a heavy commitment of men and materials.[39] Given this stark assessment, the reasonable course open to the United States was to bring the two countries together to collaborate on managing their water resources. "The Kashmir issue, as an issue in itself, may not be solvable, now, short of war," he wrote. By he hoped that "the surrounding tensions can be reduced, one by one."[40] The key to the "political future" of Kashmir and the entire region lay in strengthening the hands of the peaceful and the professional. It was by means of water sharing and hence the economic development of both countries, Lilienthal suggested, that the United States could reduce these "surrounding tensions" in a way that served its national security.

Lilienthal turned to the World Bank as the means to do so. Through its leadership, he argued, the United States should help resolve Pakistan's insecurity in the face of Indian plans for controlling the water that flowed through Kashmir. Lilienthal suggested that the Indus be managed jointly, what he called "a new and simple concrete idea" based on the seven-state TVA he'd headed.[41] In fact, his "simple" idea seemed to be much more complicated to work out than he'd acknowledged, and from the earliest days of the World Bank's involvement in the dispute the idea of managing the Indus jointly was, after some tentative efforts, quietly set aside. The fact that Pakistan and India were two sovereign nations that shared the trauma of a bloody Partition at their moment of birth meant that they were unwilling to act as if they were states within a federal system of government. The TVA could be a model for engineering, but it was difficult to depict it as a potential resolution for conflict that spanned two federal countries and not, albeit with its own complications, within a federation. This is not necessarily to disavow that cooperation does occur across international borders between sovereign nations. But in this specific case, the parties' history of hostile relations created special challenges. To help explain the difficulties of the canal waters dispute to his readers, Lilienthal sketched out what the control of water and land meant in the context of the Indus:

> The partition gave the major part of the irrigated lands of the Punjab and Sind to Pakistan; but the headwaters of some of the largest irrigation canals that feed Pakistan were left with India or Kashmir. *All the rivers* [emphasis added] upon which Pakistan depends for life originate in India or Kashmir. Two thirds of the entire water supply originates in Kashmir, where the snow-fed Indus rises. This crucial and determinative aspect of the "Kashmir issue" is rarely referred to; *it is not even an issue before the United Nations* [emphasis added]. Why the flow of the Punjab's lifeblood was so carelessly handled in the partition no one seems to know.[42]

The question of "the Punjab's lifeblood" was too important to leave to postcolonial actors alone. N. D. Gulhati, who led the Indian delegation "throughout the critical phases" of the treaty negotiations largely agreed.[43] He later wrote that, despite the best efforts of seasoned and experienced men, "inevitably several problems remained unresolved."[44]

This was an understatement. The Standstill Agreement of 1947, which had been signed pre-Partition between the two halves of the province of Punjab, was meant to give time to the new countries to resolve the issue of supplying the canals in west Punjab.[45] Just short of eight months after the still unfolding immediate upheavals such as population transfers unleashed by Partition, the Indian province of Punjab stopped the canal waters on April 1, 1948, the day after the expiration of the Standstill Agreement. That decision was perceived in Pakistan as posing an existential threat, a fledgling downstream nation with millions of refugees still in camps. Eight percent of the Punjab province's cultivable area in Pakistan was deprived of water at the start of the crucial summer planting season. After this act and during three long years of protracted negotiations before Lilienthal's visit, the threat that subsequent ad hoc arrangements would fail to hold loomed large in the nation's collective psyche. In 1948, while the new nation was still reeling from the massive displacement of peoples and an influx of refugees, the sight of the canals on which Lahore relied for its drinking water running dry left an indelible mark, and it continues to shape the quest for water security, a security the country defines as not being at the mercy of upstream territorial control by India.[46]

In Lilienthal's estimation, given the situation on the ground and the absence of the international community from an effort to help resolve the broader territorial dispute of the Kashmir issue, the United States had a special responsibility to step in. Despite what he knew of the dispute's recent history and of what he gathered on the ground after meeting Pakistanis "angry enough to fight with their bare hands," Lilienthal devised a plan to break the logjam between the two countries by suggesting that they jointly and cooperatively manage water for their greater overall development. Such a view meant that he needed to discount the recent history of national trauma. "This is not a religious or political problem, but a feasible engineering and business problem for which there is plenty of precedent and relevant experience," he wrote. "This objective, however, cannot be achieved by the countries working separately; the river pays no attention to partition—the Indus, she 'just keeps rolling along.'"[47]

That universalist view meant that the shared resource of Kashmir, India, and Pakistan must be "developed as a unit—designed, built, and operated as a unit" just as the TVA was in the United States.[48] Such a perspective is a reminder that Lilienthal had a proclivity for waxing poetic about nature and his faith in engineers and development. In *Democracy on the March*, Lilienthal had written that "all this could have happened in almost any of a thousand other valleys where rivers run from the hills to the sea. For the valleys of the earth have these things in common: the waters, the air, the land, the minerals, the forests." That common resource could be "controlled by men" in ways that yielded "a better living for people."[49] While so many of his sentiments about the commonality of the geographic features of rivers ring true, they necessarily raise questions about specific moments, histories, and places. Did he underappreciate the power of human feelings and deeply ingrained animosities? The power of colonial rule as it comes to impact controlled territory? Was he simply naïve and unwilling to see the deep antipathy of the two countries toward each other? Or was he so enamored of the rationality of the engineering profession and the commitment of engineers to its norms that he was unable to see that much had happened between the two countries that might prevent the engineers from behaving as he expected them to? What does this notion tell us about the role of technocratic expertise more broadly?

Those questions were as important as ideas about rivers as a common resource and engineers as apolitical actors. For before Lilienthal ever came to the region, the two countries had fought each other to an impasse through their engineers and other technical professionals for three long years. The post-Partition politicization of the engineering profession is a phenomenon that Daniel Klingensmith identified with the emergence of the "nationalist engineer," one that calls into question Lilienthal's belief in the technically impartial judgement of engineers.[50] Engineers may have remained technically sound professionals, but they used their knowledge and skills to recast the claims of their nations in those very same technical and legally sound terms.[51]

That dynamic led to an impasse between Pakistani and Indian engineers and diplomats. In his report, Gulhati detailed the protracted and stalled negotiations and exchange of memoranda between the two countries from 1948 to 1951. After a stalemate in bilateral engineering-focused negotiations, to protect and enforce its rights and to move the dispute to the domain of law, Pakistan began to press India to accept the jurisdiction of the International Court of Justice, so that the matter could finally be decided by a neutral, legally focused arbiter. India, as in other areas including mediation regarding the broader Kashmir dispute, continued to deny any role for a third party. This stalemate is what led Pakistan to the verge of referring the dispute to the UN Security Council.[52]

Lilienthal doubted the efficacy of turning to international law. In his logic, legal or historical arguments about the rights of claimants would not work because of Indian territorial control and sovereignty. As Daniel Haines has underscored, the control of land was at the base of India's assertion to begin with not to let waters flow to Pakistan through territory it controlled. The stoppage of water itself was an assertion of sovereignty.[53] This certainly is how Lilienthal expressed it. "Pakistan's position—that she has the *legal* right to the uninterrupted flow of water, [by virtue of the prior developed irrigation uses in Punjab that came to it] a right to a share of waters stored by India's dams upstream—is quite inadequate for this great issue," Lilienthal said, "however sound her legal claim might be if the dispute were between two farmers asserting their private rights." He admitted that the International Court of Justice might decide the legal issue in Pakistan's favor, but he doubted that India would agree to submit the issue to their jurisdiction.[54] In his brutal assessment of the state of international law and institutions he categorically acknowledged one glaring requirement, that of a sovereign willingly submitting itself to an international decision maker. Notions of having "rights" or "law" or even "history" on its side would not help downstream Pakistan.

What in fact mattered was territorial control, which came with the power to dictate what legal claims a government was willing to entertain against itself. This is a stark legal realist insight, that political power is ultimately the enforcer of the law. Even though his notion of joint technical management did not come to pass with the subsequent involvement of the World Bank in the dispute, the acceptance that "domestic" law and "international" law are inherently different has had a lasting impact when it comes to transboundary adjudication of water claims. In this critical realm at least, it seems as if a country must learn to live and work as best it can with its powerfully placed neighbors and seek the help of those willing to come to its aid to help settle outstanding disputes such that the norms and institutions of international law may not come to its aid. The implications were clear and note Lilienthal's recognition of the limits of technical expertise, even as he touted its potential power. International law and the notion of "rights" might not help Pakistan, but a powerful ally could because it could be more able to gain concessions from the other party. By all measures such tasks are easier when globally powerful actors are willing to take an interest in a transboundary dispute, as they did in the early Cold War. Another note of caution is important here: It may be that when the interests of more powerful actors shift, the "law" is unlikely to come to the aid of those hoping to press their claims. The challenge for countries without geostrategic power, then, is one of finding reliable allies through shifting conditions. The other challenge, one all too easy to lose sight of in the middle of absorbing international engagements, is that lasting change or the strengthening of local interests will be realized through the "help" of international actors, thus making it much harder at a later time for a country to shift course both because of the power of facts on the ground and because of the winds of broader international forces. This means that select internal actors and their interests will be strengthened in partnership with and through an overlap with the interests of more powerful international actors. In this pull and tug, the more powerful have a head start.

It is crucial to keep these insights in mind when considering the Indus River Basin in 1951. As we'll recall, it was Britain's creation of the integrated irrigation network that set the subcontinent on the path on which Lilienthal found it.[55] The particular path that was adopted in the 1950s was one that reinforced massive infrastructure development and the development of dams financed by the Indus Basin Development Fund Agreement, which accompanied the 1960 treaty.[56] As we'll see below, this means that for the most part a fairly sticky choice was made to commit the countries to one based on a particular vision of modernization of the economy, one that irrevocably tied local populations to global commodity value chains. In some ways, the choice was less about the fact of that engagement, which is unquestioned, but more so about the particular technologies and methods of water control that were adopted. This fact is visible in the hardware of such development programs, which remains more physically "fixed" and in place in the form of dams, barrages, and irrigation canals, as opposed to shifting geopolitical interests. What this means is that long after geopolitical interests have shifted in their focus or intensity, a particular polity is left coping with the effects of previously supported and hardwired development. To this realization we can see almost no thought being devoted at the time the ideas were being developed and executed. There was no question in Lilienthal and others' minds that to secure water supplies through a treaty predicated on sound engineering was the correct way forward. And doing so would only continue and reinforce the forms of water control developed during colonial rule.

In Lilienthal's worldview, the model that needed to be developed in the Indus was the next step of what had been put in place under the New Deal in the United States and, later, the reconstruction of postwar Europe. He advocated for the "continuing influence in the growing worldwide interest in the TVA concept," especially for the South Asian neighbors.[57] He wasn't exactly sure what mechanisms that entailed when he wrote for *Collier's* in 1951. He imagined a jointly financed "Indus Engineering Corporation" that would comprise "technical men of India, Pakistan, and the World Bank." Together they could "readily work out an operating scheme for storing water wherever dams can best store it, and for diverting and distributing water." Once the engineers designed the scheme, some group would manage it—either an "Indo-Pakistan Agency" or some "supranational agency such as the Schuman Plan provides in Europe, or by some special corporation like the Port of New York Authority."[58] The difficulty he faced in putting his finger on how to manage the engineering challenge was evidence of the political challenge he confronted; it did not extend into his vision for what the project, however administered, could achieve.

That optimism, and the place of South Asia in it, grew out of both the imperial past and the geopolitical imperatives of the Cold War. Perhaps understandably, the financing vision at the base of the scheme was but a continuation of the model the British had deployed in the Indus, the model of the "canal colonies" that relied on making previously unirrigated, "barren" "wastelands" "productive" by dividing and "settling" them with cultivators, thereby bringing them into the operation of the land revenue scheme.[59] Following the British premise, Lilienthal too assessed that the land was fertile enough to support a major push forward of agricultural development that would tie the region even further into global commodity markets and increase the likelihood of the countries living up to the aspirations and developmental needs of their citizens: "Such a plan could certainly be financed, for this now worthless unirrigated land would, with water, become immensely productive and valuable; the increased value of the land, now owned by the respective governments, would be enough to base financing." The course of action he recommended was financially feasible and perhaps would even prove to be profitable, just as the canal colonies had been during British rule. As it turned out, the World Bank had to arrange nearly a billion dollars' worth of financial commitments first under the Basin Fund to finance the called-for infrastructure.

Lilienthal was honest enough to acknowledge that ultimately his vision was of overcoming the reality of Partition and turning the clock back on it. But he also knew that, at the same time, an American-led international project would carry forward a key component of the original British colonial project by increasing the use of the Indus's waters for "development," which was now defined more broadly than just a focus on irrigated agriculture. Coming from the TVA with its ample rainfall for agriculture, he understood the relevance of hydropower and the importance of building reservoirs for flood control. He expressed his hope thus: "Such planning of the water resources (and the accompanying potential electric power) of the Indus Basin is nothing new; it was for generations largely a function of British-trained Indian engineers of the state of Punjab."[60] As David Gilmartin has shown, the precolonial contestation over Indus waters was played out on the provincial spatial scale within British India with upstream Punjab and downstream Sindh province competing for colonial investment and the development of barrages and settled, irrigated canal colonies. After Partition, in both independent countries, this spatial contestation reappeared between provinces.[61] Also after Partition, the nationalist engineer appeared to present their country's respective claims. In Lilienthal's telling, however, these subnational scales were ignored. It would be Punjabi engineers who could become the heroic figures, now on opposite sides of international boundaries, who had lain the foundation of the irrigation system. And according to him, they too saw the river basin as a natural unit. "Then partition, a politico-religious instrument, fell like an ax, and colleagues who had worked together all their lives, elbow to elbow, separated because they were Hindu and Sikh, or Moslem," he wrote. "Partition did not repeal engineering or professional principles among these engineers; it merely made them secondary, for a time, to politics and emotion."[62]

The most important political problem to surmount, then, was postcolonial nationalism. Of course the characterization of the river basin as a "unit of nature" reflects its own bias: both his and that of the engineers he attributes the claim to. As Lilienthal well knew, it was those same engineers who over the decades had trained and developed the rivers to act as if they were a "unit" in the first place. And the "unit" was one that was meant to act in the service of what were after all very human goals, perhaps attributable to nature only if one understood nature to be in the service of humans.[63] Nevertheless, by the time he came to the Indus, it was a basin on which engineers, planners, and rulers had built unprecedented "development" based on the infrastructure of canal irrigation. In fact, he sought to build on that colonial infrastructure and saw it as a potential pathway to more peaceful relations. He felt strongly about this possibility, and it informed the most moving sections of his *Collier's* articles. "Working together on a common project that is not political but functional, a part of life, and based on technical skill and human need, is the way to inject a creative decent note into the rapidly degenerating quarrel between Pakistan and India *over Kashmir*," he said. He continued: "The endless and futile arguments on political issues, such as plebiscites and the legalisms about reference to the International Court of Justice of rights to existing supplies of water, serve only to inflame these controversies, or create new ones; they 'solve' nothing. These people will live or die by the way they handle the waters of the Indus River and its six parts."[64]

Lilienthal captured how important the Indus was, especially for downstream Pakistan. Making its way from the Himalayas to the Arabian Sea, it was thought of in Pakistan as the country's lifeline. But he drew a different conclusion from that of the Pakistani negotiators in 1951. Although Pakistan was the country that had pressed its legal claims to the International Court of Justice, Lilienthal essentially advocated that it brush aside any remaining belief in international law and organizations for the implementation of its water rights. Instead, he believed that the two countries and their engineers needed to get on with the practical and common task of managing water. This occurred despite his myriad engagements in the region and his having met and heard from an American farm extension worker during his trip to Pakistan, who told him how difficult this would be. The "deliberate, conservative, typical old-line extension man" had spent considerable time "up and down the country, especially in the West Punjab, Sind, and North-West-Frontier Provinces." He emphasized how strong nationalism was to Lilienthal: "He says everywhere he went he found Kashmir—and the river waters of Kashmir—was the cause of much worry and concern among farm people."[65]

International Infrastructure Finance and the Indus Waters Treaty

After the publication of Lilienthal's seminal articles, events took on a life of their own and resulted in a series of outcomes with effects well into the present. The most important thing to fall by the wayside soon after the mediated negotiations began in earnest was the idea of joint management and development of the basin, either by the two countries or through an international organization or mechanism. This was something Lilienthal had expressly suggested as a first step toward deeper cooperation in the subcontinent, something he believed could create the conditions for greater peace and development in the region. The critical break with his idea was that the treaty *divided* the waters instead of *sharing* them when it was signed in 1961. More importantly, unlike any previous instrument of transboundary water sharing (and indeed any since), it did not divide volumes or a share of the waters of a particular river. Instead, it allocated entire rivers to one nation or the other. This itself was a function of territorial insecurities that could not be assuaged by the guarantees of an international treaty. Lilienthal acknowledged this limit when he learned of the final contours of the plan, just before its adoption: "This, of course, was very far from my proposal that India and Pakistan operate the Indus system jointly, as a unit. My object had been to bring the two nations closer together in a cooperative venture of river development—not to find a means of separating them further."[66]

Even though the Indus Waters Treaty is often touted as the world's most successful water treaty,[67] given that another attempt at such separation hasn't been tried since may indicate more about its general unworkability than any other single feature of the water-sharing arrangement between the two countries. Engineers could not overcome their nationalism, as the conditions of the treaty reveal. Pakistan's mistrust of any Indian promise to deliver a given quantity or percentage of a river's flow of water combined with the crucial issue of the timing of the flows on which so much agricultural prosperity depends was so great that it resulted in a division of the rivers: the three "eastern" rivers were assigned to India and the three "western" rivers to Pakistan without, in both theory and actual practice, any hindrance in water deliveries and supply from upstream India. To work around the fact of physical control by India of land in the Kashmir region through which the western rivers flow, the parties put in place both physical, that is, engineering and structural, and legal limitations. In short, the result cast doubt on the basic division between engineering and law that Lilienthal suggested. The very "legalisms" he warned against as false promises were accepted as the means to preserve the peace. But his exhortation to not put too much faith in unreal norms also proved prescient; tensions and conflicts have steadily increased in the decades since the treaty's signing.[68] This, too, is a result of the way that negotiators sought to work around postcolonial nationalism. Where he had proposed joint cooperative management, a physical division of severing the "naturalness" of the river basin occurred. The result could not be further from what Lilienthal envisaged and built under the TVA model that ignited the imagination of so many around the world. In the clash between the model and the realities of actual places, local constraints and histories prevailed.

To understand the importance of that lost opportunity for cooperative management, it is important to briefly examine some of the more technical aspects of the treaty. Such an analysis reveals why the story of that gap between visionary and practical idealism, not to mention the international attention that was unleashed by Lilienthal's Cold War concerns, continues to shape the history of the Indian Subcontinent as much as the Indus shapes the landscape.

The treaty accommodated the contentious issue of territorial control by giving India the right to develop certain uses on two of Pakistan's western rivers, the Jhelum and the Chenab, including the right to develop hydropower without the creation of or with minimal storage/pondage—in other words, run-of-the-river hydropower projects. The rationale of allowing hydroelectric production without a provision for the storage of water was to protect downstream Pakistan from any potential ability on India's part to control either the volume or the timing of water flows. As Lilienthal had presciently warned, a change to the timing of flows would be devastating to Pakistan's agriculture. "Pakistan includes some of the most productive food-growing lands in the world in western Punjab (the Kipling country) and the Sind," he wrote. He continued with a dramatic description of the potential consequences: "But without water for irrigation this would be desert, 20,000,000 acres would dry up in a week, tens of millions would starve. No army, with bombs and shell fire, could devastate a land as thoroughly as Pakistan could be devastated by the simple expedient of India's permanently shutting off the sources of water that keep the fields and the people of Pakistan alive. India has never threatened such a drastic step, and indeed denies any such intention—but the power is there nonetheless."[69]

Decades later, John Briscoe made a similar point about subsequent and ongoing Indian plans.[70] The treaty thus did precisely that which Lilienthal had cautioned against, with some structural restrictions hardwired into it as if nationalist engineers could at least protect if not cooperate. In the apportionment of the three western rivers to Pakistan, Lilienthal's key objective of making Partition technically irrelevant when it came to the "natural unit" of the Indus River Basin fell by the wayside. Instead, the assertion of territorial sovereignty still mattered, and Partition was perhaps made more permanent by agreeing to a division of the rivers under the control of separate countries and the attendant changes to their landscapes wrought by the treaty's terms.

But with the passage of time, the hardwired limitations on Indian's upstream hydroelectric power development has faced immense pressure.[71] Recent years have seen the treaty increasingly under attack, and a virtual war of project-by-project attrition, as it were, has become the new operational normal of water sharing between the two countries. Indeed, each new construction project by India unleashes a volley of complaints in downstream Pakistan. Typically, under the treaty's mechanisms, when India first informs Pakistan of an intended project, the downstream country in addition to raising objections to particular technical aspects also protests India's overall approach of continuous upstream hydroelectric power development, which Pakistan claims is against the very spirit of the treaty. Given the primary conditions that produce a dwindling supply of water (for example, a warming climate melting glaciers)[72] and a growing demand (population, food, and energy), there is no reason to think that the existing arrangement, based fundamentally on mistrust, can ease rising tensions.

Importantly, the treaty's dispute settlement mechanisms have been paused since 2016. World Bank Group president Jim Yong Kim stepped in to take this drastic step to avoid the risk of "contradictory outcomes," which arose from the invocation by both countries of different parts of the treaty's dispute settlement mechanisms.[73] The World Bank has further disclosed that it "has worked tirelessly to seek an amicable resolution" to recent disagreements. It "remains committed to act in good faith and with complete impartiality and transparency in fulfilling its responsibilities under the Treaty, while continuing to assist the countries."[74] Other legal instruments by which countries or states share river water apportion parts of the flow to the various parties based on principles ranging from prior appropriation and developed uses to the equitable apportionment of flows in which "first in time, first in right" need not necessarily be the governing principle.[75] None has yet undertaken the scale of the physical division the treaty unleashed. The division and the subsequent ways in which it's played out is a far cry both from what Lilienthal originally envisaged as well as from the atmosphere at the treaty's signing.

The day the treaty was finally signed—September 19, 1961—President Ayub cabled Lilienthal, "You have cause for legitimate pride in fulfillment of your cherished desire for harmony and understanding between the two neighbors."[76] Pakistan's ambassador to the United States, Aziz Ahmed, also phoned to say, "This is not India's victory nor Pakistan's victory, but yours." He told Lilienthal: "You should rejoice that you have done something so directly related to the peace of the world, and of the people of the subcontinent of India. I tell you most seriously that if you had not made your most fortunate trip to our countries, and made your grand and imaginative proposal, this dispute would never have been resolved and war would have ensued."[77]

Such celebratory language may have been hasty. The accompanying crucial elements of what Lilienthal had proposed—finance, joint irrigation development, and government revenue generation—also fell by the wayside once negotiations led by the World Bank began. The bank followed both the British imperial position and Lilienthal's position that technical expertise could overcome the problem of nationalist animosity.[78] As Eugene Black, the president of the World Bank who took up Lilienthal's proposal and used it to offer the "good offices" of the bank, saw the problem: "We wouldn't think that the settlement of the Kashmir dispute would be a proper function of the Bank. This is a political question. On the other hand, the question between India and Pakistan over water, which called for enormous expenditures for building irrigation systems and reservoirs, this was a financial question in that not only you've to get agreements on an overall plan that would be of benefit to both countries, but you've got to find out the way to raise the money to do this. That wouldn't be involved in Kashmir."[79] In this view of infrastructure finance, Black did not see the bank's intervention as a political act. But given the history of the creation of Britain's irrigation empire in the Indus, which was both deeply political and financially lucrative for the colonial government, it is hard to be as sanguine as Black in neatly categorizing actions into distinct political and financial realms. Moreover, for cash-strapped new countries, international development financing was and remains a way to fund plans and deliver on political promises of "development" and uplift to the electorate.

Lilienthal had envisaged that the necessary joint development and management of the basin could be financed with the involvement of the World Bank. And given the able administrator he was, he was deeply cognizant of the fact that sound finances based on future revenue streams from newly irrigated lands would provide the rationale for calculations of expected future profitability. But when treaty negotiations began and moved closer to the division of the western and eastern rivers between the two countries, such a notion of financing projects from future revenue streams began to look quaint. To begin with, given Pakistan was unlikely to find a sympathetic hearing of its legal and reliance interests in the international community, the country shifted its focus to seeking compensation for its loss, as well as international funding for the development of supplies it would lose to India with the proposed diversion of the eastern rivers. In the ensuing and drawn-out formal negotiations, the notion of expectation-based, nationally profitable financing gave way to a near-total reliance by Pakistan on foreign aid for a massive program of infrastructure development. That program surpassed any notions of sound financing and responsible lending and borrowing.

This near-total dependence on foreign development assistance really took off in the build-up to the anticipated signing of the treaty. It is hard to overstate the course that the negotiations set the country on. At the time of closing treaty negotiations, only one civil servant—the country's federal secretary of food and agriculture who had been trained in the famed Indian Civil Service before Partition—is known to have questioned the wisdom of the path the country was embarking on. Because he voiced his concerns, President General Ayub Khan, who had taken over in a coup just two years earlier in Pakistan, is reported to have threatened him thus: "I shall have you stand against the wall and shoot you personally."[80] Given this message from the top, it is easy to see why others with misgivings may have failed to voice them.

To capitalize on the anticipated and unprecedented windfall of international development financing under the treaty, development partners suggested in 1958 that the country create a national organization that would be capable of working with the anticipated influx of foreign experts and their full-scale regime of "technical assistance." This was the massive parastatal Water and Power Development Authority (WAPDA), at the time the West Pakistan Water and Power Development Authority. While it did not have as broad a mission as the TVA, it was certainly modeled on the idea of integrated development of water and power. Under the program of works to be undertaken as a result of the treaty, WAPDA was tasked with taking the lead on constructing and overseeing the construction of the massive infrastructure development program known as the Indus Basin Replacement Works.

The importance of the works program to the conclusion of the treaty can be seen from the fact that perhaps counterintuitively, it is the treaty that is an annex to the works program such that it was dependent on securing the necessary external funding to compensate Pakistan for the nonacceptance of, or its inability to realize, its legal and historical claims, which resulted in its negotiated loss of the three eastern rivers under the treaty. As far back as 1953, soon after the start of negotiations, it was clear that the Pakistanis were approaching the negotiations as a technical matter that required infrastructure funding. The country's embassy in Washington, D.C., reported then that joint studies were being undertaken by the two countries and the World Bank pursuant to the "Lilienthal Proposal." At the center of the transnational project was the objective to "study possible technical measures to *increase* the supplies of water available from the Indus River system." The report continued: "The object of the current meetings is to work out a comprehensive plan, including specific engineering measures, by which the supplies of water effectively available to each country will be increased substantially beyond what they have ever been." Following Lilienthal's belief in the apolitical power of engineers, the report added that "success achieved from these talks would bring to an end one of the most important causes of tension between Pakistan and India."[81]

The controversy, however, continued long after the treaty's signing, even though political dissent during military rule by definition remained muted. Only one politician, Fatima Jinnah, the sister of the country's founding father, castigated the military ruler General Ayub Khan in 1964 for signing away the country's historic water rights. "In reply to my reference to the Indus Water Treaty Mr. Ayub Khan said that he did get Rs. 900 crores for it. I ask him is that adequate price for losing permanently the water for all times? Is it not frittering away our permanent water rights?" she asked. "Is it not a fact that this treaty represents lowest ebb of his will because it signifies a lack of determination to fight for our water rights on which our prosperity, progress and future depends?"[82]

The necessary works program would be massive by any measure and one that would challenge any country's technical and administrative capacities, much less a newly emergent one on the world stage. As Aloys Michel, the preeminent chronicler of the treaty's negotiations, put it, it would be "the largest single irrigation project in history."[83] As the long negotiations continued after Lilienthal's visit in the 1950s, it became clear to all involved that the young country had no institutional structure large enough that would be up to the task of the massive undertaking that it was about to embark on. The international development community thus pushed for the creation of a sufficiently large national organization that spanned provincial boundaries. This had lasting effects on the country's already weak federal constitutional structure, but development experts believed that only an organization that attracted the best domestic engineering talent would be able to engage with international counterparts and attract foreign funding and expertise. The treaty negotiations thus further reinforced the inherited, colonial-era nostalgia with its belief in the power of engineering and engineers to build and manage massive infrastructure that would control and shape nature to human will. In many ways, this was also the TVA model, but without even a precommitment to the regional cooperative foundation or grassroots democracy to undergird it. It was instead the administrative technocratic will to engineer landscapes and tie peoples and their social relations to international expertise and global commodity markets. In the colonial era, the goal was to tie people to the state. In both cases, the ties of people to far removed centers of power were strengthened.

The distance between U.S. power and the imperial past was small. In the treaty negotiations themselves, the critical turning point came when Pakistan recognized that it would be unable to enforce its claims to water that had previously flowed to canals in the Punjab from territory that had been awarded to India by the drawing of the Partition line. This acceptance did not come easily, as all claims of established uses and rights arising from prior appropriation failed, as did claims based on being the downstream state across an international boundary with a reliable expectation to continue to receive water that had previously flowed to it. Nothing was to work, and India's claim to have a right to divert water to use in its territory triumphed over any legal and moral rights-based claims Pakistan advanced.

That path was not set in stone. In fact, Pakistan had been on the verge of taking the dispute to the UN Security Council for a recognition of its rights when the World Bank stepped in with its proposal to make the dispute a technical rather than a political one. As Lilienthal had observed, both countries had significant need of the Indus's waters. One need only to look at his account of pre- and post-Partition history and his land and water use estimates in *Collier's* to see the difficulties Pakistan faced. The Indian decision to cut off Pakistan's water supply in the spring of 1948 caused "distress, loss of crops and general disruption," he wrote. "This rankles and makes Pakistan fearful of the future." But the Partition had also left India with serious problems. It had given India upstream control but almost none of the canals and irrigation systems. Lilienthal estimated that of the twenty-two million acres irrigated in the Indus Basin, Pakistan held about eighteen million. Yet the

Indian population in the Basin, around twenty million people, was almost the same as Pakistan's total population. He estimated that some thirty-five million acres in India could be irrigated. "India, too, must have more water or starve," Lilienthal wrote. "So India is going full speed ahead with canals, headworks and dams that will divert the flow of upstream water to irrigate as many of these 35,000,000 acres as possible."[84] As far as Pakistan was concerned, when it found no help in the international community, legal fora, or diplomatic and political institutions for its arguments, its focus shifted to securing the necessary foreign aid package to fund the massive Works program. As Michel noted, the final treaty was thus "published as an Annexure to the Development Fund Agreement rather than vice versa." According to this view, "the Bank and the 'friendly Governments,' chiefly the United States had actually purchased an agreement."[85]

Under the Replacement Works program, the international community including India, which was going to be the main beneficiary of the diverted three eastern rivers, was to finance the construction of massive link canals to transfer water from the Indus river main stem to the irrigated eastern and southern areas of the Punjab on which the British had built the canal colonies. The works program also included funding for the dams that Pakistan desired, as it was clear that without such storage that would "increase" available supplies, its developmental needs could not be met. Astutely, Pakistan had buttressed its claims during treaty negotiations after hiring the services of an American engineering consulting firm, Tipton and Kalmbach, to undertake a study of the World Bank's original plan.[86] Later, Eugene Black, perhaps somewhat inadvertently given Pakistan's long effort to secure funding for dams, harked back to Lilienthal's proposal. "A large amount of this water just flowed into the sea," he recalled Lilienthal's proposal claiming. "If you could capture this water and set up these big reservoirs and have an irrigation system, you'd give both countries more water."[87] It was becoming clearer that because of India's diversion of the eastern rivers, Pakistan would have to augment its water supply by capturing and storing available water in large dams. This firmly put the country on its present path, with the government recently aiming to raise funds more broadly as it finds itself in a less favorable international development assistance climate than the heyday of Indus Waters Treaty negotiations. For our purposes, though, the important thing to note is the "stickiness" in the Indus of Lilienthal's TVA vision. Despite the fact that his initial proposal of joint management of the basin did not come to pass, the idea itself of engineering-centric management of water nevertheless has established deep roots within the geospatial scale of the nation-state and its planners. This is where the debate starts and resides and is the starting point from which any alternate discourse must begin: not transboundary cooperative management, but in-country engineering.

The creation of WAPDA was a milestone in Pakistan's development history, one that further strengthened the heavy infrastructure paradigm and reinforced the economic dependency of the economy on a vision of financially unsustainable foreign-supported water development. It soon eclipsed the importance of institutional actors that had existed before its creation, in particular the provincial irrigation and agriculture departments in the federal structure. Under the Government of India Act 1935 and the model of devolved power sharing that the British Raj had been forced to concede due to broader resistance to its rule, irrigation and agriculture in the colonial era had been provincial "subjects" under the federal structure of India's constitution. Into this overall inherited structure, which Pakistan kept in place after Partition, WAPDA was nothing short of a behemoth. Not only would it be a national organization with the ability to cut across provincial boundaries à la the TVA, but crucially it would be one with the ability to fund its ambitious plans via the accompanying financial package to the treaty, the development fund.[88] With contributions from the United States, the United Kingdom, Australia, Canada, Germany, New Zealand, India, Pakistan, and the World Bank, the fund became a massive collective postwar international financial infrastructure investment program undertaken by the nascent international community under the aegis of the World Bank—worth eventually close to $1.2 billion at the time.[89]

"It was a very difficult job and very discouraging," World Bank president Eugene Black recalled.

> It cost the Bank at least a million dollars of our own money in engineers' fees, lawyers' fees, travel expenses, not to mention time. It finally worked out. We not only had to get them to agree on a plan, which incidentally was our plan because they both submitted plans which were miles apart. The Indian plan would have given India a whole lot more water, and the Pakistan plan would have given Pakistan a whole lot more water. I said to them all one day, "We can make money but we can't make water. There's just so much water, and both of your plans are unreasonable. The hell with both of you; we'll make a plan of our own." So we worked out our own plan. Then we had to sell them on our plan and that was a terrible job. Then we

> had to go out and raise a billion dollars. That wasn't half as hard as getting them to agree, but we had to get a billion dollars. This is the biggest thing we've ever done in the world. The biggest undertaking we ever carried out.[90]

The results of the World Bank plan were as consequential as the plan was massive. James Wescoat describes WAPDA as "one of the largest river basin planning organizations in the world—a Tennessee Valley Authority on a national scale," particularly as "massive construction projects dominated water sector programs."[91] As early as 1961, only a few years after its formation, WAPDA had contracted at least 28 foreign consulting firms.[92] The hiring and construction boom in the postindependence era had well and truly begun.

In addition to its disproportionately greater powers vis-à-vis any other public entity in the federal structure of water governance, it is the combination of its twin roles of water development for both irrigation and hydropower that make WAPDA a truly formidable institutional challenge to the country's federal governance structure. The effects of long-ago Cold War actions continue to shape relations between the Pakistani state's organs, federal-provincial relations, and relations with the international development community. Most important, any other vision of water management, any vision not entirely reliant on heavy infrastructure construction and its management, continues to be marginalized.[93] Old paradigms built in colonial times reinforced by dominant international strategic security paradigms continue to colonize thinking in ostensibly independent nations. With this vise grip on development thought, from where will the independence promised at the postcolonial moment come?

* * *

The path that Pakistan undertook as a result of the Lilienthal proposal led to its embrace of the World Bank and has continued to reinforce its belief that the United States' involvement in and support of the fullest development of its water resources is critical to the successful realization of the country's plans. More recently, the country has continued to harness the vision through the realization of China's growing geostrategic interests in the form of the China Pakistan Economic Corridor under the Belt and Road Initiative that aims to tie the Asian region closer together. After independence, American and World Bank involvement with other multilateral development institutions, such as later the Asian Development Bank, reinforced the country's hopes. In 1961, a year after the treaty's signing, General Ayub Khan visited the United States and met with President John F. Kennedy. He asked for American help to tackle critical problems arising from irrigation in the Indus basin—the very same integrated irrigation network initially created by the British. President Kennedy immediately obliged by asking Secretary of the Interior Stewart L. Udall and Jerome B. Wiesner, the special assistant to the president for science and technology, to study the problem. They in turn asked the eminent Roger Revelle, Udall's science advisor, to lead what became the White House–Department of the Interior panel on waterlogging and salinity in then West Pakistan. In sharing the findings of the Revelle report, President Kennedy wrote to President Ayub, "You are determined to benefit your people through the maximum use of your land and water resource. . . . This report is a good example of how the sharing of scientific and technical knowledge can contribute to the welfare of our people and to the cause of peace and understanding. Our people learned much from your people in working on this challenging project. I hope the future will draw us closer together, as together we solve common problems."[94]

More than half a century later, President Kennedy's letter continues to resonate with Pakistani planners who desire to both fully "develop" the country's water resources as well as continue efforts to attract U.S. funding and expertise, now in the form of USAID assistance[95] and partnerships with American universities.[96] In their preface to the report, Udall and Wiesner wrote that the president's "response was characteristic of President Kennedy's readiness to utilize the best of America's expert knowledge in the solution of problems affecting the welfare not only of citizens of the United States but of peoples throughout the world."[97] Given that American foreign policy can shift relatively easily with shifts in political power within and across regions and countries, foreign governments cannot always rely on such largesse emanating from the highest levels. Nevertheless, as this case of water development shows, once a contact with American aid and influence occurs, particular types of developmentalist forces are strengthened. And continue to be built on.

In that foundational sense, as administrator of the development fund, the World Bank's comprehensive study covering nearly thirty-five volumes of the Indus Basin's water and power resources known colloquially as the Lieftinck report, named after the eminent Dutch economist, remains a starting point. The final report and supporting document were presented to the government of Pakistan as well as the World Bank in 1964. The study team was assisted by a plethora of experts at the highest levels within American academia, including those of the legendary Harvard Water Program. Its aim was to "assist the Pakistan authorities in achieving the maximum feasible rate of economic development in the fields covered." In presenting the report, Lieftinck hoped that it would "serve as a useful background document to the Pakistan Government in taking decisions about future development and to the World Bank in assessing Pakistan's progress and plans."[98] But it became more than that. Given that President General Ayub Khan had requested that the World Bank develop such a study, which thus came with its imprimatur, future governments would be particularly constrained in deviating too far from its integrated findings. Even though Lieftinck reiterated that the report's findings were not binding on either the government of Pakistan or the World Bank, functionally it became and remains to this day the starting point for water sector investment decisions. This is justified by the integrated nature of the Indus's resources. The nonbinding yet binding nature of foreign investment decisions once begun remains difficult to shake off.

As recently as 2011, long after the official end of the Cold War, the American government reiterated its stance toward the treaty. A majority staff report for the Select Committee on Foreign Affairs of the U.S. Senate under the chairmanship of then senator and later secretary of state and now special envoy for climate to President Biden, John Kerry termed it thus: "The continued peace, stability, and success of the IWT are in the national security interests of all stakeholders, including the United States."[99] While America may have retreated from its once direct role in the region, the initial Indus conflict between two South Asian neighbors nevertheless has expanded to encapsulate broader regional dynamics spanning western and central Asia that require ever more deft American balancing across a larger group of countries with competing interests. As ever, the water resources of the region provide the potential to both bind and divide. Given that the Kabul River originating in Afghanistan is the main western tributary of the Indus, any potential international aid for its development may, if not handled carefully, become an ongoing source feeding a sense of water insecurity in Pakistan. The 2011 report went on to state that the United States must be mindful of what its investments in both technology provision and infrastructure finance in one country may do to regional relations and dependence of downstream countries on river water flows that originate in upstream, perhaps less friendly countries. As this chapter shows, we have seen a consideration of these issues before: the calculus of the Cold War is alive and well in American foreign policy circles.

Donald Worster in his monumental *Rivers of Empire* captures the hydrological challenge and state-private dynamics of building a thriving society in the American West: "On its environmental base of aridity, it had erected a closely integrated system of power that included both the state and private capitalist enterprise. Neither could survive in the harsh land without the other. Working together, however, the vision of total use could be dreamed and realized: the management of every river, every obscure remote creek, for the sake of America and a greater West, for the sake of domination."[100] This is not too far from the dream of the Indus's irrigation engineers and planners, within all the countries that the basin touches—if only they could command the resources to do so.

But perhaps another way is possible. Somewhat unexpectedly given his earlier advocacy, Lilienthal became more thoughtful about the effects of human actions and development on the environment. During lunch with World Bank president Robert McNamara in 1971, Lilienthal discussed their shared concerns about international development and the growing and questionable commitment of the United States to continue funding it. Given the movement by the Nixon administration toward détente with the Soviet Union, Lilienthal noted, "advocates of foreign aid appropriations can no longer scare people with the Cold War." Lilienthal continued with an attack on "the tired phrase [of] 'cost-benefit ratio.'" In the new context of the environmental movement, the model of progress that Lilienthal had pioneered now seemed outdated. "What makes urgent our thinking through a new concept of cost is the sudden emphasis on environment," he wrote. "I reminded McNamara that great doubts have arisen about development itself—is development, after all, a 'good thing,' as has always been assumed? Or is it the very thing that has brought on this crisis of a deteriorating and perhaps fatal impairment of our physical environment?"[101] Was "Mr. TVA" rethinking the rationale of his career? Meanwhile, we continue to await Kipling's meeting of equals, working together toward sustainable shared prosperity in the realm of water management and beyond.

CHAPTER 6

Productivity as a Way of Life: USIS Propaganda Films in Cold War Italy

Giulia Crisanti

In the midst of work to reorder the dusty and messy spaces of the Trieste State Archive, Ugo Cova, at the time director of the archive, bumped into an incredible number of boxes, containing over six hundred film reels, labeled with the tag "USIS—Motion Picture Program." It was the fall of 1984 and an unknown but impressive celluloid historical treasure had just been found. The movies recorded on the film reels were all that was left of the audiovisual libraries opened by the U.S. Information Service in Italy between 1944 and 1965 and offered an incredible visual gallery of people, ideas, products, landscapes, and transformations from all over the North Atlantic world.[1] Through their restoration and subsequent digitalization, it was once again possible to project on the screen the ideologically charged (self-)representations of America and Italy made during the years of the Marshall Plan and the Cold War.[2] The films opened thereby a window on the economic and political transformations of postwar Italy, and on those American information and propaganda strategies attempting to direct such transformations.

Overall, the Fondo Audiovisivo USIS di Trieste comprises 509 short movies, almost all shot on 16-mm film and most produced between 1941 and 1966 in the United States or in Italy, with only a dozen films produced in other European countries.[3] As for the contents, the collection ranges from documentaries and newsreels to fictional short films, training/educational footage, and animated features, dedicated to a variety of topics and set in all kinds of environments. It is thus possible to find UCLA college students, farmers from the American south, Detroit workers, Italian peasants from all over the peninsula, Marshall Plan officials engaged in Italy's economic recovery, Italian immigrants and students, American and Italian housewives, modern trains and new buildings, and all kinds of leisure activities. The common thread unifying such an incredible variety of visual documents is their collective participation in the larger, U.S.-led postwar process to modernize and Americanize Italian society. Indeed, far from being part of an exclusively Italian effort, the USIS films should be inserted within the broader framework of USIS information and propaganda activities not only in Europe but throughout the world. Already during World War II, USIS centers had been opened in all areas reached by the U.S. army, in connection with the activity of the Office of War Information. After the war, USIS centers continued their activities, first under the direction of the Department of State, then, from 1953, as local branches of the U.S. Information Agency (USIA), and eventually becoming one of the main instruments of America's Cold War cultural diplomacy. The films distributed by USIS were, hence, one of the many Cold War "weapons" deployed by the United States in the bipolar struggle to win people's "hearts and minds" from predatory communism.

In this context, the goal of this essay is to propose a comparative analysis of the Italian and American films distributed by USIS and specifically dedicated to promoting productivity and democracy. It is my belief that these were the two key concepts around which the "American way of life" was defined during the Cold War, especially in a country such as Italy, where the threat posed by communism to democracy was considered inherently tied to the country's backward standing in terms of productivity. The films offer, therefore, a unique (visual) opportunity to compare the parallel ways in which postwar Americans and Italians understood and implemented concepts such as productivity and democracy.

The historiographical debate on postwar Americanization in Europe and on the role of U.S. cultural diplomacy has been going on for decades. Numerous compelling works have covered all major aspects of the developments related to the American presence in Western Europe during the Cold War. Studies such as those by Victoria De Grazia, Mary Nolan, and Charles Maier have effectively discussed the impact of American patterns of production and consumption across the North Atlantic. At the same time, scholars such as Volker Berghahn, Reinhold Wagnleitner, Uta Poiger, Penny Von Eschen, John Dower, and Laura Belmonte have analyzed the many facets of American cultural diplomacy, either from the perspective of the United States or through the examination of specific European cases. The development and impact of, and reactions to, various forms of American cultural diplomacy and imperialism in Italy, through the involvement of the United States in Italian postwar reconstruction, have been masterfully unveiled by David Ellwood, while scholars such as Mario Del Pero, Kaeten Mistry, and Federico Romero have examined U.S. strategies to effectively influence the Italian political and trade union arena after World War II. At the same time, the activity of USIS and of its broadcasting program has been analyzed by Luigi Bruti Liberati and Simonetta Tobia, while Paola Bonifazio and David Ellwood have examined many of the Italian short films produced by the Economic Cooperation Association (ECA) and distributed by USIS.

In this context, the goal of my study is to take up the challenge raised by David Ellwood in the catalogue of Trieste's archival film collection to realize an extended comparative analysis of the short films produced in Italy and those produced in the United States. In doing so, I aim at unveiling the differences, gaps, limits, and compromises that characterized the interactions between U.S. officials and Italian society. On the one side, then, the very composition of the Trieste collection (with the majority of its films produced no later than the early 1950s), together with the increasing reliance on Italian institutions to produce the films, accounts for the shift that occurred within USIS by 1953. It was then that the Motion Picture Program became marginal, as a result of abandonment of the USIS mass approach to focus instead on targeting the molders of public opinion and "Italianizing" American information services.

On the other side—and even more importantly—I believe that this incredibly various array of films represents one of the best historical sources for examining the many discrepancies between the real world—in this case the reality of Italy's postwar social, cultural, and political reconstruction—and the world projected (on the screen) by those American and Italian institutions willing to drive such reconstruction. It is the very nature of these celluloid-made sources that makes them the best—I argue—plastic and dynamic synthesis of the process of "selective appropriation," which, according to Rob Kroes, has characterized the Americanization process throughout Western Europe.[4] As a result, the analysis of USIS films can substantially enrich historians' comprehension of the goals and intents animating the sender (whether U.S. officials or the Italian government) of the political, social, and cultural messages that the films were supposed to transmit, and of the aspirations and the reception of the viewers whom the films were produced to reach.

In the context of the American Cold War in Western Europe, the specific role of the USIS short films was, in fact, to project the achievements reached by all those willing to follow the American model, or, as one official put it in 1961, to provide "a factual account of the United States and its aspirations that serves as a balance to the more highly dramatized version of America and Americans presented by Hollywood."[5] USIS movies were therefore not simply intended to parallel the clearly wider and more impactful film production realized by Hollywood. On the contrary, the existence of the USIS Motion Picture Program was consistent with the idea of not censuring commercial images of America, even when they offered negative or subversive representations of U.S. society, as for example might have been the case with gangster movies or movies for teenagers, such as *Rebel Without a Cause*. It follows that the short films produced or distributed by USIS, including some of those found in Trieste, were in constant dialogue with Hollywood film production, as they both took part in the joint Cold War effort to spread the American Dream.

Moreover, the usefulness of these short films was considered even larger in those countries, such as Italy, in which a relevant percentage of the population was still illiterate. Films were "the most effective medium for reaching all groups in all areas," one U.S. expert wrote to his superiors in 1950.[6] In Europe, the decade after 1945 saw the gradual expansion of the USIS Motion Picture Program, which eventually put USIA in control of the largest noncommercial network for the distribution of documentaries in the world, with two hundred film libraries across the globe and its films being watched by almost five hundred million people. In this sense, the films found in Trieste, especially those produced in the United States and intended to be screened in different countries, represent a visual archive whose historical relevance is not and should not be confined to Italy. On the contrary, they extend the possibility to use Italy as an illustrative case study for a more global project, an attempt to promote modernization along the model offered by "the American way of life."

* * *

A word of context is helpful to understanding the importance of productivity and democracy in the American model presented in Italy. A series of internal specificities and political circumstances made Italy central to U.S. Cold War concerns in the 1950s and 1960s and make it now, I believe, an effective case to examine the impact and limits of Americanization in Western Europe. This is especially true if one considers how dual American cultural cold wars, one against communism and one against European perceptions of American society, were fully in action in Italy.[7] First of all, then, postwar Italy hosted the largest communist party of the Western Bloc (the Partito Comunista Italiano, or PCI), supported by 30 percent of the Italian population and one of the few political actors, alongside the Democratic Christian Party, able to gain mass support in the peninsula. It follows that, differently from other Western European countries (with the partial exception of France), the communist threat appeared in Italy real and imminent. This gave particular urgency to "actively combatting Communist propaganda in Italy, by an effective US information program and by all other practicable means," as was stated in the first document issued by the U.S. National Security Council, in 1947.[8] At the same time, the lack of a strong liberal political party, together with the conservative character of most Italian businessmen and politicians, made particularly challenging the attempt to convince the Italian political and economic environment to embrace the American alternative to communism. In fact, the Italian Confindustria (the General Confederation of Italian Industry) was rather skeptical about the possibility of effectively applying American economic models to Italy and seemed to lack a capitalist mentality. In this context, the president of Confindustria, Angelo Costa, defended Italian economic policies against the charges of inefficiency raised by American reconstruction officials. Costa and others argued that in Italy, given the high cost of capital and the low cost of labor, increases in productivity levels were more likely to happen on the backs of the workers.

Moreover, it is precisely this joint communist strength and lack of a strong capitalist tradition among Italy's economic and political elites that makes Italy a particularly effective case study for analyzing the way in which the two concepts of democracy and productivity were inherently related in the U.S. definition of an American way of life. In this sense, adequate levels of productivity, alongside the full embrace of a productivity mindset, seemed the fundamental requisite for implementing democracy in a country where, based on the American interpretation given at the time, communism's success relied on persistent economic backwardness and lack of prosperity. At the same time, it was only democracy that could guarantee the correct implementation of any American-like policy of productivity. This series of considerations found translation into the USIS idea that the best way "to mobilize support for democracy in Italy" was by "convincing Italians that adoption of the principles and practices of a 'dynamic economy' (with emphasis on the concepts of 'productivity' and labor-management cooperation) will benefit their economic and social welfare."[9] This combination of "dynamic democracy" and "dynamic economy" became the core vision behind what was defined as a "People's capitalism."[10] The latter had become central to the USIS information and advertising strategy by the beginning of 1950, as documented by the increasing presence of films dedicated to the two concepts of democracy and productivity. In this regard, it is important to point out the way in which USIS activity cannot and should not be separated by the parallel activity of the Marshall Plan. On the contrary, the former's promotion of an American culture of productivity was meant to serve the same geopolitical goals as foreign aid did: converting Western Europeans to the American doctrine of mass production for mass consumption, and promoting the democratic political system considered better suited to such a doctrine.[11]

It was, therefore, out of these considerations—the troubling electoral strength of the Italian Communist Party and the lack of a capitalist mentality among Italian businessmen and politicians—that USIS officials operating in Rome called not for a mere cultural transfer, but rather for a broader transformation of the Italians mindset, according to the idea that Italy did not necessarily need the techniques of the American way of life, but did need to believe in the concepts—productivity and democracy—behind it. Being, hence, a visual translation of the "American way" and of what this could lead to, the USIS films help us understand how America was defined for those to whom the American way was projected. The screening of documentary shorts, such as those in the series *Panorami d'America: Serie di quadri* (*American Landscapes: Sequence of Portrayals*), reveals to the eye of the historian a Norman Rockwell–like depiction of American society, presented in a fully optimistic way as a honey-and-milk land of abundance and happiness. The shorts offered, in other words, a sanitized—and often unrealistic—representation of the United States as a country where everyone had a job and a good standard of living, all workers owned a nice house equipped with excellent facilities, all citizens participated in the political life of the nation, and everyone had access to consumer goods, so that social and class distinctions could be easily overcome.[12] The hope was that USIS films would thereby encourage the Italian population to follow the path traced by the United States.

To better reach this goal, the USIS Motion Picture Program in Italy made agreements to guarantee the largest possible distribution of its films across the Italian peninsula, taking advantage of the Italian legislation that prescribed the screening of a short documentary or a newsreel before every feature film.[13] Moreover, the USIS films were distributed outside commercial circuits, through the employment of an increasing number of mobile units, which enabled public screenings in Italy's remotest and smallest villages. The films were thus watched in local squares, libraries, schools, factories, parishes, museums, cultural centers, universities, and other kinds of environments. At the same time, to more easily address and reach Italian audiences, USIS offices increasingly relied on Italian-produced short films by entering a collaboration with the Centro di Documentazione, created by the Italian Council Presidency in 1951. The purpose of this institution was precisely to produce official documentaries reporting on and making the population a participant in the Italian government's reconstruction efforts. As a result, these Italian films (at least the group found in Trieste's collection) are all characterized by the same enthusiastic representation of the reconstructive effort promoted by the Italian government. This kind of representation was also meant to contrast the parallel neorealism's cinematographic production, which conversely highlighted the many contradictions that characterized Italy's postwar path toward its economic miracle.

A comparison between the short films produced by the Centro di Documentazione and those produced by ECA officials to advertise the Marshall Plan shows an interesting difference.[14] If, on the one side, the depiction of the Italian North as industrial and of the Italian South as rural is evident and recurring in the American production, differences in degrees of modernization between the North and the South are constantly downsized in the Italian production, as the films of the Centro di Documentazione took part in the Italian government's policies to modernize the Meridione and present the image of a unified modern nation. Moreover, a comparative examination of Italian and American films casts light also on the way in which USIS itself, in order to be effective, was eventually forced to abandon its triumphalist modernizing rhetoric to rather increasingly rely on Italian produced films, which offered a more familiar and reassuring representation of the modernization process underway in the peninsula. This need to somehow Italianize USIS had in fact been acknowledged by the end of 1950, as confirmed by the missive sent to Rome by the Department of State, which urged "to develop plans for the production in Italy of motion pictures," based on "previous communications from the Embassy [which] have emphasized the need for certain films made in Italy by Italian producers."[15]

* * *

If the role of the films was to somehow anticipate on the screen the destination toward which postwar Italy was allegedly directed, the abracadabra words to open the door to the New World were "democracy" and "productivity," presented as the inseparable and constitutive elements of the American way of life.[16] As we have seen, the expression which came to embody the connection between these two concepts was "people's capitalism," which the USIS office in Rome described as an ideal mix of "dynamic democracy" and "dynamic economy," strengthening each other and able to effectively contrast any form of totalitarianism, whether fascist or communist.[17] And yet, if at the end of the day it was up to capitalism to defeat communism, economic dynamism was the more important of the two. Officials and films consistently emphasized how productivity inevitably represented the *conditio sine qua non* of any democratic system: the key not only to more economic efficiency, but also to political peace and equality.

In this sense, the interpretation of PCI's popularity as the outcome of a "Communism of the belly," as it had been called by Don Luigi Sturzo, was consistent with the American idea according to which economic welfare and prosperity were a prerequisite for political and social stability. As explained by historian Charles Maier in his well-known article "The Politics of Productivity," U.S. officials believed that increasing productivity levels would have guaranteed economic abundance, and thus the ability to overcome class divisions and defeat communism.[18] Or, as Werner Sombart put it, "all socialist utopias come to nothing on roast beef and apple pie."[19] In this reference, the need to achieve economic welfare as a requisite for Italy's political stability had already been acknowledged in a specific study made in 1944, "The Treatment of Italy." At the same time, however, productivity was not to be confined to factories or within the economic field. It was conversely supposed to become a social behavior, to restructure people's private lives according to principles of order and efficiency, and to rationalize all daily moments and tasks. In the films, as in pamphlets and other USIS publications, productivity was therefore turned from an economic principle into an all-encompassing way of life.

In 1953, the Italian USIS branch drafted a list of all the films better suited to the promotion of "Dynamic Democracy and Productivity."[20] A detailed analysis of some of these short movies should provide a clearer understanding of how these two ideas were practically translated into images and narratives, and what obstacles they encountered once they landed in Italy. To this end, within the USIS audiovisual collection it is possible to identify a certain number of films intended to introduce the Italian audience to democracy and productivity.[21] At the same time, through a comparison of U.S.-produced and Italian-produced films, it will be possible to cast light on any element of convergence or divergence between the American transmitters and the Italian receptors. Consistently, however, with the idea that democracy and productivity were notions to be exported to Italy and not yet domestically rooted there, USIS short movies dedicated to such concepts are far more numerous among the U.S.-produced films than among those produced in Italy.

The majority of these short movies are educational in tone and aspiration. This was mainly the result of U.S. perceptions of postwar Italy as a backward country that, having just come out of twenty years of a Fascist regime, was inevitably unaccustomed to modernity and democratic practices. In this sense, already in 1944, the Long Range Plan for Italy had highlighted how few people in the peninsula had not been "contaminated" by Fascist political culture, so that it was "difficult for the Italians to accept any democratic perspective, let alone to translate it into practice."[22] Efforts to change such conditions began immediately after the war. In this context, the "democracy training" of Italy—to contrast both fascism and communism—was mostly built on two particular representations of American democracy, which would remain central in the documentary production of the following years, when the Cold War transformed Italy in a fundamental stage of soft power's deployment. The first of these two representations revolved around the figure of the "educated citizen" and was based on the conviction that a democratic mindset takes shape in schools, so that—in the words of a USIS official—"the concept of an educated citizenry is not only a premise of our domestic society, but also for the world order we are trying to build."[23] As a result, in 1945 U.S. officials in Italy engaged in the reconstruction and reform of the Italian school system along the lines of an American schools model. At the same time, they distributed a series of technical bulletins dedicated to "Educazione, psciologia e assistenza sociale" ("Education, psychology and social assistance"), in which it was possible to read, "Education provides an essential contribution in explaining the nature and goals of democracy. Education enables to understand the ideal, which the American nation has pursued since its very foundation: a State in which there are freedom, justice and equal possibilities for everyone. It is through education that it becomes possible to understand the importance of civic liberties and political institutions, by which the democratic ideal is expressed [. . .] Education provides the opportunity to live democracy in every moment and aspect of life."[24]

This view on the role of education as a laboratory for democracy found full expression in the U.S.-produced films of the Trieste collection. In this sense, a documentary like *La libertà di imparare* (*Freedom of Learning*), also from the *Panorami d'America* series, aimed at showing how in the United

States education was free and accessible to everyone, and how the right to it represented the key to freedom.[25] According, thus, to the background comment accompanying the images of small classrooms in rural Iowa, "freedom of learning" guarantees the formation of conscious and politically aware citizens and, consequently, the very functioning of democracy.

This idea was likewise re-presented in another documentary, called *UCLA*, that opened a window on life inside American colleges, through the personal experience of four students coming from different social backgrounds.[26] This was meant to point out what was said to be one of the most praiseworthy aspects of the U.S. college system: the equal and universal access to education, so that opportunities for social mobility are guaranteed, in America, to people from all classes. Moreover, the narration is particularly keen to emphasize how the system was organized so as to teach its students not merely a profession, but how to live peacefully together and become responsible citizens. To this end, the film shows students' rising democratic awareness, their engagement in political and electoral activities, and their personal contribution to the governance of the college community.

The representation of universities as "democracy workshops" recurred in many other films, for example, in *Il collegio di Antioch: politecnico del lavoro* (*Antioch College: A Labor Polytechinic*) and *L'università di Bryn Mawr*, which are similarly dedicated to student life in ideal American colleges. Once again then, the emphasis is on student participation in the university's governance and their consequent formation as individuals able "to live democracy in every moment and aspect of life." In particular, by entering actual classrooms, the camera allowed filmgoers to observe the centrality given in America to class debates not as confrontations but as a means to foster mutual respect. Within such a framework, each student is deliberately presented as foremost an aware citizen of a democratic nation, educated for free thought and an exchange of ideas, while America's liberal teaching tradition is praised as "the only safeguard available to democracy."[27]

The second specific representation of American democracy on which USIS officials built their effort to democratize Italian society revolved around the fundamental role played in the United States by freedom of expression and freedom of the press. The commitment to advertise these notions on the peninsula involved all kinds of information instruments, and its immediacy finds confirmation in the articles published in *Nuovo Mondo*, the magazine distributed in Italy by the U.S. government in 1945 and 1946. The commitment was also part of USIS attempts to foster the development of an independent press in a nation in which newspapers were often linked to political parties and associations. In this sense, an article in *Nuovo Mondo*'s October issue repeatedly pointed out how "objective information and news represent sources of democracy" and how "the merit for having built a strong America should be given to its strong and independent press."[28] These same ideas were expressed in USIS documentaries, either through the employment of a didactic approach to explain the U.S. political system or through fictional films on American history. A documentary like *Libertà di stampa* (*Freedom of the Press*) was therefore intended to introduce Italian audiences to the way in which the press operated in the United States and how important it is, for a democracy, to inform people and search for the truth.[29] To this end, the film shows the daily work of some of the most important American newspapers, together with their keen attention in checking the validity and accuracy of their news, so as to draw the conclusion that truth is the best shield with which to defend freedom.

The historical fiction format was also employed in the documentary *Una notizia che non si poteva stampare* (*News Which Could Not Be Published*), to similarly make a connection between freedom of the press and democratic practices.[30] In particular, the film starts by recalling the First Amendment of the American constitution—"eleven words committing the U.S. government to always live under the shining light of a free press"—and proceeds with narration of the 1734 trial against John Zenger, a New York editor and journalist.[31] Arrested for having denounced the illicit appropriations made by the state's governor, Zenger is defended by a young lawyer whose words anticipated, according to the movie's narration, the core elements of the U.S. Declaration of Independence, which "still guarantees freedom today and for which American journalists are envied all over the world." The story of this hero of the past does not seem too distant from that of the incorruptible journalist interpreted by Humphrey Bogart in *Deadline-U.S.A.*: they both aim to embody the power of an independent press, not surrendering to censorship.[32] The renowned Bogart line—"That's the press, baby. The press! And there's nothing you can do about it. Nothing!"—echoed the words of the USIS documentary, providing further confirmation of how USIS film production cannot be separated from parallel filmmaking in Hollywood.

One last example of how the American political system was employed to educate people to democratic principles is offered by the U.S.-produced documentary *Martedì di Novembre* (*A Tuesday in November*).[33] As in the previous two short films, in this one the main topic also is freedom of expression, although this time translated not into a free press but into an American citizen's right to vote. Election day becomes, thus, an opportunity to explain U.S. separation of powers, the "checks and balances" principle, and the American electoral system. Moreover, the American society seen on the screen is idyllic and sanitized of all its negative and discriminatory components: those same components that were instead constantly denounced in PCI's propaganda on American racism. To this end, the camera lingers over a few black women waiting in line to vote, while the narration explains how, in America, "each citizen has the right to vote, with no racial, gender, religious or political discrimination whatsoever."[34] Shot in 1944, the film confirms how the USIS Motion Picture Program was intended to counterbalance negative images of American society.

Overall, then, in U.S.-produced short films, democracy was presented as the shining star of U.S. society, the ultimate American achievement. On the contrary, in the USIS documentaries produced in Italy, democracy was discussed with completely different approaches and tones. This mainly resulted from the fact that—consistently with American perceptions—post-Fascist Italy still had to prove itself as a democratic nation, both domestically and internationally. In this sense, the large majority of Italian documentaries tended to present democracy more as a hope for the future: a goal to point to and to achieve resolutely, but gradually. A good example of such a vision is the one offered by *Dal Tevere al Liri* (*From the Tiber to the Liri*), a documentary commissioned by the Presidenza del Consiglio (the Premiership Office) in 1954.[35] In its presentation of the many advancements achieved in Italy since the end of the war, the sound comment hails the democratic (re)birth of the Italian nation, but tellingly concludes that "democracy has achieved much, but there is still much more to do, having faith in democracy means having faith in ourselves and in our constructive capacities." The tone is thus optimistic, as in the entire Italian production, but democracy is still something to conquer, rather than be conquered. Moreover, differently from the American production, in the Italian documentaries, democracy was presented as dependent not on citizens' responsible and cooperative behavior, but as something that should be pursued and guaranteed through the guidance of the state, which had therefore a more central role than in any U.S.-produced film.

* * *

As explained above, the series of documentaries dedicated to democracy cannot and should not be separated from the parallel and inherently connected set of short films dedicated to productivity, whose centrality in USIS propaganda in Italy vastly increased after 1950, with the onset of an extended productivity campaign. However, the mentioned lack of a strong capitalist mentality among Italian major politicians and businessmen made American efforts to explain and convert the Italians to productivity particularly challenging and should be framed within the larger endeavor "to overcome the rather prevalent misconception abroad of US capitalism," as asserted in a dispatch from the American Embassy in Rome, in 1951.[36] The same document also pointed out U.S. officials' conviction that if the "American system" consisted in a mix of "recognition of the rights of people, a sense of social responsibility, mass production, lower prices, competition, improved public service and a fair share of the profits of greater productivity," the improvements in Italians' standard of living guaranteed by such greater productivity would have been larger than those coming from any other action. It consequently is no surprise to find, among Trieste's film collection, a conspicuous number of documentaries—often commissioned by the Economic Cooperation Administration—dedicated to productivity as the "key to plenty," as one film put it.[37]

As in the case of the shorts on democracy, most documentaries concerned with explaining and exporting productivity employed a didactic approach, consequently using an extremely simple and accessible language and a large number of animated pictures. This is the case of *I nastri portanti* (*The Assembly Line*), an animated feature rich in illustrations and diagrams.[38] The documentary was commissioned by ECA's Mission in Italy and aimed at explaining the functioning mechanisms of a Ford assembly line by showing the various stages of the production of a car. The assembly line was thus credited for having enabled men to overcome "problems as ancient as humanity," for having increased their efficiency, and for having made laborers' work easier and less demanding. Such simplification of a worker's job was nonetheless also an element of concern for the many distrustful criticizers of productivity, conversely emphasizing the dark side of a machine-based system, which risked displacing and alienating workers.

In this sense, it was not sufficient to explain the technical aspects underlying the application of the politics of productivity, but the latter had also to be presented in a reassuring way. It met this purpose through documentaries like *Il segreto del progresso: la macchina al servizio dell'uomo* (*The Secret to Progress: The Machine at the Service of Men*), produced in 1950 and intentionally building on the constant juxtaposition of the antique and the modern.[39] The documentary consequently alternates old and modern working tools, to support the argument that the key to progress lies in machines and in their ability to transform people's life and win man's struggle against time and space. As further proof, the narration explains how machines, by improving productivity levels and increasing production, have not enslaved workers but rather have provided them with more free time and consumption capacity, so that men have, in fact, come to have full control over machines.

Productivity, however, was not only about modern machines and efficient methods of production. Rather, it had to do with the very organization of people's lives and the necessary "rationalization" of daily routines. In short, productivity was a cultural mindset too. Its full application required a transformation of people's social behaviors and everyday actions, toward a more productive organization of people's time. The modern individual, it was said in American propaganda, had to be ingenious, enterprising, hardworking, and able to apply a scientific approach to the resolution of all kinds of daily problems. This vision is perfectly conveyed by one of the more effective films distributed in Italy by USIS, *Tempo perduto* (*Time Lost*), a fictional short movie commissioned by ECA.[40] The footage shows the working day of a young woman, proposing and juxtaposing the same sequence of events twice, to create a marked contrast between the first sequence and the second. To this end, the first half of the short is time-lapsed and has agitated music as its soundtrack. It presents the woman's day as a constant struggle against time, most of which is lost because of poor decisions and bad organization. The second part, instead, slows down both the music and the motion to show how the same day could take place serenely and with no rush, if only everyone organized more rationally and efficiently their daily tasks and time. The narration, in this sense, explains how cooperation and less loss of time would enable people to spend only the strictly necessary amount of time in working duties and, thus, to have more time to relax and rest. The comparison with industrial work is inevitable and made explicit by the assimilation of the social organism to the factory, the activity of which can be paralyzed by the interruption of even a single component of the machinery. The film aimed thereby at encouraging an extension of the logic of productivity to all aspects and moments of life, to allow a better functioning of society as a whole.

The presence of documentaries dedicated to productivity also among the Italian production reveals how the concept was not alien to Italian officials in charge of Italy's economic recovery and growth. And yet, far fewer Italian-produced short movies were dedicated to the topic, and even those that dealt with productivity were characterized by an underlying degree of anxiety and insecurity about its implications. It followed that there was not only the constant and impelling need to demonstrate and reassure audiences about the many potential benefits of a full-range application of the politics of productivity, but also the necessity to avoid presenting productivity as an imported and innovative mindset. In other words, all Italian documentaries shared the attempt to somehow root productivity in the peninsula. In this reference, it is worth mentioning at least two documentaries of Italian origin. The first is an animated feature produced in 1950, *Meno fatica . . . e più denari: la storia del progresso umano narrata in cinque minuti da De Seta* (*Less Strain and More Money: The History of Progress Narrated in Five Minutes by De Seta*), which interprets the history of progress as driven by men's will to simultaneously work less and have a better living.[41] The key to reaching these two goals, according to the narration, is provided by productivity, a new term embodying an idea "as old as human attempts to have a better life." Both the language and the images employed by the short to celebrate modern methods of production are simple and widely accessible. The second selected short movie, *Un'idea in cammino*, has a rather different structure and was produced in 1953 by the Comitato nazionale per la produttività (National Productivity Committee) to promote the productivity campaign launched in Italian industries.[42] In this case, the fictional plot tells the story of a working class Italian family, whose members were initially skeptical and reluctant about the productivity program introduced in their factory but are eventually convinced that productivity means better working conditions and their active involvement in new proposals to improve production. Beside the persuasiveness of the rhetoric employed by the narration, the movie's value comes from the information it provides on the ways in which the U.S.-sponsored campaign of productivity was practically implemented in Italy. In particular, the movie shows the lectures delivered in Italian factories during the so-called productivity hour, and the various initiatives undertaken to engage workers in the production process, such as awards given to those who proposed innovations that increased production.

* * *

The actual effectiveness of this kind of visual propaganda in Italy is difficult to evaluate. It seems that, at least in the initial phase of USIS activity (1945–1950), the Italian branch considered the Motion Picture Program crucial to its informative and advertising effort, to the point of soliciting "a sharp increase in the film program [. . .], since films are one of the best ways of reaching the USIS target groups in Italy, particularly workers, both industrial and agricultural." According to the 1950 "country plan" for Italy, USIS films were seen "by about 10,000,000 persons yearly, at about 35,000 separate showings."[43] Other evidence of effectiveness was provided by the allegedly good disposition and cooperative spirit of the various Italian local authorities, which recurrently solicited the screening of USIS films in their villages and towns. In this reference, the capacity to reach Italian workers was further proved by a series of reported episodes such as one that occurred in Milan, where "a typical evening with the rice workers illustrates the efficacy of our films."[44] Or even in the "red" Reggio Emilia, where the director of the local popular library—a communist institution—had ended up organizing the collective screening of USIS films.[45]

The marginalization of the program soon after seems, however, to belie such arguments, which were probably as much a way to convince the Department of State to direct more money to the program as an acknowledgment of its effectiveneess. Moreover, given that the only available evidence of effectiveness is that recorded by USIS and U.S. officials themselves, additional evaluations should be looked for in local newspapers and reports. However, these are difficult to track down and often are unavailable, so that it is rather difficult to offer a straightforward evaluation of USIS films' ability to reach Italian audiences, let alone to convince them. What it is very likely, nonetheless, is that, relative to productivity and democracy, the images and the rhetoric offered by USIS in the short films diverged, at least partially, from the reality of Italy's industrial environment. And it is sure that they concealed doubts and skeptical feelings that—as already pointed out—pervaded the largely conservative Italian economic world. Such an assessment is confirmed by the very documentation left by USIS, so that, for instance, the country plan issued in 1953 seems to partially contradict the propaganda made in the contemporary *Un'idea in cammino*. Differently from the optimism expressed in the documentary, the plan identified culture as the main obstacle to the creation of a dynamic democracy in Italy. "A backward concept of business among the powerful industrialists and financiers, a lack of knowledge of the real meaning of "productivity" and a reluctance to accept its precepts for Italy, including the importance of good labor-management relations," hurt productivity and growth and limited the full potential of the American ally.[46] Two years earlier the Italian magazine *Mondo Economico* had similarly pointed out that "On the road to productivity, intended as improving plants and production, it does not seem possible to walk, at least in Italy and in the present conditions. What we need now are raw materials and exportation markets, and, most of all, an economic policy, which will make factories work at full speed."[47]

And yet, not many years later, in 1957, another newsreel distributed by USIS, but belonging to the Italian series *Oggi e Domani* (*Today and Tomorrow*), in its report of the Turin automobile fair, enthusiastically hailed the assembly line as "the most pacific revolution of the modern industrial world."[48] Productivity was thus given the credit for having transformed Italy into a modern nation and having guaranteed welfare, progress, peace, and cooperation. At the same time, however, the specifically Italian design of Fiat cars (the so-called *linea italiana*) was praised as the best counterweight to Italy's persistent gap of productivity compared to the United States.

It can be concluded that the analysis of USIS films reveals both the gradual nature and the limits of the still significant impact produced by American models in Italy, to the extent by which Italians seem to have adopted different and often contradictory attitudes toward productivity. Such a vision is in line with the dominant interpretation of Americanization as a two-way process, with influences running in both directions across the Atlantic, and subject to selective appropriation by European audiences. Italians, therefore, rather than fully embracing capitalism as packaged by U.S. officials, interacted with it and shaped their understanding and appropriation of American concepts based on what best suited their personal needs and aspirations, their national traditions and specificities. For the USIS, productivity was an American way of life, to be sure. Yet when it landed in Italy, the American way of life became what the Italians thought it was.

CHAPTER 7

Selling Cooperative Capitalism Abroad: The U.S. Cooperative Movement and International Development During the Cold War

Nicole Sackley

On June 16, 1961, Senator Hubert Humphrey followed John F. Kennedy to the podium of the grand ballroom of the Shoreham Hotel in Washington, D.C. With a critical vote on the president's $8 billion foreign aid bill pending in Congress, 1,200 representatives of the most prominent U.S. religious charities, think tanks, universities, corporations, labor unions, and cooperatives had gathered in Washington for the National Conference on International Economic and Social Development. The theme of the two-day meeting was the "Decade of Development" ahead. Delivering the keynote address, Kennedy urged the nongovernmental leaders to "channel their energies behind our new foreign aid program" by "giving those who are fighting communism the weapon to fight it."[1]

The crowd received the president warmly. But it was the senior senator from Minnesota whose impassioned closing speech roused the greatest applause. Relating his experience that very morning at a closed session of the Senate Foreign Relations Committee, Humphrey conveyed his indignation that the State Department had sent eleven military advisors to a discussion of U.S. policy toward Latin American policy but no representatives of the American cooperative movement. Americans would have to recognize, Humphrey declared, that promoting the American way in Latin America, Asia, and Africa meant more than military assistance, free trade, and corporate investment. The United States was losing the fight against communism because of its failure to hold up its own experience with social welfare, economic planning, and, especially, cooperative economic organization. Cooperatives were "the only way that I know . . . to save this area of the world from collectivism. The answer to the communist collective is the democratic cooperative. And everybody knows it," Humphrey concluded.[2]

Cooperatives represented a small but significant segment of the U.S. economy at midcentury. Concentrated in the American Midwest but located throughout the nation, cooperatives played a substantial role in U.S. agriculture, insurance, electricity, and banking. They touched the everyday lives of Americans through cooperative general stores, local credit unions, and car insurance policies. In 1960, nearly one of every four American families belonged to a cooperative. Yet, U.S. cooperatives were not merely small and local affairs. They generated more than $12 trillion in annual business, with the largest of them resembling Fortune 500 companies in the size and scope of their assets and operations.[3] Nationwide Insurance, one of the largest U.S. insurance companies, operated cooperatively, with 2.5 million policyholders, twelve thousand employees, and operations that spanned twenty-three states.[4] Large cooperatives like Nationwide along with national cooperative associations, from the Cooperative League of the United States of America (CLUSA) to the National Rural Electric Cooperative Association, also exercised considerable political clout, particularly within the Democratic Party. Cooperative leaders like Jerry Voorhis, former U.S. congressman from California; Murray Lincoln of Nationwide; and Howard Cowden, president of the giant oil-marketing cooperative Consumers Cooperative Association (CCA) headquartered in Kansas City, had the ear of influential Midwestern politicians like Humphrey and Secretary of Agriculture Orville Freeman as well as presidents Kennedy and Johnson.

When the Foreign Assistance Act of 1961 finally passed in September, Humphrey had inserted into a section on the "vital role of free enterprise" the stipulation that U.S. policy should "encourage the development and use of cooperatives, credit unions, and savings and loan associations" around the world.[5] A task force of U.S. cooperative leaders was assembled to advise the newly created United States Agency for International Development (USAID) and, over the next six years, USAID contracted with eleven of the largest U.S. cooperative associations to develop forty thousand cooperatives in fifty-three countries.[6] The Humphrey amendment opened the door to direct participation by U.S. cooperatives in U.S. development policy. But cooperative projects and cooperative talk also suffused the broader Third World initiatives of the Kennedy administration, from the Peace Corps to the strategic hamlet program in Vietnam. Cooperatives appealed as an "American" alternative to agricultural collectivism, as a means of curbing foreign aid costs by encouraging "self-help" initiatives, and as a mechanism for inculcating democracy "from the bottom up." The cooperative structure of jointly owned and operated private enterprises was said to teach the principles of democratic small group relations to peasants, workers, and other groups presumed susceptible to the communist message.[7]

This chapter examines the efforts of an influential group of U.S. cooperative leaders to promote the cooperative model as the international face of U.S. capitalism. Beginning in the mid-1950s, large banking, insurance, and oil cooperatives along with national cooperative associations joined together in a two-decade effort to shape international development throughout Asia, Latin America, and Africa. The Humphrey amendment of 1961 connected these efforts by private American actors to U.S. development policy. By 1967, ten associations of U.S. cooperatives operated under USAID contracts in fifty countries around the world.[8]

Why did U.S. cooperatives devote so much energy to the international development field in the 1950s and 1960s? In part, U.S. cooperative leaders were primed by previous international experience and strong ideological commitments. Figures like Murray Lincoln of Nationwide and Howard Cowen of the giant Kansas City oil cooperative CCA had developed their understanding of cooperatives' economic potential through interwar engagement in transnational networks that circulated cooperative ideas around the Atlantic and throughout Asia. During World War II, as the European cooperative movement collapsed, they envisioned leading this global cooperative movement. Yet, in these same years, U.S. cooperatives felt themselves under attack—economically, by accelerating corporatization, and politically, by those attacking them as "socialistic." These attacks represented a wider internal struggle over the meaning and legacies of the New Deal. It was in the face of these challenges, I argue, that cooperative leaders turned abroad to the international arena as a place to work out domestic struggles over the meaning of "the American way."

Throughout the 1950s, the Eisenhower administration had stressed the role of American corporate capitalism in the world. Although increasingly open in the final years of his presidency to the necessity of government-to-government assistance, Eisenhower saw corporate investment and international trade as the central motors of economic development. While other Eisenhower critics, such as the liberal economists John Kenneth Galbraith, Leon Keyserling, and Walt Whitman Rostow, argued that underdeveloped nations needed state planning and large-scale capital aid to take off into self-sustaining economic growth, American cooperators carved out a third position in a national debate framed as public *versus* private. The cooperative, they maintained, avoided state control and encouraged private ownership while protecting small producers and consumers from the vagaries of the market.[9] Rather than push the free enterprise system, U.S. policymakers should spread the word that millions of Americans joined together in cooperatives of their own making. Such an image could, CLUSA president Jerry Voorhis argued in 1961, change "the picture of America as seen by the people of the rest of world." It was "an image no totalitarian country could project."[10]

The U.S. cooperative movement is largely missing from the historiographies of both international development and American capitalism abroad during the second half of the twentieth century.[11] Historians of U.S. foreign relations who study the "selling" of American capitalism through psychological warfare have generally assumed that American visions of capitalism projected abroad were consistent, shared, and relatively stable during the 1950s.[12] Focused on the U.S.-Soviet struggle, they have missed the intra-American contest over the meaning of international development during the 1950s and 1960s. Meanwhile, historians of U.S. politics have, in recent years, upended the notion of a postwar liberal consensus by documenting the vociferous efforts of conservative economists, think tanks, and corporations to roll back the New Deal in the 1950s and early 1960s. Yet, these historians have ignored the interest and participation of U.S. conservatives in international development. Theirs is largely a domestic story.[13]

Examining the U.S. cooperative movement and their quest for a middle way at home and abroad between the 1940s and 1960s shows how international development became a key arena in which Americans debated and defined the nature of their own economic system. More than anywhere else in the world, India's development in the late 1950s and early 1960s became central ground on which the American contended over what defined the American way of capitalism. As I have argued elsewhere, in Nehru's India, Keynesian and neoliberal economists fought over the proper role of the state in economic development. Prominent liberal U.S. economists likened India's mixed economy to the New Deal and hailed India's second five-year plan, announced in 1956, as a model for other underdeveloped nations. By the late

1950s, their calls for U.S. aid for Indian planning had activated the resistance of an emerging counternetwork of economists and journalists, led by Milton Friedman and clustered around the Mont Pelerin Society, who opposed state restrictions on private enterprise.[14] The Eisenhower administration shared an antipathy to India's heterodoxy, critical of both Nehru's neutralism in the Cold War struggle and acceptance of Soviet economic assistance. As the first blast furnace powered up at the new million-ton-capacity, Soviet-built steel mill in Bhilai in February 1959, the United States prepared for the opening of a $2 million, five-acre American pavilion at the World Agricultural Fair in New Delhi, featuring Motorola television sets, International Harvester tractors, and Webcor tape recorders.[15]

To American cooperative leaders, neither five-year planning nor the consumer fruits of American corporations held the future of India or the rest of the developing world. Deeply anticommunist but also suspicious of corporate capitalism, they hoped to weave a global path between big government and big business while defending their own place and legitimacy in the American economic landscape. The cooperative, they maintained, avoided state control and encouraged private ownership while protecting small producers and consumers from the vagaries of the market. Fear of bigness and centralization, in both its state and corporate forms, had animated the U.S. cooperative since the early twentieth century. During the Cold War, U.S. cooperative leaders insisted that when they went abroad, they acted as private citizens and that cooperative assistance was a grassroots "people-to-people" program. Such a characterization ignored not only the role of large cooperative associations as powerful economic and political actors but also, by the early 1960s, denied the ways in which "private" cooperative assistance had become entangled in U.S. foreign policy. In its own way, the cooperative movement sold as simplified a vision of American capitalism as the one it sought to complicate.

* * *

As U.S. cooperative leaders began to assert a larger international role in the 1940s, they came under fire at home. Several corporate leaders in the Midwest went on the offensive against the success of the cooperatives and the competition they posed. In 1944, a Minneapolis grain merchant organized a nationwide campaign against the cooperatives' corporate tax exemption, arguing it unfairly benefited an "un-American" economic form. "Collectivist" cooperatives, thundered Michigan congressman Paul Shaffer in 1947, "cause irreparable harm to our whole system of free enterprise . . . it can hardly be denied that this movement, carried to its logical conclusions, would play right into the hands of the Communists."[16]

The American cooperative movement had, in fact, little affinity with and a record of outright hostility toward communism. In the years of the Popular Front, CLUSA leaders railed against the capture of Russian cooperatives by the Soviet state and denounced "statism" almost as frequently as they condemned monopoly capitalism. Cooperative democracy meant cooperative, but private, control of economics and politics. Still, cooperative leaders like Murray Lincoln and their political allies in Congress had, generally, strong political ties to Roosevelt and the New Deal.[17] In 1946, Lincoln's hometown newspaper, the *Columbus Dispatch*, suggested that Lincoln had ties to the "radical" Congress of Industrial Organizations. That same year, Congressman Jerry Voorhis, a loyal New Dealer, ardent anticommunist, and cooperative booster, was redbaited and defeated by Richard Nixon in Nixon's first campaign for political office.[18] Voorhis' defeat, and Nixon's election, symbolized a newly precarious political climate for the cooperatives. Conservative business attacks on the New Deal and the ideological conflict with the Soviet Union had placed particular forms of economic activity and association under ideological suspicion. The cooperative movement, with its antipathy to capitalist monopoly and commitment to excising the profit motive, fit uneasily into an American way increasingly conflated with the free enterprise system. Simultaneously, cooperative insurance companies, credit unions, and rural electric and marketing cooperatives struggled to compete with the exponential postwar growth of the largest corporations and banks.

Many cooperatives fought back. First, CLUSA changed how it presented itself. It established a subcommittee to review its policy and publicity. The committee recommended that the league avoid excessive criticism of capitalism and highlight instead the economic benefits of cooperative organization: private ownership that would produce an economy of abundance. Second, CLUSA entered politics more directly. It hired the defeated Voorhis, a Washington veteran, as its executive director and opened a Washington, D.C., office to defend its tax exemptions. Increasingly, the cooperative movement, which had counted supporters in both political parties, tilted toward the Democratic Party.[19] In 1948, large regional cooperatives of Minnesota turned out their members and helped put Hubert Humphrey in the Senate. From his early career as mayor of Minneapolis, Humphrey represented a vision of cooperative democracy popular in the upper Midwest that sought to align consumers and farmers in cooperatives with unionized industrial workers. In the closely contested presidential election of that year, Harry Truman recognized the importance of the cooperatives, writing support for them into the Democratic Party platform.[20]

Not merely defensive, American cooperators sought to reappropriate the term "free enterprise" and cast themselves as the keepers of the genuine American way. "On the radio one hears half-minute blurbs sandwiched into symphonies extolling the virtues of free enterprise," Lincoln explained. "Business clubs from coast to coast ply their listeners with catchwords and phrases—'freedom,' 'American tradition,' and 'initiative.' And they're convincing a lot of people." But Americans should not be fooled: "What they call 'free enterprise' has been freedom to employ the practices of monopoly, cartel agreements, [and] price fixing formulas." By contrast, cooperatives demonstrated a "practical devotion to genuinely free completion and enterprise." They were, Humphrey explained, "American citizens [who] without waiting for government action, have turned trust-busters themselves. They are joining together in cooperative democracy." They were "essential to the health of the American economy."[21]

In the late 1940s, U.S. cooperatives also began to recognize the international arena as a place to underscore their anticommunism and lay claim to the "American" nature of their work. CLUSA promoted its role in helping to "save" Europe from communism. As the Marshall Plan pumped U.S. government dollars into Western Europe, CLUSA collected private funds from its members to set up Italian credit cooperatives, an international cooperative bank in Switzerland, and the cooperative infrastructure for CARE. Under Lincoln's leadership, CARE then expanded its relief efforts to postpartition India, first through CARE packages and then, in 1950, through the U.S. sale of $10 ploughs for "guaranteed, tax-free delivery anywhere in India and Pakistan."[22] All of these efforts came bundled with a clear message about the ideological as well as the humanitarian purpose of cooperative work, both at home and abroad. *Time* magazine reported favorably in 1953 on Lincoln as a "Man with a Mission" who saw "the co-ops as an answer to Communism in Europe and Asia, and as a balance wheel against unfettered private enterprise in the U.S." The following year, Jerry Voorhis stood up at the world meeting of the International Cooperative Alliance and led a charge to refuse to seat "puppet" cooperatives from the Eastern Block. *Time* again depicted a U.S. cooperative leader as a hero who had taught the world a "lesson in democracy."[23]

Through international engagement, U.S. cooperative leaders had found a way to shore up anticommunist bona fides and remain relevant within the

United States. Defining the American way of capitalism in the world, they might be able to shape its terms at home.

* * *

India emerged at the forefront of Americans' preoccupation with international development in the early 1950s. Dire warnings of a high-stakes competition with China for the "hearts and minds" of Asia's peasants were commonplace among U.S. academics, policymakers, and journalists in the late 1950s. The Eisenhower administration, whose foreign aid and propaganda policies emphasized the virtues of free enterprise, argued that a combination of U.S. private investment and agricultural knowledge (along the lines of the USDA county agent model) would answer what was seen as India's most pressing needs: feeding its people and generating agricultural exports. But U.S. cooperative leaders put a different spin on the question, emphasizing how cooperative economic organization offered a better model than single-family or corporate farming to the problems of low agricultural productivity and hunger in Asia and Latin America. American democratic cooperative solutions were meant to counter the allure of the collectivist agricultural models proffered by the People's Republic of China. Producer and consumer cooperatives would allow impoverished peasants producing staple crops or hungry urban consumers to band together to establish a foothold in the market.[24] Rather than push the free enterprise system, cooperative leaders held that U.S. policymakers should spread the word that millions of Americans joined together in cooperatives of their own making.

The first connection between U.S. and Indian cooperatives occurred in late 1952 when Thomas Keehn, a representative of Nelson Rockefeller's American International Association for Economic and Social Development (AIA), arrived in New Delhi to investigate a "people-to-people relationship" in India.[25] Keehn saw immediate promise of a partnership with the small Indian Cooperative Union (ICU). Founded by socialist reformer Kamaladevi Chattopadhyay, the ICU had launched several handicraft and agricultural cooperative projects in and around Delhi and the planned town of Faridabad between 1947 and 1952. The fledgling ICU was an outlier in the wider Indian cooperative movement at midcentury. British colonial policy had fueled exponential growth in Indian cooperatives in the first half of the twentieth century, notably primary credit societies, but had tied these societies, financially and administratively, to the colonial state. The patterns continued after 1947.

The Reserve Bank of India and the Indian Planning Commission viewed local and regional cooperatives as well as the nominal national apex organization, All India Cooperative Union, as instruments of national development goals.[26] In contrast, the ICU operated, Rockefeller observed, with "the philosophy and function of a voluntary agency" while nonetheless maintaining strategic political support from Nehru and "outstanding business, welfare and political figures in the country."[27] Chattopadhyay and Nehru were indeed longtime allies in the noncooperation movement against British rule, and Nehru had made personal donations to the ICU. For her part, Chattopadhyay desired the technical and financial support that Rockefeller money might provide but insisted that the scion of the Rockefeller oil fortune bring on board CLUSA to create a true cooperative-to-cooperative venture.

In spring 1953, Keehn established a joint AIA-CLUSA office inside ICU's headquarters on Queensway and, over the next three years, assisted ICU secretary L. C. Jain in the creation of a fifteen-village pilot of credit and producer cooperatives on the outskirts of New Delhi. A pilot project made sense. Much of the ideas undergirding the community development program had emerged from pilot efforts. The government of India quickly endorsed the project.[28] CLUSA was now on Nehru's radar. When the prime minister arrived in New York City in December 1956, he invited Murray Lincoln to his Waldorf Astoria suite to talk over the work of CARE and CLUSA in India.[29] There is no extant record of Nehru's reaction to this first meeting with Lincoln, but we do know that Nehru approached the cooperative question with an increasing sense of urgency in 1956. The ambitious growth targets of India's Second Five-Year Plan, launched earlier that year, depended on driving capital into industrial projects and raising food productivity through the community development program. Those targets were not, however, being met, and increasingly India faced both rising food prices and an emerging foreign exchange crisis.

In this context, Nehru cast about for cooperative models for agricultural production, from the cooperative leaders of the U.S. Midwest to the People's Republic of China. In January 1954, China had announced plans for gradual collectivization of Chinese cultivators and soon began posting claims to broad strides in agriculture. Nehru and his key advisors had become increasingly convinced that the Chinese example offered possible models for India. As China announced a new plan for complete agricultural collectivization in January 1956, Nehru had already authorized Indian delegations to tour and study Chinese agricultural cooperatives.[30] The Chinese cooperatives differed fundamentally from U.S. cooperative efforts in that they proposed collective farming, whereas U.S. cooperatives operated by the pooling of resources to effect prices within a system of individual land ownership.

The visits to China initiated tensions and political debates within India. While both Indian delegations to China confirmed the necessity of cooperative farming and stressed the voluntary nature of Chinese efforts, there were dissenting voices among the Indian visitors. Nehru had faced fierce resistance to land reform efforts from Congress Party elites in the Indian states. Now the possibility of following the Chinese example threatened fundamental change in the structures of power in the Indian countryside where village elites and the most prosperous farmers controlled the rural credit cooperatives. Nehru lashed out at the Chief ministers of the Indian states:

> We have no other choice but cooperative farming. The real alternative is collective farms owned by the State, which most Communist countries have. That, I take it, is further removed from the customs and habits of the Indian farmer. Within two or three years, millions of cooperative farms have sprung up there. Now, they are being converted into collectives. We do not want to go in that direction. But the forces at work which are driving China in that direction—a vast agricultural population, the need for greater production, etc.—are at work in India, and we have to find some solution . . . we must have cooperative farming. At this stage, for anyone to challenge this surprises me.[31]

Nehru and the National Development Council continued to press for the creation of cooperative farms and the reorganization of rural business along cooperative lines, and deteriorating economic conditions gave ballast to the possibility for more radical solutions. Agricultural production had fallen, food prices had skyrocketed by 50 percent between October 1955 and August 1957, and the government was forced to import two million tons of food. When the monsoon failed in spring 1957, conditions worsened further, depleting both food and foreign capital reserves. As Indian planners were forced abroad to lobby for European and U.S. aid to save the Second Five-Year Plan, Nehru continued to urge the expansion of cooperative techniques. "The only possible way is some cooperative method which fits in with the [poor farmer's] life and is not too far removed from him," he wrote in September 1958.[32]

The Food Ministry and the state ministers of agriculture had very different ideas, proposing instead to raise agricultural productivity through greater investment in agricultural education; scientifically improved pesticides, seeds, and fertilizer; and government price supports for rice and wheat to encourage increased private investment. The village, not larger cooperative farms, would be the principal unit of the rural economy. The conflict came to a head in 1959. Indian politicians and the Indian press accused Nehru and central planners of plotting to take India on the road to collectivism. At the Forum for Free Enterprise, a clearinghouse for free market ideas in Bombay, Minoo Masani railed against "collective farming of the Sino-Chinese pattern." The prospect of cooperative farming became a final straw for the conservative Congress Party leader C. Rajagopalachari, who in 1959 broke with Nehru to found the Swatantra Party.[33] Even without these political repercussions, the basic constitutional structure of India tied Nehru's hands on the question of cooperative farming. The center could do little to enforce the resolution without legislative action from the states. By the summer of 1959, the possibility of large-scale cooperative farming was dead in India. The incursion of China into Tibet and rising tensions over the Sino-Indian border shut down all talk of Chinese models. The Indian government ultimately accepted the U.S.-backed recommendation to create the Intensive Agricultural Development Program with Ford Foundation support.

Meanwhile, the narrative of India's economic policies played in the United States as a battle between collectivism and the free enterprise system. The Eisenhower administration focused on building up the power and prestige of corporate capitalism in India. Between 1957 and 1959, studies by the International Cooperation Administration, the Government Accounting Office, and two congressional committees despaired at the low regard for capitalism in India and called for tax incentives to support Indian corporations and U.S. private investment. (The state of free enterprise in India so worried one Kansas oil executive visiting India that he deposited $30,000 at the Punjab National Bank for "young men in India" to "develop private initiative as a productive force in India.")[34] In November, as India hosted a world agricultural fair in New Delhi, the U.S. government built a $2 million exhibit on the fairgrounds that included a thirty-six by forty foot model of a typical American rural landscape, replete with a replica of a small town, seven U.S. farm families, and a massive display of consumer goods hosted by 158 U.S. corporations. Eisenhower himself visited the fair during his state visit to India and hailed it as a visual embodiment of the "ways in which American farmers multiplied their productivity; the fertility of their fields; the vigor and the value of their livestock."[35] The U.S. exhibit fit into a wider U.S. government depiction of American capitalism abroad. From international trade fairs to Voice of America broadcasts, the Eisenhower administration had advanced a vision of "people's capitalism," a reformed capitalism in which U.S. workers and farmers were no longer exploited and, in fact, shared in the rewards of the capitalist system as stockholders and consumers of corporate products. Vice President Richard Nixon's celebrated "kitchen debate" with Soviet Premier Nikita Khrushchev at the American National Exhibition, only four months earlier in Moscow, exemplified this approach.[36]

Leaders of the U.S. cooperative movement responded that this presentation of the free enterprise system as not only ineffective but potentially dangerous. Jerry Voorhis called for a change "in the picture of America as seen by the peoples of the rest of the world [of] the nature of our economic life at home. We have had much to say about a 'people's capitalism.' We can show that America is not only a nation that boasts of General Motors, and United States Steel, and Standard Oil. America is also a nation in which 14 million families use their freedom and their often-small resources to create economic institutions of their own to meet directly their own economic needs."[37]

Nowhere was this lesson more important, they felt, than in India. Raymond Miller, a professor at Harvard Business School who began his career working for marketing cooperatives in California, had attended a Food and Agriculture Organization conference on Asian cooperatives in Lucknow, India, in 1949 and then returned in 1954 to consult with the Indian Planning Commission. In a 1959 manifesto for a general audience—entitled *Can Capitalism Compete? A Campaign for American Free Enterprise*—Miller defended the cooperative as the best expression of American capitalism. He explained that the idea for the book had first come to him after verbal exchange with a Soviet diplomat at a Rotary Club dinner in New Delhi in which the Soviet official declared that communism would triumph and that capitalism was at the root of most of the world's problems. Arguing that U.S. publicity "belabor[ed] the dead devil of nineteenth century capitalism," Miller complained that few foreign leaders or ordinary people learned anything about the achievements of U.S. cooperatives. Nothing was "more capitalistic than a corporation for service without entity-profit but with profit to the members who use and own it," he said. "The Scandinavian countries are 'loved' in all parts of the world largely because of their 'middle way.' We have a similar development here, but we do not talk about it enough."[38]

Even as Miller called for new U.S. publicity about cooperatives abroad, CLUSA was putting plans into place for greater engagement in the Third World. In 1959, CLUSA established the Fund for International Cooperative Development. The fund underwrote schools for co-op leaders in Morocco and Nyasaland; sent seasoned cooperative managers and advisors to Borneo, Ghana, Basutoland, Panama, Congo, Vietnam, and the Philippines; and supported the creation of an international training center for foreign cooperative leaders at the University of Wisconsin. While CLUSA boasted that countries came calling to it, it was no accident that its focus was on nations that were often flashpoints in the Cold War conflict.[39] Indeed, the internal memos of CLUSA leaders show an awareness of international competitors and a worry that foreign cooperatives might adopt "wrong" cooperative models. CLUSA tracked the progress of a cooperative college for Southeast Asia established in New Delhi by the Swedish federation of consumer cooperatives, *Kooperativa Förbundet*, and CLUSA personnel reported on the presence of cooperative delegations from Czechoslovakia and the Soviet Union touring India.[40] In India in particular, CLUSA's local director Thomas Keehn identified an unstable situation: "Government policy at present can only be described as riding the fence . . . if the Package Program fails—then the ICA [International Cooperative Alliance] must be prepared to deal with cooperative farming and the political left."[41]

Nehru had reiterated in a November 1960 speech that he wished to "convulse India with the Cooperative Movement to make it, broadly speaking, the basic activity of India."[42] But even a cursory reading of the final version of the Third Plan, released in April 1961, revealed that he had pulled back considerably on what "cooperation" meant. The Third Plan invested in cooperative credit and agricultural inputs and consumer cooperatives but offered little structural or financial support for cooperative farming.[43] Moreover, the political and economic benefits of credit, marketing, and consumer cooperatives continued to be unequally distributed along lines of class and caste. The economist Daniel Thorner documented these realities on the ground in 1959. After a seven-month field survey of 117 cooperatives across ten Indian states, Thorner concluded, "the success of rural cooperatives presupposes a modicum of social equality, political democracy, and economic viability among the villagers. These conditions have not been present in village India and are still not present today. . . . What is happening in India today is that cooperatives are being asked to create their own pre-conditions, to reconstruct village society so that the ordinary peasants can make effective use of the cooperative method. This is too much to expect."[44]

There is no evidence that Nehru read Thorner's cautionary report. Instead of structural reforms at the village level, Nehru reached out a second time to Murray Lincoln and to the promise of technical expertise in cooperative methods. During his official state visit to the United Nations, Nehru invited Lincoln to visit India to study and make recommendations for India's cooperative movement. Lincoln accepted but asked that Nehru first send a delegation to Ohio, so that Indian officials might see what cooperatives in his state had accomplished. Within the week, Nationwide's company jet transported India's defense minister V. K. Krishna Menon and four members of the Indian parliament to Columbus. There, Menon lunched with faculty at Ohio State, lectured to Nationwide's board of directors, and toured the state's largest cooperative processing plants and stores that supplied tens of thousands of farmers with fertilizer, seed, auto supplies, oil, and insecticides. Impressed with what he saw, Menon made arrangements with Lincoln to have a delegation of Nationwide's directors and executive make a one-month tour of India's consumer, housing, marketing, purchasing, and credit cooperatives.[45] The six-foot, three-inch Lincoln—described by the press that year as "a big man who thinks big"—was delighted.[46] Nationwide Insurance, he had declared publicly in his 1960 memoir *Vice President in Charge of Revolution*, was "serious when it says that it wants to save the world."[47]

* * *

The invitation for a Nationwide team to visit India came as Nehru cast about for cooperative solutions to India's food crisis that avoided the political impossibility of cooperative farming. The team of Nationwide experts that departed for India in November 1961 could make the conservative case for cooperatives. Indeed, as he prepared for the trip, the team's leader, David Scull, argued that it seemed Nationwide and CLUSA had an opportunity to help create a unique sector of the economic machinery, neither state nor profit-capitalist, which we might call an "open-ended cooperative."[48]

While an ailing Lincoln stayed behind in Columbus, the team comprised Scull, a Nationwide director and president of several credit unions; Leslie Woodcock, a Nationwide director, former director of CLUSA, and the International Cooperative Alliance's representative to the UN Economic and Social Council; Ferris Owen, a lifelong farmer and director of the Ohio Farm Bureau Federation; Wallace Campbell, founder and vice president of CARE, longtime head of CLUSA's Washington headquarters, and Nationwide's new director of public affairs; Paul Nelson, a former National Rural Electric Cooperative Association economist and now on Nationwide's research staff; and Allie Felder, Jr., a rural sociologist on leave from the Hampton Institute who now directed the CLUSA office in New Delhi.[49] The team spent four weeks in India, visiting five Indian states and examples of every type of cooperative enterprise, consumer, housing, marketing, and purchasing, and credit organizations. In Delhi, they spoke at length with Nehru and his chief ministers.[50] By February 1962, back in Ohio, they had formulated a set of recommendations and promises of support. U.S. cooperatives would provide India with eight cooperative specialists to help the Indian Council of Agricultural Research and the Rockefeller Foundation with cooperative distribution of hybrid corn, create a new network of consumer cooperatives with the Indian Cooperative Union, and create a development loan fund to make loans to credit cooperatives.[51]

Nehru accepted the recommendations and, over the next few months, CLUSA sent three experienced cooperative leaders (in rural credit, hybrid corn, and consumer cooperatives) to Delhi. At the same time, high-ranking Indian officials began touring the cooperatives of the Midwest. These included Minister of Community Development S. K. Dey (as a guest of Senator Hubert Humphrey), Indian ambassador B. K. Nehru, and C. D. Deshmukh, former finance minister and vice chancellor of the University of Delhi. While touring the vast Consumer Cooperative Association plants in Kansas City, Missouri, on June 25, 1962, Deshmukh explained to U.S. reporters why he was there: "We want to get a glimpse of U.S. farms, farmers, co-ops, systems of marketing, study price support, fertilizer, insecticides, weedicides, prices, availability of credit to farmers [and] farm organisations. . . . [We] need for U.S. cooperatives to come to an agreement with India. Instead of U.S. private manufacturers working in India, we would like assistance from U.S. cooperatives."[52]

Prominent Indians were not the only ones trumpeting the new relationship. CLUSA and Nationwide Insurance sent copies of its official report, entitled "Mission to India," to the White House, members of Congress, the U.S. Embassy in India, and high-ranking officials in the U.S. Department of State and Department of Agriculture. They also issued press releases that depicted "strong cooperative organization" as the "missing link" in efforts to address "India's No. 1 problem" of food production. U.S. cooperative experts could help India's vast array of "small and weak" cooperatives become "economically efficient organizations." Cooperatives, explained the Nationwide report, "must be planned, organized, and established to assure economic virility... capable of employing competent managerial personnel and technicians." Indian cooperatives required "competitive efficiency [for] performing operations of greatest economic significance."[53]

Even as U.S. cooperative leaders explained their intervention in India as a provision of capitalist discipline, they touted the cooperatives as a superior face of American capitalism in India. The "Mission to India" report took care to recount the reactions of the former Indian ambassador to the United States, G. L. Mehta, to the presence of U.S. cooperative experts in India. Mehta had said that to "most of his countrymen America was a land of capitalism and big business, with a lack of social purpose and cooperative spirit. If through our trip and efforts to follow, we could let them know that a strong cooperative movement is an important part of America, he said we could have a positive political effect on India almost greater than anything else the U.S. had done or was doing in India."[54]

By 1961, the climate in Washington had warmed for greater attention to the work of U.S. cooperatives abroad. Hubert Humphrey led the charge to bring U.S. cooperatives into U.S. development policy more directly.[55] Humphrey imagined cooperatives as a key to U.S. interests in Latin America in the wake of the Cuban Revolution. "The right kind" of farmer, consumer, and housing cooperatives, Humphrey argued, would deter communist revolution better than military support for dictators and oligarchs by raising mass living standards and teaching "grassroots democracy."[56] Humphrey's amendment to the Foreign Assistance Act of 1961 led to a special advisory committee on cooperatives, composed of U.S. cooperative leaders assembled to advise the newly created USAID.

The Humphrey amendment opened the door to direct participation by U.S. cooperatives in U.S. development policy. In its first report on the Humphrey amendment, USAID administrators stressed the economic and political advantages of U.S. cooperative assistance in developing countries. Participation in cooperatives could further popular investment in capitalism by "stimulat[ing] the sense of pride and stability which stems from the knowledge of ownership," and cooperatives could "serve as laboratories for democracy" in which the "feeling of ownership and belonging [to the] cooperative can be a strong stabilizing ballast to citizenship." The report concluded that "a country covered with local cooperatives and their members—understanding owners—does not fear revolution and military coups."[57]

* * *

In 1962, Lincoln joined the USAID cooperative advisory board, but U.S. cooperative leaders maintained an ambivalent relationship to their new place in U.S. development policy. On the one hand, the Humphrey amendment and the encouragement of cooperative projects within the newly established Peace Corps meant that U.S. cooperative models were spreading globally, as CLUSA had advocated for a decade. On the other hand, U.S. cooperative leaders had ideological and practical reasons to separate their work from U.S. government efforts. A strong antistatist strain and a general distrust of "bigness" and monopoly in all of its forms had long pervaded the movement. Unlike other prominent critics of Eisenhower's development policy, such as Rostow or Kennedy, CLUSA leaders opposed large-scale transfers of U.S. capital to fund state-led planning for economic "take-off" in Asia, Africa, and Latin America.[58] Only the cooperative way, declared Murray Lincoln, could "prevent the average man from being smothered between Big Business and Big Government." Only the cooperative way could "save private capitalism from becoming state capitalism."[59]

At the ideological heart of the U.S. cooperative movement was a profound faith that economic problems could be solved, not by corporations or governments, but by ordinary citizens banding together to "help themselves." That ideology animated not only the cooperative movement but a wider landscape of community-based, self-help projects that were imagined by reformers, social scientists, activists, and government officials as mechanisms to eradicate poverty and inculcate democratic values, both inside the United States and beyond its borders. "Thinking small," as historian Daniel Immerwahr has characterized it, meant not only local cooperatives but also urban "community action," housing councils, and village community development projects. Self-help, community-led projects proved a seductive model, precisely because of their malleability. They appealed to local activists' calls for self-determination, to postcolonial leaders' efforts to nation-build from the ground up, and to U.S. policymakers seeking mechanisms for controlled modernization. Yet, we should not underestimate the extent to which self-help initiatives offered an illusion of connection and affiliation across international lines. To imagine a world organized into cooperatives, villages, and community promised a mechanism for "international understanding" even as it ignored differentials of geopolitical and national economic power and hierarchies of race, class, and gender.[60]

An appeal to international connection undergirded the cooperative campaign. U.S. cooperatives sold their international engagement as a "people-to-people" or "coop-to-coop" program, where Americans—typically, rural Midwesterners—connected personally with rural people around the world. Agents of the Mutual Insurance Company of Saint Paul, Minnesota, for example, canvased policyholders throughout the Upper Midwest who sponsored $10 plows for six Indian villages. Nationwide agents collected $200,000 for Central American cooperatives and then flew a select group of employees to work with the beneficiaries in Honduras and Costa Rica. Such connections were then replayed in CLUSA convention speeches, Kiwanis Club presentations, and feature stories in cooperative newsletters.[61]

Cooperative leaders saw psychological importance in these transnational connections. The U.S. movement, admitted David Scull, had become "a fairly comfortable middle-class movement. . . if we can bring American cooperators face-to-face with the challenge that their fellow-cooperators in India are trying to meet . . . it is just possible that we could infuse a new and much-needed element of inspiration and idealism into the American cooperative movement."[62] But the intimate, cooperative ethic also underlined for U.S. cooperative leaders what made their work a superior vision of American capitalism. The identity of the U.S. cooperative movement depended on cooperators seeing themselves as within and representing the *private* sphere of American life. Indeed, CLUSA cooperative experts in Indian critiqued the Indian movement for being too tightly tied to the Indian state. Maintaining a distance from the U.S. government and funding their own international activities offered proof of their claims to represent American capitalism and a model for cooperatives abroad.[63]

In March 1962, CLUSA launched a $1 million fundraising drive of its member cooperatives to fund its development activities.[64] CLUSA headquarters in Washington sent out letters of appeal to join the "World Co-op Partners Campaign." A campaign brochure entitled "I Fought in the Revolution" offered photographs and a first-person appeal by one cooperative expert fulfilling a "revolution of rising expectations" in Indian villages. The brochure urged U.S. cooperative members to join the revolution by "'adopt[ing]' a co-op in an underdeveloped country," volunteering to work overseas, or pledging annual contributions to the fund: "This can be your revolution. It is peaceful. It involves no conquest of one people by another only conquest of the ancient enemies of hunger and poverty. This is not charity whose benefits recede with time. This is self-help, people helping other people to help themselves. It offers hope. . . . For while other ideologies may promise much, this revolution and this alone offers freedom for men to walk upright and without fear."[65]

Publicly, CLUSA executive director Jerry Voorhis announced the campaign as "a people-to-people program aimed at helping developing countries." CLUSA would help establish "free-enterprise cooperatives," Voorhis explained, that would "grow rapidly and expand in ever-widening circles once we provide expert training and just a little initial capital."[66] Privately, however, Voorhis worried about the cooperative's private fundraising efforts. A substantial part of the fundraising campaign was earmarked for the Nationwide-CLUSA work in India, but contributions to the fund had not come close to the goal. Nationwide's board of directors had pledged an initial $50,000 for the India work, but by September 1963, they demurred on further financing. Only two of the promised eight cooperative experts were on the ground in India, and Voorhis reported he was "exceedingly worried" that their expenses were "running way beyond the estimates."[67]

With new funding failing to materialize, CLUSA joined half a dozen other U.S. cooperative associations, from the American Savings and Loan Institute to the National Rural Electrical Cooperative Association, in accepting a multiyear global contract with USAID to run their own projects in countries around the world. By 1966, U.S. cooperatives received $9.5 million from USAID to advise forty thousand cooperatives in fifty-three countries.[68] In these years, CLUSA and other regional U.S. cooperatives vastly expanded their work in India. Working with the Peace Corps program in India and the Indian Cooperative League, CLUSA established two cooperative "super bazaars" in New Delhi and assisted another seventeen wholesale consumer cooperatives on operations logistics and the training of some eight hundred Indian cooperative instructors.[69] Then in 1967, U.S. fertilizer cooperatives, led by CLUSA, joined the government of India, USAID, and a consortium of Indian state cooperatives to begin plans for construction of a massive cooperative fertilizer plant in Gujarat, capable of producing enough fertilizer to grow ten million tons of food annually. A new consortium of U.S. fertilizer cooperatives, Cooperative Fertilizers International, would "develop, coordinate, and manage [the] plants until Indians are adequately trained to take over these responsibilities." Meanwhile, the Indian state cooperatives formed a new all-India cooperative to own and operate the proposed facilities and to market and distribute the output through state cooperative warehouses. While the U.S. cooperatives provided personnel and $1 million in financing, most of the project was underwritten primarily with government funds. Although CLUSA boasted that the project placed "ownership of fertilizer production facilities in the hands of millions of farmers," there was little about the Gujarat fertilizer plant that met the ideals of private, people-to-people cooperative action.[70]

The U.S. cooperative movement continued to present itself as a private, nonstate, "co-op to co-op" movement. In the mid-1960s, the Johnson administration and the U.S. cooperative movement had mutual interests in this fiction. To the administration, facing the mounting costs of the Vietnam War and a U.S. public and Congress impatient with development aid, U.S. cooperatives promised to subcontract development work and reduce its need by teaching "self-help" abroad.[71] Even as the USAID contributed more and more funding to CLUSA operations in India, the CLUSA Delhi office continued to be housed separately. "The Mission feels," CLUSA's public affairs director Shelby Southard explained to the House Foreign Affairs Committee in 1968, "that the office's role as a private organization enables it to operate far more effectively than would be possible if it were looked upon as part of AID."[72] In Southard's framing, CLUSA's work in India was "a people-to-people program" through which Americans sent to India were "private citizens" generating "psychological transformations in individuals, which is the basis from which economic development 'takes off.'"[73] To U.S. cooperatives, such a characterization stoked their desire to be seen, in Humphrey's phrase, as "a vital part of our free enterprise system."[74]

Taking USAID funding also allowed the cooperatives to hide the anemic nature of their internal fundraising. For all the emotive appeals to the global ties between co-ops and an aggressive fundraising campaign, CLUSA was never able to raise more than $100,000 per year for international development from its member cooperatives. Instead, in May 1967, Neil Sheehan of the *New York Times* revealed that CLUSA had begun to take funding from private foundations that acted as CIA conduits. Nearly three-quarters of its Fund for International Development originated from CIA sources between 1963 and 1965.[75] The revelations came in the midst of other exposures of CIA activities in India, including reports of CIA front groups meddling in the Indian elections of the 1967 and funding the Asia Foundation. In the political outcry, the Asia foundation was forced to shutter its New Delhi office, but the cooperative work in India continued without controversy. Indeed, by tying itself to the food production strategy of the Indian government, U.S. cooperatives had become indispensable to the Indian state.

* * *

In the 1970s, much of the reform energy that had characterized the U.S. cooperative movement's international activities in the 1950s and 1960s had dissipated. Murray Lincoln stepped down as Nationwide's president in 1964, and with his departure Nationwide turned away from most of its populist and international development work. Tellingly, the company changed its advertising slogan that year from "In Service to People" to "The man from Nationwide is on your side." With Jerry Voorhis' retirement in 1967, CLUSA turned increasingly toward domestic projects.

For a decade in the middle of the twentieth century, the cooperative movement attempted to remake economic relations within a wide swath of the world's rural economy along cooperative lines. Those efforts largely failed. The 1970s and 1980s saw the ascendance of the multinational corporation and the abandonment of state-centered economic planning under World Bank and IMF-led pressures for privatization and austerity. The collapse of the Soviet Union underscored an international regime where, in British prime minister Margaret Thatcher's slogan, "there is no alternative" to free market capitalism.

But if the neoliberal order ultimately won out, the economic battlefield of the Cold War years was always more complicated than a simple bipolar struggle between competing economic systems. Reinserting the American cooperative movement into the history of international development can help us to see ideological and methodological variation within the "American way" of capitalism. The Cold War narrowed, but did not shut down, American debates over what a just and productive economic order would look like. Indeed, the cooperative movements efforts from India to Latin America demonstrate the extent to which domestic ideological contests—about corporate regulation, the role of the state, and the rights of the consumer—could find new life and new allies on foreign terrain.

CHAPTER 8

Building a Capitalist Consciousness: Japan and Visions of Capitalist Asia

Jennifer M. Miller

Throughout the early Cold War, the United States funded technical assistance and productivity programs across the globe. Premised on the belief that poverty and economic strife created fertile ground for radicalism and communism, these programs sought to export American industrial techniques, management, and labor politics. Advocates claimed that the resulting increases in productivity would lead to "higher profits, better wages, and lower consumer costs" and a new level of economic growth and sociopolitical stability; stabilizing international capitalism, U.S. policymakers believed, would also secure American power and hegemony.[1] To achieve these aims, productivity programming also sought to curb labor activism. Its proponents argued that active collaboration with management would "increase the pie" because the "the true dialectic was not one of class against class, but waste versus abundance."[2] The promoters of productivity training therefore framed both political and social progress and national and global stability as the product of the cooperative and steady pursuit of economic growth.

While productivity programming began in Europe as part of the Marshall Plan, in the early 1950s the United States began to fund similar efforts in Japan. After fifteen years of aggressive war-making and an extensive American bombing campaign over mainland Japan, productivity advocates—both American and Japanese—emphasized the need to rebuild, modernize, and expand Japan's economic and industrial capacity. They encouraged new management techniques and labor-management cooperation, celebrating productivity as the technocratic and apolitical process of building wealth through novel technological skills and technical capabilities. The success of this project seemed clear as Japan entered a period of sustained economic growth in the late 1950s and early 1960s. As the country's GNP grew at a breakneck average annual rate of 9 percent, spurring widespread talk of an "economic miracle," many policymakers claimed that American visions had been vindicated.

The core of productivity programming, however, relied not only on its framing of capitalist relations as technocratic and apolitical. As the efforts to instill these principles in Japan reveals, productivity efforts conceptualized capitalist growth and economic progress as a process of mental and psychological transformation. As its advocates consistently proclaimed, productivity required the proper mental state, a "productivity consciousness" that would direct human efforts into the peaceful and cooperative pursuit of growth. In part, productivity programming sought to counter communist economic visions by arguing that such a consciousness could only come from market-based competition wherein all actors—companies, managers, and workers—strove to continuously improve themselves and achieve individual fulfillment through wealth creation. This psychological language also targeted Japan's active and vibrant labor movement. It asserted that productivity needed people to conceive of themselves as rational individuals—individuals who would personally and economically benefit from higher wages, expanded production capacity, and new consumer products—rather than as part of an allegedly deviant and class-based collective. In this world, cooperation would come across rather than within classes; workers could only achieve productivity by channeling their desire for economic improvement into a proper labor-management hierarchy within a larger corporate and national body. Ultimately, for productivity advocates, capitalist growth was not simply the product of proper techniques and technologies. It required the necessary mental state, one that accepted capitalist hierarchies and celebrated market competition as a "natural" manifestation of healthy psychologies.

What is more, this psychological language proved important beyond Japan's shores. As foreign aid and development became vital tools in the fight against communist expansion in Asia and beyond, Americans and Japanese alike argued that Japan offered a vital model for the rest of Asia because of its historical trajectory of rapid political and economic modernization and its embrace of the spirit of productivity. Historians have often claimed that American development policies toward so-called underdeveloped countries, such as Korea and the Philippines, differed substantially from their plans for more modern states such as Japan.[3] Yet for U.S. policymakers and the officials of organizations like the Ford Foundation, Japan's experiences could show other Asians the path forward. By bridging the gap between a fully industrialized United States and an "underdeveloped" Asia, Japan simultaneously demonstrated the specific possibility of economic growth in Asia and the universal nature of the capitalist economic model. Just as Japan had benefited from American tutelage, so the logic went, other Asian states could now benefit from Japan's knowledge, technical expertise, and success in their quest to ward off Communism.

With American aid and support, the Japanese government, its bureaucracy, and private organizations and companies worked to build a technical assistance and development aid apparatus that sought to export this productivity consciousness by bringing Asian economic elites to Japan to learn the wonders of Japanese industrial, consumer, and technical progress. Indeed, conceptualizing productivity as a psychological transformation, rather than just the product of mechanical or technological change, allowed both Americans and Japanese to claim that Japan's experiences could be exported to other Asian states with very different historical experiences. Only fifteen years removed from Japan's disastrous and violent attempt to conquer much of East and Southeast Asia, Americans and Japanese alike now argued that Japan's recent economic success would offer a new path forward for postcolonial Asia. Drawing from modernization theory's claim that progress and growth necessitated the shedding of traditional mindsets, this elevation of Japan as a model argued that economic stagnation was due to Asians' own mentalities—defined as preindustrial, unproductive, irrational, and immature—rather than destructive warfare and decades of extractive American, European, and Japanese colonialism.[4]

These historical oversights meant that Japan's regional productivity and development initiatives—funded by the United States—enabled grim ironies.[5] The elevation of Japan as a model and training site resurrected Japanese imperial and wartime ideas, projects, and personnel. During the 1930s and 1940s, Japanese political, military, and economic elites routinely claimed that their country's scientific and technical superiority justified its imperialist expansion. Under Japan's benevolent rule, they proclaimed, Asia would prosper and become "modern."[6] With such ideas recast in the language of productivity and development, Japanese leaders again claimed to be agents of progress across East and Southeast Asia. Japan's regional productivity schemes therefore highlight how American development efforts relied on foreign ideas, traditions, and experiences. By conceptualizing capitalism, modernity, progress, and growth in mental and psychological terms, productivity programming not only depoliticized socioeconomic inequalities between workers and employers but also elided geopolitical hierarchies and historical legacies of violence.

* * *

In the aftermath of World War II, stabilizing international capitalism through overseas growth and prosperity became an important focus of American Cold War diplomacy. At home and overseas, U.S. policymakers proclaimed that the United States needed to help develop other countries into technologically proficient, capitalistic economies engaged in a global web of trade and commerce that centered on the United States. This approach drew in part on pre–World War II imperial and philanthropic projects through which Americans sought to "civilize" and "uplift" nations like the Philippines, Cuba, and China by exporting their own technological, educational, medical, hygienic, and economic systems. But the urgency and scope of postwar projects dwarfed these earlier efforts. In the aftermath of global depression and war, U.S. officials believed it self-evident that economic distress sent people and nations into political extremism, including communism. To prevent the reoccurrence of such horrific events, the United States had to export the knowledge, expertise, and money (both private and public) necessary to revitalize overseas economies and prevent the economic scarcities that birthed extremist ideologies.[7] Such policies would also secure American hegemony; policymakers had little doubt that the United States would naturally triumph in this integrated global economy.

One vital aspect of this effort was the dissemination of American business procedures and management methods. American political and economic leaders believed that the United States had been so successful at increasing production that the financial benefits reached business owners and workers alike, "transcend[ing] the class conflicts that arose from scarcity."[8] Through the support and participation of major corporations and business leaders, the U.S. government worked to export American management practices overseas to spark industrial growth and forestall labor activism and communist or socialist forms of political economy. As part of the Marshall Plan, U.S. officials launched a new program in 1948, the United States Technical Assistance and Productivity Mission. Among other things, this program organized American trips for European business and labor teams, offered productivity training at seminars on both sides of the Atlantic, and assisted in the founding of productivity centers across Europe. In 1953, these efforts culminated in the launch of the U.S.-funded European Productivity Agency, which disseminated techniques, publications, and information; planned trips and study missions throughout Europe and the United States; and trumpeted the ideology of productivity as the obvious resolution to class conflict, political division, and nationalist sentiments.[9]

Similar goals sparked productivity efforts in postwar Japan. The initial impetus for Japanese productivity programs rested with Japanese management organizations. Most significant was the Keizai Doyukai (KD) (Economic Friends Association), a group of younger, middle-ranking managers—most members were in their forties—that touted managerial capitalism as a necessary response to Japan's social, economic, and political difficulties.[10] The immediate postwar years were marked by vibrant and widespread labor activism and extreme poverty; against this backdrop, KD called for expanded collaboration between capital and labor to "surpass old feudalism."[11] They advocated for a "'reformed capitalism': a high-productivity, high-wage economy that avoided strikes by nurturing cooperative labor-management relations."[12] In 1953, after returning from a tour of European productivity centers, KD director Gōshi Kōhei seized on productivity as an allegedly apolitical concept that could simultaneously expand the status and influence of management and encourage collaboration with labor unions.[13] That same year, the U.S. Embassy's commercial attaché Wesley Haraldson met with Japanese business leaders, including KD, and told them that the United States hoped to fund a Japanese productivity program. This program would extend earlier U.S.-Japanese efforts to tame the Japanese labor movement and bolster U.S. support of Japan's postwar economic recovery well beyond the end of the U.S. occupation in 1952.[14]

This productivity push was institutionalized in June 1954; with the support of the Japanese government's Ministry of Trade and Industry (MITI), several private Japanese organizations, including the Japanese Chamber of Commerce and the Federation of Economic Organizations (Keidanren), pooled 800,000 yen to create the Japan Productivity Center (JPC). In its first statement, the JPC declared that its goal was to "advance the mutual interests of managers, workers and consumers, striving to . . . improve real wages and the standard of living through a reduction of costs achieved by the more effective and scientific employment of resources, manpower, and equipment."[15] By mentioning managers, workers, *and* consumers, the JPC's statement demonstrates the belief that productivity programming sought to accomplish more than simply adopting new technology or achieving new standards of efficiency. Rather, through large-scale cooperation and collaboration, productivity would expand production, increase employment, and raise Japan's standard of living; by reaching all Japanese, increases in productivity would reduce economic barriers and class divisions through the reform, rather than eschewal, of capitalism.[16] As the JPC's first managing director, Gōshi became an important partner with the United States and a prominent productivity evangelist throughout Japan. Although he regularly described the JPC as a cross-class organization, the institute's founding leadership was almost entirely made up of business leaders and executives, and no labor representatives were involved in its creation. Only five years later, the JPC had grown from a small office to a large operation staffed by 170 people. It ran an array of classes and training programs, hosted experts and consultants, distributed a wide range of publications and films, arranged foreign visits and exchange programs for management and labor, supported a network of regional centers, and ran two demonstration plants.

The JPC also became the United States' formal partner in a larger productivity program. When it signed a military assistance agreement with Japan in March 1954, the U.S. government agreed to fund programing designed to bring about the "improvement of the managerial and marketing efficiency of Japanese industrial enterprises through, among other means, technical assistance."[17] This was followed by an April 1955 agreement between Japanese foreign minister Shigemitsu Mamoru and U.S. ambassador John Allison that singled out the JPC as the United States' official partner in a formal productivity program.[18] For the next five years, along with financial support from Japanese corporations and the Japanese government, U.S. technical assistance aid funded the programming and growth of the JPC, reaching a peak of $2.5 million a year in 1958 and 1959.[19] The International Cooperation Administration (ICA), the U.S. government agency that managed technical assistance, opened a special operations mission (USOM) at the embassy in Tokyo that coordinated and administered the American portion of the program. Americans and Japanese alike hoped that this joint commitment to productivity would inaugurate a new age of growth and prosperity. As Gōshi asserted in 1955, the productivity movement was "the only way to modernize Japan, to make the lifestyle of the Japanese people wealthy and bright."[20]

Beyond spurring growth, Japanese advocates hoped that productivity would facilitate broader structural changes to Japan's economy. They based this hope, in part, on a long-standing criticism that Japan had a "dual economy." Its modern industrial trappings were built on top of shaky and feudalistic social and economic structures; both academics and commentators were particularly concerned that Japan's agricultural and small business sectors still operated through family loyalty and paternalism, semiemployment, low wages, and low productivity.[21] Prominent Japanese economists therefore supported productivity programming and worked with the JPC in the hope of resolving these issues. For example, well-known economist Arisawa Hiromi, who served on the board of the JPC, argued only modernizing Japan's industrial structure could close this gap and expand employment. As historian Laura Hein states, Arisawa believed that "productivity increases could produce high wages for large numbers of people and revenues for reinvestment through expanded export opportunities. In other words, it could diminish the barriers that created the dual economy."[22] For Arisawa, productivity programming offered a way for Japan to transcend the past. Other prominent economists, such as Nakayama Ichirō, a member of the faculty at Hitotsubashi University who chaired Japan's central labor relations commission from 1946 to 1960 and served as vice president of the JPC, thought along similar lines. Nakayama coined the concept of wage doubling that would become the inspiration for Japanese prime minister Ikeda Hayato's famed income doubling plan in the early 1960s; increasing productive capacity, he argued, was the key to substantially increasing wages.[23]

Yet for both its American and Japanese boosters, productivity programming would not just produce structural changes or economic growth. Its benefits extended beyond technological innovation, new production techniques, and economic efficiency, though all of these were central to its appeal and implementation. Equally important, both Americans and Japanese hoped that productivity programming would inspire a mental and psychological revolution. As the Eisenhower administration's policy coordination body, the Operations Coordinating Board, asserted in 1955, "the productivity programs . . . stress changes in attitudes which have inhibited economic expansion abroad as distinguished from narrow concerns with technological improvement and rationalization."[24] Indeed, both American and Japanese efforts with the JPC described productivity as a process of mental transformation; productivity both required and would encourage the psychological and spiritual attitudes necessary to growth. In particular, both American and Japanese productivity boosters emphasized the ability to overcome irrationality, collectivism, and selfishness—which they argued was especially embodied by labor unions—in favor of cooperative responsibility premised on respect for managerial leadership, a focus on economic growth, and expanded production rather than economic equality or worker representation. As one 1959 JPC pamphlet asserted, higher productivity could only come from the right "psychological climate," one that birthed a "productivity consciousness."[25] Nakayama, in the short JCP pamphlet *An Introduction to Productivity*, similarly declared, "The most general and important factor affecting long term productivity is a change in the general atmosphere of society which arises in the process of such economic development. The change in the atmosphere can be defined, in a word, as the birth of a way of life suitable for industrialization."[26] Productivity's advocates not only celebrated its material benefits, such as higher wages and lower prices. Productivity, they routinely claimed, was a process of personal transformation, which would foster the mindsets necessary for growth and modernization.

To create this productivity consciousness, productivity programming emphasized leadership, especially effective management, as fundamentally necessary to changing both practices and psychologies. As Nakayama asserted, it "goes without saying that the ability and character of leaders will affect labor production directly as well as indirectly."[27] In keeping with the thinking of KD and the midcentury elevation of management science in the United States and beyond, JPC programming sought to facilitate the creation of a new class of leaders—technocratic and professional managers—that it hoped would usher Japan into an efficient, productive, and cooperative future.[28] Improving Japanese management practices thus became a significant focal point of U.S. cooperation with the JPC. For example, the first American team to visit Japan as part of a JPC exchange tour in the summer of 1955 explicitly sought to disseminate American management ideologies and techniques. This team included William Robbins, vice president of General Foods, who discussed top management and costs; Arthur C. Nielsen, executive vice president of the marketing and public relations firm AC Nielsen; and Lee Vance, executive vice president of the David C. Cook publishing company, who spoke about production. More than three hundred Japanese upper management officials attended seminars and programming in Tokyo, Nagoya, Osaka, and Fukuoka. As one diplomat proclaimed, the goal of these workshops was to "provide Japanese industrial management with intimate contact with outstanding American management personalities."[29]

This emphasis on "personality" reiterated the belief that productivity was a process of individual and psychological improvement. JPC material echoed similar ideas. As one pamphlet claimed, utilizing the language of health and illness, "respect for managerial authority is an indispensable element in the healthy progress of business."[30] During their visit, the American team also toured factories and other workplaces; armed with charts and visual aids, its members offered their thoughts on the needs of Japanese business.[31] Alongside lectures about cost estimating, profits planning, quality control, and other technical issues, the group highlighted the importance of managerial leadership and authority in facilitating progress. Through they presented their expertise as apolitical, these businessmen claimed that such leadership best developed in an economic system premised on market-based competition, rather than extensive state regulation or state control. "Without any dogmatism," a U.S. government report on the trip gushed, "the Americans have tried to inject . . . the value of competition to able managements, consumers, and the nation as whole."[32]

This emphasis on managerial authority also stemmed from the midcentury United States' fascination with management, which was celebrated as the key to corporate prosperity, worker satisfaction, and the health and progress of American society. Celebrated management consultants like Peter Drucker repeatedly emphasized that successful management not only produced better market results, but just as important, it encouraged employees to seek personal fulfillment and satisfaction through the workplace by actively taking responsibility for the social and economic welfare of the organization, thus reducing social friction, class conflict, and the appeal of noncapitalist ideologies. Indeed, Drucker's vision was similar to that of KD; both sought "strategies in which profit making also solved social problems" by co-opting worker activism and facilitating social cohesion through the harmonization of public and private interests.[33] Throughout the second half of the 1950s, American management consultants regularly visited Japan, some under the auspices of the JPC. After his celebrated 1954 text, *The Practice of Management*, appeared in Japanese, Drucker visited Japan several times and increasingly claimed that Japanese management practices best embodied his core teachings.[34] Other management consultants included Melvin J. Evans, an advocate of the human relations management philosophy, and Walter P. Coombs, an authority on small business management.[35] In seminars and lecture halls, these figures described how effective management struck a balance between asserting authority and encouraging workers' close emotional and psychological association with the company in order to facilitate hard work and a sense of personal investment. As Evans put it, managers had to foster "character, attitude, knowledge and energy" by listening to their workers, considering their welfare, and creating "an atmosphere for employees to work voluntarily."[36]

Alongside this emphasis on management, productivity programming also heavily targeted labor unions. As Japanese foreign minister Shigemitsu Mamoru asserted in 1955, the "purpose of this program is to assist in every way possible . . . the encouragement of a healthy labor movement."[37] Officials sought to include labor in productivity programing not only to neutralize the fierce and sustained strikes and vibrant shop-floor activism that marked Japan's postwar labor movement.[38] They also hoped that the productivity movement could tame workers' intense anti–Cold War advocacy, which had exploded in protests against occupation-era economic rationalization, Japan's postwar remilitarization, and U.S. military bases, protests where labor unionists played a central role.[39] Productivity programming therefore sought to convince workers to accept loyalty to a responsible and technocratic manager, the company, and the larger mission of economic growth. As a 1955 Eisenhower administration statement explained, the United States had to "encourage the strengthening in foreign countries of free and democratic trade unions . . . in recognition of the vital role of free enterprise in achieving rising levels of production and standards of living essential to the economic progress and defensive strength of the free world." In this vision, democracy did not equal political activism or control over the workplace; democratic trade unions contributed to the broader successes of "free enterprise" by cooperating with and "function[ing] alongside free management within a free economy."[40] Given such goals, it is not surprising that Japan's largest labor federation, Sōhyō, repeatedly lambasted productivity as a capitalist and imperialist scam to subjugate workers.[41]

In part, the JPC's goal of institutionalizing amiable interclass cooperation took the form of advocacy for labor-management councils. In this vision, these councils would function alongside collective bargaining—which would deal solely with economic issues such as wages—to facilitate labor-management collaboration over other issues, such as worker safety and hygiene, employee welfare, and increasing productivity. For example, in the 1959 joint JPC-ICA publication entitled *Labor-Management Cooperation in Japan,* a management and industrial relations specialists study team that had recently returned from a trip to the United States heralded labor-management cooperation as a requirement for Japan's continued growth. To complete "the Second Industrial Revolution," the report declared, Japan must "establish a progressive labor–management co-operation system in order to solve, in peaceful and rational manners, the new problems of labor–management relations which stem from the technical revolution." As historian Andrew Gordon notes, this call for cooperation sought to replace "bargaining over demands generated from the workplace" with meetings between union leaders and company executives. The returned team argued that such a system would actually increase labor's say in company decisions. By cooperating with management in its plans about "'the increase of pies' and on 'the distribution of pies,'" explained the report, consultation puts "labor and management on equal standing and in this sense it aims at labor's participation in management."[42]

Productivity outreach further argued that by playing its "proper" role in the pursuit of growth, labor unions were contributing to the development of Japanese democracy.[43] In this argument, labor unions' participation in political protests not only hindered economic growth and prevented individual fulfillment but also undermined democratic freedoms. For example, in a 1958 JPC-sponsored panel for twelve labor unionists who had recently returned from the United States, participants drew an explicit connection between economic individualism, freedom and democracy, and cooperative industrial relations. In an article summarizing the panel, the *Japan Productivity News* claimed that "Industrial relations in American industry are a natural outcome of the economy that has been developed by the American nation who traditionally loves freedom—the spirit fostered by individualism, an ethical conception directing the individual to make decision at his responsibility." The author connected this individualism directly to the "freedom" offered to American trade unions to act according to their conscience, rather than "imposed" political or ideological beliefs: "Major labor organizations, such as AFL and CIO, devote most of their energies in preparing authoritative data, performing counseling services and offering training. They make no fighting plans for their member unions, as the Japanese labor organizations do. They issue no fighting orders, either. The American trade union does not like communism any more than fascism." By emphasizing that American unions did not issue "fighting orders," the panelists proclaimed that American labor unions allowed their members to fulfill their own economic goals rather than being distracted by the political or ideological goals of union leaders. This freedom, however, could only come from proper motivations and mindsets; the motivating force for American unions was not politics or ideology but "free competition . . . employees all fear that there would be an end to their happiness, should their business fall behind in the competition. So they are serious at work." American unions thus liberated their members from the ideology's alleged oppression to pursue "freedom and democracy" by working hard for economic gain in a capitalist society.[44]

This conception of freedom as individual fulfillment, an emotional state best achieved through capitalist competition, meant that Americans saw the main barriers to higher productivity as emotional, mental, and psychological, rather than technological or structural. Nowhere was this clearer than in a 1956 report by industrial management consultant W. S. Landes. Landes arrived in Japan in August 1955 and spent five months observing Japanese industry. In his final report, which he wrote for the USOM and which was also published by the JPC, Landes condemned Japanese productivity as "deplorably low" and in urgent need of an infusion of American ideas and techniques. The Japanese, he lamented, were still locked in backward "culture, habits, traditions, and methods of thinking." Echoing a widespread, racist American belief that Asians, especially Japanese, were incapable of individual thought, a staple of World War II propaganda, Landes argued that Japanese managers could not delegate responsibility or make individual decisions; rather, they remained dependent on the ideas and opinions of others. "In large plants frequently as many as ten or twelve representatives of various management levels might have to be called together for a discussion on problems that the average American executive would decide without any hesitation."[45]

This lack of individual confidence or responsibility among the economy's designated leaders was only part of the problem. Resurrecting racist wartime stereotypes that denigrated the Japanese as prone to emotional extremes, Landes excoriated Japanese executives for their "noticeable absence of reasoning power" and complete "failure" to successfully solve problems.[46] "In some cases, the evidence was very strong that the individual was incapable of making a decision without being influenced by emotions such as envy, pride, suspicion, personal dislike or superstition. The tendency to go from one extreme to the other was frequently noticed." Landes ultimately concluded that in order to achieve economic prosperity, the Japanese would have to go far beyond the application of new techniques and adopt profoundly new psychologies. "The Japanese way of life is pleasant in many respects," he scoffed, "but [the Japanese people] will have to depart from some of their time honored traditions, and Japanese businessmen must adopt more of the Western psychology, if we are to have the right foundation for further gains in productivity."[47]

While they likely would not agree with all aspects of Landes' analysis, Japanese productivity advocates echoed this belief that productivity was ultimately a process of mental transformation. As Japanese economic growth accelerated after 1955, JPC publications identified the "spirit" of productivity as a vital component of Japan's remarkable economic resurgence. In March 1962, a team of leaders and managers from prominent Japanese companies visited the United States. The delegation included the president of Hitachi, the president of Sanwa Bank, and several high-level executives from Nissan. These industrial and financial leaders embarked on a three-week tour that visited major corporations like Chrysler, RCA, and IBM, labor unions such as United Auto Workers, and educational institutions like Harvard University. While meeting with USAID administrator Fowler Hamilton, they presented him with a recent JPC pamphlet entitled "Growth of Japanese Economy and Productivity." This pamphlet described Japan as technologically advanced, a center of innovation that had character, determination, and a "vigorous entrepreneurial spirit." In essence, it argued that Japan's economy grew because the Japanese people *wanted* it to grow. Japan's recent economic success, the JPC declared, can "be regarded as a reflection of the determination of business to attain higher productivity. Therefore, this positive attitude for increased productivity can surely be called a driving force in the rapid economic growth of Japan."[48]

Perhaps even more satisfying for productivity advocates, productivity gained legitimacy within the Japanese labor movement. As Japan entered a prolonged period of growth in the late 1950s and early 1960s, some labor unions abandoned their earlier hostility to productivity programming, adopting its claims that productivity would secure both economic growth and democracy in Japan. In 1955, the moderate labor federation Sōdōmei partnered with the JPC. In a joint statement, it proclaimed that "the increased productivity movement in Japan bases its foundations on democratic relations between employers and workers."[49] Zenrō, another moderate labor association, quickly followed suit. By 1956, it was printing unattributed materials written by the United States Information Agency, celebrating productivity as a "national good" and declaring that "labor's participation" would enhance the people's welfare, the main goal of democracy.[50] The same year, representatives of labor unions affiliated with Sōhyō—Japan's largest and most hardline labor organization—began joining JPC trips to the United States. By 1958, the JPC reported that 37 percent of unions engaged in joint labor-management councils; even Sōhyō-affiliated unions, such as the Electrical Communication Workers Union and the Coal Mine Workers Union, were taking preliminary steps toward establishing such consultations.[51] In 1960, the JPC doubled down on its call for labor-management councils, launching a series of publications and discussion seminars promoting this system; ten years later, almost all unionized companies utilized a union-management consultation system alongside, or sometimes in place of, collective bargaining.[52]

By the dawn of the 1960s, productivity programming had become widely accepted. Contrary to its claim to be technocratic and apolitical, it served as a key site to disseminate specific ideas about economic growth and prosperity. Growth, its publications argued, was not simply the product of historical experience, financial practices, the application of new technologies, or government policies, though all of these mattered. Equally important was the proper attitude and spirit, a sense of purpose, the personal adoption of corporate objectives, progress and improvement through market competition, and cooperative respect for leadership and authority, especially in the form of management. Productivity sought to bypass divisive conflicts over redistribution with a promise of shared growth, but this growth could come only if all participants—managers, workers, consumers—made the proper mental commitment; emotional and psychological transformation was the primary goal, rather than distributive or structural equality. This transformation, productivity advocates claimed, could be achieved only through market competition, which would foster the internal drive—the "entrepreneurial spirit"—to improve one's own economic situation and seek happiness and fulfillment through internalizing the corporate and national goal of economic growth.

* * *

With the dawn of the 1960s—in the words of John F. Kennedy, the "decade of development"—both Japan and the United States increasingly sought to turn the gospel of productivity outward. Encouraged by Japan's meteoric economic growth, Americans and Japanese alike came to believe that Japan served as a crucial example for other Asian states. As Peter Drucker wrote in 1963, "The last decade in Japan proved that the methods, tools, and policies of a free economy can generate very fast economic development on non-Western soil."[53] With this goal in mind, the United States and Japan launched training programs in Japan for Asian nationals and founded the Asian Productivity Organization (APO), a multilateral international organization that sought to develop a productivity consciousness across Asia.[54] As was the case in Japan itself, American and Japanese productivity advocates argued that productivity and development required developing the "right" psychology. By learning from Japan's economic success, the people of Taiwan, Thailand, India, and South Korea would develop the mindsets required for economic prosperity. American and Japanese policymakers also hoped that Japanese development assistance would rebuild Japanese-Asian trade ties, relegitimatize Japan as a leader in Asia, and undermine the appeal of communist models and assistance. U.S. policymakers thus sought to ensure American security and economic hegemony through the reconstruction of Japanese economic power and geopolitical legitimacy.

Defining growth and productivity as a process of mental transformation, rather than historical legacies, technological advancement, or socioeconomic structures, allowed American and Japanese policymakers to argue that the Japanese "model" could be transplanted to postcolonial states with far different historical trajectories. Yet such plans relied on a series of problematic assumptions. They were premised on racial and ethnic homogenization, assuming that Asia's cultural and ethnic similarities meant that the Japanese model could be exported to other Asian states. They maintained clear hierarchies, elevating the United States and Japan as the most developed states that should be rightfully tasked with improving the rest of Asia. Most notably, these programs resurrected ideas and people once central to Japan's imperial expansion and wartime aggression. During the 1930s, Japan's political, military, intellectual, industrial, and bureaucratic leaders claimed that Japan's superior technological development entitled it to "civilize" the rest of Asia, militarily if needed. Now, with American support, Japan relaunched this ideology under the guise of Asian development, arguing that a technologically and psychologically advanced Japan could lead Asia into a productive future of growth. Indeed, this historical reconfiguration undergirded productivity's usefulness on the international stage: it recast the United States' quest for capitalist hegemony and Japan's search for rehabilitation as the benevolent modernization of other Asian societies.

As Japan's economy accelerated in the mid-1950s, U.S. policymakers quickly began to view it as an economic model for other Asian nations. Japan, they claimed, demonstrated that it was possible to actively create growth through appropriate policies within a free and capitalist system. As the State Department asserted in 1960, "Japan plays [a] unique role in Asia. Under [a] system of private enterprise it has become one of four great industrial complexes of the world and its rate of economic growth is one of the highest in the world. In addition to being a counterweight to [the] growing power of Communist China in Asia, Japan provides other Asian countries with

[an] example of rapid economic growth under [a] free system which is in clear contrast to harsh methods Chinese Communists impos[e] on people to achieve quick economic development."[55] Beyond its function as a counterweight to Communist China, Japan was also useful because it showed that Asian states could embrace the spiritual transformation advocated by Americans. Japan's embrace of a productivity consciousness offered an encouraging example of Asian capacity for mental transformation, a racist claim that simultaneously assumed that Asians were mentally deficient and that all Asians were generally the same, and thus capable of following Japan's path. U.S. officials therefore asserted that Indonesians, Vietnamese, Indians, and others would be more likely to understand "modern" ideas and models if they were transmitted through the Japanese. As one U.S. aid official proclaimed in 1958, compared to training in the United States, "Japan presents less of a cultural and psychological shock to the participants from South East Asia. The small farms of Japan offer a scale of operations comparable to the small farms of his own country. Japan offers living proof that Asian [*sic*] too can adapt."[56]

With development becoming a major focus of American governmental and private aid efforts in Asia, such claims merged the ideology of productivity with the prominent midcentury paradigm of modernization theory. In their discussions of the processes of modernization, both government officials and social scientists claimed that economic growth did not simply result from access to resources, the use of technology, or the application of new techniques. Becoming modern through industrialization and economic growth also required the proper values, norms, and attitudes; essentially, it required psychological transformation. Such thinking reflected the widespread influence of psychology in midcentury ideas about politics and economics. Modernity was not simply an economic or technological state but also a "spiritual phenomenon or kind of mentality."[57] Japan's recent experiences therefore seemed to blaze a path for other Asians to shed their mental adherence to tradition—which mired societies in a state of low productivity, superstition, and technological stagnation—by embracing modern values such as individuality, rationality, universalism, and a desire for achievement.[58] Political scientist and Japan specialist Robert Ward articulated this optimism forcefully in 1958, asserting that "Mechanical things can change easily but political attitudes are about the last things to change. In Asia there are few societies that have achieved modernity, [except] Japan."[59] The barriers to disseminating the Japanese model—such as fresh memories of Japan's violent expansion throughout Asia during the war, language difficulties, or the vastly different circumstances of a postimperial Japan versus a postcolonial Asia—rarely entered American discussions about the possibilities created by Japanese growth.

American efforts to encourage Japanese development policy began in the mid-1950s, when the United States started funding industrial and agricultural training in Japan for trainees from other Asian countries through the Third Country Training Program.[60] The trainees were selected from the agricultural, industrial, labor, and administrative sectors by their own governments and their home country USOM (later USAID mission). While the United States covered the cost of travel and meals, Japanese government agencies and private institutions provided the facilities for technical study, observation tours, and training. Third Country Training in Japan slowly expanded in the late 1950s and early 1960s. Between 1954 and 1963, 2,553 participants entered training programs in Japan, the majority from Taiwan, India, Korea, and Thailand.[61] With a larger number of Japanese language speakers because of prolonged Japanese imperialism, Taiwan was an especially active participant, sending 31 percent of all trainees between 1955 and 1960, with Thailand next at 13 percent and India sending 11 percent.[62] Unique to third-country training programs in Asia, the United States and Japan signed an agreement that granted Japan formal administrative authority in March 1960.[63]

Third Country Training in Japan offered a variety of programs, from crop development and fisheries training to highway construction, land reform, and government administration. But similar to productivity programming, U.S. officials believed that Third Country Training was not simply about spreading technical expertise and new techniques. Just as important, it sought to change attitudes and psychologies in order to create behavioral and mental transformation. William J. Parker, a USAID training officer, explained this outlook in 1963, claiming that "the learning and interchange of technical knowledge" was meant to "start an internal chain reaction" that facilitated "a change in behavior more suitable to the present and future technical and social needs of the [trainee's] country."[64] Like the JPC, Third Country Training sought to expose trainees to a new psychological order to facilitate a commitment to prosperity, efficiency, and apolitical capital-labor cooperation. It was premised on the convenient belief that years of extractive colonial dominance by Japan, Europe, and the United States could be overcome, in part, by an attitude adjustment. Third Country Training thus presented a market-based system as normal, with noncompliance stemming from a deviant, traditional, or even primitive mindset.

This growing emphasis on spreading Japanese knowledge, technological know-how, and superior production techniques was not just an imposition of American ideas. Nor was it new. For both the Japanese government and private industry, development and technical assistance served as a crucial platform and rationale in Japan's attempts to rebuild trade networks and its legitimacy as a leader in Asia, in part by resurrecting earlier imperial visions and ideologies. As historians have detailed, "techno-imperialism" was a central component of Japan's wartime imaginary. During the 1930s and early 1940s, Japanese officials, architects, business leaders, and scientists sought to implement imperial visions of Asian development through urban reform, hygiene improvement, and large-scale dam projects, especially in China; they justified these projects—and Japanese imperial expansion—by citing Japan's allegedly superior industrial, technological, and scientific prowess. With American political and financial support, Japanese officials and business leaders adapted these experiences and modes of thinking, according to Aaron Moore, to "Japan's postwar context of building a prosperous nation at home and exercising soft power abroad through developmental assistance."[65] They hoped that programs like technical assistance would not only provide access to natural resources and open (or reopen) Asian markets but also bolster Japan's international standing while forestalling more radical demands for postcolonial and postwar justice. Though Japan did pay reparations to some Asian countries—including the Philippines, Burma, and South Vietnam—such reparations largely came through technical assistance, infrastructure projects, development programming, and grants, and they did nothing to address individual victims such as comfort women.[66] As such, they also served as a site to rebuild Japanese legitimacy as a technologically advanced and "benevolent" state.[67]

Not surprisingly, Asian states were wary of Japan's forays into international assistance. Prime Minister Kishi Nobusuke, who had guided Japan's extractive and forced-labor-based colonial development policy in Manchukuo in the 1930s, was a vocal proponent of expanding Japanese overseas assistance in the late 1950s, calling for an Asian development bank. When he toured Southeast Asian countries as part of launching a "more Asia-centered diplomacy," however, newspapers in Indonesia and the Philippines raised the alarm that Japan's calls for deeper economic cooperation and trade were an effort to revive the wartime Co-Prosperity Sphere, when poorer countries provided labor and resources to imperial Japan.[68] Japanese officials hoped that the combination of reparations and development assistance would quell Asian resistance, which they dismissed as childish and antimodern. For example, Tanishiki Hiroshi, who headed MITI's reparations office, wrote in 1957 that "the newly emerging countries of Southeast Asia" were possessed by "xenophobic nationalism and apprehension about a Japanese invasion," but he rhetorically wondered, "Can there be a better way for businesses to ride safely into the storm than to justify their advance there in the name of reparations payments?"[69] U.S. officials, too, occasionally worried that the legacies of Japan's wartime aggression would hamper Japanese aid efforts and trade relationships. A 1955 memorandum by Lew B. Clark, commercial attaché to the U.S. embassy, noted that Southeast Asian countries were taking a "very cautious view" to early Japanese development and financial assistance overtures.[70] Yet such attention to the historical contradictions of elevating Japanese technological leadership as a path forward for Asia was rare. The allure of economic development was so strong that U.S. officials rarely commented on or realized the continuities with prewar and wartime goals and people.

The intertwined goals of reviving Japanese trade and securing Japanese regional legitimacy through development assistance were especially apparent through the involvement of Asia Kyokai (Asia Society), a private organization composed of Japanese businesses and private groups that coordinated the Third Country Training Program in Japan. Established by the conservative prime minister Yoshida Shigeru in 1954, Asia Kyokai described itself as a "private, non-commercial and non-political organization for the purpose of promoting friendly ties with other Asian nations and cooperating with them in social, culture, economic and technical fields."[71] Funded by government subsidies and private contributions, its board of directors was largely composed of business executives from leading Japanese companies and development experts, some of whom had played central roles in Japanese colonial and wartime development projects. Board member Kubota Yutaka, for example, had been the wartime president of Yalu Hydropower, which helped build massive hydroelectric dams and railways in in occupied Korea (with turbines supplied by Toshiba) and China during World War II. He started a development consultancy called Nippon Kōei after the war; by the 1960s, Kubota had been dubbed the Shogun of the Mekong for his role in Southeast Asia's Mekong River Development Project.[72]

Asia Kyokai's newsletters, publications, and propaganda material repeatedly proclaimed that international training would not only expand commercial and trade connections but also restore Japan to regional leadership through a new image of friendship and technical assistance. As an Asia Kyokai film script promoting training in Japan declared, "A hearty welcome to Japan! These trainees have come from all over Asia." Throughout the script, trainees repeatedly expressed their appreciation to Japan and the Japanese and extolled the benefits of Japanese friendship and assistance. As an Indian Trainee at Kubota ironworks proclaimed, "The factories and institutions at which training programs are arranged are always enthusiastic to help and cooperate. My experiences of the two big companies where I worked have also shown that the industries exchange their utmost cooperation, depute special staff and render all facilities to make the training a success . . . I am much grateful to the government of Japan for according me this opportunity." Asia Kyokai portrayed Japan, in the form of government, commerce, industry, and people, as eager to help Asians help themselves. As the film's closing narration claimed, "A farewell party for the trainees is held at the Asia Center. 'Sayonara.' But this does not mean farewell. To them, it is the greater of hope for tomorrow. It is an expression of well-wishing upon the start towards a better life for the countries of Asia, hand and hand with one another."[73]

Such messaging was remarkably heavy-handed given the ways in which Japanese imperialism had waged a violent and forceful transfer of wealth from countries throughout East and Southeast Asia. Yet it resonated with U.S. officials, who gave Asia Kyokai an increasingly active role in Third Country Training. Its formal responsibilities included selecting training facilities, contacting local government officials, and preparing the schedule for trainees.[74] By the end of the 1950s, it also conducted the training orientation for Third Country Training groups, especially groups from Taiwan that were likely to know Japanese due to prolonged Japanese colonialism.[75] This orientation course included lectures on Japanese technical cooperation in Asia, the present status of Japan's economy, the social situation in Japan, and traveling in Japan; it was followed by a sightseeing trip through Tokyo by bus. In a letter inviting U.S. officials to attend future orientations, Asia Kyokai proclaimed that the orientation course, which gave the "real picture of Japan in its economic, social, agricultural and industrial fields," was "successful and of much help for [trainees'] extensive studies in Japan. It is our belief that these lectures will make the understanding of the participants deeper and finally promote more friendly and mutual understandings among the host and guest countries."[76] For Asia Kyokai, this orientation course was the chance to tell the "real story" about Japan, one that overwrote Japan's history of imperial conquest with a sanitized and propagandistic story of technocratic benevolence and "miraculous" growth.

As international development became an increasingly important site of American-Japanese cooperation, it is not surprising that the JPC also became a leading advocate. Along with participating in the industrial components of Third Country Training, the JPC also sought to spread its productivity message through its own programming. In the fall of 1957, JPC director Gōshi Kōhei contacted several other Asian countries with the proposal for a planning conference in Japan to coordinate a regional productivity movement. Thanks to several favorable responses, particularly from India, the JPC secured funding from the United States to host a pan-Asian productivity conference, with the goal of sharing productivity techniques and laying the foundation for a regional productivity agency modeled after the European Productivity Agency.[77] In March 1959, the Asian Productivity Roundtable Conference gathered in Tokyo, including delegates from India, the Philippines, Thailand, and Taiwan. The JPC's report hyperbolically declared the conference "epoch-making" and a milestone in "Asian solidarity." The delegates "showed excellent cooperation," the author enthused, "regardless of their political and ideological backgrounds, for paving the way for realization of the unified Pan Asian productivity organization."[78] As in the domestic sphere, the JPC presented productivity as vigorously apolitical; as Gōshi declared, because the productivity movement was "politically and commercially independent and neutral," it had the ability to serve as "powerful bondage to unite Asia."[79] Yet the conference was clearly an attempt to counter communist developmental assistance, techniques, and planning. Nevertheless, U.S. observers were equally excited by the prospect of unifying Asia around a private enterprise model of productivity. U.S. officials thus hoped that a new regional organization would increase trust and cooperation, legitimatize American ideas and influence, and stabilize the region against communist incursion.[80]

Not surprisingly, when American and Japanese efforts culminated in the April 1961 founding of the APO, the new organization's eight members—Taiwan, India, Japan, South Korea, Nepal, Pakistan, the Philippines, and Thailand—were all noncommunist. The APO quickly worked to undertake programming very similar to that of the JPC: it released and translated publications and reports about productivity (its first translation was Nakayama's *An Introduction to Productivity*), held an array of seminars and workshops on subjects like training for industrial managers and assistance to small businesses, and coordinated multinational study team exchanges between member countries, the United States, and Europe around topics such as industrial development, standardization, and quality control. By 1962, the APO had sent a professor of material science from the Tokyo Institute of Technology to Taiwan to consult on glassware manufacturing, including plant surveys, lectures, and demonstrations to improve technique and quality. It held a range of training courses for Asian trainees, including a three-country marketing and training course implemented by the Japan Marketing Association in Tokyo, the Thailand Management Development and Productivity Center in Bangkok, and the China Productivity and Trade center in Taipei. The APO also started a fellowship program that allowed member countries to select individual training programs for chosen nominees; all three trainees, from the Philippines, South Korea, and Nepal, were entering JPC training programs in Japan.[81]

The APO's close relationship with the Japanese productivity program—it was headquartered in Tokyo and largely administered by the JPC—meant that its architects envisioned their goals in similar psychological and spiritual terms. Drawing on both American and Japanese emphases on proper mentalities and emotional states as a crucial motor of economic growth, many in the JPC envisaged the APO as an organization that would facilitate a "productive" psychology throughout Asia. As the JPC noted in planning the March 1959 conference, conference discussions would encourage "Asian countries, akin to one another culturally and economically [to] pull out of the state of destitution and backwardness with the consciousness that 'we, too, can prosper.'"[82] Rather than exploring alternatives to capitalism, calling for neutralism, or criticizing the importation (or imposition) of foreign knowledge and developmental models, the JPC implicitly claimed that Asian countries simply needed to foster a cooperative mindset. This psychological disposition, the JPC seemingly hoped, would also accept Japan as a friendly and technologically advanced regional leader anxious to help other Asian states for their own gain. Given these foundations, it is not surprising that both American policymakers and Japanese officials viewed the APO not so much as a multidirectional project but largely as a vehicle to transfer Japanese knowledge, skills, and techniques to other countries in Asia. Japanese Foreign Minister Kosaka Zentaro utilized the first plenary session at the formal launch of the APO in Tokyo in May 1961 to promise ample support from the Japanese government in the mission to bolster the Asia's economic development. As quoted in the *Japan Times*, Kosaka proclaimed, "When duly applied in according [*sic*] with the economic demands and circumstances of respective member countries, Japan's experiences with its own industrialization would no doubt serve for economic development of your esteemed countries."[83]

This belief that economic growth would place both Japan and Asia on the right economic, political, and psychological path helped the APO garner funding beyond the U.S. government; private American philanthropic organizations also gave the APO financial support. In the early 1960s, the Ford Foundation, the world's largest and most influential philanthropic organization, decided to expand its program in Japan. In 1962, the Ford Foundation's trustees therefore allocated $1.5 million for grants to Japan and Australia in Ford's International Affairs Division, with the possibility of an additional $2.2 million in 1964 and 1965.[84] As part of this funding stream, Ford trustees approved a $320,000 grant to the APO for an experimental training program in small business management in December 1963. This grant would fund two different multimonth programs held at the newly constructed JPC headquarters in Tokyo, which would focus on small business consulting and small business organization, topics that had been integral to JPC- and ICA-funded productivity programming in Japan.

In making this grant, Ford was explicit in its belief that the APO's strength lay in its promise to export Japan's recent experience and to reassert Japanese leadership in Asia. "The relevance of the Japanese experience in modernization and the extent of the support by the JPC give the APO a solid and practical basis for international cooperation which is lacking in many other regional organizations in Asia."[85] As one official put it, Japan's "experience of successful modernization offers important lessons" about how to achieve rapid, yet balanced, growth relevant to the "overwhelming bulk of Asian industry and the majority of employed workers."[86] For Ford, the APO could foster a new sense of Asian cooperation and political unity, premised on disseminating ideas and attitudes conducive to development. As one of its officials proclaimed, "Small industry will remain a key factor in economic growth at this stage of Asian development. The development of managerial talent and other skills and attitudes associated with small industry is also essential for balanced social and political development."[87] In making such a claim, Ford echoed APO's own argument that its proposed training programs were not just about modernizing industries but about modernizing humans. Responding to a series of questions about the proposed institute in 1963, Oshikawa Ichirō, secretary general of the APO who had previously been part of the JPC, argued that in an Asian context, productivity had to be about more than technological advancement or modern production techniques.[88] "In Asia," he said, "most of the countries are still in the stage of economic development where productivity ideas have to concentrate on the development of man and the better utilization of the existing resources. It is the stage where adequate and effective use of the talent is the concern."[89] The introduction of modern management techniques could therefore teach Asian countries how to use human talent effectively to foster "the development of the right type of men." For both Ford and members of the JPC, the APO offered an important opportunity to implement their belief that economic growth was a consequence of mental and psychological transformation.

Unsurprisingly, Asian participants in JPC and APO programming sensed these patronizing attitudes, especially the implied hierarchy between an "advanced" Japan and an "underdeveloped" Asia. For example, in a 1961 evaluation meeting at the China Productivity and Trade Center in Taiwan, attended by two Taiwanese teams who had participated in JPC training in Japan, participants were critical of their experiences, even as they acknowledged the hard work put in by the Japanese sponsors. Participants derided the training as didactic, overly simplistic, and paternalistic; "some of the lecturers were recruited from vocational schools of the high school level," one report bemoaned. "The participants felt they were being treated as immature rather than as mature adults." Moreover, it was overly focused on proselyting the experiences of Japan rather than adapting the information specifically to Taiwan because it assumed that Japan's expertise could be widely applied: "It would be better if the Japanese sponsor could make study of the industrial background of the countries from which the participants come."[90] Yet such critiques did little to change the American and Japanese focus on productivity as a fruitful path forward; the APO still exists today.

Ultimately, American-Japanese regional productivity efforts reproduced the widespread belief that development required not just new technical skills but the proper mindsets and attitudes. Like the domestic productivity program, it argued that economic growth stemmed from determination and a proper state of mind, rather than reforming or overturning structural and economic inequalities, including the legacies of American and Japanese colonialism in Asia. Such a definition of productivity, growth, and development made it intellectually possible to export the Japanese "model" to countries with far different historical trajectories and political economies. What is more, this dissemination of a productivity consciousness, both Americans and Japanese claimed, would facilitate not only material development but also a new commitment to cooperation and unity throughout Asia. Rooted in the productivity programming in the 1950s, this vision of Japanese regional leadership sought to offer a new model for political, economic, and spiritual anticommunist mobilization. It aimed to recreate Japanese regional hegemony as a benevolent, technocratic, and modern future.

Indeed, development and productivity were appealing to both Japanese and U.S. officials in part because these goals did not entail any substantial challenge to previous core assumptions and hierarchies. Endeavors like Third Country Training and the APO tantalizingly promised to tame workers' radicalism and solidify the supremacy of management while simultaneously securing U.S. and Japanese regional and even global power. Development assistance and technical training sought to revitalize Japan's role as the center of East Asia's economy, production, and trade while also restoring Japanese political, ideological, and economic influence in support of the United States' capitalist hegemony. Perhaps for this reason, the United States and Japan shared a commitment to international assistance and development for the rest of the twentieth century. Despite visible clashes over trade policies, most notably in the 1970s and 1980s, their commitments in this sphere remained; in 1989, Japan's foreign aid budget was larger than that of the United States.[91] This joint emphasis on economic growth, productivity, and development, allegedly for the good of the entire Asia region and the world, celebrated psychological transformation as the foundation of capitalist success.

CHAPTER 9

Cash for Gold: The Role of Private Finance in Shaping Decolonization in South and Central Africa, 1960–1974

Alanna O'Malley

> "In addition to mining, there is hardly any field in which British companies and their subsidiaries are not engaged. . . . The western powers are involved in Southern Africa up to their necks."

More often than not, UN expert reports are steeped in the language of bureaucracy and diplomacy, products of an interwoven system of checks and balances and, therefore, usually devoid of strong political opinion. However, in 1962, the drafters of a report analyzing the implementation of General Assembly Resolution 1514 (Declaration on the Granting of Independence to Colonial Countries and Peoples) did not mince their words about the role of private corporations in stunting the economic and political development of countries in south and central Africa.[1] The report was damning in its condemnation of the activities that companies such as the Anglo-American Corporation of South Africa (AAC) and Union Minière du Haut-Katanga (UMHK) played in the economic and political development of Congo, Rhodesia (Zimbabwe), South Africa, and South West Africa (Namibia). It concluded that "there is a complex set of interconnections between the Cape-to-Katanga miners: there are few secrets where directorships interlock, and although a group may act independently in the fields which do not impinge on the interests of the others, on most questions it must have at least the tacit agreement of the rest."[2]

The 1960s in Africa were a period of rapid political, social, and economic development as more than twenty countries gained independence from colonialism. They proceeded to mount an international campaign for the expansion of decolonization from questions of sovereignty and self-determination into issues such as regulation of the role of private companies operating in their territories and more equitable distribution of their profits to the economies in which they operated. The United Nations was the epicenter of much of their international activities as they activated the organization by formalizing their economic crusade largely in the committees of the General Assembly and the Economic and Social Council (ECOSOC). During the 1950s, postcolonial countries such as India began to meet informally with others, such as Ethiopia, Egypt, and Liberia, to form communities of interest, and they set about creating formal structures with which to progress the question of economic development. From 1958 onward, African states in particular engaged with their Asian and Latin American counterparts and asserted economic autonomy, testing the limits of economic independence and threatening to disrupt trade and finance networks that the old European colonial powers were determined to maintain. As it became gradually apparent that territorial sovereignty did not necessarily equate to economic sovereignty in many former colonies, Global South states launched a quest, finally issuing a formal declaration, the New International Economic Order (NIEO), in 1974.[3]

This chapter investigates the role that private companies, specifically the AAC and UMHK, played in this dynamic moment of Global South activity, by tracing their influence on American and British policies toward development in Central and South Africa and their role in conditioning responses to the campaign for international economic justice.[4] In particular, it demonstrates how UN efforts to regulate networks of private finance in Central and Southern Africa clashed with the expansion of American capitalism in this space. Since the regulation of private companies was a central focus of the larger campaign to reshape North-South economic relations, the role of private finance in decolonization emerges as an important feature in the landscape of postcolonial development. Much of the scholarship on the role of private companies operating across Africa focuses on the personal links between American and European policy planners, financiers, and bankers and the efforts to sustain the financial architecture of European colonialism.[5] While there is a growing literature that emphasizes the important role of international organizations in mediating the complex relations between finance and government, relatively little has so far been devoted to the question of what role the UN played in helping the Global South to organize its campaign for economic sovereignty by critically analyzing the role of private capital in political development in Africa.[6] This chapter bridges the gap and in the process examines how UN policies and resolutions affected the ways in which Britain and the United States developed economic policy toward Central Africa and, moreover, fundamentally altered the perception of the organization and its role in shaping the global economic order among policy makers. To do so, the chapter traces the development of this question at the UN during the 1960s, outlining the political foundations of the NIEO campaign. Thereby it provides an important contribution to the existing debate by showing how the expansion of American capitalism in the region was a contested process that often confronted American financiers and African actors with difficult choices around how to guarantee investment flows while balancing economic rights during these years, which precisely involved increasing regulation of the control of private companies.

Resolution 1514, which asserted the right of every nation to political and economic independence, was passed by a huge majority by the General Assembly in 1960.[7] As the special committee on the implementation of Resolution 1514 worked to ensure it was more than a rhetorical victory, the General Assembly passed the Declaration of Permanent Sovereignty over Natural Resources (PSNR), providing the first concerted achievement of Global South countries to develop their agenda for economic reform. These measures, in parallel with the campaign for economic sovereignty through the meetings of ECOSOC, the United Nations Conference on Trade and Development (UNCTAD), and the continued activities of the Committee of 24 (Special Committee on Decolonization), combined to pose a challenge to Western efforts to preserve the financial architecture of colonial systems. Against this rapidly evolving framework which accelerated decolonization, the AAC and UMHK sought at every opportunity to prevent UN resolutions from being implemented, stunting the effectiveness of UN policies. Therefore, they played an important role in conditioning both American and British responses to UN initiatives but also heightened tensions with African states who publicly branded them "neo-colonialists." Such was the strength of the position of UMHK in Congo that one Liberian delegate asked the Security Council in June 1961 "why Union Minière had hitherto been immune to the enforcement of United Nations policies."[8] Indeed, the AAC would prove similarly impervious to the effects of UN resolutions and, later, even sanctions against South Africa. In order to understand how they wielded such political power, both nationally in Congo, Rhodesia, and South Africa and internationally with governments in Britain and the United States, it is important to examine the ways in which these companies became embedded in the political economy of Africa.

This essay asserts that African economic development was not just approached by the United States as either a Cold War imperative or an altruistic effort through the United States Agency for International Development (USAID) and the Bretton Woods institutions of the International Monetary Fund and the World Bank. Rather, private finance actually played a much more influential and direct role and has gone largely underexamined in studies of American foreign policy in Africa during these years. By examining select UN efforts to regulate the behavior of private financial actors through a variety of means, this chapter presents a new perspective of the UN as an instrument that sought to monitor if not regulate the expansion of American political-economic power in Central and Southern Africa. Further, the chapter offers an original contribution to the field by emphasizing that American financiers were equally invested in the extraction and production of African raw materials as their European counterparts, if not more so. This viewpoint diversifies conventional arguments that neocolonialism was primarily defined by the relationships between former colonies and old European colonial empires, by revealing that American investors not only shaped but dominated the structure of economic relations between Africa and the rest of the world for most of the twentieth century and into the twenty-first.

The Oppenheimer Empire

The report of the Special Committee to Implement Resolution 1514 described the South African tycoon Harry Oppenheimer as "perhaps the single most powerful person in Southern Africa."[9] Alongside serving as chairman of the AAC, by far the most influential in Africa in the 1960s, he was on the boards of two other large gold groups, the Rhodesian Selection Trust copper company and Tanganyika Concessions (TANKS), a subsidiary of UMHK. Oppenheimer's mining empire included vast personal holdings in the AAC and South Africa's De Beers Consolidated Mines, one of the largest diamond producing companies in the world. In addition, he had shares in almost all of the import groups and was in a position not just to know what his rivals were doing but to influence the decisions of other companies through his vast network of friends and business associates across Britain and the United States.[10] The AAC controlled the mining of gold, diamonds, copper, platinum, uranium, and vanadium and the production of a vast array of other strategic materials across Central and South Africa, including pulp, paper, coal, potash, and beer, producing profits of £7.4 million in 1958.

The AAC was closely intertwined with a number of other major companies, most importantly De Beers, the Rand Selection Corporation, and Charter Consolidated.[11] Connected by an intricate network of joint shareholders and directors, each company owned a controlling stake in the other. Together with a host of hundreds of subsidiaries (among which were the British South Africa Company and TANKS), they became known as the Anglo-American Group, which is today involved in at least 250 companies operating in 66 countries worldwide, producing $5.5 billion in earnings in 2019.[12] At the very top of the corporate ladder, Ernest Oppenheimer, and later his son Harry Oppenheimer, enjoyed an "almost unassailable position" controlling the Anglo-American Group well into the 1990s.[13] While the group has a decentralized internal structure, the private company, E. Oppenheimer and Son, directly under the control of the Oppenheimer family, has been at the head of Anglo-American for much of the twentieth century. Exemplifying the personal influence of the Oppenheimer family in directing the group, in 1966 all the directors of the AAC were "shareholders in and nominees of E. Oppenheimer and Son."[14] Based on wealth drawn from the mining of gold and diamonds (the leading assets among the others) in eleven countries across Central and Southern Africa, the group expanded its international activities dramatically in the 1960s, placing investments around the world through the London-based Charter Consolidated. Such was the power and influence of the AAC's network in the private sector in South Africa that it was in a position to "dictate to whole industries" across the region for much of the twentieth century.[15]

The empire of the group had been established across Africa from Angola to Rhodesia and from Katanga to South Africa in a largely unrestricted manner from 1917 onward. However, when Congo erupted into violence on independence from Belgium in 1960, the activities of TANKS and UMHK in particular were brought to international attention. Britain was heavily invested in both, as well as another group called the British South Africa Company, a subsidiary, with TANKS, of the AAC.[16] The southeastern Congolese province of Katanga contained millions of dollars' worth of strategic materials including copper, diamonds, gold, and uranium, which had been used by Robert

Oppenheimer (no relation) to produce the American atomic bomb in 1942. UMHK was heavily intertwined in economic and political aspects of mining in Congo, managing an output of around 8,431 metric tons of cobalt and 280,403 metric tons of copper annually.[17] The group also controlled much of the infrastructure across Central Africa from railways, cement works, flour mills, and insurance companies to cattle ranches, hospitals, and schools.[18] The power and wealth of the group are illustrated by their remarkable profit margins: from 1950 to 1959, UMHK alone recorded a total net profit of 31 billion Belgian francs.[19]

During the period of 1955 to 1960, the extraction of resources from Katanga produced profits of £464 million for Belgian and European shareholders. Given the strategic role played by TANKS in this economic architecture, Britain adopted a conservative position toward decolonization in Africa, which had at its core the preservation of private investors and British assets. Captain Charles Waterhouse, the CEO of TANKS, had close relationships with the British foreign secretary Alec Douglas Home and other members of the Conservative Party Foreign Affairs Committee.[20] Oppenheimer himself and a range of other officials of the British South Africa Group, TANKS, and Unilever enjoyed considerable influence with British politicians as they lobbied for the protection of Katanga and British economic interests in Central Africa.[21] In 1966, the British prime minister Harold Wilson even suggested "sending a raspberry" to Oppenheimer, "who always comes to see me when he is in London," over a disagreement regarding the AAC's investments in Rhodesian nickel in light of the imposition of sanctions against Ian Smith's regime following the Unilateral Declaration of Independence in 1965.[22]

In the early 1960s, Britain had in the region of $1 billion invested in Southern Africa, while dividends paid to TANKS shareholders in 1960 alone amounted to £3 million. Meanwhile, the stockholders, including Charles Hambro, a director of the Bank of England, enjoyed a £2 million profit in 1958 from "Union Corporation," yet another AAC subsidiary.[23] While these companies had preferential associations at the top level in London and maintained their influence by supplying large dividends to investors, they also directed a network of special relationships with governments across Central Africa and South Africa and asserted substantial influence over the international markets for their products. Furthermore, through the AAC and the U.S. Export-Import Bank, millions of dollars were lent to Anglo-American subsidiaries at low interest rates in order to generate more profits.[24] Throughout the political crisis in Congo between 1960 and 1964, shareholders wielded considerable influence with British and Belgian policy makers, strengthening the resolve of those governments to limit the efforts of the UN in helping the Congolese government to assert authority over Katanga and regulate the activities of TANKS and UMHK.[25]

American officials were similarly intertwined with the Anglo-American Group. It has previously been argued by David Gibbs and John Kent, among others, that American policy toward the crisis was driven as much by an effort to maintain capitalist networks as by Cold War considerations.[26] Indeed, there were clear personal links between President John F. Kennedy's administration and private business interests in Congo. Former CIA director Allen Dulles had connections with the AMAX mining company that operated in Northern Rhodesia and South West Africa. In 1962, AMAX had a 42 percent holding in Rhodesia Selection Trust (alongside whom the AAC developed the copperbelt region from the 1920s onward), which controlled a significant amount of copper mining across Central Africa. When the independence of Zambia was declared under Kenneth Kaunda, AMAX increased its holdings to 49 percent and negotiated a concession that guaranteed the continuation of their mining activities for twenty-five years.[27]

Although diamond mining was largely controlled by De Beers under the AAC, the American diamond trading company Leon Tempelsman & Son held significant shares in the mines of Katanga, Rhodesia, and South Africa and traded through the group.[28] Kennedy's ambassador to the UN, Adlai Stevenson, managed Tempelsman's legal affairs through a law firm in which he was a major partner. Gibbs has argued that not only did Stevenson use his influence to allow this company to expand its activities in Congo after independence, but he also encouraged the U.S. government's policy of stockpiling Congolese diamonds. Tempelsman positioned itself as a middleman for this process and in exchange the Congolese were promised American agricultural commodities.[29] The Rockefeller Foundation, which in the early 1960s was also interested in expanding its activities in Africa, had multiple connections to the Africa Bureau in the State Department. Kennedy's secretary of state, Dean Rusk, was a former president of the organization, undersecretary Chester Bowles was a former trustee, and, most importantly, J. Wayne Fredericks was assistant secretary of state for African affairs.[30] Through these links and a variety of others, private business interests expanded their activities and political influence in the economic development of Congo, Rhodesia, and South Africa.

Beyond direct American links to investments in Africa, however, the importance of the AAC as an investor in the United States should not be ignored. A subsidiary called the Zambian Anglo-American Corporation that controlled interests in Zambia, most importantly copper, began to expand its activities in the late 1950s. With the revenue from Zambian copper, MINORCO was established in the tax haven of Bermuda, from where the AAC expanded activities into North America. In 1961, the AAC acquired a controlling interest in the Hudson Bay Mining and Smelting Company in Canada and undertook significant investments in the United States and Latin America. Such was MINORCO's success that by the 1980s it was the largest single foreign investor in the United States, with a total revenue of $26,750,000,000, surpassing Shell and Unilever.[31] This influence very much operated at elite political levels within various U.S. administrations. For example, when Oppenheimer met with President Johnson in 1964, he denounced UN interference in his companies, branding Africans "too emotional" in dealing with South Africa, a question in which other countries should not interfere. The State Department advised the president to encourage cooperation with the UN while praising Oppenheimer's ideas "for increasing investments in black Africa."[32]

The enlargement of the role of private finance in the postcolonial world was of course wholly compatible with American plans for the modernization of and development in the Global South. The American approach to development was driven by two fundamental tenets, a belief in the value of liberal economics and the free market and the perceived omnipresence of the Cold War, both of which served to drive a rigorous modernization campaign and bilateral aid program across Africa. The economist Walt Rostow rose to prominence in the State Department following the 1960 publication of his seminal work *The Stages of Economic Growth: A Non-Communist Manifesto*. Rostow argued that the modernization of economies across the world takes place in five stages, providing the basis for the American approach toward modernization until the rise of neoliberalism in the 1980s.[33] Key among Rostow's theories was that it was possible to roll out a worldwide model for development through aid and the promotion of liberal economic theories. This universalist approach failed to take account of the variety of national and local features that existed among Global South countries, not least the access to natural resources, labor conditions, and capital reserves. Revisionists later criticized Rostow's emphasis on rapid industrialization as a road toward development that disenfranchised large swaths of the poorest populations while enriching elites.[34]

Rostow also advocated for the extension of bilateral aid programs to newly independent countries in order to promote favorable relations. In 1961, USAID was created to manage the flow of aid to the developing world and promote social and economic development.[35] As American engineers, doctors, and technicians flowed into Global South countries, the State Department promoted the creation of a "community of free nations" whereby the industrialized countries of the world, including the European states, Japan, and the United States, would provide direct investment and technical assistance to the "rest," thereby staving off the influence of communism.[36] Through direct investment with bilateral aid and trade agreements and through USAID, from the 1960s, therefore, the United States vigorously pursued a development agenda designed to thwart the influence of the Soviet Union in the countries of the Global South.

On a wider level, the United States sought to manage, if not control, the international economic system through the Bretton Woods institutions: the International Monetary Fund and the World Bank. The effort to expand American influence through groups such as the AAC had the effect of strengthening existing European monopolies of financial control and resource extraction on a structural level across Central and South Africa, proving as if not more influential than the more altruistic programs rolled out by USAID and the World Bank. For example, the reliance of the Bretton Woods system on the gold standard (and therefore the continued supply of gold) proved a strong imperative to policy planners in the State Department. Even in 1967, 70 percent of the world's gold was still produced by South Africa, further entrenching the position of the AAC within the strategic interests of the U.S. government. Similar to the British approach, officials in the State Department viewed the AAC, and Oppenheimer, in particular as a valuable contact and a conduit for influence in the political and business communities of Central and Southern Africa. As one memo noted, in the context of the growing tensions with South Africa and Rhodesia over the issues of apartheid and sanctions in 1965, "Oppenheimer . . . is a man who might have the answers, if anyone does."[37]

Taking Back Control at the UN

Against this powerful, wealthy, and deeply entrenched network of private investment and political authority, Global South countries mounted a campaign to take back control of their economies and in the process restructure the global economic relationship between North and South. Monitoring the activities of private companies was viewed as a two-pronged strategy that would not only have a direct influence on economic development within the Global South but also wrest political control away from the industrial and business elites. Since 1950, Latin American countries had been agitating for economic reform, led by the head of the Economic Commission for Latin America, Raúl Prebisch, an Argentine economist who developed the Prebisch–Singer thesis (Hans Singer was a German-born British economist working along similar lines). Prebisch argued that the modernization theory of the West would entrap developing economies into a core-periphery relationship with the industrialized North and that what was needed was domestic industrialization and therefore direct control of natural resources.[38]

These ideas resonated with postcolonial leaders in Africa and Asia. Following the Conference of Independent States of Africa in Ghana in 1958, the Pan-Africanist George Padmore described to an Indian diplomat his plans for a regional organization for technical cooperation in the vein of the Colombo Plan, which had been developed to strengthen economic and social cooperation among countries in the Asia-Pacific region.[39] Drawing on the principles of economic cooperation between African and Asian states agreed to at the Bandung Conference in 1956, the Afro-Asian Organization for Economic Cooperation was established in Cairo just two years later.[40] India was particularly interested in economic cooperation with Ghana and on a bilateral level secured an agreement that would increase Ghanaian imports of cotton and jute in return for Indian imports of industrial diamonds, manganese, and timber.[41] Strengthening relations between the two continents on bilateral and multilateral levels through complementary regional organizations led African and Asian countries to cultivate political affinities into formal connections with the Latin American quest for economic reform at the UN from 1958 onward.

Mirroring developments on a transregional level, a host of new groups and organizations for global economic reform sprang up both inside the UN, institutionalizing the connections between African, Asian, and Latin American countries. With the cooperation of the UN Department of Economic Affairs and ECOSOC, the UN set up regional commissions for economic and social development across the Global South. Within the UN itself, representatives discussed common challenges and ideological and structural problems, laying the foundation for the first meeting of UNCTAD, the formation of the G-77 in 1964, and eventually the NIEO declaration a decade later. At the center of these initiatives was an effort to create common markets between African, Asian, and Latin American states that would "craft new forms of trade to ameliorate the effects of uneven imperialist exploitation."[42] However, before attention could be turned toward reforming world trade, African countries in particular needed to address the activities of private companies operating in their territories and assert authority over their own natural resources.

As quiet footwork was taking place at the UN to press the issue of control of private companies at ECOSOC, the Congo crisis and the ineffectiveness of the UN to oblige UMHK to turn their profits over to the Congolese government put the question on the agenda of the General Assembly and the Security Council. The wealth and influence of UMHK, and its connections with both the Belgian and the British governments, and the Katangese regime, allowed officials to heavily influence political developments and resist the implementation of UN resolutions. A draft Security Council report for the year from July 1961 to July 1962 noted that it was increasingly clear that in their role as political advisors and their supply of resources and mercenaries to Katanga, the company remained impervious to UN resolutions and was largely able to operate with a policy of "business as usual."[43] The activities of UMHK, as well as of the AAC and Unilever, not only led to widespread accusations of neocolonialism from African states but also gave those actors a point of reference with which to accelerate the campaign for the passing of a resolution declaring permanent sovereignty over natural resources.

The whole issue of how to challenge the intricate and powerful network of private capital and its influence over political and economic development was raised by events in the Congo but had ramifications for postcolonial state-building across Africa. The experience produced two important realizations among the Afro-Asian group. The first was that the acquisition of political independence and territorial sovereignty did not necessarily imply economic and social autonomy from former colonial powers, as evidenced by their continued stranglehold over African social and economic development. The second, related to the first, was that much of this control hinged on the role and position of private companies and industries invested in the extraction of the vast natural resources of both regions. In response, Global South countries began to generate support in the General Assembly for proposals which would expand the meaning of sovereignty to assert the right of countries to declare control over their natural resources and simultaneously to undermine the power of private companies that operated with relative autonomy from newly independent states.

Discussions about sovereignty over natural resources had already been taking place at the UN since 1952, when a General Assembly declaration asserted the right of underdeveloped countries to use their natural resources for economic development.[44] This issue was tied with human rights claims about the meaning of self-determination during debates at the Commission on Human Rights that asserted that "the right of peoples to self-determination shall also include permanent sovereignty over their natural resources."[45] Following the establishment of the Commission on Permanent Sovereignty over Natural Resources, the UN Secretariat produced a report on the status of the question in 1961.[46] On the basis of this report, and a draft declaration of principles presented by Chile, the question was passed to the General Assembly where, with Global South lobbying, it was adopted by a vote of eighty-seven to two with twelve abstentions on December 14, 1962.[47]

This was a significant development not just in representing the first attempt of the countries of the Global South to take back control of their resources and redefine relationships with, if not assert their authority over, companies operating in their territories, but it also displayed initial efforts to enhance the meaning of sovereignty to include economic sovereignty and to remake international law in their favor.[48] This progress should be viewed in parallel with the agenda for economic development spearheaded by Prebisch many years before, but it was important because it represented the first political development that challenged the economic interests of the Western powers and solidified the connection between political economy and sovereign equality. Interestingly, however, Britain and the United States, which had both voted in favor of the resolution, interpreted it as a positive step in affirming "the importance and the legal rights of private investors in the less developed countries."[49] Although the resolution was crystal clear about the rights of countries to control their natural resources, it had also declared that "Foreign investment agreements freely entered into by or between sovereign states shall be observed in good faith."[50] Thereby, both sides regarded the PSNR as a victory, placing the struggle for control over private investment at the center of the debate about international economic reform, which would continue through the 1960s and into the 1970s, leading to initiatives such as the UN Capital Investment Fund, the Special United Nations Fund for Economic Development (SUNFED), and further efforts to regulate transnational corporations by UNCTAD and later by the NIEO.

The trajectory of efforts to regulate the activities of private companies, including those that acted in complicity with and often on behalf of the U.S. government, therefore can be viewed as having longer and deeper roots than the NIEO campaign of the 1970s. Rather, what becomes evident is that the NIEO was the pinnacle of much longer institutional and transregional efforts to utilize international organizations, particularly the various organs of the UN, to monitor and regulate private financial actors from the West. The permanent structural and normative developments that arose from early efforts in the 1950s and 1960s came about through resistance toward U.S. and European economic dominance through private companies, rather than by the much more piecemeal and less impactful attempts to alter the global political economy on the state level. The formation of lasting political and economic transnational networks sought to shape how American capitalism affected postcolonial state development, but it also revealed that while the debate about private finance tended to be framed in imperialist language, in fact the actors were American and European liberals whose activities and policies created economic frameworks that governed the inequitable political and economic development of Central and Southern Africa.

* * *

The PSNR declaration was the first assertion of economic rights by the Global South and the accompanying institutional developments outlined above were important in laying the foundations for the NIEO, as part of which the emphasis on the role of private capital in economic and political development became a central focus. The issue now started to spread from the institutions designed to deal with economic questions into the creation of transnational organizations and, crucially, the use of the General Assembly to remake international rules in order to redress the North-South economic imbalance.[51] By coupling the use of rights rhetoric with material claims to assert views about development at the UN, the beginning of the process of the longer assertion of a right to development began to foment between nations of the Global South as they used the legal and political framework of the UN to advance their claims.[52] As Adeoye Akinsanya and Arthur Davies have argued, the Global South sought to use "the whole weight of the UN to achieve an alteration of the norms governing the conduct of international economic relations and to have these norms codified into a legal document."[53]

The focus on regulating private companies therefore provided an important moral and political imperative that helped initiate the campaign for the NIEO. Crucially, however, it also led the UN to examine the activities of companies like the AAC that up to this point had operated without any oversight. It shed light on the role of industrialists like Oppenheimer in shaping economic development in Central and South Africa and highlighted the extent of his and others' influence with Britain and the United States in encouraging them to resist efforts to reform the global economic order. As the UN expert report concluded in 1962, "This deep financial and economic involvement helps to explain the concern of the metropolitan powers not to jeopardize 'economic stability' in the countries of Southern Africa, and their tendency to help perpetuate the political status quo. It is not only treaty obligations which concern Governments, but also economic commitments, and the pressures of private lobbies—most of the activities of the company chiefs go unnoticed behind the scenes and can only be guessed at, except when crisis such as that in the Congo and the present one in the Federation bring them out into the light."[54]

CHAPTER 10

Courting American Capital: Public Relations and the Selling of Ivorian Capitalism in the United States, 1960–1980

Abou B. Bamba

This chapter is an invitation to reimagine the roles assigned to players in the history of capitalism on the global stage. It challenges aspects of the historiography of capitalism in the twentieth century, which tend to center on historical actors and institutions of the Global North. Even when actors in the Global South are discussed, it is usually to portray them as passive victims of an intractable system. By focusing on the Ivory Coast and its economic diplomacy toward the United States, I seek to destabilize this general picture. While American investors, corporations, and advertising agencies are still important in this story, the plans, strategies, and actions of the Ivorians take the center stage. To be sure, this is not to deny the leading role of the United States in the world capitalist economy, especially after the Second World War. As historians have shown, the United States government certainly orchestrated many of the global institutions that emerged in the wake of the war. On the other end, American businesses strove to further their operations, not just in Latin America, which had traditionally served a U.S. sphere of influence, but also in Europe, Asia, and even Africa.[1] While the U.S. government and American corporations took the initiative in numerous foreign countries, they did not always run the show, as a number of contributions in this volume demonstrate.[2]

This should not come as a surprise. American economic hegemony in foreign lands did not play out in a *tabula rasa*. Indeed, local agents, politicians, and impresarios more often than not used the coming of the United States as an opportunity to strike new alliances in an effort to advance their own interests. In that, the power of the United States was contingent on the consent and even the invitation of national states and regional leaders. Geir Lundestad has explored this theme in the case of reconstruction of Western Europe in the aftermath of World War II.[3] In the context of twentieth-century decolonization, one sees similar processes at work in Algeria, where nationalists sought U.S. investment in their country to reduce the influence of the French.[4] That local interest groups were instrumental in the expansion of American capitalism abroad is also highlighted in Julio Moreno's insightful study of American business culture in Mexico.[5]

What is even more interesting is Moreno's discussion of the singular importance of advertising in the operation of an American-inflected capitalism. Unfortunately, his focus on development *within* Mexico gives the impression that the power of transnational advertising is one-directional: from the Global North to the Global South. There is a long tradition among media scholars of pointing to this phenomenon that some of them have called advertising imperialism.[6] Unlike these scholars, I underline in this chapter a series of instances in which the government of Ivory Coast and its diplomats posted in the United States—all actors from the Global South—deploy advertising and public relations to target an audience in the Global North. This not only confirms that the circulation of information in the operation of capitalism is all-important,[7] but it also suggests that actors in decolonizing Africa and elsewhere were willing to embrace and mobilize public relations to reach their own goals. Indeed, like Marta Musso in her work on Algeria, I highlight the efforts of the Ivorians to reduce their reliance on the French, whom, in the wake of decolonization, foreign observers and radical Ivorian activists increasingly saw as overbearing in the Ivorian drive to postcolonial modernity.[8]

The public relations campaign that the Ivorian leadership launched in the 1960s in the United States to attract investors was the cornerstone of this strategy of diversifying Ivory Coast's economic partners. The campaign lubricated the global operation of capitalism in the respective countries. Shifting the focus away from the traditional story of the Cold War or the scholarship on Franco-African relations and economic diplomacy, and the *Françafrique* paradigm, my contribution thus suggests that Francophone Africa was the arena of a different, but no less instructive, cold war that pitted the United States against France. Even more, I argue that Africans remained instrumental in the operation and the global reach of U.S. capitalism, and not necessarily as its victims.

What strategies did the Ivorian authorities use? Who were their American strategists? What were the ultimate dividends of their public relations initiatives? A central part of this chapter is devoted to answering these questions. While it will be hard to pin down the actual outcomes of the marketing ploys that Ivory Coast mobilized, I suggest that any effort to answer the questions will allow us to reimagine American capitalism and the role of Africa and Africans in its development in the twentieth century, especially in nonstrategic areas of the Global South. In many ways, this detour through the international statecraft of the Ivorians and their American public relations experts contributes to the decentering of the history of capitalism. It might serve then, to use a formulation offered by Jessica Gienow-Hecht, as part of a broader project to "dethrone the United States as a principal agent in international history."[9]

* * *

In November 1959, Félix Houphouët-Boigny led the French delegation to the United Nations General Assembly meeting. Ever since his political organization—the Rassemblement Démocratique Africain—decided to work with the French imperial state in the early 1950s, the Ivorian politician had emerged as an influential member of the Franco-African polity.[10] In 1956, indeed, he was admitted as a member of the French cabinet of the Fourth Republic. He would subsequently assume various ministerial posts in successive French governments until the independence of Ivory Coast in 1960.[11] While this situation added to the charisma of the Ivorian statesman, Houphouët-Boigny's collaboration with Paris deepened the chasm between him and the more radical members of his political movement, including Sékou Touré—the leader of the newly independent state of Guinea and one of his erstwhile lieutenants. In fact, the Guinean leader had followed the lead of his compatriots in a resounding No vote to the 1958 Franco-African referendum that Houphouët-Boigny supported. This rejection of Charles de Gaulle's brainchild vision of Franco-African relations resulted not only in the independence of Guinea but also the expulsion of the country from both the Franco-African community and the transterritorial political movement over which Houphouët-Boigny presided.[12]

The ostracization of Touré and his country was a preview of things to come. Capitalizing on his presence on U.S. soil, Houphouët-Boigny went out of his way to give a diplomatic punch to the Guinean statesman who, because his country was being isolated by France and its allies, had made overtures to socialist countries. Touré also used his presence in the United States for the United Nations gathering to rally support from the Americans.[13] True to his reputation as the "traveling salesman of French colonialism," Houphouët-Boigny attempted to sabotage Guinean diplomacy toward Washington, insisting that the American decision makers should assist only their "true friends." In particular, the Ivorian statesman told President Dwight Eisenhower not to provide any help to those "African countries that have asked and obtained aid from the communists. We, your friends and who have already chosen to be by your side in the Western Bloc, we should be able to count on you."[14]

In many ways, Houphouët-Boigny's move during his sojourn in the United States prefigured his postcolonial politics in the global arena. In 1966, for instance, he would send an envoy to Washington and hire the services of columnist Drew Pearson to undermine a plan that anticipated an increase in U.S. aid to Guinea.[15] The Ivorian statesman's mobilization of the Cold War fault lines to advance his own agenda is quite remarkable. Equally significant is the premium he placed on the United States as an ally to be courted in global politics. I have elaborated elsewhere on the importance of American ideals and ideas in providing a model of development that fired the imagination of many Ivorian modernizers.[16] The paragraphs below provide an additional layer to the story of the place of Washington in Ivory Coast's bid for modernity. This is achieved not only through an approach that decenters the power of U.S.-based multinationals as the primary agents of this historical unfolding but also through a foregrounding of the economic diplomacy of the Ivorians as enablers of the transnationalization of American business and capitalism in their country.

What made this conjuncture possible was not only the strident anticommunism of the Ivorian government and its embrace of capitalist ideology. It was also the case that Ivory Coast had emerged as an economic miracle in West Africa—a feat that can be dated to the postwar productivity politics and the cash cropping revolution that took place in the country. When Ivory Coast was amalgamated to the group of French colonies in West Africa in 1893, there were few signs to the eyes of the first imperial bureaucrats that the territory would become a colony with a sound economic future: there was no reliable seaport, passable roads in the hinterland did not go beyond a few miles upcountry, and many of the people and polities of the coast were reputed to be inhospitable. [17] Contemporaries were adamant that this situation impeded the implementation of colonial exploitation and its associated trading economy. By the interwar period, however, the ingredients for an agricultural revolution of sorts were put into place—especially when the colonial authorities began to create the rudiments of an economic infrastructure geared toward the world capitalist economy, and both white colonists and African entrepreneurs took up commercial farming.[18]

Subsequently, agriculture and the businesses related to its operation would come to dominate the economy of the colony. Even more remarkable, these transformations magnified in the aftermath of the Second World War when the French Fonds d'Investissement pour le Développement Economique et Social began implementing its modernization of France's overseas territories, including huge infrastructural projects and the mobilization of agronomic research to improve crop productivity.[19] Taking advantage of the assistance of crop scientists and the high prices for commodities such as coffee and cocoa, African planters consolidated their position as leading producers of cash crops and boosted Ivorian exports. Not only did they displace the white settler planters, but in the process the local agricultural entrepreneurs ultimately turned Ivory Coast into the El Dorado of French West Africa and the poster child of capitalist development on the continent.[20]

Even as the French colonial authorities doubled down on investment in the colonies and began an ingenious propaganda push to sell French modernization efforts, some Africans were already envisioning the enlistment of American assistance in the drive for postwar modernity. Such was the case of Kouamé Binzème—a lawyer acting as the mouthpiece of the Syndicat des planteurs et éleveurs africains de la Côte d'Ivoire. In early September 1948, he wrote to American officials who managed the Marshall Plan for European postwar reconstruction, enclosing in his letter an action plan for the economic development of Ivory Coast.[21] The keystone of Binzème's modernization vision was the implementation of what he called the "principle of *partnership* (*association*) between American *capital* and African *labor*."[22] This certainly was a subtle critique of the French doctrine of colonial *mise en valeur*, which he implied was unfair to the colonial subjects. More significantly in Binzème's document was the belief that American capital was the crucial means of promoting "freedom, economic progress, and social betterment for the Africans."[23]

The Ivorian lawyer and the people he represented were not the only party that was interested in American dollars. Anticipating the transformations that decolonization might bring, French companies operating in the colonies had begun the internationalization of their capital. Moreover, in a context marked by the rise of U.S. financial power and incessant calls for more private investment in the French colonies, the postwar authorities in Abidjan too could not avoid appealing the American financiers.[24] Houphouët-Boigny continued this open-door policy vis-à-vis American capital and businesses, especially in the wake of the Loi-cadre (framework law) of 1956 that devolved much power to Africans for the management of domestic issues. It was at this juncture that overtures were made to various U.S. corporations, including the Plymouth Oil Company for drilling and the Development and Resources Corporation, which ultimately became involved in the planning of key modernization projects in postindependence Ivory Coast.[25]

From this overview of the early years of the so-called economic miracle of Ivory Coast, it is clear that the United States exerted an appeal on the would-be architects of the Ivorian economy. The examples of Kouamé Binzème and Félix Houphouët-Boigny in the postwar period, regardless of the differing positions of these leaders in the Ivorian political spectrum, encapsulate this point quite vividly. What is more is that if the American charm was only nascent in the late colonial period, the end of formal French rule would allow it to grow in Ivory Coast. As we shall see, the causes for such growth have to deal not only with what was seen as the attractive modernity of the United States but also the actions of some activist decision makers in an effort to emancipate the economy of their country from its dependence on France.

* * *

Despite its remarkable development since the Second World War, the Ivorian economy was still dominated by French interests at the time of independence. And Houphouët-Boigny, as the first president of postcolonial Ivory Coast, knew this too well. In contradiction to the conclusions of the extant historiography on his early policies, which emphasize the continuities between late colonialism and early independence, he attempted to take action—especially since the overbearing presence of the French in his country was proving to be a liability. Although the structural features of the Ivorian economy limited the outcomes of his emancipatory moves, it is worth underlining them.

On August 19, 1960, for instance, the Ivorian statesman wrote to Washington through the American ambassador in Abidjan. His aim was to solicit U.S. aid and to ask the Americans to help his government build "with [the] greatest speed [the] economic power of [the Ivorian] state and thereby to reinforce its political independence."[26] This was the first installment of the efforts of the postindependence authorities of Ivory Coast in their request for direct American involvement in the postcolonial development of their country. During the immediate aftermath of decolonization, the Ivorians took other actions, including entreaties to potential investors during the state visit that Houphouët-Boigny made to the United States in the spring of 1962.[27]

Arguably, the most remarkable aspect of the Ivorian strategy to court U.S. economic support was the deployment of public relations techniques. Aware of the power of public relations in twentieth-century transnational statecraft, Ivorian diplomats posted in Washington hired a number of publicity and public relations agencies to lobby on behalf of Ivory Coast. This was the case of former *Time* magazine correspondent Anatole Visson, who served as an agent for the country in the United States from 1960 through the early 1980s. Other public relations agencies such as the Hamilton Wright Organization of New York were also used for specific promotional campaigns whose ultimate aim was to reach out to the American financial market. By the late 1970s, no fewer than four firms had offered their services to the West African country.[28]

The lobbying activities of Ivorian diplomats were not lost on keen contemporary observers. As early as May 1962, journalists at the *Wall Street Journal* had highlighted that a number of foreign countries, including Ivory Coast, Liberia, and Nigeria, had "signed contracts with American public relations firms" to help them "cultivate the goodwill of Americans." According to the reporters, these deals were part of a transnational campaign to "sway Uncle Sam" in favor of newly independent states.[29] The Ivory Coast Development Office in New York, the Ivorian embassy in Washington, D.C., and especially Ambassador Henri K. Bédié played important roles in this effort. This is revealed in a memoir written by Bédié decades later, wherein he reported that he indeed first hired the Hamilton Wright group in late 1962 to lobby on behalf of his country and brand Ivory Coast for American investors.[30]

The publicity agents at Hamilton Wright began their lobbying campaign promptly. In particular, they followed up on their promise to the Ivorian government that they would flood American and European newspapers with ad displays that sold Ivory Coast as a sound destination for U.S. investment capital. Examples abound. In early 1964, for instance, an advertisement featuring Ivory Coast (along with other African countries) appeared in the *New York Times*. Using the heads of state of eight countries as a visual anchor, the display claimed that the highlighted countries were "profitable opportunities for trade and investment in Africa."[31] Another ad installment in the same issue of the paper showcased Ivorian policy choices as a "Plan for Economic Growth . . . that Works."[32] In early 1965, a new ad display was placed in the newspaper. Titled "Business Opportunities in the Ivory Coast Republic," this public relations piece was part of a series that characterized Houphouët-Boigny's country as "One of Africa's Soundest Economies."[33] In 1968, yet another ad display appeared. It unabashedly claimed that "as economic progress continues in the Ivory Coast, the government welcomes American private investments."[34] Perhaps the culmination of this public relations campaign of the first decade of independence was the "16-page color advertising supplement" in a mid-December 1969 issue of the *New York Times*. Although the actual supplement is yet to be located, a series of announcements gives a preview of what it might have been marketing to the public: Ivory Coast as "Africa's New Rivera," next to a drawing of a happy couple splashing in the ocean, and "Africa's Economic Miracle," next to a drawing of a tractor. Each touted the investment opportunities present in "West Africa's Most Prosperous Country."[35]

There is little doubt that these advertisements were meant to brand Ivory Coast as an attractive destination for American investment. In each of the ads, the designers made sure to include a list of investment opportunities whether in the textile or palm oil industries (cf. the January 25, 1965, ad) or in the manufacturing of cocoa butter and powdered cocoa (cf. the January 26, 1968, ad). At a time when the eyes of the Ivorian government were on industrialization, some of the ads encouraged investment in the emerging industrial sector. In late January 1971, a series of installments was featured in the *New York Times*, including one that focused attention on the newly created Atlantic port of San Pedro and one that celebrated the Ivorian success at capitalist development.[36]

However, Ivory Coast was not alone in this deployment of international public relations tools to advance its economic agenda. For instance, the Nigerian authorities resorted to this strategy in making their country visible. Consider two examples. In October 1960, just a day after the proclamation of independence from Britain, an ad display appeared in the *New York Times*. In November 1965, another installment was placed with the revealing title "NIGERIA: A Virile Republic; A Contributor to Progress."[37] Similarly, starting in January 1965, the Senegalese government began to showcase investment opportunities in Senegal to potential American investors.[38] Thus at stake is not so much that newly independent countries targeted the United States but how they sold themselves and with what outcomes. Addressing this issue will allow us to see the distinctiveness of the Ivorian foray into public economic diplomacy.

* * *

Paying close attention to the texts of the various advertising pieces, it is clear that the Ivorian authorities behind the ads were looking for ways to diversify the base of their country's economy. Toward the last years of the formal colonial era, youth and radical activists had been denouncing the dominant position of the French interests in the Ivorian economy.[39] After independence, such a critique was echoed by an increasing number of observers. In mid-September 1960 a visiting delegation of American experts drew attention to this situation. U.S. diplomats posted in Abidjan appropriated their analysis, going as far as to suggest that reliance of France was the "basic weakness" of the otherwise sound economy of Ivory Coast. They were not alone. Even some bureaucrats and analysts in the employ of the French Ministry of Foreign Affairs reached a similar conclusion in 1965, especially with regard to the industrial sector of the West African country.[40] Capping these critiques was the release of Samir Amin's *Le Développement du capitalisme en* Côte d'Ivoire in 1967 and the dissemination of its main argument in the columns of the well-circulated *Jeune Afrique* magazine.[41] Even though the authorities in Ivory Coast attempted to provide a rebuttal to Amin's leftist take, they knew too well that diversification was a necessity for the future of the Ivorian economy.[42]

The ad campaign has to be placed within this larger context—all the more so since the calls for weaning Ivory Coast's economic development from its reliance on French investment and assistance continued through the 1970s, notably among Ivorian academics who were becoming more and more vocal against Houphouët-Boigny's visions and Francophilia that they readily called neocolonialism.[43] The ad display of January 1971 underlined this intent of diversifying foreign investment: "The Ivorian economy is oriented toward foreign trade and international investments. Of course, France, the old colonial power, is still very much the principal economic and financial partner, but her relative importance is constantly diminishing in favor of other industrialized countries, mainly the United States, which is now the Ivory Coast's second biggest trading partner. American interests are represented in the major banks established in the Ivory Coast and in insurance companies."[44] Indeed, as early as 1964, Ivorian economic planners had made overtures to American businesses that resulted in U.S. entry into Ivory Coast's budding energy sector. While this conjuncture led some French impresarios to accuse the Ivorian leader of distancing himself from France to become the "right-hand man of the Americans" (cf. "*l'homme des Américains,*"), the bid to appeal to the United States continued.[45] In 1965, Chase International Investment and Lazard Freres & Co. of New York pulled their support together to become the "principal sponsors of a new development finance company" that aimed to boost Ivorian industrialization.[46] By the late 1960s, "interest for Ivory Coast in certain American economic circles," according to a French diplomat, had become quite "indisputable." In fact, reported the French chargé d'affaires, roughly "a third of all visas granted by the Embassy of Ivory Coast in Washington were connected to business trips."[47]

The diversification of economic partners could also be conjugated with the policy of expanding the range of cash cropping products. Since the colonial period, the economy of the country had banked on coffee and cocoa. While these became the engine of the so-called Ivorian miracle, such reliance came with obvious limitations, including food shortages and vulnerability to commodity price volatility. Within the country itself, the planners of the postindependence economy promoted the cultivation of food crops such as rice, yam, cassava, and banana. To break the dominance of coffee and cocoa, the timber industry was further expanded.[48] The Ivorian authorities also sought foreign assistance in the development of new cash crops, including a variety of palm products and rubber. The ad campaign of the late 1960s was deployed for this cause, as exemplified in July 1967 and 1968, when two ad displays on behalf of SODEPALM—an Ivorian state company—were placed in the *Wall Street Journal*. The underwriters of the announcement invited interested parties to bid for land clearance in coastal Ivory Coast in view of the creation of coconut and oil palm plantations.[49]

Another type of advertising that promoted the idea of diversification of the Ivorian economy was sponsored by third parties that had already become involved in the Ivorian bid for modernization. Placed in numerous periodicals in early October 1968, this form of endorsement reinforced the idea that the Ivorian economy was reliable. By associating the name Ivory Coast with established financial institutions, the ads invited, if obliquely, other companies to trust the country.[50] Given the complex nature of public relations and especially its reception, it is hard to gauge definitively the outcomes of Ivory Coast's advertising campaign in the United States. What is certain is that the Ivorian authorities continued to appeal to American investors through the 1970s and even the early 1980s.[51] And such sustained effort seems to have borne some results. Although France was still a major player in Ivory Coast's economy, American economic and financial role had improved tremendously. This became clearer by the end of the decade. In 1977, for instance, Houphouët-Boigny's country had emerged as the United States' second trading partner in West Africa. More significantly, the country had become the first destination of U.S. direct private investment in Francophone West Africa.[52] As it turned out, this development that facilitated Ivorian easy access to international capital markets had a price tag, especially since American investment in Ivory Coast came in the form of commercial loans that weighed on the country's worsening foreign debt crisis.[53]

The transformation in the oil and gas sectors of Ivory Coast singularly put into relief some of the most insightful points regarding the Ivorian effort to court American investment, especially at the time when the country's economic growth was losing momentum. Not only had the successive oil shocks of the 1970s demonstrated the vulnerability of Ivory Coast to foreign oil, but the same global conjuncture also had forced American commercial banks to look for ways to recycle their surpluses of petrodollars.[54] It is quite telling that this was the very moment when U.S. private investment in Ivory Coast began to focus on the expansion of the Ivorian oil/petroleum sector. Although it is premature to point to a direct correlation, one cannot miss the coincidence of U.S. involvement in the nascent Ivorian oil exploitation industry paired with the latest advertisement campaign that Ivory Coast mounted in the late 1970s that specifically invited American money interests to invest in oil exploration and drilling in the country.[55]

Consider the new advertising pieces that the Ivorian Ministry of Economy, Finance, and Planning placed in the *New York Times* in February 1978. With a short, catchy title, the main display announced, "Ivory Coast with Oil," calling attention to the discovery of oil deposits "large enough [. . .] to satisfy all the country's needs by 1980." Even more, the new resource would "help develop the country's industrial base, by enabling us to build a petrochemical industry, so important in achieving overall economic progress."[56] Adjoining this display was an inset that laid out clearly the advantages that investing in Ivory Coast offered, including the "large facilities for transferring capital from Ivory Coast, a very supple taxation, [and] exoneration of entry taxes on materials or raw materials used for production."[57] The use of ad displays that marketed the oil sector to potential American investors continued through the early 1980s. In 1983, as Houphouët-Boigny prepared for another state visit to the United States, a new series of ad displays were released. In addition to New York City's celebrated daily paper, the *Washington Post* served as an outlet for one of these latest installments.[58]

To ensure that the advertising of Ivorian oil resources was effective, authorities in Ivory Coast kept tight control over the dissemination of information. Although a consortium of companies led by Exxon affiliate ESSO Côte d'Ivoire had discovered offshore oil deposits as early as 1974, the government did not publicize it immediately. Rather, it opted for "holding off on official announcement," presumably until there was confirmation that the find was commercially viable. That confirmation came in 1977, even though the exact size of the deposit remained in dispute.[59] In an attempt to spin matters and "probably to sustain investor and lender confidence in the Ivory Coast," Paul Gui Dibo (Ivorian minister of mines) and Adama Toungara (director general of the Ivorian national oil company) reportedly made "insistent demands on the exploration companies to make the most optimistic statements possible."[60] The oil companies seem to have heeded the demand—at least, with regard to the release and the strategic management of the information *within* Ivory Coast.[61]

In the United States, the initial media coverage of the Ivorian oil find was anything but effusive. Yet the Ivorian information campaign appeared to have piqued the interest of some potential investors. Indeed, not only did a number of American firms begin to enquire about the Ivorian oil sector, but some of them, including Chem-Oil Industries Limited, even sent representatives to visit the Ivory Coast.[62] Moreover, in the early 1980s, another consortium led by the American company Phillips made a discovery of an even larger deposit of oil and gas off the Ivorian shores.[63] Thus, by the time production came on line and Ivory Coast began dreaming of becoming an oil exporter, it was clear that U.S. firms were playing a key role in the country's oil and petrochemical industries.[64]

* * *

Admittedly, there is nothing unusual about advertising in the operation of capitalism. Media scholars have long recognized this fact, leading some to dub advertising "an entrenched institution bent on keeping the wheels of capitalism rolling."[65] What is intriguing, however, in the current analysis is the deployment of this marketing tool by a postcolonial country from the Global South to advance its own agenda in the Global North. In fact, while global communication scholars have usually been interested in mapping the transnational media flow, it is almost without exception in the other direction. As this contribution has demonstrated, Ivorian economic planners were active in appealing to American capital investment through their mobilization of mass marketing techniques. While the United States is still important in this story of the mediated operation of capitalism, it is also clear that a focus on the agency of the Ivorians succeeds in decentering the narrative away from American historical actors. This is much in line with the insight of historian Stefan Schwarzkopf, who has cautioned us not to assume that the rise of the "American century" necessarily led to an Americanization of the world through the expansion of U.S. mass marketing ploys.[66]

To be sure, the emergence of the United States as a global power opened new opportunities for many businesses in the world at large. But the reverse was also true. In an era marked by the maturation of capitalism, the United States itself was not immune to the redeployment of advertising from abroad to sell foreign goods or to simply brand countries as a safe and attractive destination for American capital. The case of deploying Ivorian advertisement campaigns in the United States to tap American investment capital is but one example in this fluidity of media flows that facilitated the growth of twentieth-century capitalism.

CHAPTER 11

Nuclear Reaganomics: Corporate Lobbying After Three Mile Island, 1979–1985

Jayita Sarkar

On the morning of November 4, 1980, a high-ranking Bechtel Corporation official circulated a thirty-seven-page action plan within Ronald Reagan's Energy Policy Task Force. Titled "Recommended Action Plan for the New Administration," it contained detailed instructions to reorient U.S. foreign and domestic policies on nuclear energy to steer them away from what the U.S. nuclear industry perceived as Carter-era "antigrowth" and "political" impediments.[1] It was the blueprint to facilitate a "virtual 180-degree reversal of the Carter administration policy" to get the "U.S. nuclear industry back on its feet."[2] The document originated within the top echelons of Bechtel, the San Francisco–based engineering giant that had received the bulk of construction contracts for U.S. power reactors since the Eisenhower years. The action plan's specific goal was to increase U.S. nuclear exports, which it equated with U.S. global power. The document bluntly stated, "The influence of the U.S. on international nonproliferation policies is in direct proportion to its role as a leading supplier. The less we sell overseas, the less influence we have."[3]

Circulated from the office of W. Kenneth Davis, Bechtel's vice president for nuclear development and a member of Reagan's Energy Policy Task Force, the action plan had three top-tier Bechtel executives in copy: Harry O. Reinsch, Caspar W. Weinberger, and Bechtel's president, George P. Shultz. Even though preelection polls had depicted a fairly close election, on the morning of election day the note accompanying the action plan expressed "every confidence" that the Energy Policy Task Force would imminently reconvene to devise policies of "President-Elect Reagan."[4] Later that day, Reagan won by a landslide, and the Republican Party took back control of the Senate for the first time in 28 years. According to the *New York Times*, at 9:50 P.M. Eastern time on election day, Jimmy Carter made the earliest concession statement of a major presidential candidate since 1904, when Alton B. Parker had conceded defeat to Theodore Roosevelt.[5] In 1981, several of the "Bechtellians" referenced in the action plan would go on to hold key positions in foreign, defense, energy, and economic policies in the Reagan administration.

During the Carter years, Reagan had emerged as a staunch critic of the president's foreign and domestic policies. The former governor of California claimed that Jimmy Carter had endangered U.S. national interests abroad by continuing with détente with the Soviet Union and jeopardized interests of the white working class at home by imposing higher taxes and failing to manage stagflation. Reagan's message had attracted evangelical Christians, social conservatives, fiscal conservatives, libertarians, and business leaders such that both the New Right and the Religious Right came together in support of his 1980 presidential campaign.[6]

The ongoing Iran hostage crisis, which was exactly a year old on the day of the election, had dealt a huge blow to Carter's popularity as president, as had the Soviet invasion and occupation of Afghanistan. Reagan's proposed solution was to increase defense spending, reduce taxes, and drastically curtail the institutional capacity of the federal government. The Reagan revolution ushered in supply-side economics as the guiding practice of government policies, thereby formally replacing demand-driven Keynesian economics of the postwar years.[7]

In the midst of falling domestic demand for nuclear reactors, the Carter administration had passed stricter regulations on U.S. nuclear exports for nonproliferation, which upset the industry.[8] The 1978 Nuclear Non-Proliferation Act, crafted in response to India's nuclear explosion, exacerbated the industry's sense of crisis because it constrained its export potential by demanding full-scope safeguards from countries that bought U.S. nuclear materials and technologies.[9] Economic duress of the nuclear industry meant bad business for both reactor suppliers like General Electric, Westinghouse, and Babcock & Wilcox as well the building corporation Bechtel, which handled the majority of infrastructure projects related to reactor construction.

The Three Mile Island accident in March 1979 in Middletown, Pennsylvania, thus aggravated the woes of an already struggling industry. After only one year of operation, the second reactor at Three Mile Island nuclear power plant experienced severe core damage, leading to radiation leaks that caused a public health scare among rural Pennsylvanians living close to the plant. The

Kemeny Commission, formed by President Carter to independently investigate the causes of the reactor accident, found technological flaws in the reactor design as well as human operator errors. In October 1979, the commission's report publicly criticized the nuclear industry and the Nuclear Regulatory Commission (NRC) for what it called an avoidable accident. The commission's report affected public trust in nuclear power at home and confidence in U.S. reactor safety standards abroad.[10] As antinuclear activists and environmental groups began to agitate against nuclear power after the reactor accident, the U.S. nuclear industry could not use rising oil prices during the Iranian revolution to promote itself as a viable energy alternative, as it had done during the 1973 oil shock. Against this backdrop, industry leaders sought a turnaround through increased government support—financial aid and deregulation—and found a willing advocate in presidential candidate Ronald Reagan.

Before his political career, Reagan spent over a decade as the national spokesperson for General Electric as host of *General Electric Theater*, broadcast on CBS radio and television from 1953 to 1962.[11] The Reagan family, from their ranch house in Pacific Palisades in Los Angeles, California, appeared with General Electric home appliances in three-minute commercials with the slogan, "live better electrically."[12] Reagan even toured the company's facilities for several weeks each year as its goodwill ambassador. By the time he became the governor of California in 1967, Reagan's reputation as being probusiness and antiregulation was well established. He lost his presidential bid to incumbent Gerald Ford at the Republican National Convention in 1976 but emerged as a clear favorite of conservatives in the primaries in western and southeastern states.

Four years later, in Reagan's 1980 presidential campaign, not only were business leaders closely involved, but several high-ranking executives also took up prominent positions in his administration. The "boys from Bechtel" courted considerable public controversy for casting overwhelming influence on government policy during the Reagan years.[13] After all, Bechtel's president, George Shultz, served as the secretary of state from 1982 to 1989 after chairing the President's Economic Recovery Policy Advisory Board in 1981 and 1982. The company's general counsel, Caspar Weinberger, was appointed secretary of defense in 1981, a position he held until 1987, while Bechtel's top executive for nuclear power, W. Kenneth Davis, served as deputy secretary of energy from 1981 to 1983. All three were also involved in canvassing for reduced government oversight of the U.S. nuclear industry in the aforementioned action plan for Reagan's Energy Policy Task Force.

Scholarly efforts to foreground the role of economics in U.S. foreign relations is not new; they were inaugurated by Charles Beard and expanded through economic critiques of U.S. global power by William Appleman Williams along with his fellow exponents of the Wisconsin School.[14] In U.S. foreign relations historiography, the predominant narrative about proliferation and nonproliferation is that of national security, mainly understood through the prism of arms control.[15] The global atomic marketplace is hardly present in the historical scholarship even though capitalist forces are intrinsic to both the circulation of nuclear technologies that can lead to "proliferation" and the efforts to prevent that from happening, or "nonproliferation."[16] That economic statecraft has been integral to U.S. nonproliferation, such that the relationship between U.S. diplomacy and capitalism has significant implications for U.S. empire, merits a deeper inquiry. Emily Rosenberg's foundational work on state-corporate association to promote U.S. financial interests abroad, Kim Phillips-Fein's study of the role of businesses in the U.S. conservative movement, and Paul Kramer's notion of the United States as a "commodifying empire" are particularly relevant for capturing the role of capitalist actors and processes in U.S. nonproliferation policy.[17]

This essay discusses how economic statecraft has been integral to U.S. nonproliferation, such that the analytical framework of American "capitalist diplomacy," as invoked in the introduction to this volume, is essential to fully understand its intricacies. In this volume, Jason Scott Smith's essay on neoliberal legacies of the New Deal (Chapter 4), Erum Khalid Sattar's work on the U.S. export of expertise in dams (Chapter 5), and Alanna O'Malley's piece on the role of private corporations in decolonizing Southern and Central Africa (Chapter 9) directly intersect with the themes of this essay, particularly with reference to the nature of state-corporate networks, how those changed over time, and how the changes led to dispossession and inequality in society.

Covering up Three Mile Island

"Yes, I am scared of the possibility of a nuclear accident. Yes, I am scared of the possible impact of nuclear power plants on the environment," declared John G. Kemeny in his opening convocation speech as president of Dartmouth College in September 1978.[18] He was addressing his young audience at the beginning of the academic year about "the growth of complexity in our civilization." Within six months, Kemeny would find himself as the chairman of President Carter's Commission on the Accident at Three Mile Island.

On March 28, 1979, the second reactor at Three Mile Island (TMI-2) experienced the worst accident in the history of U.S. commercial nuclear power. The accident began just before four o'clock in the morning, when the cooling valve malfunctioned, leading to a partial meltdown of the reactor core. The plant operator, Metropolitan Edison, did not inform Richard Thornburgh, the governor of Pennsylvania, about the accident until around seven o'clock that morning.[19] Civil defense officials were called in. Much confusion ensued regarding evacuation of the area among rural Pennsylvanians who lived in the area. To avert panic and save its own reputation, Metropolitan Edison claimed that there was no radiation leak from the accident and that the site was "contained." In reality, the core of the reactor was severely damaged, and radiation was released into the atmosphere.

A Congressional Research Service brief later noted that "there was some exposure of nearby residents to comparatively small amounts of radiation," while "some workers received excessive exposures," though "not enough to cause short-term injury."[20] The residents of Middletown were not convinced. Over the next months and years, disgruntled residents filed lawsuits seeking compensation for lost business, while public health fears of radiation-caused cancers fueled a burgeoning antinuclear movement.

The partial meltdown of TMI-2 grabbed headlines worldwide. The reactor accident not only contributed to mistrust of nuclear power and the industry but also demonstrated the lack of coordination in emergency preparedness at local, state, and federal levels. Lacking adequate information on nuclear accidents, and receiving mixed signals from Metropolitan Edison, Governor Thornburgh vacillated about whether to evacuate residents from the area. He evacuated only pregnant women and preschool children within a five-mile radius of the nuclear power plant but advised those within a ten-mile radius to stay.[21] An evacuation of two hundred thousand to three hundred thousand people, although planned, was never executed, which led to public controversy about the governor's decisions.[22]

On April 11, 1979, by executive order, President Carter appointed mathematician John Kemeny to chair the President's Commission on the Accident at Three Mile Island. Commonly known as the Kemeny Commission, the twelve-member team's task was to provide an independent assessment of "what happened at Three Mile Island.... how the accident could have been prevented.... [and] how the Government and others responded" and to make recommendations to "prevent any future nuclear accidents."[23] The Kemeny Commission's scrutiny of the U.S. nuclear industry was restricted to the utility (Metropolitan Edison Company, a subsidiary of General Public Utilities), the manufacturer of the nuclear reactor (Babcock & Wilcox), the engineering company that built the Three Mile Island plant (Burns and Roe), and the NRC.

Within months, the Kemeny Commission found that "fundamental changes in the industry, especially—but not only in the NRC, will be required if nuclear accidents as serious as that at Three Mile Island are to be prevented."[24] The commission discovered that as a result of an incident in the Davis-Besse plant in Ohio in September 1977, engineers at Babcock & Wilcox and an NRC inspector had "relatively clearly identified the potential for accident which became a reality at Three Mile Island." The commission took the view that "had appropriate action resulted at Babcock and Wilcox, the NRC, or in the utility industry, it is highly unlikely the accident would have happened."[25] Two engineers from Babcock & Wilcox testified to the commission that they had warned their superiors in separate memorandums that equipment malfunctions could lead to accidents in reactors like at Three Mile Island, a year before the actual accident.[26] However, Babcock & Wilcox ignored the warnings and sent no guidance to the utility company, Metropolitan Edison. Even after the partial meltdown of TMI-2, Babcock & Wilcox sent guidance to Metropolitan Edison on how to handle such emergencies after waiting a full week.

The star-studded movie *The China Syndrome*, released only weeks before the Three Mile Island accident, encapsulated the fears and mistrust of the public when it came to nuclear power. In the plot, an unsafe reactor is running at full capacity in California because otherwise the utility company would lose millions of investment dollars. The inspector has tampered with the radiographs to hide the technical flaw in the reactor. When the plant supervisor (John Lemmon) finds out, he advises that the reactor should be shut down but is met with strong resistance from his colleagues and the company. To inform the public, the supervisor reaches out to a reporter (Jane Fonda) and her cameraman (Michael Douglas), who had earlier witnessed an accident being averted in the same nuclear power plant caused by the unsafe reactor. In his desperation, the plant supervisor takes the nuclear power plant hostage to broadcast his message about the unsafe reactor to the public. The film tragically ends with the plant supervisor being shot dead inside the reactor's control room by a SWAT team called in by the utility company.

The chilling similarity between the film and their own nightmare was not lost on residents near Three Mile Island, especially as information about the negligence of Metropolitan Edison, Babcock & Wilcox, and the NRC became public knowledge. Citizens organized through environmental and antinuclear groups to hold the powerful accountable—the companies and the federal government. The antinuclear groups that already existed in the area before the accident, such as Three Mile Island Action Alert and the Environmental Coalition on Nuclear Power, saw their memberships rise. Numerous new civil society groups emerged in the wake of the accident, such as People Against Nuclear Energy, the Campaign to Stop the Restart, Concerned Citizens of Londonderry, and the Susquehanna Valley Alliance.[27]

In the era of post-Vietnam mistrust of big government and large corporations, nuclear power entered the popular imagination as antidemocratic, secretive, and dangerous. Nuclear power represented the epitome of power over people, which in the latter half of the 1970s attracted popular opposition from both the political left and the right. Nowhere was this more pronounced than in the public health effects of radiation from accidents caused by poor reactor safety standards.

The murder of Karen Silkwood, a technician at a Kerr-McGee plutonium fuel fabrication plant in Crescent, Oklahoma, had made national headlines just a few years before in November 1974.[28] In the weeks leading up to her death, she had been gathering evidence on safety standards at the plant to prove Kerr-McGee's willful negligence.[29] Even though the NRC closed the plant in 1975, Silkwood's heirs demanded compensation. The lawsuit continued well into 1979, when a federal jury awarded her estate $10.5 million in damages, which made it to the front page of the *New York Times.* Litigation gave some hope, although it did not alleviate all problems. In the case of Three Mile Island, in 1981 the nuclear industry settled claims worth $20 million for economic loss to businesses and individuals within twenty-five miles of the site and paid another $5 million to establish a public health fund to study the health impact of the reactor accident.[30]

There were no radiation-related casualties in the Three Mile Island accident, but the Kemeny Commission found "deficiencies in instrumentation for measuring the radioactivity released, particularly during the early stages of the accident."[31] The commission's report also found that three plant workers received radiation doses of about 3 to 4 rems, which exceeded the NRC's maximum permissible quarterly dose of 3 rems.[32] Jacob I. Fabrikant, renowned environmental radiologist and then senior scientist at the Donner Laboratory at Berkeley, directed the Kemeny Commission's Public Health and Safety Task Force. He confirmed at the Senate hearings of the Subcommittee on Health and Scientific Research in April 1979 that little information was available on the effects of low-dose radiation on the human body. He stated, "We do not know what the health effects are at dose rates as low as a few hundred millirem per year. It is probable that if health effects do occur, they will be masked by environmental or other factors that produce similar effects. . . . it has been necessary to estimate human cancer risk at low doses primarily from observations at relatively high doses."[33] In his 1980 address at a conference organized by the industrial lobbying group Atomic Industrial Forum, Fabrikant repeated his position by reminding his audience that very little human data was available from epidemiological surveys of exposure to low-level radiation from which to draw conclusions for public health policy.[34] Nevertheless, in the report of the Kemeny Commission, Fabrikant concluded that radiation doses received by the population were so small that "there will be no detectable additional cases of cancer, developmental abnormalities, or genetic ill-health as a consequence of the accident at TMI." According to him, the major health effect of the accident was on "the mental health of the people" living in the area and the workers at the plant.

The Three Mile Island accident and the Kemeny Commission report were disastrous for an already struggling U.S. nuclear industry. In March 1980, the utility company Metropolitan Edison sued the reactor supplier Babcock & Wilcox for $500 million for its inability to warn the utility company after the incident at Davis-Besse.[35] Metropolitan Edison also sued the NRC for $4 billion for negligence, albeit unsuccessfully. In response to the Kemeny Commission's recommendations, the nuclear power industry formed the Institute of Nuclear Power Operations (INPO) in December 1979, headquartered in Atlanta, Georgia. The industry also created the Nuclear Safety Analysis Center within the Electric Power Research Institute to discuss technical changes to improve reactor safety.[36] Formed as a nonprofit organization incorporated in the state of Delaware, INPO, which still exists, called itself an independent safety organization for the promotion of excellence in the operation of U.S. nuclear power plants. However, it promoted safety culture through self-evaluation of the nuclear power plants, namely, by the utility companies themselves. INPO's funding came from the industry while it maintained independence from the government.

Lobbying the State

President Eisenhower's 1953 Atoms for Peace proposal pushed forward civilian nuclear energy in foreign markets, thereby transforming U.S. power reactors into tools of economic statecraft.[37] Under the 1954 U.S. Atomic Energy Act, large amounts of information concerning civilian nuclear technologies were declassified for the first time. This permitted U.S. businesses to own nuclear know-how and trade in it, which had previously been the sole preserve of the U.S. government.[38] From the mid-1950s onward, as the Eisenhower administration encouraged civilian nuclear energy at home and abroad, large corporations, like General Electric, Westinghouse, and Bechtel, had a natural advantage as they could withstand the sizeable financial risks in this new source of electricity. More importantly, it was only with the 1957 Price-Anderson Act, which limited corporate liability in nuclear accidents, that the industry finally became eager to participate in commercial nuclear power.[39]

Many large U.S. firms had prior experience in nuclear technologies through their participation in the Manhattan Project during the Second World War.[40] Companies such as DuPont, Union Carbide, Allis-Chalmers, and others worked on government contracts in nuclear fission research during the war. Both General Electric and Westinghouse provided electrical equipment for the Manhattan Project, among other things. Notably, Bechtel developed infrastructure for the Hanford site in Washington state, while Westinghouse built reactors to power ships and submarines for the U.S. Navy under the stewardship of Hyman Rickover.

The U.S. nuclear industry had historically depended on federal funding, and state patronage was the key to its emergence. Government-led capitalist growth of the New Deal era created a nurturing environment for U.S. firms, many of which later played a significant role in the nuclear industry. Established in 1898, Bechtel gained its initial experience in infrastructure projects of the New Deal years with its first major undertaking, the Hoover Dam. Similarly, General Electric and Westinghouse, also founded in the Gilded Age, benefited from New Deal–era policies such as the Rural Electrification Administration, which brought electricity to America's farms.

Reactors were expensive products—selling them abroad required large loans for their buyers. Those loans were provided by the U.S. Export-Import Bank, the taxpayer-funded financial institution established in the New Deal era to provide public credit to encourage private participation in economic activities outside the United States.[41] After Atoms for Peace, while the Price-Anderson Act underwrote financial risks from nuclear accidents, the Export-Import Bank became indispensable for selling U.S. power reactors in foreign markets. When U.S. companies competed with their European and Canadian counterparts in selling reactors abroad, their offers would be sweetened by Export-Import Bank loans on generous terms.

* * *

After his electoral victory, Ronald Reagan formed a transition team for the NRC headed by Richard T. Kennedy. A former Army colonel, proindustry Kennedy was nominated in 1975 by President Gerald Ford as a commissioner to the NRC, where he frequently disagreed with fellow NRC commissioner Victor Gilinsky over nonproliferation matters. Kennedy was also a member of Reagan's advisory group for nuclear power regulation that was heavily composed of business leaders such as Arthur Randol of Exxon and Frank Staszesky of Bechtel.[42] With Kennedy's leadership of the NRC Transition Team, business leaders communicated their concerns about specific NRC regulations with requests to disband them once Reagan was sworn in.

In one such letter, Norval E. Carey, vice president of General Atomics, wrote to Kennedy complaining about the NRC's security "upgrade rule" that required companies to improve infrastructure of nuclear facilities to prevent theft, sabotage, and other forms of unauthorized access of special nuclear materials. For Carey, the NRC requirement increased costs even though the "derived benefits are very abstract, highly subjective and unquantifiable."[43] Carey called for a reexamination of the rule and "considerations of cost/benefit" because the NRC's "overzealous regulation imposes unwarranted penalty upon the sector of private industry."[44] The industry thus opposed nuclear security measures on grounds of costs.

The Reagan administration responded positively to corporate lobbying by the nuclear industry. The administration's actions in 1981 were made according to the blueprint provided in "Recommended Action Plan for the New Administration" from November 1980. The plan, prepared by the subcommittee on nuclear power and electric utilities of Reagan's Energy Policy Task Force, had directed the administration to develop a policy that "includes support of accelerated licensing of light water reactors, the reprocessing of spent fuel, demonstration of high-level waste disposal, continued development and demonstration of the fast breeder reactor and, when timely, fusion."[45]

The industry wanted limited government oversight, not reduced funding. In October 1981 when Reagan announced several measures to limit the regulatory capacity of the federal government in civilian nuclear power, he spoke with one voice with industry leaders. He declared, "Nuclear power has become entangled in a morass of regulations that do not enhance safety but that do cause extensive licensing delays and economic uncertainty."[46] The administration removed the federal ban on commercial reprocessing of plutonium and on breeder reactor technologies—two major Carter-era polices to manage the proliferation-prone plutonium economy that were extremely unpopular with the industry—and promised a business-friendly environment for the "revitalization of the U.S. industry's efforts to develop nuclear power."[47]

While the administration slashed government funds for social services like public housing, it increased funding for nuclear energy. At a time when every other Department of Energy program witnessed budget cuts, such as solar energy and conservation, the budget for nuclear energy increased by 36 percent to $1.6 billion.[48] His administration even endorsed funding for the Clinch River breeder reactor in Tennessee, which his predecessor had opposed on grounds of nonproliferation and economics.[49]

The biggest concern of the industry as a consequence of Three Mile Island was NRC's prerogative of granting export licenses.[50] Their target was to make the NRC toothless. Frank M. Staszesky Jr. of Bechtel Power wanted to shift "the export licensing function from NRC to the Executive Branch" through the president's executive order.[51] The proposal consisted of the executive branch determining an export license on the basis of the Carter-era Nuclear Non-Proliferation Act. Such a mechanism, Staszesky argued, would "eliminate the existing confusion and uncertainties" and be "conducted in a timely manner."[52] Despite the U.S. nuclear industry's dislike of the Carter-era domestic legislation, any amendment would have been difficult to move through the Democratic-controlled House Foreign Relations Committee. As a result, both the nuclear industry and proindustry Republican lawmakers, such as John Wydler of New York, recommended that the president decide export licenses through executive order "while a strategy is worked out with the White House" to deal with the Non-Proliferation Act.[53]

Stripping the NRC of its regulatory power while concentrating that authority in the hands of a proindustry president was representative of what economists would call "regulatory capture." The nuclear industry and proindustry lawmakers saw it as working toward an agenda to help "the U.S. to regain its worldwide leadership in nuclear development" and dismantle the "bankruptcy of the Carter administration's nonproliferation policy."[54]

The relationship between civilian nuclear exports and U.S. nonproliferation was obvious to the corporate actors. The U.S. nuclear industry needed to sell power reactors abroad to control the recipient countries' nuclear programs. If the United States did not, some other country would, like France, West Germany, or the Soviet Union. To business leaders, the Carter-era policy of denial through strict export regulations was misguided, and it could only be corrected by a new approach to "rejuvenate the Eisenhower 'Atoms for Peace' concept thru [*sic*] aggressive nuclear leadership in the framework of assured energy supply."[55]

John Wydler recommended to Richard Kennedy that key appointments in the Departments of State, Energy, and Commerce as well as the National Security Council, the Arms Control and Disarmament Agency, and the NRC be filled with "energy supply advocates" who believed that "aggressive nuclear cooperation can help recapture U.S. influence on other nations."[56] That the industry got its way became obvious when, in 1981, Caspar Weinberger of Bechtel became the secretary of defense and Kenneth Davis, also of Bechtel, was appointed deputy secretary of energy. The following summer, George Shultz, the former president of Bechtel, was named secretary of state following the resignation of Alexander Haig. Later that September, Richard Kennedy himself, proindustry NRC commissioner and chair of the NRC Transition Team, became the Reagan administration's ambassador-at-large for nonproliferation and special adviser on nuclear energy.[57]

When Shultz became the third Bechtel executive to join the Reagan administration in July 1982, the company's influence over government policy came up for review at the Senate Foreign Relations Committee during his confirmation.[58] Bechtel had large infrastructure contracts in many parts of the world, including Saudi Arabia, a kingdom it had been particularly close to since the 1940s.[59] After the 1973 oil shock, when oil-rich nations in the Middle East had large spendable surpluses, Bechtel bagged construction contracts worth billions of dollars, like the Jubail industrial city and the King Khalid International Airport, both in Saudi Arabia.[60] At his Senate confirmation, while describing the family-owned San Francisco–based multinational construction company as a "truly remarkable organization," Shultz lost his composure when Alan Cranston, Democratic senator from California, produced letters from Bechtel official Joseph A. Damm that showed Bechtel's willingness in 1975 to sell the "entire gamut" of sensitive nuclear technology related to uranium enrichment to Brazil. Shultz himself was then Bechtel's president.

At the time, the Ford administration was trying to stop West German company Kraftwerk Union from exporting similar technologies to Brazil.[61]

Cranston asked Shultz whether he would reverse the Carter-era policy of restricting exports of nuclear technology as secretary of state. Cranston claimed that Bechtel's offer to Brazil in 1975 was an attempt to undermine the U.S. government's nonproliferation policy. Shultz retorted that Cranston's question was a "kind of smear on Bechtel." He claimed to have learned about the Brazil offer "only after the fact" and blamed it on the Bechtel official for being an "overenthusiastic business development person."[62] Despite concerns about Bechtel's overwhelming influence on the Reagan administration's policy, the Republican-controlled Senate unanimously voted 97 to 0 to confirm George Shultz as secretary of state in July 1982, a position in which he would serve until January 1989.

The Reagan administration indeed implemented the nuclear industry's recommendations for pursuing an aggressive nuclear export policy. By the end of 1982, the Reagan administration was seeking new markets, such as the People's Republic of China.[63] The administration worked around the Nuclear Non-Proliferation Act's requirement of full-scope safeguards by finding third-party suppliers such as France to keep prior U.S. commitments of nuclear exports, as in the case of India and South Africa.[64] It reversed earlier policies of not providing nuclear materials and technologies to countries suspected of proliferation. The administration approved the sale of 143 tons of U.S.-produced heavy water to Argentina through West Germany and did away with the ban on providing reactor spare parts to India.[65]

Despite the Reagan administration's proactive support for the nuclear industry, the export of U.S. power reactors did not increase. A large part of the reason was the long-term social and political effects of the nuclear accident at Three Mile Island. Public knowledge of negligence by the NRC and the nuclear industry in the wake of the accident led social movements on the antistatist conservative right and the proregulation political left to come together in a bipartisan backlash against nuclear power.[66]

Nuclear Power and American Capitalist Diplomacy

The Reagan administration did not trade nonproliferation for geopolitics, but the two went hand in hand, mediated through the capitalist diplomacy of the U.S. nuclear industry. The administration did not dismantle the NRC and the Nuclear Non-Proliferation Act. It neither permanently withdrew from the International Atomic Energy Agency nor challenged the nonproliferation treaty.[67] It simply worked to make sure that the institutions, legislation, and treaty mechanisms of nonproliferation *worked* for U.S. business interests at home and abroad. The tensions between the state and corporate actors of the Ford and Carter years were thus transcended in favor of increased coordination and cooperation between businesses and the government in the realm of nonproliferation. National Security Decision Directive 6 represented the essence of numerous memos and much correspondence from businesses to the Reagan campaign and the transition team on what government policy on nonproliferation should be like: "remove any unnecessary impediments to commercial relations in the field of nuclear energy."[68]

Scholarship on the Reagan years is dominated by narratives of nuclear deterrence, the nuclear war scare, and arms control, such as Able Archer, the Strategic Defense Initiative, and the Intermediate-Range Nuclear Forces Treaty, while most accounts of Reagan-era U.S. nonproliferation policy focus on the government's neglect of proliferation concerns for geopolitical ends.[69] The administration's benign neglect of Pakistan's nuclear weapons development as CIA-funded mujahideen fought the Soviets in Afghanistan, its tacit support for Israel's 1981 airstrike on Iraq's Osirak reactor, and an informal understanding with South Africa to not conduct nuclear weapon tests are notable examples.[70] This essay has shown that the above is only a small part of the full picture. U.S. capitalist diplomacy holds the key to comprehensively understanding the Reagan administration's nuclear nonproliferation policy.

As social movements against nuclear power and nuclear weapons reduced public support for the industry within the United States, its business leaders looked abroad for markets. New markets were hard to come by in an age of wars, civil wars, and insurgencies raging from the Middle East to Central America to southern Asia. Despite a nuclear cooperation agreement with China, congressional approval did not arrive during the Reagan years. In 1983, the industry launched an extensive public relations campaign to clean up its image, called "Nuclear Power: Time for a Comeback," in its efforts to educate what it perceived to be a misguided public.[71] In 1985, nuclear reactor accidents took place at Davis-Besse in Ohio, Rancho Seco in California, and Brown's Ferry in Tennessee, which exacerbated popular mistrust of nuclear power.[72] That year, a *Forbes* front-page article titled "Nuclear Follies" wondered, "Can a technology as rigorous and demanding and, for all that, as useful as nuclear power find a place in a society as open as the U.S.?"[73]

It was not until the 1986 Chernobyl accident in Soviet Ukraine that the U.S. nuclear industry could claim to have a superior reactor design and better safety standards than that of the other superpower. The specter of the RBMK reactor, Soviet red tape and misinformation, and the radiation release that spread over Europe made the plight of the residents near Three Mile Island far less jarring to the general public.

The dispossession caused by state-corporate networks were not insignificant at Three Mile Island. Fearful of radiation-caused illnesses and deeply distrustful of nuclear power, the residents near Three Mile Island organized themselves in 1985 to oppose the restart of the TMI-1 reactor. To them, nuclear power reactors were large projects for which big government acted with big corporations. Nuclear power was secretive, was managed by technocrats, and reeked of being antidemocratic. Despite the community's efforts to influence government policy, the NRC voted four to one in favor of restarting the reactor.[74] As for TMI-2, Bechtel, which had been in charge of the cleanup of the reactor, was accused of mismanagement and neglect of safety standards.[75] Even though the utility company dismissed the allegations, the NRC found evidence in March 1986 that Bechtel had indeed harassed the engineer who had complained about its safety procedures.[76] One month later, Pripyat would wake up to what would become the worst nuclear reactor accident in the twentieth century. For the U.S. nuclear industry, media criticism of Soviet reactor technologies and their opaque organizational culture would provide some temporary relief.

NOTES

Introduction

1. Draft Telegram, Secretary of State to American Embassy Jidda, August 9, 1967, National Security File, Box 155, Lyndon Baines Johnson Presidential Library. On U.S.-Saudi relations and Cold War defense spending in U.S. politics, respectively, see Victor McFarland, *Oil Powers: A History of the U.S.-Saudi Alliance* (New York: Columbia University Press, 2020), and Michael Brenes, *For Might and Right: Cold War Defense and the Remaking of American Democracy* (Amherst: University of Massachusetts Press, 2020).

2. Rusk to Johnson, "Release of Arms for Saudi Arabia," January 19, 1968, *Foreign Relations of the United States, 1964-1968,* vol. XXI, *Near East Region; Arabian Peninsula* (Washington, DC: Government Printing Office, 2000), document 308.

3. Davies to Talbot, "Sale of Advanced Aircraft and Hawk Missiles to Saudi Arabia," March 23, 1965, *Foreign Relations of the United* States, *1964-1968,* vol. XXI, *Near East Region; Arabian Peninsula* (Washington, DC: Government Printing Office, 2000), document 240.

4. Paul B. Johnson to Lyndon Baines Johnson, August 21, 1967, White House Central Files, EX NR 6, Box 13, Lyndon Baines Johnson Presidential Library.

5. Memo to Walt Rostow, "Project Gasbuggy," December 6, 1967, White House Central Files, EX NR 6, Box 13, Lyndon Baines Johnson Presidential Library. On the foreign policies of Interior, see Megan Black, *The Global Interior: Mineral Frontiers and American Power* (Cambridge, MA: Harvard University Press, 2018).

6. Stewart Udall to Lyndon Baines Johnson, "The Good News for the Day!" February 6, 1968. White House Central Files, EX NR 6, Box 13, Lyndon Baines Johnson Presidential Library.

7. Judith Stein, *Pivotal Decade: How the United States Traded Factories for Finance in the Seventies* (New Haven: Yale University Press, 2010); Daniel Sargent, *A Superpower Transformed: The Remaking of American Foreign Relations* (Oxford University Press, 2015); Meg Jacobs, *Panic at the Pump: The Energy Crisis and the Transformation of American Politics in the 1970s* (New York: Hill and Wang, 2016).

8. Among others, historians of oil have been closely attuned to this connection: Michael B. Stoff, *Oil, War, and American Security: The Search for a National Policy on Foreign Oil, 1941-1947* (New Haven: Yale University Press, 1980); David S. Painter, *Oil and the American Century: The Political Economy of U.S. Foreign Oil Policy, 1941-1954* (Baltimore, MD: Johns Hopkins University Press, 1986); Toby Craig Jones, *Desert Kingdom: How Oil and Water Forged Modern Saudi Arabia* (Cambridge, MA: Harvard University Press, 2010); Elisabetta Bini, Giuliano Garavini, and Frederico Romero, eds., *Oil Shock: The 1973 Crisis and Its Economic Legacy* (London: I.B. Tauris, 2016).

9. For a thoughtful discussion on grand strategy, political economy, and history, see Katherine C. Epstein, "A Useful Category of Analysis?," in Elizabeth Borgwardt, Christopher McKnight

Nichols, and Andrew Preston, eds., *Rethinking American Grand Strategy* (New York: Oxford University Press, 2021), 123–142.

10. Marc William Palen, *The "Conspiracy" of Free Trade: The Anglo-American Struggle over Empire and Economic Globalisation, 1846-1896* (Cambridge University Press, 2016); A. G. Hopkins, *American Empire: A Global History* (Princeton, NJ: Princeton University Press, 2018); Adam Tooze, *The Deluge: The Great War, America, and the Remaking of the Global Order* (New York: Penguin Books, 2014); Benjamin A. Coates, *Legalist Empire: International Law and American Foreign Relations in the Early Twentieth Century* (Oxford University Press, 2016); Thomas Zeiler, *Free Trade, Free World: The Advent of GATT* (Chapel Hill: University of North Carolina Press, 1999); Gabrielle Hecht, *Being Nuclear: Africans and the Global Uranium Trade* (Cambridge, MA: MIT Press, 2012).

11. William Appleman Williams, *The Tragedy of American Diplomacy* (Cleveland: World Publishing Company, 1959); Walter LaFeber, *The New Empire: An Interpretation of American Expansion, 1860-1898* (Ithaca, NY: Cornell University Press, 1963); Katherine C. Epstein, *Torpedo: Inventing the Military-Industrial Complex in the United States and Great Britain* (Cambridge, MA: Harvard University Press, 2014); William McNeil, *The Pursuit of Power: Technology, Armed Force, and Society Since A.D. 1000* (Chicago: University of Chicago Press, 1982); Mona Domosh, *American Commodities in an Age of Empire* (New York: Routledge, 2008).

12. Mary Renda, *Taking Haiti: Military Occupation and the Culture of U.S. Imperialism, 1915-1940* (Chapel Hill: University of North Carolina Press, 2001); Paul A. Kramer, *The Blood of Government: Race, Empire, the United States, and the Philippines* (Chapel Hill: University of North Carolina Press, 2006); Peter James Hudson, *Bankers and Empire: How Wall Street Colonized the Caribbean* (Chicago: University of Chicago Press, 2017); Bradley Simpson, *Economists with Guns: Authoritarian Development and U.S-Indonesian Relations, 1960-1968* (Stanford, CA: Stanford University Press, 2008); Samantha Iyer, "Colonial Population and the Idea of Development," *Comparative Studies in Society and History* 55, no. 1 (2013): 65–91; Julia Irwin, *Making the World Safe: The American Red Cross and a Nation's Humanitarian Awakening* (Oxford University Press, 2013); Hal Brands, *Making The Unipolar Moment: U.S. Foreign Policy and the Rise of the Post-Cold War Order* (Ithaca, NY: Cornell University Press, 2016).

13. Francis J. Gavin, *Gold, Dollars and Power: The Politics of International Monetary Relations, 1958-1971* (Chapel Hill: University of North Carolina Press, 2004); Marc-William Palen, "British Free Trade and the International Feminist Vision for Peace, c. 1846-1956," in David Thackery, Andrew Thompson, Richard Toye, eds., *Imagining Britain's Economic Future, c. 1800-1975* (London: Palgrave Macmillan, 2018), 115–131.

14. Emily Rosenberg, *Spreading the American Dream: American Economic and Cultural Expansion, 1890-1945* (New York, 1982); Walter LaFeber, "The Tension Between Democracy and Capitalism During the American Century," *Diplomatic History* 23, no. 2 (Spring 1999): 264–284; Jessica Elkind, *Aid Under Fire: Nation Building and the Vietnam War* (Lexington: University Press of Kentucky, 2016).

15. Erez Manela, *The Wilsonian Moment: Self-Determination and the International Origins of Anticolonial Nationalism* (New York: Oxford University Press, 2007); William Roger Louis and Ronald Robinson, "The Imperialism of Decolonization," *Journal of Imperial and Commonwealth History* 22, no. 3 (1994): 462–511.

16. Charles S. Maier, "The Politics of Productivity: Foundations of American International Economic Policy After World War II," *International Organization* 31, no. 4 (Autumn 1977): 607–633; Angus Burgin, *The Great Persuasion: Reinventing Free Markets Since the Depression*

(Cambridge, MA: Harvard University Press, 2012); Daniel Stedman-Jones, *Masters of the Universe: Hayek, Friedman, and the Birth of Neoliberal Politics* (Princeton, NJ: Princeton University Press, 2012); David Engerman, *Modernization from the Other Shore: American Intellectuals and the Romance of Russian Development* (Cambridge, MA: Harvard University Press, 2003); Justin Hart, *Empire of Ideas: The Origins of Public Diplomacy and the Transformation of U.S. Foreign Policy* (New York: Oxford University Press, 2013).

17. Lawrence Glickman, *Free Enterprise: An American History* (New Haven, CT: Yale University Press, 2019); Quinn Slobodian, *Globalists: The End of Empire and the Birth of Neoliberalism* (Cambridge, MA: Harvard University Press, 2018); Daniel T. Rodgers, *Age of Fracture* (Cambridge, MA: Belknap Press of Harvard University Press, 2011); Kim Phillips-Fein, *Invisible Hands: The Making of the Conservative Movement from the New Deal to Reagan* (New York: Norton, 2009).

18. Frank Costigliola, *Awkward Dominion: American Political, Economic, and Cultural Relations with Europe, 1919-1933* (Ithaca, NY: Cornell University Press, 1985); Jennifer Mittelstadt, *The Military Welfare State* (Cambridge, MA: Harvard University Press, 2015); Dara Orenstein, *Out of Stock: The Warehouse in the History of Capitalism* (Chicago: University of Chicago Press, 2019).

19. Arturo Escobar, *Encountering Development: The Making and Unmaking of the Third World* (Princeton, NJ: Princeton University Press, 1994); Emily Rosenberg, *Financial Missionaries to the World: The Politics and Culture of Dollar Diplomacy* (Durham, NC: Duke University Press, 2003); Michael Latham, *Modernization as Ideology: American Social Science and "Nation Building" in the Kennedy Era* (Chapel Hill: University of North Carolina Press, 2000); Nils Gilman, *Mandarins of the Future: Modernization Theory in Cold War America* (Baltimore, MD: Johns Hopkins University Press, 2003); Nicholas Cullather, *The Hungry World: America's Cold War Battle Against Poverty in Asia* (Cambridge, MA: Harvard University Press, 2013).

20. Barry Eichengreen, *The Populist Temptation: Economic Grievance and Political Reaction in the Modern Era* (New York: Oxford University Press, 2018); Tony Smith, *America's Mission: The United States and the Worldwide Struggle for Democracy* (Princeton, NJ: Princeton University Press, 2012); Mark Bradley, *Imagining Vietnam and America: The Making of Postcolonial Vietnam, 1919-1950* (Chapel Hill: University of North Carolina Press, 2003).

21. Michael J. Hogan, *The Marshall Plan: America, Britain, and the Reconstruction of Western Europe, 1947-1952* (Cambridge, UK: Cambridge University Press, 1987); Eric Helleiner, *Forgotten Foundations of Bretton Woods: International Development and the Making of the Postwar Order* (Ithaca, NY: Cornell University Press, 2014).

22. Eva-Maria Muschik, "The Art of Chameleon Politics: From Colonial Servant to International Development Expert," *Humanity: An International Journal of Human Rights and Development* 9, no. 2 (2018): 219–244; Amanda Kay McVety, *Enlightened Aid: U.S. Development as Foreign Policy in Ethiopia* (New York: Oxford University Press, 2012); Amy L. S. Staples, *The Birth of Development: How the World Bank, Food and Agriculture Organization and the World Health Organization Changed the World, 1945–1965* (Kent, OH: Kent State University Press, 2006).

23. Mark Blyth, *Austerity: The History of a Dangerous Idea* (New York: Oxford University Press, 2013); Greta Krippner, *Capitalizing on Crisis: The Political Origins of the Rise of Finance* (Cambridge, MA: Harvard University Press, 2011); Ngaire Woods, *The Globalizers: The IMF, the World Bank, and Their Borrowers* (Ithaca, NY: Cornell University Press, 2007).

24. Elizabeth Borgwardt, *A New Deal for the World: America's Vision for Human Rights* (Cambridge, MA: Harvard University Press, 2005); Daniel Immerwahr, *Thinking Small: The*

United States and the Lure of Community Development (Cambridge, MA: Harvard University Press, 2015); Patrick Sharma, *Robert McNamara's Other War: The World Bank and International Development* (Philadelphia: University of Pennsylvania Press, 2017).

25. Jason C. Parker, *Hearts, Minds, Voices: U.S. Cold War Public Diplomacy and the Formation of the Third World* (New York: Oxford University Press, 2016); Julio Moreno, *Yankee Don't Go Home: Mexican Nationalism, American Business Culture, and the Shaping of Modern Mexico, 1920-1950* (Chapel Hill: University of North Carolina Press, 2003); Nathan Citino, *Envisioning the Arab Future: Modernization in U.S.-Arab Relations, 1945-1967* (Cambridge, UK: Cambridge University Press, 2017).

26. Kara Moskowitz, "'Are You Planting Trees or Are You Planting People?' Squatter Resistance and International Development in the Making of a Kenyan Postcolonial Political Order (c. 1963–78)," *Journal of African History* 56, no. 1 (March 2015): 99–118; Gregory Brew, "'What They Need Is Management': American NGOs, the Second Seven Year Plan, and Economic Development in Iran, 1954-1963," *International History Review* 41, no. 1 (Jan. 2019): 1–22; Suzanna Reiss, *We Sell Drugs: The Alchemy of U.S. Empire* (Berkeley: University of California Press, 2014).

27. Thomas C. Field, *From Development to Dictatorship: Bolivia and the Alliance for Progress in the Kennedy Era* (Ithaca, NY: Cornell University Press, 2014); Charles A. Beard, *The Idea of National Interest: An Analytical Study in American Foreign Policy* (New York: Macmillan, 1934).

28. Barbara Weinstein, "Developing Inequality," *American Historical Review* 113, no. 1 (2008): 1–18; Max Paul Friedman, "Anti-Americanism and U.S. Foreign Relations," *Diplomatic History* 32, no. 4 (2008): 497--514; Jessica Chapman, *Cauldron of Resistance: Ngo Dinh Diem, the United States, and 1950s Southern Vietnam* (Ithaca, NY: Cornell University Press, 2013); Daniel Bessner, *Democracy in Exile: Hans Speier and the Rise of the Defense Intellectual* (Ithaca, NY: Cornell University Press, 2018).

29. Peter Schulman, *Coal and Empire: The Birth of Energy Security in Industrial America* (Johns Hopkins University Press, 2015); Christopher Jones, *Routes of Power: Energy and Modern America* (Cambridge, MA: Harvard University Press, 2015); Robert Vitalis, *America's Kingdom: Mythmaking on the Saudi Oil Frontier* (Stanford, CA: Stanford University Press, 2007); Julie Greene, *The Canal Builders: Making America's Empire at the Panama Canal* (New York: Penguin Press, 2009); Ashley Carse, *Beyond the Big Ditch: Politics, Ecology and Infrastructure at the Panama Canal* (Cambridge, MA: MIT Press, 2014).

30. Matthew K. Shannon, *Losing Hearts and Minds: American-Iranian Relations and International Education During the Cold War* (Ithaca, NY: Cornell University Press, 2017); Jason M. Colby, *The Business of Empire: United Fruit, Race, and U.S. Expansion in Central America* (Ithaca, NY: Cornell University Press, 2011).

31. Jennifer Bair, "On Difference and Capital: Gender and the Globalization of Production," *Signs: Journal of Women in Culture and Society* (2010): 203–226; Mae Ngai, Sophie Loy-Wilson, and Justin Jackson, "Crossing Islands and Oceans in Labor Histories of American Empire: Capital, Commodities, Coolies and Consumers," *International Labor and Working-Class History* (2017): 180–196; Elisabetta Bini, "From Colony to Oil Producer: U.S. Oil Companies and the Reshaping of Labor Relations in Libya During the Cold War," *Labor History* (2019): 44–56; April Merleaux, *Sugar and Civilization: American Empire and the Cultural Politics of Sweetness* (Chapel Hill: University of North Carolina Press, 2015); Beth Lew-Williams, *The Chinese Must Go: Violence, Exclusion, and the Making of the Alien in America* (Cambridge, MA: Harvard University Press, 2018).

32. Tehila Sasson, "Milking the Third World? Humanitarianism, Capitalism, and the Moral Economy of the Nestlé Boycott," *American Historical Review* 121, no. 4 (2016): 1196–1224; Stephen Macekura, *Of Limits and Growth: The Rise of Global Sustainable Development in the Twentieth Century* (Cambridge, UK: Cambridge University Press, 2015); Gavin Benke, *Risk and Ruin: Enron and the Culture of American Capitalism* (Philadelphia: University of Pennsylvania Press, 2018).

33. Patricia Clavin, *Securing the World Economy: The Reinvention of the League of Nations, 1920-1946* (New York: Oxford University Press, 2013); Gabrielle Hecht, ed., *Entangled Geographies: Empire and Technoplitics in the Global Cold War* (Cambridge, MA: MIT Press, 2011); Aihwa Ong, *Neoliberalism as Exception: Mutations in Citizenship and Sovereignty* (Durham, NC: Duke University Press, 2006); Joseph Hodge, *Triumph of the Expert: Agrarian Doctrines of Development and the Legacies of British Colonialism* (Athens: Ohio University Press, 2010); Frederick Cooper and Ann Laura Stoler, eds., *Tensions of Empire: Colonial Cultures in a Bourgeois World* (Berkeley: University of California Press, 1997).

34. Alan L. McPherson, *The Invaded: How Latin Americans and Their Allies Fought and Ended U.S. Occupations* (New York: Oxford University Press, 2014); Lior Sternfeld, "Iran Days in Egypt: Mosaddeq's Visit to Cairo in 1951," *British Journal of Middle Eastern Studies* 43, no. 1 (2016): 1–20.

35. Kenneth A. Rodman, *Sanctity vs. Sovereignty: The United States and the Nationalization of Natural Resource Investments* (New York: Columbia University Press, 1988); Tanya Harmer, *Allende's Chile and the Inter-American Cold War* (Chapel Hill: University of North Carolina Press, 2011); Richard H. Immerman, *The CIA in Guatemala: The Foreign Policy of Intervention* (Austin: University of Texas Press, 1982); Dustin Walcher, "Petroleum Pitfalls: The United States, Argentine Nationalism, and the 1963 Oil Crisis," *Diplomatic History* 37, no. 1 (Jan. 2013): 24–57.

36. J. A. Hobson, "The Scientific Basis of Imperialism," *Political Science Quarterly* 17, no. 3 (Sept. 1902): 472.

Chapter 1

The author thanks Paul Behringer and Cory Waltrip for their research assistance and the indispensable archivists Alba Lombardi, Archivo del Ministerio de Relaciones Exteriores y Culto, Buenos Aires (AMREC); Adolfo Froilan Mecca, Archivo General de la Nación, Buenos Aires (AGN); Jorge Fuentes, Archivo Histórico Genaro Estrada, Secretaría de Relaciones Exteriores, Mexico City (AHGE); Niurbis Ferrer, Archivo Nacional de la República de Cuba, Havana (ANRC); Françoise Watel and Eric Trouilleux at the Ministère des Affaires Etrangères, Paris (MAE); Andrew Murphy and Bill Brooke of the National Archives in Kew, UK (NA-K); and Marty McGann of the U.S. National Archives and Records Administration in College Park, Maryland (NARA).

1. Eduardo Galeano, *Open Veins of Latin America; Five Centuries of the Pillage of a Continent* (New York: Monthly Review Press, 1973).

2. Faisal Z. Ahmed, Laura Alfaro, and Noel Maurer, "Lawsuits and Empire: On the Enforcement of Sovereign Debt in Latin America," *Law and Contemporary Problems* 73, no. 39 (2010): 39–46.

3. Lars Schoultz, *Beneath the United States: A History of US Policy Toward Latin America* (Cambridge, MA: Harvard University Press, 1998).

4. Christopher R. W. Dietrich, *Diplomacy and Capitalism: The Political Economy of U.S. Foreign Relations* (Philadelphia: University of Pennsylvania Press, 2022), 16.

5. Hans Schmidt, *The United States Occupation of Haiti, 1915-1934* (New Brunswick, NJ: Rutgers University Press, 1995 [1971]), 118.

6. Dietrich, *Diplomacy and Capitalism* (Philadelphia: University of Pennsylvania Press, 2022), 17.

7. Carlos Calvo, *Le droit international théorique et pratique*, 4th ed. (Paris: Guillaumin et Cie, 1887 [1868]), 266.

8. D. R. Shea, *The Calvo Clause: A Problem of Inter-American and International Law and Diplomacy* (Minneapolis: University of Minnesota Press, 1955), 18ff. For a different interpretation of this process that emphasizes the transnational intellectual links among diplomats who sought to contest U.S. hegemony by "Pan-Americanizing the Monroe Doctrine," see Juan Pablo Scarfi, "In the Name of the Americas: The Pan-American Redefinition of the Monroe Doctrine and the Emerging Language of American International Law in the Western Hemisphere, 1898-1933," *Diplomatic History* 40 (2016), and *The Hidden History of International Law in the Americas: Empire and Legal Networks* (New York: Oxford University Press, 2017).

9. Leandro Morgenfeld, *Vecinos en conflicto. Argentina y Estados Unidos en las Conferencias Panamericanas (1880–1955)* (Buenos Aires: Ediciones Continente, 2011), 84–86; Pablo Yankelevich, *La diplomacia imaginaria: Argentina y la revolución mexicana, 1910–1916* (Mexico City: Acervo Histórico Diplomático, 1994), 28–30.

10. Luis María Drago, *La República Argentina y el caso de Venezuela* (Buenos Aires: Coni Hermanos, 1903). See also Alberto A. Conil Paz, *Historia de la Doctrina Drago* (Buenos Aires: Academia Nacional de Derecho y Ciencias Sociales de Buenos Aires, 1975), and Gerardo Bra, *La doctrina Drago* (Buenos Aires: Centro Editor de América Latina, 1990).

11. Theodore Roosevelt, "Annual Message to Congress," 6 December 1904, www.ourdocuments.gov/doc.php?flash=true&doc=56&page=transcript. Emphasis added.

12. Drago to Martín García Mérou, 29 December 1902, microfilm M47, reel 4, "Notes from the Argentine Legation in US to Department of State, 1811-1906," NARA.

13. Penfield to Hay, 5 February 1903, microfilm M47, reel 4, "Notes from the Argentine Legation in US to Department of State, 1811-1906," NARA.

14. Isidro Fabela to Eduardo Hay, "Memoranda sobre diversos temas del programa de la Conferencia Interamericana de Consolidación de la Paz," 26 October 1936, L-E-337, Conferencia Interamericana sobre la Consolidación de la Paz, AHGE.

15. Louis A. Pérez, *Cuba Under the Platt Amendment 1902-1934* (University of Pittsburgh Press, 1986), 44.

16. There would be voices raised against Dollar Diplomacy in the United States, as well. For excellent treatments of the intersection of private capital and public force in the Dollar Diplomacy era, see Emily Rosenberg, *Financial Missionaries to the World: The Politics and Culture of Dollar Diplomacy, 1900-1930* (Cambridge, MA: Harvard University Press, 1999); Mary Renda, *Taking Haiti: Military Occupation and the Culture of U.S. Imperialism, 1915-1940* (Chapel Hill: University of North Carolina Press, 2001); Cyrus Veeser, *A World Safe for Capitalism: Dollar Diplomacy and America's Rise to Global Power* (New York: Columbia University Press, 2007); Ellen D. Tillman, *Dollar Diplomacy by Force: Nation-Building and Resistance in the Dominican Republic* (Chapel Hill: University of North Carolina Press, 2016); Peter James Hudson, *Bankers and Empire: How Wall Street Colonized the Caribbean* (Chicago: University of Chicago Press, 2017).

17. Elihu Root, Robert Bacon, and James Brown Scott, eds., *Latin America and the United States: Addresses by Elihu Root* (Cambridge, MA: Harvard University Press, 1917), 11.

18. Root, Bacon, and Scott, 86–93.

19. Bruwaert to Bourgeois, 12 September 1906, Argentina, 137CPCOM/8, Correspondance politique et commerciale, Nouvelle Série, MAE, Paris.

20. Root, Bacon, and Scott, 97–102. Emphasis added.

21. U.S. Department of State, *Papers Relating to the Foreign Relations of the United States* (Washington, DC: Government Printing Office, 1909), II: 1205.

22. Durand to Grey, 31 August 1906, 371/158, FO, NA-K; "Note on General Points Which Might Be Raised at the Hague Conference," Dec. 14, 1906, 881/9328, FO, NA-K, London.

23. Fry to Grey, 23 July 1907, Second Peace Conference at The Hague, 881/9061, FO, NA-K.

24. Reginald C. McGrane, *Foreign Bondholders and American State Debts* (New York: Macmillan, 1935), 202. See also Amos S. Hershey, "The Venezuelan Affair in the Light of International Law," *American Law Register* 51, no. 5 (1903): 249–267.

25. Andrew Newcombe and Lluís Paradell, *Law and Practice of Investment Treaties: Standards of Treatment* (London: Kluwer Law International, 2009), 13–14.

26. The phrase is from Steven Palmer's study of public health innovation. See his *From Popular Medicine to Medical Populism: Doctors, Healers, and Public Power in Costa Rica, 1800-1940* (Durham, NC: Duke University Press, 2003), 157.

27. Rubén Darío, *Prosa política (Las repúblicas americanas)* (Madrid: Mundo Latino, 1911), 3.

28. Godoy to Secretaría de Relaciones Exteriores (SRE), "Entrevista con el Señor Presidente Roosevelt," 5 October 1905, L-E-1846, AHGE, Mexico City; Casasus to SRE, "Entrevista con el Señor Presidente—Doctrina Monroe," 16 November 1905, L-E-1846, AHGE. See also Jürgen Buchenau, *In the Shadow of the Giant: The Making of Mexico's Central America Policy, 1876–1930* (Tuscaloosa: University of Alabama Press, 1996), 60–61.

29. "Notable Address by Woodrow Wilson," *Pan American Union Bulletin* 37 (1913): 684–687. Known as Wilson's Mobile speech, it was delivered before the Southern Commercial Congress on 27 October 1913 at Mobile, Alabama.

30. Woodrow Wilson, "Address at Independence Hall: The Meaning of Liberty," 4 July 1914, http://www.presidency.ucsb.edu/ws/?pid=65381.

31. Leslie Bethell, *The Cambridge History of Latin America: 1870-1930* (New York: Cambridge University Press, 1986), 107.

32. Quoted in Isidro Fabela, *La política interior y exterior de Carranza* (Mexico City: Editorial Jus, 1979), 221.

33. Isidro Fabela to Eduardo Hay, "La Doctrina Carranza como tema de la conferencia de Buenos Aires," 6 April 1936, L-E-333, Conferencia Interamericana sobre la Consolidación de la Paz, AHGE.

34. Ahmed, Alfaro, and Maurer, "Lawsuits and Empire," 45.

35. Kellogg to Morgan, 11 May 1927, FRUS 1927, I: 367–368.

36. Donativos y Remisiones. Fondo Orestes Ferrara. Caja 406. Número 18, 161, ANRC, Havana.

37. Ibid.

38. Scott and Reeves to Kellogg, 10 June 1927, FRUS 1927 I: 394.

39. Ibid., 395–396.

40. "Compte-Rendu" [January 1928], Caja 0027, Asuntos Políticos, Conferencias Panamericanas, AMREC.

41. Hipólito Yrigoyen, *Pueblo y gobierno: La función argentina en el mundo. Americanismo*, vol. VIII (Buenos Aires: Editorial Raigal, 1956), 112–115.

42. Yrigoyen, *Pueblo y gobierno*, VIII: 118.

43. Quoted in Alexander DeConde, *Herbert Hoover's Latin-American Policy* (Stanford, CA: Stanford University Press, 1951), 59.

44. Alan McPherson, *The Invaded: How Latin Americans and Their Allies Fought and Ended US Occupations* (New York: Oxford University Press, 2014).

45. Puig to Saavedra Lamas, 29 August 1933, L-E-246, Séptima Conferencia Internacional Panamericana, AHGE.

46. J. M. Puig Casauranc to Saavedra Lamas, 29 August 1933, Caja 0030, Asuntos Políticos, Conferencias Panamericanas, AMREC.

47. Puig circular telegram, 11 September 1933, L-E-246, Séptima Conferencia Internacional Panamericana, AHGE.

48. Coral Aguirre, *Cartas del Sur. La correspondencia Victoria Ocampo-Alfonso Reyes y sus implicaciones en el perfil cultural de América Latina* (Nuevo León, Mexico: Universidad Autónoma de Nuevo León, 2012), 67.

49. Puig to Alfonso Reyes, 14 August 1933, L-E-246, Séptima Conferencia Internacional Panamericana, AHGE.

50. Reyes to Puig, 18 August 1933, L-E-246, Séptima Conferencia Internacional Panamericana, AHGE, and Puig to Reyes, 2 September 1933, L-E-246, Séptima Conferencia Internacional Panamericana, AHGE.

51. Gonzalo de la Parra, "Puntos de Vista," *El Universal*, 27 December 1935.

52. Puig, "Expocisión verbal de Puig," 4 Decemebr 1933, Caja 39, Exp. 253, Secretaria Particular, AHGE.

53. Christy Thornton, "Sovereignty and Solidarity: The Mexican Revolution and the Origins of the Postwar Order, 1919-1948" (Ph.D. diss., New York University, 2015).

54. Carlos Marichal, *A Century of Debt Crises in Latin America: From Independence to the Great Depression, 1820-1930* (Princeton, NJ: Princeton University Press, 1989), 212–213.

55. Reyes to Puig, 4 September 1933, L-E-246, Séptima Conferencia Internacional Panamericana, AHGE.

56. On the key role of Latin American delegates in getting economic and social rights written into the charter of the United Nations at the 1945 San Francisco Conference, as well as more broadly the South-North impact of Latin American progressive thought in this era, see Greg Grandin, "Your Americanism and Mine: Americanism and Anti-Americanism in the Americas," *American Historical Review* 111, no. 4 (October 2006): 1042–1066.

57. Isidro Fabela to Eduardo Hay, "Memoranda sobre diversos temas del programa de la Conferencia Interamericana de Consolidación de la Paz," 26 October 1936, L-E-337, Conferencia Interamericana sobre la Consolidación de la Paz, AHGE.

58. Samuel Guy Inman, *Inter-American Conferences, 1826–1954: History and Problems* (University Press of Washington, DC, 1965), and G. Pope Atkins, *Encyclopedia of the Inter-American System* (Westport, CT: Greenwood, 1997), 102.

59. David Haglund, *Latin America and the Transformation of US Strategic Thought* (Albuquerque: University of New Mexico Press, 1984), 45.

60. Daniels to Roosevelt, 11 April 1938, Roosevelt Papers, PSF, Box 44, Diplomatic Correspondence, FDRL, quoted in John J. Dwyer, "The End of US Intervention in Mexico: Franklin Roosevelt and the Expropriation of American-Owned Agricultural Property," *Presidential Studies Quarterly* 28, no. 3 (1998): 495–509.

61. Press conference 614-A, 12 January 1940, Press Confs, XV, 78, FDR Library, Hyde Park, NY.

62. Isidro Fabela to SRE, 28 April 1936, L-E-333, Conferencia Interamericana sobre la Consolidación de la Paz, AHGE.

63. 1936 memo quoted in Isidro Fabela, *Intervención* (Mexico City: Universidad Nacional Autónoma de México, 1991 [1957]), 235.

64. Dietrich, *Diplomacy and Capitalism* (Philadelphia: University of Pennsylvania Press, 2022), 30.

Chapter 2

1. Smedley D. Butler, "America's Armed Forces, 2. 'In Time of Peace': The Army," *Common Sense* 4, no. 11 (Nov. 1935): 8–12.

2. Examples include Andrew Bacevich, *American Empire: The Realities and Consequences of U.S. Diplomacy* (Cambridge, MA: Harvard University Press, 2002), 280, note 37; Howard Zinn and Anthony Arnove, *Voices of a People's History of the United States*, 2nd edition (New York: Seven Stories Press, 2009), 252; Michael Mann, *The Sources of Social Power. Volume 3: Global Empires and Revolution, 1890-1945* (Cambridge, UK: Cambridge University Press, 2012), 97; Laurent Dubois, *Haiti: Aftershocks of History* (New York: Holt, 2012), 246; Marilyn B. Young, "'I Was Thinking, as I Often Do These Days, of War': The United States in the Twenty-First Century," *Diplomatic History* 36, no. 1 (Jan. 2012), 3.

3. Butler, "America's Armed Forces," p. 8.

4. On liberal capitalism and its trials and triumph in the twentieth century, see Eric Hobsbawm, *Age of Extremes: The Short Twentieth Century, 1914-1991* (London: Michael Joseph, 1994). See also John Gray, *False Dawn: The Delusions of Global Capitalism* (London: Granta, 2009 [1998]); Nancy Fraser and Rachel Jaeggi, *Capitalism: A Conversation in Critical Theory* (Cambridge,UK: Polity, 2018), and Branko Milanovic, *Capitalism, Alone: The Future of the System That Rules the World* (Cambridge, MA: Belknap Press of Harvard University Press, 2019).

5. Some of the most exciting recent work on the capitalism of the era has problematized the liberalism of liberal capitalism. See April Merleaux, *Sugar and Civilization: American Empire and the Cultural Politics of Sweetness* (Chapel Hill: University of North Carolina Press, 2015); Marc-William Palen, *The "Conspiracy" of Free Trade: The Anglo-American Struggle over Empire and Economic Globalization, 1846-1896* (Cambridge, UK: Cambridge University Press, 2016); A. G. Hopkins, *American Empire: A Global History* (Princeton, NJ: Princeton University Press, 2018). See also Eric Helleiner, "Economic Nationalism as a Challenge to Economic Liberalism? Lessons from the 19th Century," *International Studies Quarterly* 46, no. 3 (Sept. 2002): 307–329. On liberalism and empire and capitalism, see Uday Singh Mehta, *Liberalism and Empire: A Study in Nineteenth Century British Liberal Thought* (Chicago: University of Chicago Press, 1999); Jennifer Pitts, *A Turn to Empire: The Rise of Imperial Liberalism in Britain and France* (Princeton, NJ: Princeton University Press, 2005); Domenico Losurdo, *Liberalism: A Counter-History*, trans. Gregory Elliott (London: Verso, 2011); Greg Grandin, "The Liberal Traditions in the Americas: Rights, Sovereignty, and the Origins of Liberal Multilateralism," *American Historical Review* 117, no. 1 (Feb. 2012): 68–91; Andrew Sartori, *Liberalism in Empire: An Alternative History* (Berkeley: University of California Press, 2014); Nikhil Pal Singh, "Liberalism," in Bruce Burgett and Glenn Hendler, eds., *Keywords for American Cultural Studies*, second edition (New York: New York University Press, 2014).

6. On the history of globalization, see A. G. Hopkins, ed., *Globalization in World History* (London: Pimlico, 2002); Jürgen Osterhammel, *Globalization: A Short History* (Princeton, NJ: Princeton University Press, 2005); Jeffry A. Frieden, *Global Capitalism: Its Fall and Rise in the Twentieth Century* (New York: Norton, 2006); Emily S. Rosenberg, ed., *A World Connecting, 1870-1945* (Cambridge, MA: Belknap Press of Harvard University Press, 2012); Roland Wenzlhuemer, *Connecting the Nineteenth-Century World: The Telegraph and Globalization* (Cambridge, UK: Cambridge University Press, 2013).

7. For a sense of the vast literature on questions of imperialism, see Wolfgang J. Mommsen, *Theories of Imperialism*, trans. P. S. Falla (New York: Random House, 1980); Mommsen and Jürgen Osterhammel, eds., *Imperialism and After* (Boston: Allen & Unwin, 1986); Carl Parrini, "Theories of Imperialism," in Lloyd C. Gardner, ed., *Redefining the Past: Essays in Diplomatic History in Honor of William Appleman Williams* (Corvallis: Oregon State University Press, 1986); E. J. Hobsbawm, *The Age of Empire, 1875-1914* (London: Weidenfeld & Nicolson, 1987), 67–74; Frank Ninkovich, "The United States and Imperialism," in Robert D. Schulzinger, ed., *A Companion to American Foreign Relations* (Malden, MA: Blackwell, 2003), 79–102; John Darwin, *After Tamerlane: The Global History of Empires Since 1405* (London: Allen Lane, 2007); Ann Stoler, Carole McGranahan, and Peter C. Perdue, eds., *Imperial Formations* (Santa Fe, NM: School for Advanced Research Press, 2007); Mark F. Proudman, "Words for Scholars: The Semantics of 'Imperialism,'" *Journal of the Historical Society* 8, no. 3 (Sept. 2008): 395–433; Jane Burbank and Frederick Cooper, *Empires in World History: Power and the Politics of Difference* (Princeton, NJ: Princeton University Press, 2010); Hopkins, *American Empire*; Daniel Immerwahr, *How to Hide an Empire: A History of the Greater United States* (New York: Farrar, Straus and Giroux, 2019). See also Emily Rosenberg, "'The Empire' Strikes Back," *Reviews in American History* 16, no. 4 (1988): 585–590; Paul A. Kramer, "Power and Connection: Imperial Histories of the United States in the World," *American Historical Review* 116, no. 5 (Dec. 2011): 1348–1391.

8. The classic statement is J. A. Hobson, *Imperialism: A Study* (London: James Nisbet & Co., 1902).

9. In addition to Hobson, consider Rudolf Hilferding, *Finance Capital: A Study in the Latest Phase of Capitalist Development*, trans. Morris Watnick and Sam Gordon (London: Routledge & Kegan Paul, 1981); Rosa Luxemburg, *The Accumulation of Capital*, trans. Agnes Schwarzchild (London: Routledge & Kegan Paul, 1951); V. I. Lenin, *Imperialism. The Highest Stage of Capitalism: A Popular Outline* (1917; New York: International Publishers, 1939); Hannah Arendt, *The Origins of Totalitarianism* (New York: Harcourt, Brace, 1951).

10. See D. A. Farnie, *East and West of Suez: The Suez Canal in History, 1854-1956* (Oxford, UK: Clarendon Press, 1969), 259–470; Tony Ballantyne and Antoinette Burton, "Empires and the Reach of the Global," in Rosenberg, ed., *World Connecting*, 285–434. See also Shigeru Akita, ed., *Gentlemanly Capitalism, Imperialism, and Global History* (Houndsmills, UK: Palgrave Macmillan, 2002); A. G. Hopkins, "Globalization With and Without Empires: From Bali to Labrador," in Hopkins, ed., *Globalization in World History*, 221–243; C. A. Bayly, *The Birth of the Modern World, 1780-1914: Global Connections and Comparisons* (Malden, MA: Blackwell, 2004); Manu Goswami, *Producing India: From Colonial Economy to National Space* (Chicago: University of Chicago Press, 2004); Mark Metzler, *Lever of Empire: The International Gold Standard and the Crisis of Liberalism in Prewar Japan* (Berkeley: University of California Press, 2006); Kristin L. Hoganson, *Consumers' Imperium: The Global Production of American Domesticity, 1865-1920* (Chapel Hill: University of North Carolina Press, 2007); Sugata Bose, *A Hundred Horizons: The Indian Ocean in the Age of Global Empire* (Cambridge, MA: Harvard University

Press, 2009); Ritu Birla, *Stages of Capital: Law, Culture, and Market Governance in Late Colonial India* (Durham, NC: Duke University Press, 2009); Jun Uchida, *Brokers of Empire: Japanese Settler Colonialism in Korea, 1876-1945* (Cambridge, MA: Harvard University Press, 2011); Manu Karuka, *Empire's Tracks: Indigenous Nations, Chinese Workers, and the Transcontinental Railroad* (Oakland: University of California Press, 2019).

11. On soldiers and empire, see Brian McAllister Linn, *Guardians of Empire: The U.S. Army and the Pacific, 1902-1940* (Chapel Hill: University of North Carolina Press, 1997); Mary A. Renda, *Taking Haiti: Military Occupation and the Culture of U.S. Imperialism, 1915-1940* (Chapel Hill: University of North Carolina Press, 2001); Paul A. Kramer, "Race-Making and Colonial Violence in the U.S. Empire: The Philippine-American War as Race War," *Diplomatic History* 30, no. 2 (April 2006): 169–210; Kyle Kajihiro, "The Militarizing of Hawai'i: Occupation, Accommodation, and Resistance," in Candace Fujikane and Jonathan Y. Okamura, eds., *Asian Settler Colonialism: From Local Governance to the Habits of Everyday Life in Hawai'i* (Honolulu: University of Hawai'i Press, 2008), 170–194; Christopher Capozzola, "Minutemen for the World: Empire, Citizenship, and the National Guard, 1903-1924," in Alfred W. McCoy and Francisco Scarano, eds., *Colonial Crucible: Empire in the Making of the Modern American State* (Madison: University of Wisconsin Press, 2009), 421–430; Alfred W. McCoy, *Policing America's Empire: The United States, the Philippines, and the Rise of the Surveillance State* (Madison: University of Wisconsin Press, 2009); Joshua B. Freeman, "Militarism, Empire, and Labor Relations: The Case of Brice P. Disque," *International Labor and Working-Class History* 80 (Fall 2011): 103–120; Simeon Man, *Soldiering through Empire: Race and the Making of the Decolonizing Pacific* (Oakland: University of California Press, 2018); Christopher Capozzola, *Bound by War: How the United States and the Philippines Built America's First Pacific Century* (New York: Basic Books, 2020).

12. For a recent study of imperialism attentive to the roles of violence, see Andrew J. Rotter, *Empire of the Senses: Bodily Encounters in Imperial India and the Philippines* (New York: Oxford University Press, 2019).

13. On commodity chains, see Steven C. Topik and Allen Wells, "Commodity Chains in a Global Economy," in Rosenberg, ed., *World Connecting*, 593–814.

14. Hans Schmidt, *Maverick Marine: General Smedley D. Butler and the Contradictions of American Military History* (Lexington: University of Kentucky Press, 1998), 6–7.

15. Lowell Thomas, *Old Gimlet Eye: The Adventures of Smedley D. Butler* (New York: Farrar & Rinehart, 1933), 6–7. On the relationship of white manhood to the war, see Kristin L. Hoganson, *Fighting for American Manhood: How Gender Politics Provoked the Spanish-American and Philippine-American Wars* (New Haven, CT: Yale University Press, 1998). See also Gail Bederman, *Manliness and Civilization: A Cultural History of Gender and Race in the United States, 1880-1917* (Chicago: University of Chicago Press, 1995); and Jackson Lears, *Rebirth of a Nation: The Making of Modern America, 1877-1920* (New York: HarperCollins, 2009). On turn-of-the-century Cuba, see Louis A. Pérez, Jr., *Cuba Between Empires, 1878-1902* (Pittsburgh: University of Pittsburgh Press, 1983); and Pérez, *The War of 1898: The United States and Cuba in History and Historiography* (Chapel Hill: University of North Carolina Press, 1998).

16. Thomas, *Old Gimlet Eye*, 13.

17. See Paul A. Kramer, *The Blood of Government: Race, Empire, the United States, and the Philippines* (Chapel Hill: University of North Carolina Press, 2006).

18. Recent scholarship on U.S. colonialism in the Philippines includes Yoshiko Nagano, *State and Finance in the Philippines, 1898-1941: The Mismanagement of an American Colony* (Singapore: National University of Singapore Press, 2015); Rebecca Tinio McKenna, *American*

Imperial Pastoral: The Architecture of US Colonialism in the Philippines (Chicago: University of Chicago Press, 2017); Rotter, *Empires of the Senses*; and Capozzola, *Bound by War*. See also Julian Go and Anne L. Foster, eds., *The American Colonial State in the Philippines: Global Perspectives* (Durham, NC: Duke University Press, 2003).

19. Owen and Eleanor Lattimore, *The Making of Modern China: A Short History* (New York: Norton, 1944), 112; and Rebecca E. Karl, *The Magic of Concepts: History and the Economic in Twentieth-Century China* (Durham, NC: Duke University Press, 2017).

20. Scott Nearing and Joseph Freeman, *Dollar Diplomacy: A Study in American Imperialism* (New York: B. W. Huebsch and the Viking Press, 1925), 173; and Walter LaFeber, *The New Cambridge History of American Foreign Relations. Volume 2: The American Search for Opportunity, 1865-1913* (Cambridge, UK: Cambridge University Press, 2013), 141.

21. George Marion, *Bases & Empire: A Chart of American Expansion*, 3rd edition (New York: Fairplay Publishers, 1949), 86.

22. Owen J. Lynch, "The U.S. Constitution and Philippine Colonialism: An Enduring and Unfortunate Legacy," in Alfred W. McCoy and Francisco A. Scarano, eds., *Colonial Crucible: Empire in the Making of the Modern American State* (Madison: University of Wisconsin Press, 2009), 355.

23. Schmidt, *Maverick Marine*, 11–12.

24. On the Boxer Rising, see Joseph W. Esherick, *The Origins of the Boxer Uprising* (Berkeley: University of California Press, 1987); Paul A. Cohen, *History in Three Keys: The Boxers as Event, Experience, and Myth* (New York: Columbia University Press, 1997); Lanxin Xiang, *The Origins of the Boxer War: A Multinational Study* (Oxfordshire, UK: Routledge, 2003); Robert Bickers and R. G. Tiedemann, eds., *The Boxers, China, and the World* (Lanham, MD: Rowman & Littlefield, 2007); Susanne Kuss, *German Colonial Wars and the Context of Military Violence*, trans. Andrew Smith (Cambridge, MA: Harvard University Press, 2017), 15–36. See also Peter Duus, Ramon H. Myers, and Mark R. Peattie, eds., *The Japanese Informal Empire in China, 1895-1937* (Princeton, NJ: Princeton University Press, 1989); Akira Iriye, *China and Japan in the Global Setting* (Cambridge, MA: Harvard University Press, 1992); and Rebecca E. Karl, *Staging the World: Chinese Nationalism at the Turn of the Twentieth Century* (Durham, NC: Duke University Press, 2002).

25. See C. K. Leung, *China: Railway Patterns and National Goals* (Chicago: University of Chicago Department of Geography, 1980), 17–49.

26. On the pre-Shimoneseki Chinese economy, see Takeshi Hamashita, *China, East Asia and the Global Economy: Regional and Historical Perspectives* (New York: Routledge, 2008). See also William T. Rowe, *China's Last Empire: The Great Qing* (Cambridge, MA: Belknap Press of Harvard University Press, 2009); and Charles Holcombe, *A History of East Asia: From the Origins of Civilization to the Twenty-First Century*, 2nd edition (Cambridge, UK: Cambridge University Press, 2017), 220–231.

27. Frank H. H. King, *The History of the Hongkong and Shanghai Banking Corporation. Volume 2: The Hongkong Bank in the Period of Imperialism and War, 1895-1918: Wayfoong, the Focus of Wealth* (Cambridge, UK: Cambridge University Press, 1988), 239–312.

28. Thomas J. McCormick, *China Market: America's Quest for Informal Empire, 1893-1901* (Chicago: Quadrangle Books, 1967), 67–68.

29. E. J. Hobsbawm, *The Age of Empire, 1875-1914* (London: Weidenfeld & Nicolson, 1987), 281.

30. Thomas, *Old Gimlet Eye*, 69.

31. Schmidt, *Maverick Marine*, 23.

32. Ibid., 24; Thomas, *Old Gimlet Eye*, 75.

33. Jonathan D. Spence, *The Search for Modern China* (New York: Norton, 1990), 235. See King, *History of the Hongkong and Shanghai Banking Corporation*, 313–377.

34. Or, again, even the category of "market." On distinguishing modern "external" markets from local market(place)s, see Karl Polanyi, *The Great Transformation: The Political and Economic Origins of Our Time* (Boston: Beacon Press, 2001).

35. Quoted in David Milne, *Worldmaking: The Art and Science of American Diplomacy* (New York: Farrar, Straus and Giroux, 2015), 64.

36. On the discourse of sexual aggression and gender domination that the U.S. imperialists trafficked in, see Hoganson, *Fighting for American Manhood,* and Renda, *Taking Haiti.* See also Nerissa S. Balce, "The Filipina's Breast: Savagery, Docility, and the Erotics of the American Empire," *Social Text* 24, no. 2 (June 2006): 89–110. To think of Butler's comments in their world historical context, see Antoinette Burton, ed., *Gender, Sexuality, and Colonial Modernities* (London: Routledge, 1999); Philippa Levine, ed., *Gender and Empire* (Oxford, UK: Oxford University Press, 2004); Tony Ballantyne and Antoinette Burton, eds., *Bodies in Contact: Rethinking Colonial Encounters in World History* (Durham, NC: Duke University Press, 2005), of which see in particular Jennifer L. Morgan, "Male Travelers, Female Bodies, and the Gendering of Racial Ideology, 1500-1700," 54–66, and Mire Koikari, "Gender, Power, and U.S. Imperialism: The Occupation of Japan, 1945-1952," 342–362.

37. Thomas, *Old Gimlet Eye*, 126, 132.

38. Schmidt, *Maverick Marine*, 40.

39. Thomas D. Schoonover, *The United States in Central America, 1860-1911: Episodes of Social Imperialism and Imperial Rivalry in the World System* (Durham, NC: Duke University Press, 1991), 141–143.

40. U.S. Congress, Senate, Subcommittee of the Committee on Foreign Relations, *Foreign Loans: Hearings*, 69th Cong., 2nd sess., Jan. 26, 1927, p. 42.

41. Horacio Blanco Fombona, *Crímenes del imperialismo norteamericano* (Mexico City: Ediciones "Churubusco" [1927]), 5; Thomas, *Old Gimlet Eye*, 127.

42. John Kenneth Turner, "Nicaragua," *The Nation* 114 (May 31, 1922): 646. See Michael Gismondi and Jeremy Mouat, "Merchants, Mining and Concessions on Nicaragua's Mosquito Coast: Reassessing the American Presence, 1895-1912," *Journal of Latin American Studies* 34, no. 4 (Nov. 2002): 845–879.

43. Smedley D. Butler to Father, June 10, 1910, Bluefields, Nicaragua, box 3, Smedley D. Butler Family Correspondence, Special Collections, Green Library, Stanford University (hereafter SDBFC).

44. Schmidt, *Maverick Marine*, 39.

45. Smedley D. Butler to Father, July 14, 1910, Bluefields, Nicaragua, box 3, SDBFC.

46. Smedley D. Butler to Father, June 10, 1910, Bluefields, Nicaragua, box 3, SDBFC.

47. Subcommittee, *Foreign Loans*, 35.

48. See Emily Rosenberg, "Foundations of U.S. International Financial Power: Gold Standard Diplomacy, 1900-1905," *Business History Review* 59, no. 2 (Summer 1985): 169–202; Emily S. Rosenberg, *Financial Missionaries to the World: The Politics and Culture of Dollar Diplomacy, 1900-1930* (Durham, NC: Duke University Press, 2003); Eric Helleiner, *The Making of National Money: Territorial Currencies in Historical Perspective* (Ithaca, NY: Cornell University Press, 2003), 163–185. See also Edwin Kemmerer, *Modern Currency Reforms* (New York: Macmillan, 1916).

49. Butler, "America's Armed Forces," 8.

50. On the Knox-Castrillo convention, see Richard D. Challener, *Admirals, Generals, and American Foreign Policy, 1898-1914* (Princeton, NJ: Princeton University Press, 1973), 302. On the U.S. intervention in Nicaragua, see Nearing and Freeman, *Dollar Diplomacy*; Charles A. Beard, *The Idea of National Interest: An Analytical Study in American Foreign Policy* (New York: Macmillan, 1934); Rosenberg, *Financial Missionaries to the World*; and Michael Gobat, *Confronting the American Dream: Nicaragua Under U.S. Imperial Rule* (Durham, NC: Duke University Press, 2005), esp. 100–122, 125–127.

51. *Papers Relating to the Foreign Relations of the United States, 1912* (Washington, 1919), 1075 (hereafter FRUS).

52. Turner, "Nicaragua," 647.

53. "Butler Declares Marines 'Always Win' in Nicaragua," *Pittsburgh Post-Gazette*, Dec. 6, 1929, p. 11.

54. Smedley Darlington Butler, in Anne Cipriano Venzon, ed., *The Letters of a Leatherneck, 1898-1931* (New York: Praeger, 1992), 132; Schmidt, *Maverick Marine*, 54.

55. "Butler Assails Army as Bank Bill Collector," *New York Herald Tribune*, Jan. 2, 1933, p. 19; *Nation*, Jan. 18, 1933, p. 49.

56. Peter James Hudson, *Bankers and Empire: How Wall Street Colonized the Caribbean* (Chicago: University of Chicago Press, 2017), 84.

57. Suzy Castor, *La ocupación norteamericana de Haití y sus consecuencias (1915-1934)* (Mexico City: Siglo Veintiuno Editores, 1971), 98.

58. U.S. Congress, Senate, Select Committee on Haiti and Santo Domingo, *Inquiry into Occupation and Administration of Haiti and Santo Domingo: Hearings*, 67th Cong., 1st and 2nd sess., Aug. 5, 1921, vol. 1, p. 4.

59. Robert Lansing to Woodrow Wilson, August 2, 1915, in Arthur S. Link, ed., *The Papers of Woodrow Wilson*, vol. 34 (Princeton, NJ: Princeton University Press, 1980), 60.

60. FRUS, 1914 (Washington, 1922), 365–369.

61. The specifics of the gold removal are given in fascinating detail in Hudson, *Bankers and Empire*, 104.

62. Nearing and Freeman, *Dollar Diplomacy*, 136.

63. Hans van de Ven, *Breaking with the Past: The Maritime Customs Service and the Global Origins of Modernity in China* (New York: Columbia University Press, 2014), 10.

64. Challener, *Admirals, Generals, and American Foreign Policy*, 132–133; Cyrus Veeser, *A World Safe for Capitalism: Dollar Diplomacy and America's Rise to Global Power* (New York: Columbia University Press, 2002).

65. J. Fred Rippy, "The Initiation of the Customs Receivership in the Dominican Republic," *Hispanic American Historical Review* 17, no. 4 (Nov. 1937), 442.

66. Select Committee, *Inquiry*, 21. See Alex Dupuy, *Haiti in the World Economy: Class, Race, and Underdevelopment Since 1700* (Boulder, CO: Westview Press, 1989).

67. See Georges Anglade, *Atlas critique d'Haïti* (Montreal: ERCE & CRC, 1982); Gérard Barthélemy, *Le pays en dehors: Essai sur l'univers rural haïtien* (Port-au-Prince: Deschamps, 1990), esp. 20–23; Mimi Sheller, *Democracy After Slavery: Black Publics and Peasant Radicalism in Haiti and Jamaica* (Gainesville: University Press of Florida, 2000); Jean Casimir, *La culture opprimée* (Delmas, Haiti: Impr. Lakay, 2001); Dubois, *Haiti*; Kate Hodgson, "'Internal Harmony, Peace to the Outside World': Imagining Community in Nineteenth-Century Haiti," *Paragraph* 37, no. 2 (2014): 178–192.

68. This "struggle against peasant economy" is laid out in Luxemburg, *Accumulation of Capital*, 395–418.

69. See, for example, Ian J. Kerr, *Building the Railways of the Raj, 1850-1918* (Delhi: Oxford University Press, 1995).

70. Select Committee, *Inquiry*, 513.

71. Daniel E. Bender and Jana K. Lipman, eds., *Making the Empire Work: Labor and United States Imperialism* (New York: New York University Press, 2015). See Julie Greene, *The Canal Builders: Making America's Empire at the Panama Canal* (New York: Penguin, 2009); Jana Lipman, *Guantánamo: A Working-Class History Between Empire and Revolution* (Berkeley: University of California Press, 2009); Jason M. Colby, *The Business of Empire: United Fruit, Race, and U.S. Expansion in Central America* (Ithaca, NY: Cornell University Press, 2011); Julie Greene, "Movable Empire: Labor, Migration, and U.S. Global Power during the Gilded Age and Progressive Era," *Journal of the Gilded Age and Progressive Era* 15, no. 1 (Jan. 2016): 4–20.

72. See Julie Greene, "The Wages of Empire," in Leon Fink, ed., and Eileen Boris, John French, Julie Greene, Joan Sangster, and Shelton Stromquist, assoc. eds., *Workers Across the Americas: The Transnational Turn in Labor History* (New York: Oxford University Press, 2011), 57–80.

73. Smedley D. Butler to Father, June 10, 1910, Bluefields, Nicaragua, box 3, SDBFC.

74. See Luxemburg, *Accumulation of Capital*, 452–453. For a parallel history, see Frederick Cooper, *From Slaves to Squatters: Plantation Labor and Agriculture in Zanzibar and Coastal Kenya, 1890-1925* (New Haven, CT: Yale University Press, 1980).

75. Butler, *Letters of a Leatherneck*, 167.

76. Select Committee, *Inquiry*, 530.

77. James Weldon Johnson, "Self-Determining Haiti" II, *The Nation*, September 4, 1920, p. 265.

78. Select Committee, *Inquiry*, 28; Kethly Millet, *Les paysans haïtiens et l'occupation Américaine 1915-1930* (La Salle, QC: Collectif paroles, 1978), 84–89.

79. Elisabeth Köll, *Railroads and the Transformation of China* (Cambridge, MA: Harvard University Press, 2019), 38.

80. Smedley Butler to Sweethearts, October 23, 1915, Grande Rivière, Haiti, box 3, SDBFC.

81. Renda, *Taking Haiti*, 142–143.

82. Butler, *Letters of a Leatherneck*, 154. On global racial ideologies of the era, see Marilyn Lake and Henry Reynolds, *Drawing the Global Colour Line: White Men's Countries and the International Challenge of Racial Equality* (Cambridge, UK: Cambridge University Press, 2008).

83. I am here, again, indebted to Luxemburg, *Accumulation of Capital*, 454–467.

84. Select Committee, *Inquiry*, 28–31; Ernest H. Gruening, "The Senators Visit Haiti and Santo Domingo," *The Nation*, January 4, 1922, 8.

85. Butler, "America's Armed Forces," 8.

86. "Smedley D. Butler Gives Views on Philippines in United Press Interview," *Olean Times-Herald*, Jan. 18, 1933, p. 8.

87. Smedley D. Butler, *War Is a Racket* (New York: Round Table Press, 1935), 38–42.

Chapter 3

1. Michael Fabre, *The Unfinished Quest of Richard Wright* (Chicago: University of Illinois Press, 1993), 352; "Giles Hubert Interview," Patrick Gilpin Oral History Collection, Fisk University Special Collections, Nashville, TN. Transcript in author's possession.

2. Jumelle received a master's degree in sociology from Fisk in 1945, writing a thesis entitled "Competitive Position of Haitian Products in the American Market." "Higher Degrees in Sociology Conferred," *American Journal of Sociology* 52, no. 1 (July 1946), 49.

3. Denis Lorimer and François Duvalier, quoted in Matthew J. Smith, *Red and Black in Haiti: Radicalism, Conflict, and Political Change, 1934-1957* (Chapel Hill: University of North Carolina Press, 2009), 105.

4. On the U.S. occupation, see Hans Schmidt, *The United States Occupation of Haiti, 1915-1934* (New Brunswick, NJ: Rutgers University Press, 1971); Peter James Hudson, *Bankers and Empire: How Wall Street Colonized the Caribbean* (Chicago: University of Chicago Press, 2017), 81–116; Mary Renda, *Taking Haiti: Military Occupation and the Culture of U.S. Imperialism, 1915-1940* (Chapel Hill: University of North Carolina Press, 2001); Laurent Dubois, *Haiti: The Aftershocks of History* (New York: Picador, 2012), 204–264.

5. W. E. B. Du Bois, *The Negro* (New York: Cosimo, 2007 [1915]), 106.

6. On the counter-plantation tradition, see Yvonne Acosta and Jean Casimir, "Social Origins of the Counter-Plantation System in St. Lucia," in P. I. Gomes, ed., *Rural Development in the Caribbean* (New York: St. Martin's Press, 1985), 34–59. For the concept's application to the broader history of the Caribbean, see Laurent Dubois and Richard Lee Turits, *Freedom Roots: Histories from the Caribbean* (Chapel Hill: University of North Carolina Press, 2019). For a history of peasant resistance in Haiti during the U.S. occupation, see Marvin Chochotte, "The Twilight of Popular Revolutions: The Suppression of Peasant Armed Struggles and Freedom in Rural Haiti During the US Occupation, 1915-1934," *Journal of African American History* 103, no. 3 (2018), 277–308.

7. Chantalle F. Verna, *Haiti and the Uses of America: Post-U.S. Occupation Promises* (New Brunswick, NJ: Rutgers University Press, 2017).

8. Verna, "Maurice Dartigue, Educational Reform, and Intellectual Cooperation with the United States as a Strategy for Haitian National Development," *Journal of Haitian Studies* 13, no. 2 (2007), 24–38.

9. Suzy Castor, "Veneer of Modernization," in Laurent Dubois et al., *The Haiti Reader: History, Culture, Politics* (Durham, NC: Duke University Press, 2020), 245–248.

10. Dubois and Turits, *Freedom Roots*, 168–169.

11. Mats Lundahl, *The Haitian Economy: Man, Land and Markets* (New York: St. Martin's Press, 1983), 99.

12. Smith, *Red and Black in Haiti*, 44.

13. For an overview of U.S. foreign policy in the Caribbean and Latin America in this period, see Lars Schoultz, *Beneath the United States: A History of U.S. Policy Toward Latin America* (Cambridge, MA: Harvard University Press, 1998), 316–348.

14. The early 1930s saw the creation of the Haitian Afro-American Chamber of Commerce, which in 1935 issued a report on the economic potential of inter-American commercial exchange. See Haitian Afro-American Chamber of Commerce, *Official Report of the Haitian Afro-American Chamber of Commerce's Commission to Study the Commercial, Agricultural and Industrial Possibilities of the Haitian Republic* (1935). For a discussion of African American links to Haiti before the 1930s, see Brandon Byrd, *The Black Republic: African Americans and the Fate of Haiti* (Philadelphia: University of Pennsylvania Press, 2019).

15. Millery Polyné, *From Douglass to Duvalier: U.S. African Americans, Haiti, and Pan Americanism, 1870-1964* (Gainesville: University of Florida Press, 2010), 104.

16. Claude Barnett, *News of Haiti*, March 15, 1951, 9; Haitian Tours, Barnett's Promotions 1949-1951 folder, box 205, Claude Barnett Papers, Chicago History Museum.

17. Recent work in this burgeoning literature has focused on the links between African Americans' anticolonial and antiracist work, including John Munro, *The Anticolonial Front: The African American Freedom Struggle and Global Decolonization, 1945-1960* (Cambridge, UK: Cambridge University Press); Keisha Blain, *To Set the World on Fire: Black Nationalist Women and the Global Struggle for Freedom* (Philadelphia: University of Pennsylvania Press, 2018); Nicholas Grant, *Winning Our Freedoms Together: African Americans and Apartheid, 1945-1960* (Chapel Hill: University of North Carolina Press, 2017); Judy Tzu-Chun Wu, *Radicals on the Road: Internationalism, Orientalism, and Feminism During the Vietnam Era* (Ithaca, NY: Cornell University Press, 2013). In this vibrant subfield, only one major work focuses on black intellectuals and the transformation in global agriculture after the end of slavery. See Andrew Zimmerman, *Alabama in Africa: Booker T. Washington, the German Empire, and the Globalization of the New South* (Princeton, NJ: Princeton University Press, 2010).

18. For other accounts of U.S. agricultural policy's global reverberations, see Tore Olsson, *Agrarian Crossings: Reformers and the Remaking of the US and Mexican Countryside* (Princeton, NJ: Princeton University Press, 2017); Daniel Immerwahr, *Thinking Small: The United States and the Lure of Community Development* (Cambridge, MA: Harvard University Press, 2015). On the transnational New Deal, see Elizabeth Borgwardt, *A New Deal for the World: America's Vision for Human Rights* (Cambridge, MA: Harvard University Press, 2005); Kiran Klaus Patel, *The New Deal: A Global History* (Princeton, NJ: Princeton University Press, 2016).

19. Orme Wilson to Hugh Acheson, August 18, 1946, in *Foreign Relations of the United States, Volume XI, The American Republics* (Washington, DC: Government Printing Office, 1969), 912.

20. For an overview of the history of global development in the postwar world, see Sara Lorenzini, *Global Development: A Cold War History* (Princeton, NJ: Princeton University Press, 2019). For a helpful introduction to work on the global history of assisted modernization and the Green Revolution, see Kumar et. al., "Roundtable: New Narratives of the Green Revolution," *Agricultural History* 91, no. 3 (2017), 397–422.

21. On the transnational origins of development theory and practice, see Amy C. Offner, *Sorting Out the Mixed Economy: The Rise and Fall of Developmental States in the Americas* (Princeton, NJ: Princeton University Press, 2019); Joseph L. Love, *Crafting the Third World: Theorizing Underdevelopment in Rumania and Brazil* (Stanford, CA: Stanford University Press, 1996).

22. One important exception is Jason C. Parker, "'Made-in-American Revolutions'? The 'Black University,' and the American Role in the Decolonization of the Black Atlantic," *Journal of American History* 96, no. 3 (Dec. 2009), 727–750.

23. On the conference and the broader intellectual context, see Tony Martin, "Eric Williams and the Anglo-American Caribbean Commission, 1942-1944," *Journal of African American History* 88, no. 3 (2003), 274–290. For the conference proceedings, see E. Franklin Frazier and Eric Williams, eds., *The Economic Future of the Caribbean* (Dover, MA: The Majority Press, 2004).

24. Sarah Phillips, *This Land, This Nation: Conservation, Rural America, and the New Deal* (New York: Cambridge University Press, 2007), 243. Bruce Schulman terms the Jim Crow South's model of economic transformation "Herrenvolk development." See Schulman, *From Cotton Belt to Sunbelt: Federal Policy, Economic Development, and the Transformation of the South, 1938-1980* (Durham, NC: Duke University Press, 1994), 47.

25. Frederick Cooper, "Development, Modernization, and the Social Sciences in the Era of Decolonization: The Examples of British and French Africa," *Revue d'Histoire des Sciences Humaines* 1, no. 4 (2004), 9–38.

26. "Hubert, Zachary Taylor (1904)," http://scua.library.umass.edu/youmass/doku.php?id=h:hubert_zachary_taylor (accessed February 8, 2018); "Rites Held for Zachary Hubert," *Chicago Defender,* October 18, 1958, 2.

27. "Southern Teachers Study at the University of Iowa," *Chicago Defender*, August 23, 1930, 2; "Outstanding Educators to Plight Troth: Muriel Patillo to Wed Giles A. Hubert," *Chicago Defender*, January 31, 1931.

28. Giles Hubert oral history.

29. Ibid.

30. For an overview of Johnson's training and contributions to the field of sociology, see Alice O'Connor, *Poverty Knowledge: Social Science, Social Policy, and the Poor in Twentieth Century U.S. History* (Princeton, NJ: Princeton University Press, 2002), 78–84.

31. Charles S. Johnson, quoted in Patrick Gilpin and Marybeth Gasman, *Charles S. Johnson: Leadership Beyond the Veil in the Age of Jim Crow* (Albany: State University of New York Press, 2003), 95–96.

32. Edgar T. Thompson, "Sociology and Sociological Research in the South," in *In Search of the Regional Balance of America*, ed. Howard W. Odum and Katharine Jochner (Chapel Hill: University of North Carolina Press, 1945), 114–123.

33. Jess Gilbert, *Planning Democracy: Agrarian Intellectuals and the Intended New Deal* (New Haven, CT: Yale University Press, 2015), 88.

34. "Will Study in Europe: Wife of Professor Goes with Him," *New York Amsterdam News*, September 18, 1937, 8.

35. "Fisk Teacher Appointed to Federal Post," *Chicago Defender*, May 20, 1939, 11.

36. On New Deal land policy and the USDA reformers that drove the agrarian New Deal, see Gilbert, *Planning Democracy*, 80–112. The best elaboration of their vision remains *Farm Tenancy: Report of the President's Committee* (Washington, DC: Government Printing Office, 1937).

37. Gilbert, *Planning Democracy*, 88.

38. Giles A. Hubert, quoted in *Leadership Beyond the Veil*, 120.

39. Giles A. Hubert to James G. Maddox, October 10, 1940, GHP, Box 1, Folder 3.

40. Zachary T. Hubert to Giles Hubert, May 5, 1938, GHP, Box 1, Folder 1.

41. Giles A. Hubert to Zachary T. Hubert, July 19, 1939, GHP, Box 1, Folder 1.

42. Paul V. Maris to Giles A. Hubert, August 16, 1939, GHP, Box 1, Folder 1.

43. Giles A. Hubert, "The Negro on the Agricultural Front," *Journal of Negro Education* (Summer 1943), 397–404.

44. U.S. Department of Agriculture, *Food-for-Freedom Goals for 1942 and 1943* (Washington, DC: U.S. Department of Agriculture, 1943).

45. Hubert, "The Negro on the Agricultural Front," 402.

46. Hubert, "The Negro on the Agricultural Front," 402.

47. Hubert, "The Negro on the Agricultural Front," 402–403.

48. Giles Hubert, "The FSA County Purchasing and Marketing Association and Its Significance to Race Relations," [n.d.], folder 4, box 7, GHP.

49. "Hubert Resigns FSA Post: Returns to Fisk U.," *Arkansas State Press* September 17, 1943.

50. On the creation of this program, see "New African Classes Draw Heavy Fisk Registration," *Chicago Defender,* October 16, 1943, 6.

51. Johnson, quote in Gilpin and Gasman, *Leadership Beyond the Veil*, 103.

52. Gilpin and Gasman, *Leadership Beyond the Veil*, 103.

53. Beyond the aforementioned Turnier and Jumelle, a number of other Fisk students returned from the United States to serve in the administration of President Dumarsais Estimé (1946–1950), including Franck Le Gendre (underminister of state for labor) and Max L. Etheart (chief statistician in the coffee bureau). In addition, Fisk student Roger Dorsainville served as the Haitian consul general in New York City.

54. Clovis Charlot to Allen [name unclear], May 5, 1946, folder 8, box 1, GHP.

55. Bond would later attempt, unsuccessfully, to secure the ambassadorship to Haiti, with the assistance of Claude Barnett.

56. Gerald Horne, *The Rise and Fall of the Associated Negro Press: Claude Barnett's Pan-African News and the Jim Crow Paradox* (Urbana: University of Illinois Press, 2017), 3.

57. Claude Barnett to Giles Hubert, February 5, 1945, folder 7, box 1, GHP.

58. Horne, *The Rise and Fall of the Associated Negro Press*, 121.

59. For a useful summary of structuralist economic theory, see Love, *Crafting the Third World*, 1–5.

60. On Raúl Prebisch's contribution to structuralism and the economic theory of the underdeveloped world, see Edgar J. Dosman, *The Life and Times of Raúl Prebisch, 1901-1986* (Montreal: McGill-Queens University Press, 2008).

61. Giles A. Hubert, "A Framework for the Study of Peripheral Economic Areas," *Journal of Farm Economics* 28, no. 3 (Aug. 1946), 804–820.

62. Gras wrote to Hubert that his essay was a "Good piece of work," and that "In these days of super-political emphasis, getting down to the fundamentals of social and economic organization is a necessary antidote and, I believe, a valuable stimulant to clear thinking." N. S. B. Gras to Giles Hubert, February 13, 1946, folder 8, box 1, GHP.

63. Hubert, "A Framework," 819.

64. Hubert, "A Framework," 818–819.

65. Smith, *Red and Black in Haiti*, 9.

66. Giles Hubert to Louis Decatrel, October 16, 1945, folder 7, box 1, GHP.

67. Giles Hubert to Lloyd Hughes, August 6, 1945, folder 7, box 1, GHP.

68. A. Ogden Pierrot to Tom Stewart, August 19, 1947, RG 59, Department of State Central Files (National Archives II, College Park, MD).

69. Giles Hubert to Mary McLeod Bethune, October 17, 1946, folder 8, box 1, GHP.

70. Mary McLeod Bethune to Giles Hubert, October 21, 1946, folder 8, box 1, GHP.

71. Mary McLeod Bethune, "Pinder and Hubert Blaze New Trails in the Foreign Service," *Chicago Defender*, September 1, 1951, 6.

72. Dubois, *Haiti*, 314 316.

73. Giles Hubert to Emmett J. Kellogg, July 9 1948, folder 10, box 1, GHP.

74. Giles Hubert to Edward L. Tanner, September 10, 1948, folder 10, box 1, GHP.

75. Dubois, *Haiti*, 316.

76. Matthew J. Smith, *Red and Black in Haiti*,103–112.

77. On this history, see Millery Polyné, *From Douglass to Duvalier*, 131–153.

78. Giles A. Hubert to Bonita Valien, April 9, 1948, folder 10, box 1, GHP.

79. Giles Hubert to Charles Johnson, May 28, 1948, folder 10, box 1, GHP.

80. Francois Duvalier to Giles Hubert, March 26, 1949, folder 11, box 1, GHP.

81. Giles Hubert to Francois Duvalier, April 7, 1949, folder 11, box 1, GHP.

82. Charles Johnson to Giles Hubert, March 19, 1949, folder 11, box 1, GHP.

83. Charles S. Johnson, "Haiti as a Laboratory for Cultural Research," *Phylon* 8, no. 3 (1947), 259, 262.

84. Huggins, quoted in Polyné, *From Douglass to Duvalier*, 104.

85. For an explanation of the TVA's global influence and trajectory, see David Ekbladh, "'Mr TVA': Grass-Roots Development, David Lillenthal, and the Rise and Fall of the Tennessee Valley Authority as a Symbol for U.S. Overseas Development, 1933-1973," *Diplomatic History* 26, no. 3 (2002), 335–374.

86. Giles Hubert to Marshall Harris, March 27, 1950, folder 12, box 1, GHP.

87. Giles Hubert to Marshall Harris, March 27, 1950, folder 12, box 1, GHP.

88. Inter-American Institute of Agricultural Sciences, *Report on the Proposed Artibonite Valley Project of Haiti* (January 1952), iii, 2.

89. A. J. Wakefield to W. C. Brister, July 31, 1950, folder 12, box 1, GHP.

90. Giles A. Hubert, "Some Problems of a Colonial Economy: A Study of Economic Dualism in Haiti," *Inter-American Economic Affairs* 3, no. 4 (Spring 1950), 3–30.

91. David McCord Wright to Giles Hubert, March 21, 1949, folder 11, box 1, GHP.

92. Hubert, "Some Problems," 4.

93. Hubert's work cites two texts in particular: J. H. Boeke, *The Structure of Netherlands Indian Economy* (1942), and Sir Allen Pim, *Colonial Agricultural Production* (1946).

94. Robert Tignor, *W. Arthur Lewis and the Birth of Development Economics* (Princeton, NJ: Princeton University Press, 2006), 80. For an effective summary of Lewis's essay's significance to the broader field of development economics, see Douglas Gollin, "The Lewis Model: A 60-Year Retrospective," *Journal of Economic Perspectives* 28, no. 3 (Summer 2014), 71–88.

95. W. Arthur Lewis, "Economic Development with Unlimited Supplies of Labor," *The Manchester School* 22, no. 2 (1954), 149.

96. Hubert, "Some Problems," 11.

97. Hubert, "Some Problems," 29.

98. Smith, *Red and Black*, 164.

99. "Bon Papa," *Time*, February 22, 1954.

100. Smith, *Red and Black*, 164–165; Dubois, *Aftershocks*, 317–319.

101. Lundahl, *The Haitian Economy*, 237.

102. "Profiles in the News," *Chicago Defender*, April 14, 1951.

103. Daniel Immerwahr, *Thinking Small*, 10.

104. Eric Williams, *The Negro in the Caribbean* (Greenwich, CT: Greenwood Press, 1969 [1942]), 46. Hubert later acknowledged that turning down an offer from Williams to work for the Anglo-American Caribbean Commission was one of the biggest regrets of his career. See "Giles Hubert Interview."

105. Patel, *The New Deal*, 145–171.

106. Edgar T. Thompson, "The South in Old and New Contexts," in *Plantation Societies, Race Relations, and the South: The Regimentation of Populations: The Selected Papers of Edgar T. Thompson* (Durham, NC: Duke University Press, 1975), 314.

Chapter 4

1. Alan Brinkley, *The End of Reform: New Deal Liberalism in Recession and War* (New York: Alfred A. Knopf, 1995). For a brief treatment of the relationship between capitalism and democracy, see Walter LaFeber, "The Tension Between Democracy and Capitalism During the

American Century," *Diplomatic History* 23, no. 2 (Spring 1999): 264–284. For more recent treatments of this theme, see Amy C. Offner, *Sorting Out the Mixed Economy: The Rise and Fall of Welfare and Developmental States in the Americas* (Princeton, NJ: Princeton University Press, 2019), and Melvyn Leffler, *Safeguarding Democratic Capitalism: U.S. Foreign Policy and National Security, 1920-2015* (Princeton, NJ: Princeton University Press, 2017). Much has been written about anticommunism during the twentieth century; I have found particularly helpful Ellen Schrecker, *Many Are the Crimes: McCarthyism in America* (Boston: Little, Brown, 1998); Robert Justin Goldstein, *Political Repression in Modern America: From 1870-1976*, rev. ed. (Urbana: University of Illinois Press, 2001); and Luis Herrán Ávila, "Anticommunism, the Extreme Right, and the Politics of Enmity in Argentina, Colombia, and Mexico, 1946-1972" (Ph.D. diss., The New School for Social Research, 2017).

2. Jordan A. Schwarz, *Liberal: Adolf A. Berle and the Vision of an American Era* (New York: The Free Press, 1987); Jason Scott Smith, *Building New Deal Liberalism: The Political Economy of Public Works, 1933-1956* (Cambridge, UK: Cambridge University Press, 2006); David Ekbladh, *The Great American Mission: Modernization and the Construction of an American World Order* (Princeton, NJ: Princeton University Press, 2010); Ngaire Woods, *The Globalizers: The IMF, The World Bank, and Their Borrowers* (Ithaca, NY: Cornell University Press, 2006); Patrick Sharma, *Robert McNamara's Other War: The World Bank and International Development* (Philadelphia: University of Pennsylvania Press, 2017); Alfred E. Eckes, Jr., *A Search for Solvency: Bretton Woods and the International Monetary System, 1941-1971* (Austin: University of Texas Press, 1975); Eckes, Jr., *Opening America's Market: U.S. Foreign Trade Policy since 1776* (Chapel Hill: University of North Carolina Press, 1995); Eric Rauchway, *The Money Makers: How Roosevelt and Keynes Ended the Depression, Defeated Fascism, and Secured a Prosperous Peace* (New York: Basic Books, 2015); Douglas A. Irwin, *Clashing over Commerce: A History of U.S. Trade Policy* (Chicago: University of Chicago Press, 2017).

3. Daniel Immerwahr, *Thinking Small: The United States and the Lure of Community Development* (Cambridge, MA: Harvard University Press, 2015), 137. For more on the circulation of ideas across borders, see Offner, Sorting Out the Mixed Economy; Tore C. Olsson, Agrarian Crossings: Reformers and the Remaking of the U.S. and Mexican Countryside (Princeton, NJ: Princeton University Press, 2017); Alyosha Goldstein, Poverty in Common: The Politics of Community Action During the American Century (Durham, NC: Duke University Press, 2012); Manuel R. Rodríguez, A New Deal for the Tropics: Puerto Rico During the Depression Ear, 1932-1935 (Princeton, NJ: Markus Wiener, 2011); Stuart Schrader, Badges Without Borders: How Global Counterinsurgency Transformed American Policing (Berkeley: University of California Press, 2019); and Julie M. Weise, "La revolución institucional: The Rise and Fall of the Mexican New Deal in the U.S. South, 1920-1990," in Shaped by the State: Toward a New Political History of the Twentieth Century, ed. Brent Cebul, Lily Geismer, and Mason B. Williams (Chicago: University of Chicago Press, 2019), 162–185.

4. Frederick Cooper, "Conflict and Connection: Rethinking Colonial African History," *American Historical Review* 99 (Dec. 1994): 1533. "Weapons of the strong" is a rejoinder to James C. Scott, *Weapons of the Weak: Everyday Forms of Peasant Resistance* (New Haven, CT: Yale University Press, 1985). For an insightful critique of Scott's oeuvre, see Samuel Moyn, "Barbarian Virtues," in *The Nation*, October 23, 2017.

5. Betsy A. Beasley, "Service Learning: Oil, International Education, and Texas's Corporate Cold War," *Diplomatic History* 42 (April 2018): 177–203; Thomas F. O'Brien, *Revolutionary Mission: American Enterprise in Latin America, 1900-1945* (Cambridge, UK: Cambridge University

Press, 1999); O'Brien, *The Century of U.S. Capitalism in Latin America* (Albuquerque: University of New Mexico Press, 1999); Darlene Rivas, *Missionary Capitalist: Nelson Rockefeller in Venezuela* (Chapel Hill: University of North Carolina Press, 2002); Jason Scott Smith, "The Great Transformation: The State and the Market in the Postwar World," in Boundaries of the State in US History, ed. James T. Sparrow, William J. Novak, and Stephen W. Sawyer (Chicago: University of Chicago Press, 2015), 127–151; Smith, "The Liberal Invention of the Multinational Corporation: David Lilienthal and Postwar Capitalism," in *What's Good for Business: Business and Politics Since World War II*, ed. Kim Phillips-Fein and Julian E. Zelizer (Oxford, UK: Oxford University Press, 2012), 107–122.

6. Ferdinand Eberstadt quoted in "7 to 10 Billion Exports Seen Possible by 1948," *New York Herald Tribune*, October 22, 1944, 15, in box 174, Ferdinand Eberstadt Papers, MC 021, Seeley G. Mudd Manuscript Library, Princeton University.

7. Ibid.

8. Panamericus (William LaVarre), "Latin America's New ism," syndicated column clipping, no date (probably 1940), in "Re Bretton Woods 1944-1945" folder, box 28, Ferdinand Eberstadt Papers.

9. Artemy M. Kalinovsky, *Laboratory of Socialist Development: Cold War Politics and Deconlonization in Soviet Tajikistan* (Ithaca, NY: Cornell University Press, 2018); Tanya Harmer, *Allende's Chile and the Inter-American Cold War* (Chapel Hill: University of North Carolina Press, 2011); Jeffrey James Byrne, *Mecca of Revolution: Algeria, Decolonization and the Third World Order* (Oxford, UK: Oxford University Press, 2016); David C. Engerman, *The Price of Aid: The Economic Cold War in India* (Cambridge, MA: Harvard University Press, 2018). See also Joseph Hodge, "Writing the History of Development (The First Wave)," *Humanity* 6 (Winter 2015): 429–463, and Hodge, "Writing the History of Development (Part 2: Longer, Deeper, Wider)," *Humanity* 7 (Spring 2016): 125–174; Amy L. S. Staples, *The Birth of Development: How the World Bank, Food and Agriculture Organization and the World Health Organization Changed the World, 1945–1965* (Kent, OH: Kent State University Press, 2006); Bradley Simpson, *Economists with Guns: Authoritarian Development and U.S-Indonesian Relations, 1960-1968* (Stanford, CA: Stanford University Press, 2008); Arturo Escobar, *Encountering Development: The Making and Unmaking of the Third World* (Princeton, NJ: Princeton University Press, 2011); Vijay Prashad, *The Darker Nations: A People's History of the Third World* (New York: New Press, 2007); Odd Arne Westad, *The Global Cold War: Third World Interventions and the Making of Our Times* (Cambridge, UK: Cambridge University Press, 2005); and Westad, "Epilogue: The Cold War and the Third World," in *The Cold War and the Third World: Reinterpreting History*, ed. Robert J. McMahon (Oxford, UK: Oxford University Press, 2013), 208–219.

10. "Memorandum on Seminar for Junior Executives," no date (probably February 1952), folder 5, "Seminars for Business Executives, 1939-1941, 1952-1953," box 576, Council on Foreign Relations Records, MC 104, Seeley G. Mudd Manuscript Library, Princeton University. For more on Point Four, see Amanda MacVety, *Enlightened Aid: U.S. Development as Foreign Policy in Ethiopia* (Oxford, UK: Oxford University Press, 2012). For more on the intersection of government and corporate enterprise in the context of U.S. global expansion during this period, see Megan Black, *The Global Interior: Mineral Frontiers and American Power* (Cambridge, MA: Harvard University Press, 2018), and Joy Rohde, *Armed with Expertise: The Militarization of American Social Research during the Cold War* (Ithaca, NY: Cornell University Press, 2013).

11. As Jordan Schwarz has argued, we might readily consider the New Deal, when viewed as a whole, as "a massive governmental recapitalization for purposes of economic development,"

one that "sought to create long-term markets by building an infrastructure in undeveloped regions." Jordan A. Schwarz, *The New Dealers: Power Politics in the Age of Roosevelt* (New York: Alfred A. Knopf, 1993), xi. Indeed, we might think of the New Deal as a variation on what Jo Guldi has termed "the infrastructure state." Jo Guldi, *Roads to Power: Britain Invents the Infrastructure State* (Cambridge, MA: Harvard University Press, 2012).

12. Cary Reich, *The Life of Nelson A. Rockefeller: Worlds to Conquer, 1908-1958* (New York: Doubleday, 1996), 408.

13. Ibid. For more on the idea of the corporation as an instrument of progress, see Emily S. Rosenberg, *Financial Missionaries to the World: The Politics and Culture of Dollar Diplomacy* (Cambridge, MA: Harvard University Press, 1999); Rosenberg, *Spreading the American Dream: American Economic and Cultural Expansion, 1890-1945* (New York: Hill and Wang, 1982); Steve Striffler, *In the Shadows of State and Capital: The United Fruit Company, Popular Struggle, and Agrarian Restructuring in Ecuador, 1900-1995* (Durham, NC: Duke University Press, 2002); and Marcos Cueto, ed., *Missionaries of Science: Rockefeller Foundation and Latin America* (Bloomington: Indiana University Press, 1994).

14. Ekbladh, *Great American Mission*; Sarah Phillips, *This Land, This Nation: Conservation, Rural America, and the New Deal* (Cambridge, UK: Cambridge University Press, 2007), esp. 242–283; Wayne G. Broehl, Jr., *The International Basic Economy Corporation* (Washington, DC: National Planning Association, 1968).

15. Barbara Weinstein, *For Social Peace in Brazil: Industrialists and the Remaking of the Working Class in São Paulo, 1920-1964* (Chapel Hill: University of North Carolina Press, 1996); Elizabeth A. Cobbs, *The Rich Neighbor Policy: Rockefeller and Kaiser in Brazil* (New Haven: Yale University Press, 1992).

16. Inderjeet Parmar, *Foundations of the American Century: The Ford, Carnegie, and Rockefeller Foundations in the Rise of American Power* (New York: Columbia University Press, 2012), viii; italics in original. William Novak has made a similar set of claims about the public-private nature of the state, see his "The Myth of the 'Weak' American State," *American Historical Review* 113 (June 2008): 752–772.

17. Leslie Bethell and Ian Roxborough, "Introduction: The Postwar Conjuncture in Latin America: Democracy, Labor, and the Left," in *Latin America Between the Second World War and the Cold War, 1944-1948*, ed. Leslie Bethell and Ian Roxborough (Cambridge, UK: Cambridge University Press, 1992), 5, 7. For the more recent history of Venezuelan politics, see Alejandro Velasco, *Barrio Rising: Urban Popular Politics and the Making of Modern Venezuela* (Berkeley: University of California Press, 2015), and Fernando Coronil, *The Magical State: Nature, Money, and Modernity in Venezuela* (Chicago: University of Chicago Press, 1997).

18. Nelson A. Rockefeller to Romulo Betancourt, June 19, 1947 [English translation], in "VBEC (Venezuelan Basic Economy Corporation)" folder 92, box 10, Nelson A. Rockefeller Papers, AIA-IBEC, Series B (FA33), Rockefeller Archive Center, Sleepy Hollow, NY (hereafter referred to as RAC).

19. Steve Ellner, "Venezuela," in *Latin America Between the Second World War and the Cold War*, 147–169, and Reich, 411.

20. Reich, 416.

21. Reich, 414.

22. John Lockwood to NAR and Wallace Harrison, February 14, 1949, in "IBEC Technical Services Corporation-Caracas LaGuaira Highway," folder 41, box 5, Nelson A. Rockefeller papers, AIA-IBEC, Series B (FA 339), RAC.

23. Ibid., Robert Moses to Wallace Harrison, April 11, 1949.

24. Ibid., William Machold to John Lockwood, June 2, 1949.

25. William H. Alton to NAR, November 11, 1947, in "AIA-Alton, W.H.," folder 3, box 1, Nelson A. Rockefeller Papers, AIA-IBEC, Series B (FA339), RAC.

26. Melissa Teixeira, "Making a Brazilian New Deal: Oliveira Vianna and the Transnational Sources of Brazil's Corporatist Experiment," *Journal of Latin American Studies* 50 (Aug. 2018): 614; for more on the international significance of the New Deal, see Kiran Klaus Patel, *The New Deal: A Global History* (Cambridge, UK: Cambridge University Press, 2016), and Jason Scott Smith, "Understanding the New Deal in an Age of Trump and Brexit," *Reviews in American History* 46 (March 2018): 121–127. For examples of how U.S. ideas about urban infrastructure and housing circulated in Latin America, see Helen Gyger, *Improvised Cities: Architecture, Urbanization, and Innovation in Peru* (Pittsburgh: University of Pittsburgh Press, 2019); Leandro Benmergui, "The Transnationalization of the 'Housing Problem': Social Sciences and *Developmentalism* in Postwar Argentina," in *The Housing Question: Tensions, Continuities, and Contingencies in the Modern City*, ed. Edward Murphy and Najib B. Hourani (Burlington, VT: Ashgate, 2013), 35–56; and Marcio Siwi, "The Making of New York's Avenue of the Americas: Transnational Circuits of Urban Renewal," *Journal of Urban History* 47 (2021).

27. Memorandum, "Suggestions Re Financing of Brazilian Road Building Program," September 29, 1948, in "AIA-Brazil-Highway Construction" folder 8, box 2, Nelson A. Rockefeller Papers, AIA-IBEC, Series B (FA339), RAC.

28. Ibid.

29. Ibid. For more on the history of public authorities and public-private partnerships, see Gail Radford, *The Rise of the Public Authority: Statebuilding and Economic Development in Twentieth-Century America* (Chicago: University of Chicago Press, 2013); Radford, "From Municipal Socialism to Public Authorities: Institutional Factors in the Shaping of American Public Enterprise," *Journal of American History* 90 (Dec. 2003); and Brent Cebul, "Creative Competition: Georgia Power, the Tennessee Valley Authority, and the Creation of a Rural Consumer Economy, 1934-1955, *Journal of American History* 105 (June 2018): 45–70. On the history of the corporation, see William J. Novak and Naomi R. Lamoreaux, eds., *Corporations and American Democracy* (Cambridge, MA: Harvard University Press, 2017); Thomas K. McCraw, ed,. *Creating Modern Capitalism: How Entrepreneurs, Companies, and Countries Triumphed in Three Industrial Revolutions* (Cambridge, MA: Harvard University Press, 1997); Neil J. Mitchell, *The Conspicuous Corporation: Business, Public Policy, and Representative Democracy* (Ann Arbor: University of Michigan Press, 1997); and William G. Roy, *Socializing Capital: The Rise of the Large Industrial Corporation in America* (Princeton, NJ: Princeton University Press, 1997); for the intersection of public and private entities in a Latin American context, see Offner, *Sorting Out the Mixed Economy*.

30. NAR to John Lockwood, November 3, 1948, in "AIA-Brazil-Highway Construction," folder 8, box 2, Nelson A. Rockefeller Papers, AIA-IBEC, Series B (FA339), RAC.

31. Ibid. On the overlap between state and nonstate actors and their capacities to shape society, see, for example, Brian Balogh, *The Associational State: American Governance in the Twentieth Century* (Philadelphia: University of Pennsylvania Press, 2015), and James T. Sparrow, *Warfare State: World War II Americans and the Age of Big Government* (Oxford, UK: Oxford University Press, 2011).

32. See "Biographic Information on Teodoro Quartim Barbosa" (1963). *Opening the Archives: Documenting U.S.-Brazil Relations, 1960s-80s*, Brown Digital Repository, Brown University Library, https://repository.library.brown.edu/studio/item/bdr:352801/.

33. NAR to Teodoro Quartim Barbosa, January 14, 1949, in "AIA-Brazil-Highway Construction," folder 8, box 2, Nelson A. Rockefeller Papers, AIA-IBEC, Series B (FA339), RAC.

34. Ibid., Teodoro Quartim Barbosa to NAR, January 21, 1949.

35. Daniel Immerwahr, "Polanyi in the United States: Peter Drucker, Karl Polanyi, and the Midcentury Critique of Economic Society," *Journal of the History of Ideas* 70 (July 2009): 445–466; Howard Brick, *Transcending Capitalism: Visions of a New Society in Modern American Thought* (Ithaca, NY: Cornell University Press, 2006). Also see the essays collected in *American Capitalism: Social Thought and Political Economy in the Twentieth Century*, ed. Nelson Lichtenstein (Philadelphia: University of Pennsylvania Press, 2006).

36. Arthur M. Schelsinger, Jr., *The Vital Center: The Politics of Freedom* (Boston: Houghton Mifflin, 1949), 233. See also Nick Cullather, "Damming Afghanistan: Modernization in a Buffer State," *Journal of American History* 89 (Sept. 2002): 512–537; the essays collected in David C. Engerman, Nils Gilman, Mark H. Haefele, and Michael E. Latham, eds., *Staging Growth: Modernization, Development, and the Global Cold War* (Amherst: University of Massachusetts Press, 2003), and Michael A. Bernstein, *A Perilous Progress: Economists and Public Purpose in Twentieth-Century America* (Princeton, NJ: Princeton University Press, 2001). For the TVA, see Erwin C. Hargrove, *Prisoners of Myth: The Leadership of the Tennessee Valley Authority, 1933-1990* (Princeton, NJ: Princeton University Press, 1994), and Thomas K. McCraw, "The Hubris of the Engineers," *Technology and Culture* 36 (Oct. 1995): 1007–1014.

37. On the definition and history of neoliberalism, I have found helpful Kim Phillips-Fein, "The History of Neoliberalism," in *Shaped by the State*, ed. Cebul, Geismer, and Williams, 347–362; Daniel Rodgers, "The Uses and Abuses of 'Neoliberalism,'" *Dissent* (Winter 2018), with responses by Julia Ott, Mike Konczal, N. B. D. Connolly, and Timothy Shenk, and reply by Rodgers, at https://www.dissentmagazine.org/online_articles/debating-uses-abuses-neoliberalism-forum (accessed March 14, 2020); Brent Cebul's conception of "supply-side liberalism" and its connections to neoliberalism, as outlined in Cebul, "Supply-Side Liberalism: Fiscal Crisis, Post-Industrial Policy, and the Rise of the New Democrats," *Modern American History* 2 (2019): 139–164; and Cebul, "'They Were the Moving Spirits': Business and Supply-Side Liberalism in the Postwar South," in *Capital Gains: Business and Politics in Twentieth-Century America*, ed. Richard R. John and Kim Phillips-Fein (Philadelphia: University of Pennsylvania Press, 2017), 139–156; Gary Gerstle, "The Rise and Fall (?) of America's Neoliberal Order," *Transactions of the Royal Historical Society* 28 (Dec. 2018): 241–264; and Vanessa Ogle, "Archipelago Capitalism: Tax Havens, Offshore Money, and the State," *American Historical Review* 122 (Dec. 2017): 1431–1458.

Chapter 5

1. Sir Zafarullah Khan, "Meeting of East and West," in *UNESCO: The First Nine Years—An American Appraisal and Forecast*, U.S. National Commission for UNESCO, 1955, 2.

2. V. B. Singh, *Economic History of India, 1857-1956* (Bombay: Allied Publishers, 1965); Hamza Alavi, *Capitalism and Colonial Production* (London:Croom Helm, 1982); Robert I. Rhodes, *Imperialism and Underdevelopment: A Reader* (New York: Monthly Review Press, 1971); Deepak Kumar, Vinita Damodaran, and Rohan D'Souza, *The British Empire and the Natural World: Environmental Encounters in South Asia* (New Delhi: Oxford University Press, 2011); M. H. Panhwar, *Six Thousand Years of History of Irrigation in Sindh* (Karachi: Department of Culture, Government of Sindh, 2011); E. Walter Coward, *Irrigation and Agricultural Development in Asia: Perspectives from the Social Sciences* (Ithaca, NY: Cornell University Press, 1980); Malcolm Darling, *Wisdom and Waste in the Punjab Village* (London: Oxford University Press,

1934); Romesh Chunder Dutt, *The Economic History of India.* (New York: A. M. Kelley, 1969); David Reed, *Water, Security and U.S. Foreign Policy* (London: Routledge, 2017); Eric Stokes, *The English Utilitarians and India.* (Oxford, UK: Clarendon Press, 1959); E. A. G. Robinson, Michael Kidron, and International Economic Association, *Economic Development in South Asia: Proceedings of a Conference Held by the International Economic Association at Kandy, Ceylon* (London: Macmillan, 1970); Malcolm Yapp, *Strategies of British India: Britain, Iran, and Afghanistan, 1798-1850* (Oxford, UK: Clarendon Press, 1980); Daniel Thorner, *Land and Labour in India* (Bombay: Asia Publishing House, 1962); Benjamin Robert Siegel, *Hungry Nation: Food, Famine, and the Making of Modern India* (Cambridge, UK: Cambridge University Press, 2018); Nick Cullather, *The Hungry World: America's Cold War Battle Against Poverty in Asia* (Cambridge, MA: Harvard University Press, 2013); Narendra Singh Sarila, *The Shadow of the Great Game: The Untold Story of India's Partition* (New York: Carroll & Graf, 2006); Mithi Mukherjee, *India in the Shadows of Empire: A Legal and Political History, 1774-1950* (New Delhi: Oxford University Press, 2010); Department of the Interior Panel on Waterlogging and Salinity in West Pakistan, *Report on Land and Water Development in the Indus Plain* (Washington, DC: Government Printing Office, 1964).

3. David Ekbladh, "'Mr. TVA': Grass-Roots Development, David Lilienthal, and the Rise and Fall of the Tennessee Valley Authority as a Symbol for U.S. Overseas Development, 1933–1973," *Diplomatic History* 26, no. 3 (2002): 335–374, esp. 336–337. See also Steven M. Neuse, *David E. Lilienthal: The Journey of an American Liberal* (Knoxville: University of Tennessee Press, 1996).

4. Donald Worster, *Rivers of Empire: Water, Aridity, and the Growth of the American West* (New York: Pantheon Books, 1985); Karl August Wittfogel, *Oriental Despotism: A Comparative Study of Total Power* (New Haven, CT: Yale University Press, 1957); Jerome Delli Priscoli, "Water and Civilization: Using History to Reframe Water Policy Debates and to Build a New Ecological Realism," *Water Policy* 1, no. 6 (March 9, 2000): 623–636; Jerome Delli Priscoli, "Reflections on the Nexus of Politics, Ethics, Religion and Contemporary Water Resources Decisions," *Water Policy; Oxford* 14, no. S1 (March 2012): 21–40.

5. John F. Kerry et al., "Avoiding Water Wars: Water Scarcity and Central Asia's Growing Importance for Stability in Afghanistan and Pakistan," Committee on Foreign Relations, U.S. Senate, February 22, 2011, https://www.foreign.senate.gov/imo/media/doc/Senate%20Print%20112-10%20Avoiding%20Water%20Wars%20Water%20Scarcity%20and%20Central%20Asia%20Afgahnistan%20and%20Pakistan.pdf.

6. Joshua Busby, "Water and U.S. National Security," Council on Foreign Relations, Center for Preventive Action, January 2017; Alper Baba et al., eds., *Climate Change and Its Effects on Water Resources: Issues of National and Global Security*, vol. 3, NATO Science for Peace and Security Series C: Environmental Security (Dordrecht: Springer Netherlands, 2011); *Himalayan Glaciers: Climate Change, Water Resources, and Water Security* (Washington, DC: National Academies Press, 2012); Salman M. A. Salman and Kishor Uprety, *Shared Watercourses and Water Security in South Asia: Challenges of Negotiating and Enforcing Treaties*, (Leiden: Brill, 2018); Mara Tignino, "Water, International Peace, and Security," *International Review of the Red Cross* 92, no. 879 (Sept. 2010): 647–674.

7. "Fact Sheet: The Indus Waters Treaty 1960 and the Role of the World Bank," World Bank, June 11, 2018.

8. Robert W. Oliver, *Transcript of Oral History Interview with Mr. Eugene R. Black*, World Bank Group Oral History Program, August 6, 1961, 48, https://oralhistory.worldbank.org/transcripts/transcript-oral-history-interview-eugene-r-black-held-august-06-1961-main-transcript.

9. David E. Lilienthal, *TVA: Democracy on the March* (New York: Harper, 1953).

10. Ekbladh, "Mr. TVA," 337.

11. Neuse, *Lilienthal,* 145.

12. William U. Chandler, *The Myth of TVA: Conservation and Development in the Tennessee Valley, 1933-1983* (Cambridge, MA: Ballinger, 1984); E. C. Hargrove and P. K. Conkin, *TVA: Fifty Years of Grass-Roots Bureaucracy* (Champaign: University of Illinois Press, 1984); Steven M. Neuse, "TVA at Age Fifty—Reflections and Retrospect," *Public Administration Review* 43, no. 6 (1983): 491–499.

13. "Tennessee Across the World," address by Justice William O. Douglas before the General Assembly of the State of Tennessee, February 22, 1951, reported in Lilienthal, TVA, 211.

14. Neuse, *Lilienthal,* 133.

15. Ibid.

16. Quoted in Lilienthal, *TVA,* 210.

17. David E. Lilienthal, *The Journals of David E. Lilienthal, Volume III: Venturesome Years 19501955* (New York: Harper & Row, 1964), xi.

18. Rakesh Ankit, "1948: The Crucial Year in the History of Jammu and Kashmir," n.d., 12; Rakesh Ankit, "Great Britain and Kashmir, 1947–49," *India Review* 12, no. 1 (Jan. 2013): 20–40; Sumona Dasgupta, "Kashmir and the India-Pakistan Composite Dialogue Process," n.d., 28; "UN Chief Urges India, Pakistan to Come Together to Resolve Kashmir Dispute," January 29, 2021, https://www.dawn.com/news/1604303.

19. Abdul Gafoor Noorani, *Article 370: A Constitutional History of Jammu and Kashmir* (New Delhi: Oxford University Press, 2011).

20. Lilienthal, *Journals,* 121.

21. David C. Engerman, *The Price of Aid: The Economic Cold War in India* (Cambridge, MA: Harvard University Press, 2018).

22. Saiyid Ali Naqvi, *Indus Waters and Social Change: The Evolution and Transition of Agrarian Society in Pakistan* (Karachi: Oxford University Press, 2013), 100.

23. Ibid.

24. Neuse, *Lilienthal,* 258; Lilienthal, *Journals,* 54–73, McGhee quotation on 63.

25. N. D. Gulhati, *Indus Waters Treaty: An Exercise in International Mediation* (Bombay: Allied Publishers, 1973), 91.

26. Naqvi, *Indus Waters,* 100.

27. David E. Lilienthal, "Are We Losing India?," *Collier's,* June 23, 1951; Lilienthal, "Another Korea in the Making?," *Collier's,* August 4, 1951.

28. Waseem Ahmad Qureshi, "Dispute Resolution Mechanisms: An Analysis of the Indus Waters Treaty," *Pepperdine Dispute Resolution Law Journal* 18 (2018): 75–116; Muhammad Uzair Qamar, Muhammad Azmat, and Pierluigi Claps, "Pitfalls in Transboundary Indus Water Treaty: A Perspective to Prevent Unattended Threats to the Global Security," *npj Clean Water* 2, no. 1 (Dec. 2019); "Fact Sheet: The Indus Waters Treaty 1960 and the Role of the World Bank," World Bank, https://www.worldbank.org/en/region/sar/brief/fact-sheet-the-indus-waters-treaty-1960-and-the-world-bank (accessed October 13, 2020).

29. William Norman Brown, "The Quarrel Over Kashmir" in *United States and India, Pakistan, Bangladesh* (Cambridge, MA: Harvard University Press, 2013), 159.

30. "World Bank Declares Pause to Protect Indus Waters Treaty," World Bank, https://www.worldbank.org/en/news/press-release/2016/12/12/world-bank-declares-pause-protect-indus-water-treaty (accessed February 14, 2021).

31. Lilienthal, *Journals,* 83.

32. Lilienthal, "Another Korea?," 56.

33. Lilienthal, "Losing India?," 13–14.

34. Oliver, *Transcript of Oral History Interview with Mr. Eugene R. Black,* 48–49.

35. Lilienthal, "Another Korea?," 23.

36. Imran Ali, *The Punjab Under Imperialism, 1885-1947* (Karachi: Oxford University Press, 2003).

37. Lilienthal, *TVA,* 2.

38. Lilienthal, "Another Korea?," 56.

39. For an excellent summary of the Kashmir dispute see William Norman Brown, "The Quarrel Over Kashmir," in *United States and India, Pakistan, Bangladesh* (Cambridge, MA: Harvard University Press, 2013), 159–173. The author calls it "the most critical of all between India and Pakistan," 159.

40. Lilienthal, "Another Korea?," 57.

41. Ibid.

42. Ibid, 58; emphasis added.

43. Gulhati, *Indus Waters,* xvi.

44. Ibid, xvii.

45. Daniel Haines,*Rivers Divided: Indus Basin Waters in the Making of India and Pakistan* (New York: Oxford University Press, 2016), 42.

46. Ibid.

47. Lilienthal, "Another Korea?,"58.

48. Lilienthal, "Another Korea?,"58.

49. Lilienthal, *TVA,* 1–2.

50. Daniel Klingensmith, *One Valley and a Thousand: Dams, Nationalism, and Development* (New Delhi: Oxford University Press, 2007); see in particular his chapter on nationalist engineering, 211–253.

51. As Daniel Haines has shown, the pre-Partition build-up to the Standstill Agreement had its fair share of complexity and opacity. This was compounded by the religious demography of the Punjab, with Sikhs demanding territorial division from the colonial authorities that recognized that water rights attached to them on the basis of their past labor. See Haines, *Rivers Divided,* 40–44.

52. Gulhati, *Indus Waters*; see especially Chapter IV, The Partition, and Chapter V, Abortive India-Pakistan Discussions.

53. Haines, *Rivers Divided.*

54. Lilienthal, "Another Korea?," 58 (emphasis in original).

55. David Gilmartin,*Empire and Islam: Punjab and the Making of Pakistan* (London: Tauris, 1988).

56. Indus Basin Development Fund Agreement, September 19, 1960, https://iea.uoregon.edu/treaty-text/1960-indusbasindevelopmentfundentxt (accessed February 20, 2020).

57. Lilienthal, *Journals,* xi.

58. Lilienthal, "Another Korea?,"58.

59. For a masterful analysis of British settlement policy in the Punjab involving giving agricultural lands to the military and the lasting effects of the military's role in the rural economy of what became Pakistan, see generally Ali, *Punjab Under Imperialism.*

60. Lilienthal, "Another Korea?," 58.

61. David Gilmartin, *Blood and Water: The Indus River Basin in Modern History* (Oakland: University of California Press, 2015); see particularly Chapters 6 and 7.

62. Lilienthal, "Another Korea?," 58.

63. David Blackbourn, *The Conquest of Nature: Water, Landscape, and the Making of Modern Germany* (New York: Norton, 2006).

64. Lilienthal, "Another Korea?," 58, emphasis added.

65. Lilienthal, *Journals,* 81.

66. Lilienthal, *Journals,* 470.

67. Saad Sultan, "The Indus Waters Treaty: An Exemplar of Cooperation," *South Asia@ LSE,* June 25, 2018, https://blogs.lse.ac.uk/southasia/2018/06/25/the-indus-waters-treaty-an-exemplar-of-cooperation/; Christopher Rossi, "Blood, Water, and the Indus Waters Treaty," *Minnesota Journal of International Law* 29, No. 2 (2020).

68. Ashfaq Mahmood, *Hydro-Diplomacy: Preventing Water War Between Nuclear-Armed Pakistan and India* (Islamabad: Institute of Policy Studies, 2018).

69. Lilienthal, "Another Korea?,"58.

70. John Briscoe, "Troubled Waters: Can a Bridge Be Built over the Indus?," *Economic and Political Weekly* 45, no. 50 (Dec. 2010).

71. Ijaz Hussain in *Indus Waters Treaty: Political and Legal Dimensions* (Karachi: Oxford University Press, 2017) details the project-by-project legal claims and counterclaims between the countries, leading to the conclusion that this form of international relations is the new normal.

72. Damian Carrington, "A Third of Himalayan Ice Cap Doomed, Finds Report," *The Guardian,* February 4, 2019, https://www.theguardian.com/environment/2019/feb/04/a-third-of-himalayan-ice-cap-doomed-finds-shocking-report; Kenneth Pomeranz, "Asia's Unstable Water Tower: The Politics, Economics, and Ecology of Himalayan Water Projects," *Asia Policy* 16, no. 1 (2013): 4–10; Suhaib Bin Farhan et al., "Assessing the Impacts of Climate Change on the High Altitude Snow- and Glacier-Fed Hydrological Regimes of Astore and Hunza, the Sub-Catchments of Upper Indus Basin," *Journal of Water and Climate Change* 11, no. 2 (June 2020): 479–490; "Billions Rely on Himalayan Glaciers for Water. But They're Disappearing," https://www.globalcitizen.org/en/content/himalayas-melting-climate-change/ (accessed January 10, 2021); Pratap Singh, S. K. Jain, and Naresh Kumar, "Estimation of Snow and Glacier-Melt Contribution to the Chenab River, Western Himalaya," *Mountain Research and Development* 17, no. 1 (Feb. 1997): 49; Damian Carrington, "Himalayan Glacier Melting Doubled Since 2000, Spy Satellites Show," *The Guardian,* June 19, 2019, https://www.theguardian.com/environment/2019/jun/19/himalayan-glacier-melting-doubled-since-2000-scientists-reveal; Erica Thorson, "Sharing Himalayan Glacial Meltwater: The Role of Territorial Sovereignty," *Duke Journal of Comparative & International Law* 19, no. 3 (April 1, 2009): 487–514; "The Costs of Heightened Conflict in the Himalayas," https://www.eco-business.com/news/the-costs-of-heightened-conflict-in-the-himalayas/ (accessed October 6, 2020).

73. "Fact Sheet: The Indus Waters Treaty 1960 and the Role of the World Bank," World Bank, June 11, 2018.

74. Ibid.

75. The Colorado River Compact between seven western states and the federal government signed in 1922 divides the flow of the rivers to upper and lower basin states; see https://www.usbr.gov/lc/region/pao/pdfiles/crcompct.pdf. As the protracted history of the Colorado River Compact demonstrates, predicting future flows from previous records and apportioning it among a

river's co-sharers is rife with uncertainty. With the increasing uncertainty resulting from climate change, this work of observation and prediction is becoming more complex.

76. David E. Lilienthal, *The Journals of David E. Lilienthal, Volume V: The Harvest Years 1959-1963* (New York: Harper & Row, 1964), 116.

77. Ibid., 117.

78. Ali, *Punjab Under Imperialism*, 158–205.

79. Oliver, *Transcript of Interview with Mr. Eugene R. Black*, 43.

80. Bashir A. Malik, *Indus Waters Treaty in Retrospect* (Lahore: Brite Books, 2005), 153.

81. *Indus Basin Irrigation Water Dispute*, Embassy of Pakistan, Washington, DC, 1953; author's emphasis.

82. Quoted in Malik, *Indus Waters Treaty in Retrospect*, 153.

83. Arthur Michel Aloys, *The Indus Rivers: A Study of the Effects of Partition* (New Haven, CT: Yale University Press, 1967), 270.

84. Lilienthal, "Another Korea?," 8.

85. Aloys, *The Indus Rivers*, 254.

86. Reported in Haines, *Rivers Divided*, 126.

87. Oliver, *Transcript of Interview with Mr. Eugene R. Black*, 48.

88. Indus Basin Development Fund Agreement, 19 September 1960, https://iea.uoregon.edu/treaty-text/1960-indusbasindevelopmentfundentxt (accessed, February 20, 2020).

89. Majed Akhter, "The Hydropolitical Cold War: The Indus Waters Treaty and State Formation in Pakistan." *Political Geography* 46 (2015): 65–75.

90. Oliver, *Transcript of Interview with Mr. Eugene R. Black*, 49–50.

91. James Wescoat, "The Historical Geography of Indus Basin Management: A Long-Term Perspective, 1500-2000," in *The Indus River: Biodiversity, Resources, Humankind*, ed. A. Meadows and P. S. Meadows (Karachi: Oxford University Press, 1999), 424.

92. Edwin Bock and Albert Gorvine, *A Scientific Panel in Foreign Affairs: The Revelle Report*, Inter-University Case Program, 1962, 5.

93. Kaiser Bengali and Nafisa Shah, "Introduction," in *The Politics of Managing Water*, ed. Kaiser Bengali (Islamabad: Oxford University Press, Sustainable Development Policy Institute, 2003), xi–xxiv.

94. Department of the Interior Panel on Waterlogging Salinity in West Pakistan, *Report on Land and Water Development in the Indus Plain* (Washington, DC: Government Printing Office, 1964), Preface, 1.

95. USAID, "Economic Growth & Agriculture," November 13, 2020, https://www.usaid.gov/pakistan/economic-growth-agriculture.

96. U.S.-Pakistan Center for Advanced Studies in Water, The U Water Center, https://water.utah.edu/uspcasw (accessed February 15, 2021).

97. Department of the Interior panel.

98. P. Lieftinck, *Water and Power Resources of West Pakistan: A Study in Sector Planning* (Baltimore: Johns Hopkins University Press, 1968), Foreword.

99. *Avoiding Water Wars: Water Scarcity and Central Asia's Growing Importance for Stability in Afghanistan and Pakistan*, https://www.foreign.senate.gov/imo/media/doc/Senate%20Print%20112-10%20Avoiding%20Water%20Wars%20Water%20Scarcity%20and%20Central%20Asia%20Afgahnistan%20and%20Pakistan.pdf (accessed February 20, 2020).

100. Donald Worster, *Rivers of Empire: Water, Aridity and the Growth of the American West* (New York: Oxford University Press, 1992), 284–285.

101. David E. Lilienthal, *The Journals of David E. Lilienthal, Volume VII: Unfinished Years, 1968-1981* (New York: Harper & Row, 1964), 203–204.

Chapter 6

1. As part of its information activities in Italy, USIS opened centers and film libraries in all major Italian cities. None of the other film collections, however, have been found.

2. For more information on the restoration work, see the video produced by AAMOD and available on YouTube: https://www.youtube.com/watch?v=ZM_RZKhJYbA (accessed February 2020).

3. For more information on the film collection, see the catalogue: Giulia Barbera and Giovanna Tosatti, eds., *United States Information Service. Catalogo del fondo cinematografico (1941-1966)* (Rome: Ministero per i beni e le attività culturali—Direzione Generale degli Archivi, 2007).

4. Rob Kroes, *If You've Seen One, You've Seen the Mall. Europeans and American Mass Culture* (Chicago: University of Illinois Press, 1996).

5. William Dizard, *The Strategy of Truth. The Story of the United States Information Service* (Washington, DC: Public Affairs Press, 1961).

6. NARA, RG59, Department of State 1950-54, Central Decimal File, from 51165/5-550 to 51165/12-2850, box 2464, Foreign Service of the United States, Confidential, subject: USIE Country Papers, to the Department of State, from Rome, June 30, 1950.

7. The idea of the two parallel cultural Cold Wars is borrowed from Volker R. Berghahn, *American and the Intellectual Cold Wars in Europe* (Princeton, NJ: Princeton University Press, 2001).

8. Foreign Relation of the United States, 1948, Western Europe, Volume III, Document 440-NSC 1/1, *Report by the National Security Council,* Washington, November 14, 1947.

9. NARA RG59 Department of State 1950-54, Central Decimal File, from 511651/4-153 to 511652/3-3154, box 2467, Confidential, Desp. No. 2619, subject: IIA Country Plan for Italy, from the American Embassy, Rome, to the Department of State, Washington, May 29, 1953.

10. For more on the concept and role of "people's capitalism," see Laura A. Belmonte, *Selling the American Way: U.S. Propaganda and the Cold War* (Philadelphia: University of Pennsylvania Press, 2010); David M. Potter, *The American Round Table, Discussions on People's Capitalism, Part II: An Inquiry into the Social and Cultural Trends in America Under Our System of Widely Shared Material Benefits at the Yale Club, New York, May 22, 1957* (New York: Advertising Council, 1957); Rudolph L. Weissman, "Toward a People's Capitalism," *Challenge* 7, no. 6 (March 1959): 8–12.

11. In this reference, Lizabeth Cohen has effectively shown the relationship established between consumption and democratic participation through the extension of the consumer's freedom of choice to the political arena. Lizabeth Cohen, *A Consumers' Republic: The Politics of Mass Consumption in Postwar America* (New York: Vintage Books, 2003).

12. Laura Belmonte makes a good analysis of the negative implications of this gap between U.S. reality and the way in which America was represented by USIS. See Belmonte, *Selling the American Way.*

13. The prescription had been introduced by the so-called Legge Andreotti in 1949.

14. The Economic Cooperation Administration began producing documentaries to advertise its reconstruction effort in Western Europe in the second half of 1948. It constantly collaborated with the USIS Motion Picture Program, leveraging the latter's distribution networks.

15. NARA RG59, Department of State, Decimal File, 1950-1954, from 511654/10-251 to 511655/2-2651, box 2470, *Restricted, Outgoing airgram A-537*, from the Department of State, to AmEmbassy, Rome, December 9, 1950.

16. *Operaio a Detroit,* 16 mm, 0.21.00 min, 1950, Fondo USIS—Archivio Centrale dello Stato; available online on AAMOD's YouTube channel: https://www.youtube.com/watch?v=FvcznG1TW6A (accessed February 2020).

17. NARA, RG59 Department of State 1950-54, Central Decimal file, from 51165/1-352 to 51165/3-1453, box 2466, Secret Security Information, Desp. No. 1714, subject: IIA—The combined (USIS/MSA) Information Service: A Progress Report, from AmEmbassy, Rome, to the Department of State, Washington, February 24, 1953.

18. Charles S. Maier, "The Politics of Productivity: Foundations of American International Economic Policy After World War II," *International Organization* 31, no. 4 (1977): 607–633.

19. Werner Sombart, *Why Is There No Socialism in the United States?* (White Plains, NY: M. E. Sharpe, 1976).

20. NARA, RG59 Department of State 1950-54, Central Decimal file, from 51165/1-352 to 51165/3-1453, box 2466, Secret Security Information, Desp. No. 1714, subject: IIA—the combined (USIS-MSA) Information Services: A Progress Report, from Rome to the Department of State, February 24, 1953.

21. I have identified five different thematic lines. Besides the films dedicated to democracy and productivity, it is possible to distinguish a set of films dedicated to Italy's economic recovery and later boom; one concerned with daily life and the social role of families and women; a third group more directly engaged in anticommunist propaganda; and a relevant number of films aimed at encouraging European integration along the U.S. model. See Giulia Crisanti, "Modernizzazione in celluloide. Le politiche d'informazione americane in Italia e il Fondo USIS di Trieste (1941-1966)" (master's diss., University of Pisa, 2015).

22. The quote from the plan is reported in Italian in Gian Piero Brunetta, ed., *Identità italiana e identità europea nel cinema italiano dal 1945 al miracolo economico* (Torino: Edizioni della Fondazione Giovanni Agnelli, 1996), 31. The translation is mine.

23. William Dizard, *The Strategy of Truth*, 159.

24. The original text of the bulletin is in Italian and is reported in Luigi Bruti Liberati, "*Words, Words, Words.*" *La Guerra Fredda dell'USIS in Italia* (Milan: CUEM, 2004), 49–50. The translation in English is mine.

25. *La libertà di imparare,* 16 mm, 0.19.00 min, 1942-1945, Fondo USIS—Archivio Centrale dello Stato; available online on AAMOD's YouTube channel: https://www.youtube.com/watch?v=qrvUmn78ul4 (accessed February 2020).

26. UCLA, 16 mm, 0.41.00 min, 1950, Fondo USIS—Archivio Centrale dello Stato; available online on AAMOD's YouTube channel: https://www.youtube.com/watch?v=G0ZGw62uJH4 (accessed February 2020).

27. The quote is taken from the narration of another film: *L'università di Saint-John,* 16mm, 0.26.00min, 1955, Fondo USIS—Archivio Centrale dello Stato; available online on AAMOD's YouTube channel: https://www.youtube.com/watch?v=syKWUH1I7ss (accessed February 2020).

28. "La libertà di stampa in America," *Nuovo Mondo*, no. 16 (Oct. 15, 1945). The original text is in Italian; the translation in English is mine.

29. *Libertà di stampa,* 16 mm, 0.20.00 min, 1950, Fondo USIS—Archivio Centrale dello Stato; available online on AAMOD's YouTube channel: https://www.youtube.com/watch?v=WA6mZw-UoUM (accessed February 2020).

30. *Una notizia che non si poteva stampare*, 16 mm, 0.10.00 min, 1950, Fondo USIS—Archivio Centrale dello Stato; available online on AAMOD's YouTube channel: https://www.youtube.com/watch?v=73e4vSWlbcg (accessed February 2020).

31. The translation of the quotation from the film is mine.

32. The film, directed by Richard Brooks, was distributed in 1952.

33. *Martedi di Novembre*, 16 mm, 0.14.00 min, 1944, Fondo USIS—Archivio Centrale dello Stato; available online on AAMOD's YouTube channel: https://www.youtube.com/watch?v=ztG8T6iKLgY (accessed February 2020).

34. The translation from Italian to English is mine. It is worth pointing out how similar representations were also intended to contrast criticisms of racism at home.

35. The analysis of this documentary is based on the one proposed by David Ellwood in the catalogue of the collection.

36. NARA, RG59 Department of State 1950-54, Central Decimal File, from 5116521/1-1050 to 5116521/2-354, box 2468, Confidential, Desp. No. 1036, subject: Efforts to overcome misconception abroad of US capitalism, from AmEmbassy, Rome, to the Department of State, October 29, 1951.

37. The expression is borrowed from the title of one of the USIS documentaries dedicated to productivity.

38. *I nastri portanti*, 16 mm, 0.10.00 min, 1948-1953, Fondo USIS—Archivio Centrale dello Stato; available online on AAMOD's YouTube channel: https://www.youtube.com/watch?v=B_Hrg-J3888 (accessed February 2020).

39. *Il segreto del progresso: la macchina al servizio dell'uomo*, 16 mm, 0.12.00 min, 1950, Fondo USIS—Archivio Centrale dello Stato; available online on AAMOD's YouTube channel: https://www.youtube.com/watch?v=fe2WtNAK40Q (accessed February 2020).

40. *Tempo perduto*, 16 mm, 0.12.00 min, 1948-1950, Fondo USIS—Archivio Centrale dello Stato; available online on AAMOD's YouTube channel: https://www.youtube.com/watch?v=MwV_ds9ovH8 (accessed February 2020).

41. *Meno fatica.e più denari: la storia del progresso umano narrata in cinque minuti da De Seta*, 16 mm, 0.05.30 min, 1950, Fondo USIS—Archivio Centrale dello Stato; available online on AAMOD's YouTube channel: https://www.youtube.com/watch?v=o_2SvD0uAb0 (accessed February 2020).

42. *Un'idea in cammino*, 16 mm, 0.13.00 min, 1953, Fondo USIS—Archivio Centrale dello Stato; available online on AAMOD's YouTube channel: https://www.youtube.com/watch?v=lswd9oVJGhc (accessed February 2020).

43. NARA, RG59, Department of State 1950-54, Central Decimal File, from 51165/5-550 to 51165/12-2850, box 2461, Foreign Service of the United States, Confidential, subject: USIE Country Papers, to the Department of State, from Rome, June 30, 1950.

44. NARA, RG59, Department of State, Decimal File, 1950-1954, from 511654/10-251 to 511655/2-2651, box 2470, Foreign Service of the United States of America, Unclassified, subject: USIE Evidence of Effectiveness–Films, to the Department of State, from Rome, January 12, 1951.

45. In this respect, it is worth pointing out how, in fact, USIS documentation points toward both successes and episodes of communist violent attacks against USIS mobile units, so that any clear evaluation of the reception and effectiveness of the films, including among communists, is problematic.

46. NARA, RG59 Department of State 1950-54, Central Decimal File, from 511651/4-153 to 511652/3-3154, box 2467, Confidential, Desp. No. 2619, subject: IIA Country Plan for Italy, from the American Embassy, Rome, to the Department of State, Washington, May 29, 1953.

47. The original text is in Italian and is reported in Pier Paolo D'Attorre, "Anche noi possiamo essere prosperi," in *Quaderni storici*, no. 58 (April 1985): 73. The translation is mine.

48. *Oggi e domani no. 33,* 16 mm, 0.10.00 min, 1957, Fondo USIS—Archivio Centrale dello Stato; available online. on AAMOD's YouTube channel: https://www.youtube.com/watch?v=fSY9zO1bY_E (accessed February 2020).

Chapter 7

1. Office of the White House Press Secretary, "Remarks of the President at the National Conference on International Economic and Social Development," Washington, DC, June 16, 1961, Series 3, Speech Files, President's Office Files, Presidential Papers, Papers of John F. Kennedy, John F. Kennedy Library, Boston, MA [hereafter JFK]; Conference Program, "A Decade of Development: Eighth National Conference on International Economic and Social Development," Washington, DC, June 15-16, 1961, Series 3, Speech Files, President's Office Files, JFK.

2. Hubert H. Humphrey, "A Time for Compassion, A Time for Excellence," Transcription of Address to National Conference on International Economic and Social Development, Washington, DC, June 16, 1961, Box 10, Speech Text Files, Hubert H. Humphrey Papers, Minnesota Historical Society, St. Paul, MN [hereafter HHP]; "Humphrey Scores Plan on Latin Aid," *New York Times*, June 19, 1961, 14; Felix Belair, Jr., "Kennedy Bids U.S. Back Foreign Aid to Combat Reds," *New York Times*, June 17, 1961, 1.

3. Joseph G. Knapp, "The Scope of Farmer Cooperatives—Present and Future," *Journal of Farm Economics* 44, no. 2 (May 1962), 476–488; Jerry Voorhis, *American Cooperatives: Where They Come From, What They Do, Where They Are Going* (New York: Harper, 1961), 82–86.

4. "Personality: Co-Op Man a Rugged Idealist," *New York Times*, July 16, 1961, F3.

5. *Section 601, Public Law 87-195: Foreign Assistance Act of 1961, September 4, 1961* (Washington, DC: Government Printing Office, 1961), 438.

6. *Development of Cooperative Enterprises 1967: Implementation of the Humphrey Amendment to the Foreign Assistance Act of 1961. Sixth Annual Report to Congress* (Washington, DC: Government Printing Office, 1968), 3.

7. Proponents of community development, an allied movement in international development with different constituencies, made similar arguments about the democratic potential of community development strategies. On the history of community development, see Nicole Sackley, "Village Models: Etawah, India and the Making and Remaking of Development in the Early Cold War," *Diplomatic History* 37, no. 4 (Sept. 2013): 749–778; Matthew S. Hull, "Communities of Place, Not Kind: American Technologies of Neighborhood in Postcolonial Delhi," *Comparative Studies in Society and History* 53, no. 4 (2011): 757–790.

8. *Development of Cooperative Enterprises 1967: Implementation of the Humphrey Amendment to the Foreign Assistance Act of 1961. Sixth Annual Report to the Congress* (Washington, DC: Government Printing Office, 1968).

9. Burton I. Kaufman, *Trade and Aid: Eisenhower's Foreign Economic Policy, 1953-1961* (Baltimore: Johns Hopkins University Press, 1982); Walt W. Rostow, *Eisenhower, Kennedy, and Foreign Aid* (Austin: University of Texas Press, 1985).

10. Voorhis, *American Cooperatives*, 210–211.

11. Histories of international development have focused largely on the work of U.S. university-based experts, the Ford and Rockefeller foundations, government officials, and NGOs. Nathan J. Citino, *Envisioning the Arab Future: Modernization in US-Arab Relations* (New York: Cambridge University Press, 2017); Matthew Connelly, *Fatal Misconception: The Struggle*

to Control World Population (Cambridge, MA: Belknap Press of Harvard University, 2008); Nick Cullather, *The Hungry World: America's Cold War Battle Against Poverty in Asia* (Cambridge, MA: Harvard University Press, 2010); David Ekbladh, *The Great American Mission: Modernization and the Construction of an American World Order* (Princeton, NJ: Princeton University Press, 2009); David C. Engerman, *The Price of Aid: The Economic Cold War in India* (Cambridge, MA: Harvard University Press, 2018); Stephen J. Macekura and Erez Manela, eds., *The Development Century: A Global History* (New York: Cambridge University Press, 2018).

12. Laura A. Belmonte, *Selling the American Way: U.S. Propaganda and the Cold War* (Philadelphia: University of Pennsylvania Press, 2008); Robert H. Haddow, *Pavilions of Plenty: Exhibiting American Culture Abroad in the 1950s* (Washington, DC: Smithsonian Institution Press, 1997).

13. Wendy L. Wall, *Inventing the "American Way": The Politics of Consensus from the New Deal to the Civil Rights Movement* (New York: Oxford University Press, 2008); Kevin M. Kruse, *One Nation Under God: How Corporate America Invented Christian America* (New York: Basic Books, 2015); Nancy McClean, *Democracy in Chains: The Deep History of the Radical Right's Stealth Plan for America* (New York: Viking, 2017). Important recent work has traced transnational intellectual networks that gave rise to neoliberalism. See Johanna Bockman, *Markets in the Name of Socialism: The Left-Wing Origins of Neoliberalism* (Stanford, CA: Stanford University Press, 2011); Angus Burgin, *The Great Persuasion: Reinventing Free Markets Since the Depression* (Cambridge, MA: Harvard University Press, 2012); Juan Gabriel Valdes, *Pinochet's Economists: The Chicago School in Chile* (New York: Cambridge University Press, 1995).

14. Nicole Sackley, "The Road from Serfdom: Economic Storytelling and Narratives of India in the Rise of Neoliberalism," *History and Technology* 31, no. 4 (2016): 397–419.

15. Julius Duscha, "US Farmers to Answer Queries at Fair in India," *Washington Post*, November 1, 1959, B19; Arlen J. Large, "India's Sensitivities Sway U.S. Plans for New Delhi Farm Fair," *Wall Street Journal*, December 9, 1959, 1.

16. Grain merchant Ben McCabe organized the National Tax Equality Association (NETA) in 1944 with headquarters in Chicago. NTEA solicited contributions from all over the country and provoked multiple congressional investigations in the late 1950s and early 1950s. Paul W. Schater, "Co-Op Tax Exemption: A Threat to Free Enterprise," *Public Utilities Fortnightly*, August 28, 1947, 268; Thomas L. Stokes, "Tax Question is Mixed into Fight Made upon Cooperatives in US," *Toledo Blade*, August 21, 1947, 18.

17. James Peter Warbasse, *Cooperative Democracy: Through Voluntary Association of the People as Consumers*, 3rd edition (New York: Harper & Row, 1936), 47.

18. Peter D. Franklin, *On Your Side: The Story of the Nationwide Insurance Enterprise* (Columbus, OH: The Enterprise, 1994), 62–63; Jerry Voorhis, *Confessions of a Congressman* (Garden City, NY: Doubleday, 1947), 220, 229, 335.

19. U.S. farmers in cooperatives in many Midwest and plains states voted Republican. Ezra Taft Benson, Eisenhower's Secretary of Agriculture from 1953 to 1961, led the more conservative National Council of Farmer Cooperatives from 1939 to 1943. Edward L. Schapsmeier and Frederick H. Schapsmeier, "Eisenhower and Ezra Taft Benson: Farm Policy in the 1950s," *Agricultural History* 44, no. 4 (Oct. 1970): 369–378.

20. In 1944, Humphrey helped found Minnesota's Democratic-Farmer-Labor Party. On Humphrey, see Arnold Offner, *Hubert Humphrey: The Conscience of the Country* (New Haven, CT: Yale University Press, 2018); John Earl Haynes, "Farm Coops and the Election of Hubert Humphrey to the Senate," *Agricultural History* 57, no. 2 (April 1983), 201.

21. Murray D. Lincoln, "Agriculture in America's Crisis," *Antioch Review* 4, no. 2 (Summer 1944): 607–615; Hubert H. Humphrey, "Cooperatives," 1948, Box 2, Speech Text Files, HHP; "Cooperative League Broadcast," Transcript, April 13, 1953, Box 3, Speech Text Files, HHP.

22. Wallace J. Campbell, *The History of CARE: A Personal Account* (New York: Praeger, 1990), 140; "C.A.R.E. to Send Plows," *New York Times*, January 28, 1950, 23.

23. "Man with a Mission," *Time*, August 17, 1953, 84–86; "Lesson in Democracy," *Time*, September 20, 1954.

24. Cooperatives distinguished themselves from corporations in that they aimed to obtain financial benefit for their members as users rather than maximize profits for shareholders and they distributed any profits to members in proportion to their use of its service rather than in proportion to investment in the enterprise. See Joseph G. Knapp, "Are Cooperatives Good for Business?" *Harvard Business Review*, January 1, 1957, 58.

25. In 1952, Rockefeller decided to expand the work of AIA, focused initially on Brazil and Venezuela, to India. Nelson A. Rockefeller to Murray Lincoln, February 2, 1953, and Murray Lincoln to Nelson A. Rockefeller, February 5, 1953, Rockefeller Family Archives, Public Relations Department Papers, Series 1, Box 5, Folder 50, Rockefeller Archives Center, Tarrytown, NY.

26. On the early history of the Indian Cooperative Union, see Kamaladevi Chattopadhyay, *Inner Recesses, Outer Spaces* (New Delhi: Navrang, 1986), 307–320; L. C. Jain, *Civil Disobedience: Two Freedom Struggles, One Life* (New Delhi: Book Review Literary Trust, 2010). On the Indian cooperative movement, see Nikolay Kamenov, "The Place of the 'Cooperative' in the Agrarian History of India, 1900-1970," *Journal of Asian Studies* 79, no. 1 (2020): 103–128; Eleanor M. Hough, *The Cooperative Movement in India*, 5th rev. edition (Calcutta: Oxford University Press, 1966).

27. "Project Statement for the India Program of the American International Association for Economic and Social Development and the Cooperative League of the USA," March 12, 1953, Rockefeller Family Archives, Public Relations Department Papers, Series 1, Box 5, Folder 50, Rockefeller Archives Center, Tarrytown, NY.

28. "Nehru Convinced Security Pacts Can't Preserve Peace: India Premier Ends U.S. Visit Today," *Reading Eagle*, December 21, 1956, 17. CLUSA provided seed money to a cooperative the farmers owned: "Money was lent to groups of farmers who pool resources get better prices, buy good seeds, tools, and fertilizer at lower prices. . . . As farm production loans were repaid, money was relent to other farmers." By the end of 1960, the Mehrauli project had extended credit and technical assistance to two thousand farmers with a revolving loan fund of $63,435. Allie C. Felder, Jr., "I Fought in the Revolution," Brochure, ca. 1962, Box 62, Wallace J. Campbell Papers, Harry S. Truman Library, Independence, MO (hereafter WCP).

29. Douglas Ensminger, Ford Foundation Program Letter No. 25, April 22, 1953, Ford Foundation Archives, Rockefeller Archives Center, Tarrytown, NY; Walter L. Crawford to Board of Directors of AIA and the Cooperative League of the USA, "Report on Cooperatives and the AIA-Cooperative League Work in India," April 13, 1955, Box 4, Folder 34, Series B, AIA-IBCC, Nelson A. Rockefeller Papers, Harry S. Truman Library, Independence, MO; Nicole Sackley, "Village Models: Etawah, India and the Making and Remaking of Development in the Early Cold War," *Diplomatic History*, 37, no. 4 (Sept. 2013): 749–778.

30. Francine R. Frankel, *India' Political Economy, 1947-1977: The Gradual Revolution* (Princeton, NJ: Princeton University Press, 1978), 124–125; Ministry of Food & Agriculture, *Report of the Indian Delegation to China on Agricultural Planning and Techniques* (New Delhi: Government of India, 1956); Planning Commission, *Report of the Indian Delegation to China on*

Agrarian Cooperatives (New Delhi: Government of India, 1957); "China Farm Plan Urged for India," *New York Times*, June 3, 1957, 5.

31. H. Y. Sharada Prasad, ed., *Selected Works of Jawaharlal Nehru, Second Series, Vol. 34, 21 June-31 August, 1956* (New York: Oxford University Press, 2006), 51–52.

32. Nehru to Chief Ministers, September 6, 1958, Jawaharlal Nehru, *Letters to Chief Ministers, 1947-1964, vol. 5 1958-1964* (New Delhi: Oxford University Press, 1990), 120.

33. Frankel, *India's Political Economy*, 147, 154, 163–167; Sisir Gupta, "The Retreat from Nagpur," *Economic Weekly* 11 (July 1959): 933–936; Howard L. Erdman, *The Swatantra Party and Indian Conservatism* (New York: Cambridge University Press, 1967), 66–67; Sucheta Dalal, *A.D. Shroff: Titan of Finance and Free Enterprise* (New York: Viking, 2000), 69.

34. By 1959, such reports were tempered with assurances that the recent foreign exchange crisis had forced India into "a whole bevy of tax concessions" that had smoothed the way for tens of millions in new investment by such major U.S. corporations as Firestone, Goodyear Tire, and Kaiser Steel. Richard Neff, "Creeping Capitalism," *Christian Science Monitor*, July 18, 1961, 12; Keyes Beech, "Private Dollars Flowing to India," *Washington Post*, November 2, 1959, A10. For reports advocating private enterprise in India, see Lewis Webster Jones, "Survey No. 8: South Asia," in *Foreign Aid Program: Compilation of Studies and Surveys Prepared Under the Direction of the Special Committee to Study the Foreign Aid Program, United States Senate.* (Washington, DC: Government Printing Office, July 1957), 1465–1504; U.S. General Accounting Office, *Examination of Economic and Technical Assistance Program for India, International Cooperation Administration, Department of State, 1955-1958* (Washington, DC: Government Printing Office, 1959), 25; Henry R. Lieberman, "Bill Graham, a Kansas Oilman, Conducts Own Crusade in India," *New York Times*, August 2, 1957, 3.

35. Carroll Kilpatrich, "U.S. Plans Farm Exhibit at Fair to be Held in India," *Washington Post*, September 19, 1959, C6; Arlen J. Large, "India's Sensitivities Sway U.S. Plans for New Delhi Farm Fair," *Wall Street Journal*, December 9, 1959, 1; Julius Duscha, "U.S. Farmers to Answer Queries at Fair in India," *Washington Post*, November 1, 1959, B19; Josephine Ripley, "U.S. Accents Farmer at Fair in India," *Christian Science Monitor*, November 24, 1959, 9; Dwight D. Eisenhower, "Remarks at the Opening of the World Agricultural Fair in New Delhi," December 11, 1959, in *Papers of the Presidents of the United States: Dwight D. Eisenhower* (Washington, DC: Government Printing Office, 1960): 839–842

36. On "people's capitalism," see Belamonte, *Selling the American Way*, 118–134; Haddow, *Pavilions of Plenty*, 39–52; Wall, *Inventing the "American Way,"* 189–198.

37. Voorhis, *American Cooperatives*, 210.

38. A. Ladru Jensen, "Raymond W. Miller, Cooperative Advocate," in *Great American Cooperators*, ed. Joseph G. Knapp (Washington, DC: American Institute of Cooperation, 1967), 351; Raymond W. Miller, *Can Capitalism Compete? A Campaign for American Free Enterprise* (New York: Ronald Press Company, 1959), 4–6, 235–236.

39. Voorhis, *American* Cooperatives, 216; Felder, "I Fought in the Revolution," Brochure, Box 62, WCP.

40. In a later report from July 1963, a CLUSA cooperative expert noted, "I was somewhat concerned by the fact that the Indians are planning to send a few people to Czechoslovakia for cooperative training," but they were not able "to participate in our cooperative training program at the University of Wisconsin. Certainly, if Indians are willing to pay for transportation to Czechoslovakia, possibly something could be worked out for them to use Air India to come to the United States." Samuel F. Ashelman, Jr., to Jerry Voorhis, July 1, 1963, Box 62, WCP;

R. C. Dwivedi, *Asia in ICA: Participation of Asian Cooperatives in ICA Congresses, 1900-1988* (New Delhi: International Cooperative Alliance, Regional Office for Asia, 1989), 95, 125, 127; Thomas B. Keehn, "Indian Cooperative Politics," January 1961, Box 64, WCP.

41. Thomas B. Keehn to Wallace J. Campbell, July 18, 1961, Box 64, WCP.

42. International Cooperative Alliance, *Cooperative Leadership in South-East Asia* (Bombay: Asia Publishing House, 1963), 1.

43. Frankel, *India's Political Economy,* 183; Planning Commission, *Third Five Year Plan* (New Delhi: Government of India, 1961), 201, 211.

44. Daniel Thorner, *Agricultural Cooperatives in India: A Field Report* (New York: Asia Publishing House, 1964), 36–37.

45. "Mission to India: A Report of the Nationwide Cooperative Study Team," Nationwide Insurance, Columbus, OH, February 1962, Box 62, WCP; H. W. Culbreth to Douglas Ensminger, September 8, 1961, Box 64, WCP.

46. "Personality: Co-Op Man a Rugged Idealist," *New York Times*, July 16, 1961, F3.

47. Murray D. Lincoln and David Karp, *Vice President in Charge of Revolution* (New York: McGraw-Hill, 1960), 308.

48. David H. Scull, "Report to the Nationwide Insurance Board by the International Development Committee," August 3, 1961, Box 64, WCP.

49. "Mission to India: A Report of the Nationwide Cooperative Study Team," Nationwide Insurance, Columbus, OH, February 1962, Box 62, WCP.

50. David H. Scull, "Cooperative in India: Challenge to America," ca. 1962, Box 63, WCP.

51. "Mission to India: A Report of the Nationwide Cooperative Study Team," Nationwide Insurance, Columbus, OH, February 1962 Box 62, WCP.

52. Ray Newton to Ferris Owen and Wallace Campbell, September 12, 1962, Box 63, WCP; Wallace J. Campbell to B. K. Nehru [Indian Ambassador], August 1, 1962, Box 63, WCP.

53. Press Release, Nationwide Insurance, January 9, 1962, Box 63, WCP; "Mission to India" Report, Box 62, WCP.

54. "Mission to India" Report, Box 62, WCP.

55. Hubert H. Humphrey, "A Time for Compassion, A Time for Excellence," Transcription of Address to National Conference on International Economic and Social Development, Washington, DC, June 16, 1961, Box 10, Speech Text Files, HHP; Felix Belair, Jr., "Kennedy Bids U.S. Back Foreign Aid to Combat Reds," *New York Times*, June 17, 1961, 1.

56. "Instead of having all these fine men in this room in uniform," Humphrey declared angrily in a closed session of the Foreign Relations Committee, "we ought to have this room filled with people on the housing cooperatives, consumer cooperatives and credit union cooperatives." "Humphrey Scores Plan on Latin Aid," *New York Times*, June 19, 1961, 14.

57. United States Agency for International Development, *Implementation of the Humphrey Amendment to the Foreign Assistance Act of 1961* (Washington, DC: Government Printing Office, 1962).

58. Max F. Millikan and Walt Rostow, *A Proposal: Key to an Effective Foreign Policy* (New York: Harper & Brothers, 1957); Rostow, *Eisenhower, Kennedy, and Foreign Aid.*

59. Lincoln and Karp, *Vice President*, 87, 305.

60. On self-help projects in the U.S. domestic and international contexts, and the circulation between them, see Alyosha Goldstein, *Poverty in Common: The Politics of Community Action During the American Century* (Durham, NC: Duke University Press, 2012); Nicole

Sackley, "The Village as Cold War Site: Experts, Development, and the History of Rural Reconstruction," *Journal of Global History* 6, no. 3 (Nov. 2011): 481–504; Daniel Immerwahr, *Thinking Small: The United States and the Lure of Community Development* (Cambridge, MA: Harvard University Press, 2015). On aided self-help housing, see Helen Gyger, *Improvised Cities: Architecture, Urbanization, and Innovation in Peru* (Pittsburgh, PA: University of Pittsburgh Press, 2019); Richard Harris and Ceeinwen Giles, "A Mixed Message: The Agents and Forms of International Housing Poilicy, 1945-1973," *Habitat International* 27 (2003): 167–191; Nancy H. Kwak, *A World of Homeowners: American Power and the Politics of Housing Aid* (Chicago: University of Chicago Press, 2015); Amy C. Offner, *Sorting Out the Mixed Economy: The Rise and Fall of Welfare and Developmental States in the Americas* (Princeton, NJ: Princeton University Press, 2019).

61. Campbell, *History of CARE,* 206; "Gifts of Farm Tools from Midwest Reach India," *New York Times*, March 28, 1954, F1.

62. Lincoln and Karp, *Vice President*, 308; Wallace J. Campbell to Harry Culbreth, January 15, 1962, Box 63, WCP; David H. Scull, "Cooperative in India: Challenge to America," ca. 1962, Box 63, WCP.

63. The Mission to India report "urge[d] U.S. cooperative movement to make as substantial an effort as possible out of their own and other private resources. We made the point, and everywhere in India found agreement, that the independent stature of the co-ops needs to be increased relative to government supervision and control, and that this could be aided most by stressing the co-op to co-op nature of our efforts." Mission to India Report, February 1962, Box 62, WCP.

64. "Bold Assistance Programme for Indian Co-Operation," Co-operative News Service, No. 4, April 1962, Box 64, WCP.

65. Allie C. Felder, Jr., "I Fought in the Revolution," Brochure, ca. 1962, Box 62, WCP; H. W. Culbreth to Nationwide Board of Directors, October 19, 1962, Box 62, WCP; Jerry Voorhis to H. W. Culbreth, December 31, 1962, Box 62, WCP.

66. "Co-op Group Maps Program Abroad," *New York Times*, September 23, 1962, 70.

67. Jerry Voorhis to Allie C. Felder, Jr., September 25, 1963, Box 63, WCP; Wallace J. Campbell to B. K. Nehru [Indian Ambassador], August 1, 1962, Box 63, WCP; Wallace J. Campbell to Harry Culbreth, July 31, 1962, Box 62, WCP.

68. United States Agency for International Development, *Implementation of the Humphrey Amendment to the Foreign Assistance Act of 1961* (Washington, DC: Government Printing Office, 1962); *Development of Cooperative 1967: Implementation of the Humphrey Amendment to the Foreign Assistance Act of 1961. Sixth Annual Report to the Congress* (Washington, DC: Government Printing Office, 1968).

69. Shelby Edward Southard, "Assistance of Cooperative League of the U.S.A. to the Cooperative Movement of India, 1954-67," in *Foreign Assistance Act of 1968: Hearings Before the Committee on Foreign Affairs House of Representatives,* 19th Cong., 2nd session on H.R. 15263, February 28, 29, March 4, 5, 6, and 7, 1968 (Washington, DC: Government Printing Office, 1968), 1076.

70. Between 1967 and 1974, USAID contributed $21 million, while the government of India poured $110 million into the project, nearly $18 million from loans from the British and Dutch governments and U.S private banks. Southard, "Assistance of Cooperative League of the U.S.A. to the Cooperative Movement of India, 1954-67," 1079–1080; *Foreign Assistance Act of 1968: Hearings Before the Committee on Foreign Affairs House of Representatives,* 19th Congress, 2nd

session on H.R. 15263, February 28, 29, March 4, 5, 6, and 7, 1968 (Washington, DC: Government Printing Office, 1968), 1060.

71. Lyndon Johnson, "Statement by the President upon Appointing a Committee to Review Foreign Aid Programs," December 26, 1963, *Papers of the Presidents of the United States: Lyndon B. Johnson 1963–1964* (Washington, DC: Government Printing Office, 1965), 84.

72. Southard, 1075.

73. Ibid.

74. Senator Humphrey speaking on S. 1643, on July 25, 1961 in 87th Cong., 1st session, *Congressional Record,* 107, pt. 10, 13222.

75. Jerry Voorhis to H. W. Culbreth, December 31, 1962, Box 62, WCP; "Co-Op Group Maps Program Abroad,"70; Neil Sheehan, "Co-Op Group Got C.I.A. Conduit AID," *New York Times* May 16, 1967, 37.

Chapter 8

1. William M. Tsutsui, *Manufacturing Ideology: Scientific Management in Twentieth-Century Japan* (Princeton, NJ: Princeton University Press, 1998), 137.

2. Charles S. Maier, *In Search of Stability: Explorations in Historical Political Economy* (Cambridge, UK: Cambridge University Press, 1987), 130.

3. For a prominent example, see David Ekbladh, *The Great American Mission: Modernization and the Construction of an American World Order* (Princeton, NJ: Princeton University Press, 2010).

4. On tradition, see Nils Gilman, *Mandarins of the Future: Modernization Theory in Cold War America* (Baltimore: Johns Hopkins University Press, 2003), 5–11, 98–101, and Robin Averbeck, *Liberalism Is Not Enough: Race and Poverty in Postwar Political Thought* (Chapel Hill: University of North Carolina Press, 2018), 17–24.

5. See Aaron Stephen Moore, "Japanese Development Consultancies and Postcolonial Power in Southeast Asia: The Case of Burma's Balu Chang Hydropower Project," *East Asian Science, Technology and Society: An International Journal* 8, no. 3 (Sept. 2014): 297–322.

6. See Janis Mimura, *Planning for Empire: Reform Bureaucrats and the Japanese Wartime State* (Ithaca, NY: Cornell University Press, 2011); Hiromi Mizuno, *Science for the Empire: Scientific Nationalism in Modern Japan* (Stanford, CA: Stanford University Press, 2009); Aaron Stephen Moore, *Constructing East Asia: Technology, Ideology, and Empire in Japan's Wartime Era, 1931-1945* (Stanford, CA: Stanford University Press, 2013).

7. See Leffler, *Safeguarding Democratic Capitalism,* 118–119. On Japan specifically, see Aaron Forsburg, *America and the Japanese Miracle: The Cold War Context of Japan's Postwar Economic Revival* (Chapel Hill: University of North Carolina Press, 2000), and Sayuri Shimizu, *Creating People of Plenty: The United States and Japan's Economic Alternatives* (Kent, OH: Kent State University Press, 2001).

8. Quote from Maier, *In Search of Stability,* 128. See also Michael J. Hogan, *The Marshall Plan: America, Britain and the Reconstruction of Western Europe, 1947–1952* (New York: Cambridge University Press, 1989), 135–188, and Jacqueline McGlade, "The U.S. Technical Assistance Program: From Revolutionary Vision to Production Drive," in *Catching Up with America: Productivity Missions and the Diffusion of American Economic and Technological Influence After the Second World War,* ed. Dominique Barjot (Paris: Press de l'Université de Paris-Sorbonne, 2002), 73–74.

9. John Foster Dulles to the American Embassy, New Delhi, Subject: European Productivity Agency, January 10, 1958. RG 286 Agency for International Development, USAID/Bureau for Far East, Office of Indonesia Affairs, Entry #P 368, Closed Project Files, 1955–1964, Box 17. Folder: An Asian Productivity Agency–Pros and Cons. National Archives and Records Administration, College Park, MD (hereafter NARA).

10. Mark Metzler, *Capital as Will and Imagination: Schumpeter's Guide to the Postwar Japanese Miracle* (Ithaca, NY: Cornell University Press, 2013), 98.

11. Tsutsui, *Manufacturing Ideology*, 125.

12. Andrew Gordon, *Wages of Affluence: Labor and Management in Postwar Japan* (Cambridge, MA: Harvard University Press, 2008), 36.

13. Tsutsui, *Managing Ideology*, 135; Bai Gao, *Economic Ideology and Japanese Industrial Policy: Developmentalism from 1931–1965* (New York: Cambridge University Press, 1997), 217.

14. John G. Harlan to Clinton Morrison, Subject: Report on Trip to Japan, September 1954, to Consult with Embassy and Japanese Officials re Productivity and Technical Exchange Programs, September 30, 1954. RG 286 Agency for International Development, USAID/Bureau for Far East, Office of Indonesia Affairs, Entry #P 368, Closed Project Files, 1955–1964, Box 9. Folder: Productivity Harlan Report. NARA.

15. Quoted in Tsutsui, *Managing Ideology*, 136.

16. Laura Hein, *Reasonable Men, Powerful Words: Political Culture and Expertise in Twentieth-Century Japan* (Berkeley: University of California Press, 2004), 144–146, 151. See also Scott O'Bryan, *The Growth Idea: Purpose and Prosperity in Postwar Japan* (Honolulu: University of Hawai'i Press, 2009), 164–168.

17. Quoted in Simon Partner, *Assembled in Japan: Electrical Goods and the Making of the Japanese Consumer* (Berkeley: University of California Press, 2009), 124.

18. United States Operations Mission to Japan, "Exchange of Notes Between the Government of Japan and the Government of the United States Regarding the Productivity Program," April 7, 1955. RG 286 Agency for International Development, USAID/Bureau for Far East, Office of Indonesia Affairs, Entry #P 368, Closed Project Files, 1955–1964, Box 2. Folder: Agreements: Original Notes etc., Meyer Report etc. NARA.

19. Report on Examination of the United States Operations Mission to Japan, as of June 30, 1960, 3. RG 286 Agency for International Development, USAID/Bureau for Far East, Office of Indonesia Affairs, Entry #P 368, Closed Project Files, 1955–1964, Box 7. Folder: Japan Phase Out. NARA.

20. Partner, *Assembled in Japan*, 125.

21. O'Bryan, *The Growth Idea*, 88, 156.

22. Hein, *Reasonable Men, Powerful Words*, 151.

23. Metzler, *Capital as Will and Imagination*, 69, 170, 200–201. See also Hein, *Reasonable Men, Powerful Words*, 78–79.

24. Operations Coordinating Board, "Statement of the Existing United States Policy in the International Labor Field," October 20, 1955. White House Office, National Security Council Staff: Papers, 1948–1961, OCB Central Files Series, Box 14, Folder: OCB 004.06 [Overseas Labor Activity] (File #1) (5) [August 1955–June 1956]. Dwight D. Eisenhower Library, Abilene, KS.

25. Japan Productivity Center, *Japan Productivity Activities*, 1959. RG 286 Agency for International Development, USAID/Bureau for Far East, Office of Indonesia Affairs, Entry #P 368, Closed Project Files, 1955–1964, Box 6. Folder: Japan Productivity Activities. NARA.

26. Nakayama Ichirō, *An Introduction to Productivity* (Tokyo: Asian Productivity Organization, 1963), 37.

27. Ibid., 39.

28. On management science, see Stephen P. Waring, *Taylorism Transformed: Scientific Management Theory Since 1945* (Chapel Hill: University of North Carolina Press, 1991), 28, 85–94.

29. Tokyo Telegram no. 339, Subject: "Press Announcement and Seminars," June 20, 1955. RG 469 Records of the U.S. Foreign Assistance Agencies, 1948–1961, Office of Far Eastern Operations, Japan Subject Files, 1950–59, Box 28, Folder: Japan Productivity. NARA.

30. Quoted in Tsutsui, *Manufacturing Ideology*, 139–140. For more on the JPC's claims about the politically neutral content of contemporary management ideology, see *Manufacturing Ideology*, 143.

31. Partner, *Assembled in Japan*, 125.

32. Charles Hatton to Grant Whitman, Subject: "Report on the J.P.C.'s Top Management Seminar at the Fujiya Hotel, Mianosita, July 6–8, 1955," July 11, 1955. RG 286 Agency for International Development, USAID/Bureau for Far East, Office of Indonesia Affairs, Entry #P 368, Closed Project Files, 1955–1964, Box 9. Folder: Report * Landes Productivity. NARA.

33. Waring, *Taylorism Transformed*, 90–94.

34. Ibid., 90.

35. Ibid., 90.

36. "U.S. Expert Gives Advice–Seminar on Human Relations," in *Productivity: The Bulletin of Japan Productivity Center*, December 1, 1959. RG 286 Agency for International Development, USAID/Bureau for Far East, Office of Indonesia Affairs, Entry #P 368, Closed Project Files, 1955–1964, Box 6. Folder: Japanese Govt–Kishi Visit–Jan 1960. NARA.

37. John M. Allison to Shigemitsu Mamoru, April 7, 1955. RG 286 Agency for International Development, USAID/Bureau for Far East, Office of Indonesia Affairs, Entry #P 368, Closed Project Files, 1955–1964, Box 2, Folder: Agreements: Original Notes etc., Meyer Report etc. NARA.

38. See Gordon, *Wages of Affluence*.

39. On labor's participation in postwar protest movements, see Gordon, *Wages of Affluence*; Christopher Gerteis, *Gender Struggles: Wage-Earning Women and Male Dominated Unions in Postwar Japan* (Cambridge, MA: Harvard University Asia Center, 2010); Nick Kapur, *Japan at the Crossroads: Conflict and Compromise After Anpo* (Cambridge, MA: Harvard University Press, 2018); Jennifer M. Miller, *Cold War Democracy: The United States and Japan* (Cambridge, MA: Harvard University Press, 2019); Mari Yamamoto, *Grassroots Pacifism in Postwar Japan: The Rebirth of a Nation* (New York: RoutledgeCurzon, 2004).

40. Operations Coordinating Board, "Statement of the Existing United States Policy in the International Labor Field," October 20, 1955. White House Office, National Security Council Staff: Papers, 1948–1961, OCB Central Files Series, Box 14, Folder: OCB 004.06 [Overseas Labor Activity] (File #1) (5) [August 1955–June 1956]. Eisenhower Library.

41. Tsutsui, *Manufacturing Ideology*, 142.

42. On labor-management councils, see Gordon, *The Wages of Affluence*, 80, 143. Management and Industrial Relations Specialists Study Team, *Labor–Management Cooperation in Japan, 1959* (Japan Productivity Center/International Cooperation Administration, 1959), 1.

43. For a more detailed exploration of the connection between thinking about productivity and visions of democracy in the U.S.-Japanese relationship, see Jennifer M. Miller, *Cold War Democracy: The United States and Japan* (Cambridge, MA: Harvard University Press, 2019), 227–272.

44. Tokyo to the International Cooperation Administration. Excerpts from *Japan Productivity News* No. 101 issued June 16, 1958. RG 469 Records of the U.S. Foreign Assistance Agencies, 1948–1961, Office of Far Eastern Operations, Japan Subject Files, 1950–1959, Box 58. Folder: Japan—Productivity 1958. NARA.

45. W. S. Landes, "Survey of Japanese Industrial Productivity," January 1, 1956. RG 286 Agency for International Development, USAID/Bureau for Far East, Office of Indonesia Affairs, Entry #P 368, Closed Project Files, 1955–1964, Box 6. Folder: Landes Report. NARA. Ironically, by the 1980s, Japanese communalism and consensual decision making was celebrated by American and Japanese alike as a core reason behind Japan's economic success. See, for example, Frank Gibney, *Miracle by Design: The Real Reasons Behind Japan's Economic Success* (New York: Times Books, 1982); Ezra Vogel, *Japan as Number One: Lessons for America* (Cambridge, MA: Harvard University Press, 1979); Yamamoto Shichihei, *The Spirit of Japanese Capitalism and Other Selected Essays*, trans. Lynne E. Riggs and Takechi Manabu (Lanham, MD: Madison Books, 1992).

46. See, for example, Headquarters, U.S. Army Service Forces, *Civil Affairs Handbook, Japan, Section 2: Government and Administration* (Washington, DC: Government Printing Office, 1945), 78, and Ruth Benedict, *The Chrysanthemum and the Sword: Patterns of Japanese Culture* (Boston: Houghton Mifflin, 1946), 13, 224–225.

47. W. S. Landes, "Survey of Japanese Industrial Productivity," January 1, 1956. RG 286 Agency for International Development, USAID/Bureau for Far East, Office of Indonesia Affairs, Entry #P 368, Closed Project Files, 1955–1964, Box 6. Folder: Landes Report. NARA.

48. Japan Productivity Center, Seventh Top Management Team, *Growth of Japanese Economy and Productivity*, December 1, 1961. RG 286 Agency for International Development, USAID/Bureau for Far East, Office of Indonesia Affairs, Entry #P 368, Closed Project Files, 1955–1964, Box 14. Folder: Japan FY 1962 January June phase-out, Folder 5. NARA.

49. U.S. Operations Mission to Japan to International Cooperation Administration, Washington, DC Subject: Joint Declaration Regarding the Increased Productivity Movement, September 28, 1955. RG 286 Agency for International Development, USAID/Bureau for Far East, Office of Indonesia Affairs, Entry #P 368, Closed Project Files, 1955–1964. Box 9, Folder: Report * Landes Productivity. NARA.

50. U.S. Information Service, Tokyo to U.S. Information Agency, Washington, Subject: Pamphlet on Promotion of Productivity Sponsored by Zenro and Financed Jointly by USIS and USOM, April 13, 1956. RG 469 Records of the U.S. Foreign Assistance Agencies, 1948–1961, Office of Far Eastern Operations, Japan Subject Files, 1950–1959, Box 41. Folder: Japan—Productivity 1956. NARA.

51. Management and Industrial Relations Specialists Study Team, *Labor-Management Cooperation in Japan*, 7–8.

52. Gordon, *The Wages of Affluence*, 143.

53. Peter F. Drucker, "Japan Tries for a Second Miracle," *Harper's*, March 1, 1963, 72.

54. Japan also had its own development initiatives, such as reparations programs, foreign loans and investments, and participation in the Colombo Plan and the United Nations Economic Commission for Asia and the Far East (ECAFE). However, this chapter focuses on joint initiatives between the United States and Japan and on Japanese initiatives that received American funding.

55. Christian Herter Circular, March 23, 1960. RG 286 Agency for International Development, USAID/Bureau for Far East, Office of Indonesia Affairs, Entry #P 368, Closed Project Files, 1955–1964, Box 3. Folder: Development Assistance Group. NARA.

56. JJM, Purpose of the Tokyo International Training Center, April 5, 1958. RG 286 Agency for International Development, USAID Mission to Japan/Training Office, Entry #P 516, Subject Files, 1955–1963, Box 8. Folder: Miscellaneous Conferences, Seminars, Workshops, Meetings. NARA.

57. Gilman, *Mandarins of the Future*, 95. See also Ellen Herman, *The Romance of American Psychology: Political Culture in the Age of Experts* (Berkeley: University of California Press, 1996).

58. Gilman, *Mandarins of the Future*, 100.

59. Quoted in *Mandarins of the Future*, 145.

60. Japan also carried out training programs through international aid programs like the Colombo Plan.

61. Far East Region (Japan), Program Support 488, September 10, 1963. RG 286 Agency for International Development, USAID/Bureau for Far East, Office of Indonesia Affairs, Entry #P 368, Closed Project Files, 1955–1964, Box 2. Folder: #Rpts. NARA.

62. United States Operations Mission to Japan, International Cooperation Administration, Summary of Operations 1955–1960, December 1960. RG 286 Agency for International Development, USAID/Bureau for Far East, Office of Indonesia Affairs, Entry #P 368, Closed Project Files, 1955–1964, Box 7. Folder: Briefing Book United States/Japan Productivity Program Background Material and Current Problems. NARA.

63. Ibid.

64. William J. Parker, Report on Official Visit to Hiroshima, Osaka and Sendai, 1963. RG 286 Agency for International Development, USAID Mission to Japan/Training Office, Entry #P 516, Subject Files, 1955–1963, Box 1. Folder: Field Trip Reports. NARA.

65. Moore, *Constructing East Asia*, 227. See also Aaron Stephen Moore, "Japanese Development Consultancies and Postcolonial Power in Southeast Asia," *East Asian Science, Technology and Society: An International Journal* 8, no. 3 (Sept. 2014): 297–322; Louise Young, *Japan's Total Empire: Manchuria and the Culture of Wartime Imperialism* (Berkeley: University of California Press, 1998), 183–306.

66. Hiromi Mizuno, "Introduction: A Kula Ring for the Flying Geese: Japan's Technology Aid and Postwar Asia," in *Engineering Asia: Technology, Colonial Development and the Cold War Order*, eds. Hiromi Mizuno, Aaron S. Moore, and John DiMoia (London: Bloomsbury Academic, 2018), 33–35.

67. Reparations became a prominent form of Japanese overseas development efforts, totaling $1 billion. Shinji Takagi, *From Recipient to Donor: Japan's Official Aid Flows, 1945 to 1990 and Beyond* (Princeton, NJ: International Finance Section, Department of Economics, Princeton University, 1995), 12. See also Mizuno et al., *Engineering Asia*, 43–164.

68. Seuhiro Akira, "The Road to Economic Re-Entry: Japan's Policy Towards Southeast Asian Development in the 1950s and 1960s," *Social Science Japan Journal* 2, no. 1 (April 1999): 97–98.

69. Quoted in Suehiro, 92.

70. U.S. Embassy, Tokyo (Lew B. Clark) to Department of State, Washington, Subject: Japan's Ability to Participate in Development of South and Southeast Asia, March 29, 1955. RG 469 Records of the U.S. Foreign Assistance Agencies, 1948–1961, Office of Far Eastern Operations, Japan Subject Files, 1950–1959, Box 26, Folder: Japan—Industry. NARA. See also Shimizu, *Creating People of Plenty*, 198–199.

71. Seuhiro, "The Road to Economic Re-Entry," 92.

72. Moore, *Constructing East Asia*, 235.

73. Asia Kyokai, "Hope for Tomorrow," 1957. RG 286 Agency for International Development, USAID Mission to Japan/Training Office, Entry #P 516, Subject Files, 1955–1963, Box 1. Folder: General Correspondence I. NARA.

74. "Duties and Responsibilities of the Asia Kyokai." RG 286 Agency for International Development, USAID Mission to Japan/Training Office, Entry #P 516, Subject Files, 1955–1963, Box 1. Folder: Asia Kyokai. NARA.

75. Asia Kyokai, Contents of the 8th Orientation Case for the ICA Participants from the Republic of China, August 18, 1958. RG 286 Agency for International Development, USAID Mission to Japan/Training Office, Entry #P 516, Subject Files, 1955–1963, Box 1. Folder: Asia Kyokai. NARA.

76. Katsuhiko Miyaji, Chief Operations Division, Asia Kyokai to International Cooperation Administration, August 18, 1958. RG 286 Agency for International Development, USAID Mission to Japan/Training Office, Entry #P 516, Subject Files, 1955–1963, Box 1. Folder: Asia Kyokai. NARA.

77. Tokyo to International Cooperation Agency, Washington, Subject: Asian Productivity Agency, June 2, 1958. RG 286 Agency for International Development, USAID/Bureau for Far East, Office of Indonesia Affairs, Entry #P 368, Closed Project Files, 1955–1964, Box 17. Folder: An Asian Productivity Organization–Pros and Cons. NARA.

78. "Technical Exchange Seen on the Upswing: Asian Nations Pushing Plans in Wake of Recent Meeting," in *Productivity: The Bulletin of the Japan Productivity Center* 7 (Dec. 1959). RG 286 Agency for International Development, USAID/Bureau for Far East, Office of Indonesia Affairs, Entry #P 368, Closed Project Files, 1955–1964, Box 6. Folder: Japanese Govt–Kishi Visit–Jan 1960. NARA.

79. Quoted in Toshihiro Higuchi, "How U.S. Aid in the 1950s Prepared Japan as a Future Donor," in *The Rise of the Asian Donors: Japan's Impact on the Evolution of Emerging Donors*, ed. Jin Sato and Yasutami Shimomura (New York: Routledge, 2013), 45.

80. "An Asian Productivity Agency–Pros and Cons." RG 286 Agency for International Development, USAID/Bureau for Far East, Office of Indonesia Affairs, Entry #P 368, Closed Project Files, 1955–1964, Box 17. Folder: An Asian Productivity Organization–Pros and Cons. NARA.

81. Asian Productivity Organization, *Asian Productivity: Monthly Bulletin*, no. 15 (Nov. 1962). RG 286 Agency for International Development, USAID/Bureau for Far East, Office of Indonesia Affairs, Entry #P 368, Closed Project Files, 1955–1964, Box 14. Folder: Japan FY 1962 January June Phase Out. NARA.

82. Tokyo to International Cooperation Administration, Washington, Subject: Excerpts from the Japan Productivity News Newspaper No. 129 dated January 1, 1959, January 30, 1959. RG 469 Records of the U.S. Foreign Assistance Agencies, 1948–1961, Office of Far Eastern Operations, Japan Subject Files, 1950–1959, Box 58, Folder: Japan–Productivity 1959. NARA.

83. "Asian Productivity Body Inaugurated in Tokyo," *Japan Times*, quoted in Tokyo office to International Cooperation Administration, Washington, Subject: Asian Productivity Organization, May 25, 1961. RG 286 Agency for International Development, USAID/Bureau for Far East, Office of Indonesia Affairs, Entry #P 368, Closed Project Files, 1955–1964, Box 2. Folder: Agreements. NARA.

84. Ford Foundation, International Affairs, "Development of Associations Abroad in Japan and in Australia," December 1962. Ford Foundation Archives, International Division, Program Area 1, Series III. Herbert Passin Subject Files (1960–1966), Box 5, Folder: Japan Program–Basic Dockets, Memos 1963–1966. Rockefeller Archives Center, Sleepy Hollow, NY (hereafter RAC).

85. Ford Foundation, International Affairs, "Asian Productivity Organization–Experimental Training Program in Small Business Management," December 1963. Ford Foundation Archives, Ford Foundation Grants A–B, Reel 0685, Asian Productivity Organization (06400115). RAC.

86. Ibid.

87. Ford Foundation, International Affairs, "Asian Productivity Organization–Experimental Training Program in Small Business Management," December 1963. Ford Foundation Archives, Ford Foundation Grants A–B, Reel 0685, Asian Productivity Organization (06400115). RAC.

88. Oshikawa was a veteran of Japanese imperial development; he had worked as a researcher for the South Manchuria Railway Company crafting development plans for Manchukuo in the 1930s. See Young, *Japan's Total Empire*, 298.

89. Oshikawa Ichirō, "Clarifications on the Enquiries in Mr. Slater's letter dated 4th June," July 1963. Ford Foundation Archives, Ford Foundation Grants A–B, Reel 0685, Asian Productivity Organization (06400115). RAC.

90. International Cooperation Administration (Haraldson), Subject: Evaluation–International Small Industry Training Program, February 24, 1961. Ford Foundation Archives, Ford Foundation Grants A–B, Reel 0684, Asian Productivity Organization (06400115). RAC.

91. Robert M. Orr, *The Emergence of Japan's Foreign Aid Power* (New York: Columbia University Press, 1990), 1.

Chapter 9

Note to epigraph. "Special Committee on the Implementation of 1514 (1962) Vol. IV," 6, Verbatim records of the Committee, 2 August 1962, Chapter 6, Tshombe's Katanga, BAA/RLAA/502, George Padmore Library, Accra, Ghana (hereafter GPL).

1. The report, drafted by the committee, was presented to the General Assembly by Dr. Frene Ginwalla, a South African journalist and activist who went on to become the speaker of the National Assembly of South Africa in 1994.

2. "Special Committee on the Implementation of 1514 (1962) Vol. IV," 6.

3. UN General Assembly Resolution 3201 (S-VI), Declaration on the Establishment of a New International Economic Order, http://www.un-documents.net/s6r3201.htm (accessed 3 March 2018). On the NIEO see Nils Gilman, "The New International Economic Order: A Reintroduction," *Humanity: An International Journal of Human Rights, Humanitarianism, and Development* 6, no. 1 (Spring, 2015): 1–16; Vanessa Ogle, "State Rights Against Private Capital: The New International Economic Order and the Struggle over Aid, Trace and Foreign Investment, 1962-1981," *Humanity: An International Journal of Human Rights, Humanitarianism and Development* 5, no. 2 (Winter 2014): 211–234.

4. See also "Twenty-Five Years of the Declaration on the Granting of Independence to Colonial Countries and Peoples," United Nations Department of Political Affairs, Trusteeships and Decolonization, No. 26, December 1985, http://www.un.org/en/decolonization/pdf/decolonization/decon_num_26-1.pdf (accessed 3 March 2018).

5. David N. Gibbs, *The Political Economy of Third World Intervention, Mines, Money and U.S. Policy in the Congo Crisis* (Chicago: University of Chicago Press, 1991); Catherine Hoskyns, *The Congo Since Independence: January 1960-December 1961* (Oxford, UK: Oxford University Press, 1965); John Kent, *America, the UN and Decolonization: Cold War Conflict in the Congo* (London: Routledge, 2010).

6. For a brief selection see Christopher R. W. Dietrich, *Oil Revolution: Anticolonial Elites, Sovereign Rights and the Economic Culture of Decolonization* (Cambridge, UK: Cambridge

University Press, 2017); Alan L. McPherson and Yannick Wehrli, eds., *Beyond Geopolitics: New Histories of Latin America at the League of Nations* (Albuquerque: University of New Mexico Press, 2015); José Antonio Sánchez Román, "From the Tigris to the Amazon: Peripheral Expertise, Impossible Cooperation and Economic Multilateralism at the League of Nations, 1920-1946," in *The Institution of International Order, From the League of Nations to the United Nations*, ed. Simon Jackson and Alanna O'Malley (London: Routledge, 2018), 43–65.

7. UN General Assembly resolution 1514 (XV) of 14 December 1960, Declaration on the Granting of Independence to Colonial Countries and Peoples, http://www.un.org/en/decolonization/declaration.shtml (accessed 3 March 2018).

8. Comment from the representative of Liberia, Draft Report of the Security Council to the General Assembly, July 1961-July 1962, 330/8-162, State Department Files, Congo, National Archives and Records Administration, College Park, Maryland (hereafter NARA).

9. "Special Committee on the Implementation of 1514 (1962) Vol. IV," 7, Verbatim records of the Committee, 2 August 1962, Chapter 6, Tshombe's Katanga, BAA/RLAA/502, GPL.

10. On the Oppenheimers see Theodore Gregory, *Ernest Oppenheimer and the Economic Development of South Africa* (Oxford, UK: Oxford University Press,1962); Gary Hocking, *Oppenheimer and Son* (New York: McGraw Hill, 1973). See generally Raymond E. Dumett, ed., *Mining Tycoons in the Age of Empire, 1870-1945: Entrepreneurship, High Finance, Politics and Territorial Expansion* (London: Ashgate, 2009).

11. David Pallister, Sarah Stewart, and Ian Lepper, *South Africa Inc.: The Oppenheimer Empire* (New Haven, CT: Yale University Press, 1988), 4–7.

12. Anglo American Group, Press Release, 25 July 2019, https://www.angloamerican.com/media/press-releases/2019/25-07-2019 (accessed 25 February 2020).

13. Duncan Innes, *Anglo-American and the Rise of Modern South Africa* (London: Heinemann Educational Books, 1984), 231. See also Duncan Innes, "The Exercise of Control in the Diamond Industry of South Africa—Some Preliminary Remarks," in *Perspectives on South Africa, A Collection of Working Papers*, ed. T. Adler (Johannesburg: African Studies Institute, University of Witwatersrand Johannesburg, 1977), 195–242; John Suckling, Ruth Weiss, and Duncan Innes, *Foreign Investment in South Africa, The Economic Factor, Study Project Paper Nos. 5 to 9* (Uppsala: Africa Publications Trust, 1975). See generally Dumett, *Mining Tycoons in the Age of Empire*.

14. Innes, *Anglo-American*, 230.

15. Pallister, Stewart and Lepper, *South Africa Inc.*, 15.

16. Gibbs, *The Political Economy of Third World Intervention*, 61. Nigel J. Ashton, *Kennedy, Macmillan and the Cold War, The Irony of Interdependence* (Basingstoke, UK: Palgrave Macmillan, 2002), 113.

17. John Hillman, "Chartered Companies and the Development of the Tin Industry in Belgian Africa, 1900-1939," *African Economic History* 25, no. 1 (1997): 152.

18. Hoskyns, *The Congo Since Independence*, 17.

19. Conor Cruise O'Brien, *From Katanga and Back: A UN Case History* (New York: Simon and Schuster, 1962), 173.

20. "Republic of Congo": Newspaper Clippings (Congo), Jan 1963, Bureau of African Affairs, "Africans Must Solve the Congo Problem, the Imperialists Are Doing Their Worst," Fenner Brockway, *Ghanaian Times*, 10 January 1963, BAA/RLAA/691, GPL. See also Philip Murphy, *Party Politics and Decolonization: The Conservative Party and British Colonial Policy in Tropical Africa* (Oxford, UK: Clarendon Press, 1995), 94.

21. "Special Committee on the Implementation of 1514 (1962) Vol. IV," 6, Verbatim records of the Committee, 2 August 1962, Chapter 6, Tshombe's Katanga, BAA/RLAA/502, GPL.

22. Confidential note, 9 October 1967, PREM 13/2346, Rhodesia 1967-68, National Archives, London.

23. "Special Committee on the Implementation of 1514 (1962) Vol. IV," 6, Verbatim records of the Committee, 2 August 1962, Chapter 6, Tshombe's Katanga BAA/RLAA/502, GPL.

24. William Becker and William McClenahan, *The Market, the State, and the Export-Import Bank of the United States* (New York: Cambridge University Press, 2003): 10–40.

25. Alanna O'Malley, *The Diplomacy of Decolonisation: America, Britain and the United Nations During the Congo Crisis 1960-64* (Manchester, UK: Manchester University Press, 2018), 200–212.

26. Gibbs, *The Political Economy of Third World Intervention;* John Kent, *America, the UN and Decolonisation: Cold War Conflict in the Congo* (Routledge: London, 2011).

27. On copper mining in Central Africa see Mwelwa C. Musambachime, *Before the Rise of the Modern Copperbelt* (Bloomington, IN: Xlibris, 2017); Grietjie Verhoef, *The History of Business in Africa: Complex Discontinuity to Emerging Markets* (Berlin: Springer, 2017).

28. On De Beers and diamond mining see Colin Newbury, *The Diamond Ring: Business, Politics and Precious Stones in South Africa, 1867-1947* (Oxford, UK: Clarendon Press, 1989); Janine Roberts, *Glitter & Greed, The Secret World of the Diamond Cartel* (New York: The Disinformation Company, 2007); Todd Cleveland, *Stones of Contention: A History of Africa's Diamonds* (Athens: Ohio University Press, 2014).

29. On Tempelsman, see Gibbs, *The Political Economy of Third World Intervention,* 107–112.

30. Gibbs also points out that Fredericks went on to be a vice president at Chase Manhattan Bank, "where he probably helped arranged Congo's commercial loans." Gibbs, *The Political Economy of Third World Intervention,* 113–114.

31. Innes, *Anglo-American*, 236.

32. William Minter, *King Solomon's Mines Revisited, Western Interest and the Burdened History of Southern Africa* (New York: Basic Books, 1988), 200.

33. For an overview of how he shaped the State Department's approach to modernization and Africa under the Kennedy administration, see Robert B. Rakove, *Kennedy, Johnson, and the Nonaligned World* (Cambridge, UK: Cambridge University Press, 2013), 41–55. For more on U.S. modernization theories during the 1960s see also Larry Grubbs, *Secular Missionaries: Americans and African Development in the 1960s* (Amherst, MA: University of Massachusetts Press, 2010); Philip E. Muehlenbeck, *Betting on the Africans: John F. Kennedy's Courting of African Nationalist Leaders* (Oxford, UK: Oxford University Press, 2012).

34. Frederick Cooper, "Writing the History of Development," *Journal of Modern European History* 8 (2010): 5–23; Frederick Cooper, *Africa in the World: Capitalism, Empire, Nation State* (Cambridge, MA: Harvard University Press, 2014); Nick Cullather, "Development? It's History," *Diplomatic History* 24, no. 4 (2000): 641–653; Nils Gilman, *Mandarins of the Future: Modernization Theory in Cold War America* (Baltimore: Johns Hopkins University Press, 2007); Benjamin Knutsson, "The Intellectual History of Development: Towards a Widening Potential Repertoire," *Perspectives* 13 (2009): 1–47; Michael E. Latham, *Modernization as Ideology: American Social Science and "Nation Building" in the Kennedy Era* (Durham, NC: University of North Carolina Press, 2000); Vijay Prashad, *The Poorer Nations, A Possible History of the Global South* (New York: Verso, 2014); Amartya Sen, *Development as Freedom* (New York: Anchor, 2000).

35. Provision of aid should not be viewed as a solely altruistic endeavor. The World Bank identified this practice as essential to the expansion of overseas markets for American exports, the development of markets of U.S. companies, and the overall expansion of the free trade system, which was directly beneficial to the U.S. economy. Vijay Prashad, *The Darker Nations: A People's History of the Third World* (New York: The New Press, 2007), 71.

36. Rakove, *Kennedy, Johnson. and the Nonaligned World*, 43.

37. Memorandum from the President's Special Assistant for National Security Affairs (Bundy) and Ulrich Hayes of the National Security Council Staff to President Johnson, 10 June 1965,FRUS, https://history.state.gov/historicaldocuments/frus1964-68v24/d215.

38. "Tariffs would stimulate a domestic industry, and capital for industrialization could come from foreign air or a better utilization of the domestic surplus." See Prashad, *The Darker Nations*, 67–70. More generally see Nico Schrijver, *Sovereignty over Natural Resources: Balancing Rights and Duties* (Cambridge, UK: Cambridge University Press, 2008).

39. Letter from Narendra Singh, Accra, to R. K. Tandon, I.F.S. Joint Secretary, MEA, Delhi, 19 January 1928, on Conference of Independence States of Africa. CON-3-58-AFR II, 1958, Conference of Independent States of Africa, at Accra (Ghana) April 1958, AFR II, Ministry of External Relations Files, National Archives of India, New Delhi (hereafter NAI). For more on the Colombo Powers, see Cindy Ewing, "The Colombo Powers: Crafting Diplomacy in the Third World and Launching Afro-Asia at Bandung," *Cold War History* 19, no. 1 (2019), 1–19.

40. For more on AFRASEC see M. A. Rifaat, "Afro-Asian Organization for Economic Cooperation (AFRASEC)," *Civilisations* 15, no. 1 (1965), 73–81.

41. Memo on a meeting of Nehru and Nkrumah, M. J. Desai, MEA, 24 December 1958, F. 19(45)57: AFR II, 1958–1959, Visit of Nkrumah to India, AFR II, Ministry of External Relations Files, NAI.

42. Prashad, *The Darker Nations*, 70.

43. Even by November 1961, the representative of Liberia queried, "it would be interesting to know what steps Belgium was taking to implement the Council resolution of 21 February, particularly with respect to mercenaries and the activities of Union Miniére." Comment from the representative of Liberia, Draft Report of the Security Council to the General Assembly, July 1961–July 1962, 330/8-162, State Department Files, Congo, NARA.

44. UN General Assembly Declaration 523 (VI) Integrated Economic Development and Commercial Agreements, 6th session, 12 January 1952, http://www.un.org/ga/search/view_doc.asp?symbol=A/RES/523%28VI%29 (accessed 5 March 2018).

45. UN ECOSOC Official Records, Supplement No. 4, Commission on Human Rights, 8, http://www.un.org/ga/search/view_doc.asp?symbol=E/CN.4/669 (accessed 5 March 2018).

46. "I. The Status of Permanent Sovereignty over Natural Wealth and Resources," in *Study by the Secretariat II. Report of the Commission on Permanent Sovereignty over Natural Resources* (New York: United Nations Printing Office, 1962).

47. UN General Assembly Resolution 1803 (XVII), 14 December 1962, Permanent Sovereignty over Natural Resources, http://www.un.org/ga/search/view_doc.asp?symbol=a/res/1803(XVII) (accessed 5 March 2018).

48. For more on the legal importance of PSNR see Karol N. Gess, "Permanent Sovereignty over Natural Resources: An Analytical Review of the United Nations Declaration and Its Genesis," *International and Comparative Law Quarterly* 13, no. 2, (1964): 398–449.

49. Memorandum from Secretary of State Rusk to President Kennedy, the 17th General Assembly Summary Roundup, undated, FRUS, https://history.state.gov/historicaldocuments/frus1961-63v25/d232 (accessed 5 March 2018).

50. UN General Assembly Declaration 1803 (XVII), 14 December 1962, Permanent Sovereignty over Natural Resources, http://www.un.org/ga/search/view_doc.asp?symbol=a/res/1803(XVII) (accessed 5 March 2018).

51. Anthony Anghie, *Imperialism, Sovereignty and the Making of International Law* (Cambridge, UK: Cambridge University Press, 2007); Vijayashri Sripati, "Hammarskjold and International Executive Rule: A Third World Perspective on International Law," in *Peace Diplomacy, Global Justice and International Agency, Rethinking Human Security and Ethics in the Spirit of Dag Hammarskjold,* ed. Carsten Stahn and Henning Melber (Cambridge, UK: Cambridge University Press, 2014): 477–507.

52. For further see Marc A. Williams, "The Third World and Global Reform," *Review of International Studies* 10, no 1 (1984): 79–84; Stephen D. Krasner, "A Reply," *Review of International Studies*, 10, no. 1 (1984): 85–88.

53. Adeoye Akinsanya and Arthur Davies, "Third World Quest for a New International Economic Order: An Overview," *International and Comparative Law Quarterly* 33, no. 1 (1984), 211.

54. "Special Committee on the Implementation of 1514 (1962) Vol. IV," 9, Verbatim records of the Committee, 2 August 1962, Chapter 6, Tshombe's Katanga, BAA/RLAA/502, GPL.

Chapter 10

1. Benn Steil, *The Battle of Bretton Woods: John Maynard Keynes, Harry Dexter White, and the Making of a New World Order* (Princeton, NJ: Princeton University Press, 2013); Victoria de Grazia, *Irresistible Empire: America's Advance Through Twentieth-Century Europe* (Cambridge, MA: Belknap Press of Harvard University Press, 2005); Gilbert M. Joseph et al., eds., *Close Encounters of Empire: Writing the Cultural History of U.S.-Latin American Relations* (Durham, NC: Duke University Press, 1998); Michael Hogan, "American Marshall Planners and the Search for a European Neocapitalism," *American Historical Review* 90, no. 1 (Feb. 1985): 44–72; Charles Maier, "The Politics of Productivity: Foundations of American International Economic Policy after World War Two," in *Between Power and Plenty*, ed. Peter J. Katzenstein (Madison: University of Wisconsin Press, 1978), 23–49.

2. See in particular Max Paul Friedman's and Jennifer Miller's contributions.

3. Geir Lundestad, "'Empire by Invitation' in the American Century," *Diplomatic History* 23, no. 2 (1999): 189–217; Geir Lundestad, "Empire by Invitation? The United States and Western Europe, 1945-1952," *Journal of Peace Research* 23, no. 3 (Sept., 1986): 263–277.

4. Marta Musso, "'Oil Will Set Us Free': The Hydrocarbon Industry and the Algerian Decolonization Process," in *Britain, France and the Decolonization of Africa: Future Imperfect?*, ed. Andrew W. M. Smith and Chris Jeppesen (London: UCL Press, 2017), 62–84.

5. Julio Moreno, *Yankee Don't Go Home: Mexican Nationalism, American Business Culture, and the Shaping of Modern Mexico, 1920-1950* (Chapel Hill: University of North Carolina Press, 2003).

6. See, for instance, Michael H. Anderson, *Madison Avenue in Asia: Politics and Transnational Advertising* (London: Associated University Presses, 1984); Herbert Schiller, "Madison Avenue Imperialism," *Trans-Action* 8, no. 5 (March-April 1971): 52–64. For an instructive application of this approach to the Ivory Coast, see Pierre Thizier Seya, "Transnational Capitalist

Ideology and Dependent Societies: A Case Study of Advertising in the Ivory Coast" (Ph.D. diss., Stanford University, 1981).

7. There is currently a renewed interest in the significance of information in the unfolding of capitalism. For an overview, see Duncan K. Foley, "Rethinking Financial Capitalism and the 'Information' Economy," *Review of Radical Political Economics* 45, no. 3 (2013): 257–268; Christian Fuchs, "A Contribution to the Critique of the Political Economy of Transnational Informational Capitalism," *Rethinking Marxism* 21, no. 3 (2009): 387–402; John Bellamy Foster and Ellen M. Wood, *Capitalism and the Information Age: The Political Economy of the Global Communication Revolution* (London: Monthly Review Press, 1997); Manuel Castells, *The Informational City: Information Technology, Economic Restructuring, and the Urban-Regional Process* (Oxford, UK: Blackwell, 1989); Woodruff D. Smith, "The Function of Commercial Centers in the Modernization of European Capitalism: Amsterdam as an Information Exchange in the Seventeenth Century," *Journal of Economic History* 44, no. 4 (1984): 985–1005. For works that anticipated this trend, with a special focus on advertising, see Michael Schudson, *Advertising, the Uneasy Persuasion: Its Dubious Impact on American Society* (New York: Basic Books, 1984).

8. Thomas Molnar, "Neo-Colonialism in Africa?" *Modern Age* (Spring 1965): 175–186; "Political Uncertainties in the Ivory Coast," *London Times*, 3 April 1964, 10; "Côte d'Ivoire: Les anti-Houphouët," *Jeune Afrique*, 18–24 February 1963, 12; Andrew Borowiec, "Ivory Coast Charges Red Take-Over Plot," *Washington Post*, 8 February 1963, A7; "Côte d'Ivoire: Un éléphant caché par un chapeau," *Jeune Afrique*, 21–27 January 1963, 11.

9. Jessica C. E. Gienow-Hecht, "Introduction: Decentering American History," in *Decentering America*, ed. Jessica Gienow-Hecht (New York: Berghahn Books, 2007), 7.

10. For more on the life of Houphouët-Boigny, see Fréderic Grah Mel, *Félix Houphouët-Boigny* (Abidjan: Editions du CERAP/Maisonneuve & Larose/Karthala, 2003, 2010). See also Paul-Henri Siriex, *Houphouët-Boigny: An African Statesman* (Paris: NEA and Nathan, 1987).

11. "French Cabinet Gets 1st Negro," *Chicago Daily Defender*, 6 February 1956, 10; "Mollet Outlines a French Cabinet," *New York Times*, 29 January 1956, 3.

12. "Le PDG quitte le RDA," *Paris-Dakar*, 20 October 1958, 1; "Awakening Africa," *Wall Street Journal*, 10 October 1958, 1, 8; "Guinea Formally Ends French Rule," *Washington Post*, 3 October 1958, A4; "French Guinea Votes for Full Independence," *Christian Science Monitor*, 29 September 1958, 6. See also Elizabeth Schmidt, *Cold War and Decolonization in Guinea 1946-1958* (Athens: Ohio University Press, 2007); Schmidt, *Mobilizing the Masses: Gender, Ethnicity, and Class in the Nationalist Movement in Guinea 1939-1958* (Portsmouth, NH: Heinemann, 2005).

13. For Touré's trip to the UN, which French diplomats monitored closely, see "Voyage de M. Sékou Touré," 2 December 1959, Afrique-Levant (A-L)/Guinée, Carton 16, Archives du Ministère des Affaires Etrangères, Paris (hereafter AMAE); "Revue de la presse américaine," 6 November 1959, A-L/Guinée, Carton 18, AMAE.

14. "Le Président Houphouët-Boigny aux Américains: 'Aidez vos vrais amis,'" *Fraternité*, 27 November, 1959, 7; "L'Afrique au premier rang de la délégation française," *Fraternité*, 13 November 1959, 1. On the portrayal of Houphouët-Boigny as salesperson of French imperialism, see Frantz Fanon, *Toward the African Revolution: Political Essays* (New York: Grove Press, 1967 [1964]), 113–119. This Fanonian pronouncement should be read in the context of the radical politics of its author. As a number of historians have shown, some colonial subjects viewed decolonization in terms of a renewed, if more egalitarian, Franco-African alliance. For details, see Gary Wilder, *Freedom Time: Negritude, Decolonization, and the Future of the World*

(Durham, NC: Duke University Press, 2015); Frederick Cooper, *Citizenship Between Empire and Nation: Remaking France and West Africa, 1945-1960* (Princeton, NJ: Princeton University Press, 2014).

15. Jacques Baulin, *La politique africaine d'Houphouët-Boigny* (Paris: Editions Eurafor-Press, 1980), 70–73.

16. Abou B. Bamba, *African Miracle, African Mirage: Transnational Politics and the Paradox of Modernization in Ivory Coast* (Athens: Ohio University Press, 2016).

17. Alain Tirefort, "La Côte des Males Gens ou l'anti-hospitalité de l'enfer vert ivoirien: Une image de la colonie dans le premier quart du XXe siècle," *Afrique-Genève* 18, no. 1 (1980): 91–100; Georges Niamkey Kodjo, "Samori et la France, un nouvel enjeu Bandama-Comoé," in *La Côte d'Ivoire: Regards croisés sur les relations entre la France et l'Afrique*, ed. Rémi Fabre and Alain Tirefort (Nantes: Presses Académiques de l'Ouest/Ouest Editions, 1999), 83–93; Timothy C. Weiskel, *French Colonial Rule and the Baule People: Resistance and Collaboration, 1889-1911* (Oxford, UK: Clarendon Press, 1980).

18. René-Pierre Anouma, *Aux origines de la nation ivoirienne, 1893-1946, Volume 1: Conquêtes coloniales et aménagements territoriaux, 1893-1920* (Paris: L'Harmattan, 2005); Jean-Pierre Chauveau, "Cocoa as Innovation: African Initiatives, Local Context and Agro-Ecological Conditions in the History of Cocoa Cultivation in West African Forest Lands (c. 1850-1950)," *Paideuma* 43 (1997): 121–142; David H. Groff, "Carrots, Sticks, and Cocoa Pods: African and Administrative Initiatives in the Spread of Cocoa Cultivation in Assikasso, Ivory Coast," *International Journal of African Historical Studies* 20, no. 3 (1987): 401–416.

19. Bamba, *African Miracle, African Mirage*, 7–9, 24–36. For an overview of the French Fonds d'Investissement pour le Développement Economique et Social and its major projects, see Ambassade de France (USA), *French Africa: A Decade of Progress, 1948-1958* (New York: Service de presse et d'information, 1958). For the productivity of Ivorian agriculture, see Territoire de Côte d'Ivoire, *Inventaire économique de la Côte d'Ivoire, 1947-1956* (Abidjan: Ministère du Plan/Service de la Statistique, 1958), 33–49, 88–89; Jean Lebeuf, "L'évolution des productions agricoles," *Marchés coloniaux*, 28 April 1951, 1171–1173.

20. John Rapley, *Ivoirien Capitalism: African Entrepreneurs in Côte d'Ivoire* (London: Lynne Rienner, 1993), 28–31; Robert M. Hecht, "The Transformation of Lineage Production in Southern Ivory Coast, 1920-1980," *Ethnology* 23, no. 4 (Oct. 1984): 261–277; Laurent Gbagbo, *Côte d'Ivoire: Economie et société à la veille de l'indépendance, 1940-1960* (Paris: L'Harmattan, 1982).

21. Maître Kouamé Binzème, "Le développement économique de la Côte d'Ivoire: Plan d'action," 2 September 1948, RG 469, Box 7, National Archive and Records Administration, College Park, MD (hereafter USNA); Maître Kouamé Binzème to ECA/Paris, 2 September 1948, RG 469, Box 7, USNA.

22. Maître Kouamé Binzème to ECA/Paris, 2 September 1948, RG 469, Box 7, USNA (emphasis in the original).

23. Maître Kouamé Binzème to ECA/Paris, 2 September 1948, RG 469, Box 7, USNA.

24. Henrik S. Marcussen and Jens E. Torp, *Internationalization of Capitals: Prospects for the Third World* (London: Zed Press, 1982), 32–47; Laurent Péchoux, "Ivory Coast Governor Hails Territory's Great New Port," *New York Herald Tribune*, 29 March 1951, 6–7; Paul Santerne, "Les investissements privés étrangers sont une nécessité pour l'Union française d'Outre-mer I," *Marchés coloniaux*, 7 January 1950, 1–3, and "Les investissements privés étrangers sont une nécessité pour l'Union française d'Outre-mer II," *Marchés coloniaux*, 14 January 1950, 54–55;

Catherine Hodeir, *Stratégies d'empire: Le grand patronat colonial face à la décolonisation* (Paris: Belin, 2003), 236–247.

25. "Plymouth Oil Net Now Above '57," *Wall Street Journal*, 18 September 1958, 25; "Oil Venture Planned," *Wall Street Journal*, 13 January 1958, 40; David E. Lilienthal, *The Journals of David E. Lilienthal, Volume 5: The Harvest Years, 1959-1963* (New York: Harper & Row, 1964), 50; Lilienthal to Diffre, 7 December 1959, David E. Lilienthal Papers, Box 413, Seeley Mudd Library, Princeton University, Princeton, NJ.

26. Abidjan to Secretary of State, 20 August 1960, 770M.5-MSP/8-2060, USNA.

27. "Le Président Houphouët explique la Côte d'Ivoire aux Américains," *Fraternité*, 25 May 1962, 3; "Le discours du Président de la République au déjeuner de la Westinghouse Electric Corporation," *Abidjan Matin*, 19 May 1962, 6; Béchir Ben Yahmed, "Le présent et l'avenir," *Jeune Afrique*, 4–10 June 1962, 6; T. Bakele, "Voyages," *Jeune Afrique*, 4–10 June 1962, 6–7. For a thorough analysis of the visit and its diplomatic ramifications, see Philip Muehlenbeck, *Betting on the Africans: John F. Kennedy's Courting of African Nationalist Leaders* (New York: Oxford University Press, 2012), 145-149; Abou B. Bamba, "At the Edge of the Modern? Diplomacy, Public Relations, and Media Practices during Houphouët-Boigny's 1962 Visit to the United States," *Diplomacy & Statecraft* 22 (June 2011): 219–238.

28. *Report of the Attorney General to the Congress of the United States on the Administration of the Foreign Agents Registration Act of 1938, as Amended for the Calendar Year 1979* (Washington, DC: Government Printing Office, 1980), 259; *Report of the Attorney General to the Congress of the United States on the Administration of the Foreign Agents Registration Act of 1938, as Amended for the Calendar Year 1966* (Washington, DC: Government Printing Office, 1967), 132; *Report of the Attorney General to the Congress of the United States on the Administration of the Foreign Agents Registration Act of 1938, as Amended for the Calendar Year 1962* (Washington, DC: Government Printing Office, 1963), 201; *Report of the Attorney General to the Congress of the United States on the Administration of the Foreign Agents Registration Act of 1938, as Amended for the Calendar Year 1960* (Washington, DC: Government Printing Office, 1961), 137–139.

29. Jerry Landauer, "Swaying Uncle Sam: Foreign Lobbying Here Grows," *Wall Street Journal*, 21 January 1963, 18; Edmund K. Faltermayer, "Propaganda Push: Foreign Efforts to Win Support in U.S. Grow," *Wall Street Journal*, 8 May 1962, 1.

30. Henri K. Bedié, *Les chemins de ma vie: Entretiens avec Eric Laurent* (Paris: Plon, 1999), 73–74; Landauer, "Swaying Uncle Sam," 18.

31. "Profitable Opportunities for Trade and Investment in Africa," *New York Times*, 20 January 1964, 12E.

32. "The Republic of the Ivory Coast: A Plan for Economic Growth . . . that Works!" *New York Times*, 20 January 1964, 79.

33. "Business Opportunities in the Ivory Coast Republic," *New York Times*, 25 January 1965, 61.

34. "The Republic of the Ivory Coast: As Economic Progress Continues in the Ivory Coast, Government Welcomes American Private Investments," *New York Times*, 26 January 1968, 67.

35. "The Ivory Coast: Investment Made Easy," *New York Times*, 14 December 1969, F17; "The Ivory Coast: Africa's Economic Miracle," *New York Times*, 14 December 1969, 82; "The Ivory Coast: Africa's New Riviera," *New York Times*, 14 December 1969, E4.

36. "Ivory Coast Republic Success Formula: Political Stability Spurs Economic Progress," *New York Times*, 29 January 1971, 59; "San Pedro: New Ivory Coast Atlantic Port," *New York Times*, 29 January 1971, 61.

37. "Nigeria: A Virile Republic; A Contributor to Progress," *New York Times*, 7 November 1965, sec. 13; "Birth of a Nation: Nigeria, October 1, 1960," *New York Times*, 2 October 1960, sec. 11.

38. "Senegal: The Horatio Alger of Africa," *New York Times*, 31 January 1966, 78; "Senegal Welcomes New Industry," *New York Times*, 20 June 1965, E7; "Senegal Investment Law," *New York Times*, 25 January 1965, 63.

39. Bamba, *African Miracle, African Mirage*, 63–64, 73.

40. "L'industrialisation ivoirienne: réalisations et perspectives," June 1965, série: DAM/sous-série: CI, Carton 1888, AMAE; Abidjan to Secretary of State, 11 August 1961, 2, 5, 770M.5-MSP/8-1161, USNA; Ministre des Affaires Etrangères to Secrétaire d'Etat aux relations avec les états de la Communauté, 16 December 1960, Amérique/Etats-Unis, Carton 453, AMAE; Secrétaire d'Etat aux relations avec les états de la Communauté to Ministre des Affaires Etrangères, 12 September 1960, série: DAM/sous-série: CI, Carton 1881, AMAE.

41. Samir Amin, "Côte d'Ivoire: Valeur et limites d'une expérience," *Jeune Afrique*, 1 October 1967, 26–35. See also Justin Vieyra, Preface to "Côte d'Ivoire: Valeur et limites d'une expérience," *Jeune Afrique*, 1 October 1967, 26; Samir Amin, *Le développement du capitalisme en Côte d'Ivoire* (Paris: Editions de Minuit, 1967).

42. "Réponse à *Jeune Afrique*," *Bulletin de liaison du Ministère de l'Agriculture*, October 1967, 1–9; Raphaël-Leygues to Ministre des Affaires Etrangères, 22 February 1968, DAM/CI, Carton 1888, AMAE.

43. Laurent Gbagbo, "La décolonisation: Essai de définition d'une problématique," *Annales de l'Université d'Abidjan*, sér. I (*Histoire*), 6 (1978): 53–87; Kevin P. Phillips, "Neo-Colonialism in West Africa," *Washington Post*, 19 August 1971, A21; B. Diallo, "Côte d'Ivoire: Les chômeurs se fâchent," *Jeune Afrique*, 8-14 October 1969, 32. See also Grah Mel, Félix Houphouët-Boigny, *Volume 3: La fin & la suite* (Abidjan & Paris: CERAP/Karthala, 2010), 361–369.

44. "Ivory Coast Republic Success Formula," 59.

45. Ambassadeur de France (Abidjan) to [unidentified] correspondent, 25 June 1964, DAM/CI, Carton 1885, AMAE.

46. "Finance Company for the Ivory Coast," *London Times*, 17 February 1965, 20.

47. Jacques Leprette (chargé d'affaires/Washington) to Ministre des Affaires Etrangères, 3 August 1967, Amérique/Etats-Unis, Carton 626, AMAE.

48. Jean-Louis Chaléard, "Fronts pionniers et ravitaillement des villes en Côte d'Ivoire," in *Comment nourrir le monde? Les politiques alimentaires face à la libéralisation des économies et des échanges*, ed. C. Cohen (Montpellier: Solagral, 1990), 323–328; Michel Lesourd, "Mise en valeur agricole et organisation de l'espace en zone pionnière: Les Baoulés dans le sud-ouest de la Côte d'Ivoire," in *Le développement rural en questions: Paysages, espaces ruraux, systèmes agraires*, ed. Chantal Blanc-Pamard et al. (Paris: ORSTOM, 1984), 353–380.

49. "Notification of Invitation to Bid," *Wall Street Journal*, 29 July 1968, 16; "Submission for the Preparation of 7,050 Hectar[e]s Land in Ivory Coast," *Wall Street Journal*, 13 July 1967, 22.

50. "Republic of the Ivory Coast: $10,000,000 Five-Year Loan," *The Economist*, 5 October 1968, 44; "Republic of the Ivory Coast: $10,000,000 Five-Year Loan," *Wall Street Journal*, 2 October 1968, 26; "Republic of the Ivory Coast: $10,000,000 Five-Year Loan," *Washington Post*, 2 October 1968, D11.

51. William Eaton, "Ivory Coast Invites U.S. Business Bids," *Los Angeles Times*, 11 September 1979, F11.

52. Maurice C. Ernst to Karl Inderfurth, 1 April 1977, NSA, Brzezinski Material: Inderfurth & Gates Chron File, Box 1, Carter Library, Atlanta, GA.

53. Abidjan to State Department, 10 February 1978, Donated Historical Material: Mary King, Box 1, Carter Library; CIA, "LDC Positions on the Debt Relief Issues," February 1978, NSC Institutional Files—1977-81, Box 68, Carter Library; Esieloghene Esu, "Big Ivory Coast Loans Stir Fears of Foreign Control," *Afro-American*, 16 July 1977, 16.

54. Abidjan to Washington, 11 January 1974, Record Group [RG] 59, Access to Archival Databases [online, hereafter AAD], Document Number [#]: 1974ABIDJA00190, USNA. For more on the issue of the petrodollar surpluses, see David E. Spiro, *The Hidden Hand of American Hegemony: Petrodollar Recycling and International Markets* (Ithaca, NY: Cornell University Press, 1999).

55. For an overview of the development of the Ivorian oil industry, see Frédéric Grah Mel, Félix Houphouët-Boigny, *Volume 2: L'épreuve du pouvoir* (Abidjan: CERAP/Karthala, 2010), 390–395.

56. "Ivory Coast with Oil," *New York Times*, 5 February 1978, IES20.

57. "How To Invest in Ivory Coast," *New York Times*, 5 February 1978, IES20.

58. "Ivory Coast: An Invitation to Free Enterprise," *Washington Post*, 7 June 1983, A9; "A Strong U.S. Ally in Black Africa: Felix Houphouet-Boigny, President of the Republic of the Ivory Coast Visits the United States," *New York Times*, 7 June 1983, D17.

59. Abidjan to Washington, 07 May 1977, RG 59, AAD#1977ABIDJA04577, USNA; Accra to Abidjan, 10 January 1975, RG 59, AAD#1975ACCRA00226, USNA.

60. Abidjan to Washington, 05 May 1977, RG 59, AAD#1977ABIDJA04526, USNA.

61. Abidjan to Washington, 19 October 1977, RG 59, AAD#1977ABIDJA10277, USNA. In the Ivorian media, the announcement of the discovery of crude oil was quite loquacious even though some local journalists evoked the risk of resource curse that might befall the country. For details, see "Houphouët annonce: 'Du pétrole chez nous,'" *Fraternité Matin*, 19 October 1978, 1; Raphaël N'Guessan, "Grand-Bassam à l'heure du pétrole: L'espoir de la renaissance," *Fraternité Matin*, 20 October 1978, 10; Kinimo K. Man Jusu, "Pétrole. Les Ivoiriens: Notre joie est totale . . .," *Fraternité Matin*, 21 October 1978, 21.

62. Abidjan to Washington, 29 November 1977, RG 59, AAD#1977ABIDJA11601, USNA; Abidjan to Washington, 13 September 1977, RG 59, AAD#1977ABIDJA09047, USNA. For the first news of the oil discovery in the U.S. press, see "Exxon Affiliate Says 3 Wells Find Oil, Gas Offshore Ivory Coast," *Wall Street Journal*, 14 April 1977, 31.

63. "Phillips Petroleum Confirms Oil, Gas Find off Ivory Coast," *Wall Street Journal*, 22 April 1981, 8; Robert Metz, "Market Place: Analysts Assess Phillips Oil Find," *New York Times*, 5 May 1981, D8; William Ellington, "Phillips Petroleum Asks Loan to Explore off Ivory Coast," *Wall Street Journal*, 4 November 1980, 30; "Ivory Coast Oilfield," *New York Times*, 25 June 1980, D6; "Phillips Petroleum Co., Two Other Firms Set Ivory Coast Venture," *Wall Street Journal*, 12 March 1980, 36.

64. "Phillips Petroleum Starts Oil Production Offshore Ivory Coast," *Wall Street Journal*, 3 September 1982, 4; "Ivory Coast Plans to Be Oil Exporter," *Los Angeles Times*, 17 February 1981, E9; "Interview: Une fois de plus, les 'prophètes de malheur' en sont pour leur frais," *Fraternité Matin*, 12 December 1978, 10–11.

65. Hazel G. Warlaumont, *Advertising in the 60s: Turncoats, Traditionalists, and Waste Makers in America's Turbulent Decade* (Westport, CT: Praeger, 2001), xii. In the same vein, Roland

Marchant argued that advertising "rationalized and lubricated impersonal marketplace of vast scale." For details, see his *Advertising the American Dream: Making Way for Modernity, 1920-1940* (Los Angeles: University of California, 1985), 9.

66. Stefan Schwarzkopf, "Who Said 'Americanization'? The Case of Twentieth-Century Advertising and Mass Marketing from a British Perspective," in *Decentering America*, ed. Gienow-Hecht, 23–72.

Chapter 11

Acknowledgment: The author is grateful to Fredrik Logevall and the 2020–21 Ernest May Fellows in History and Policy for insightful comments on an earlier draft.

1. Subcommittee on Nuclear Power and Electric Utilities, Recommended Action Plan for the New Administration, sent as enclosure by F. M. Staszesky., Jr, at Bechtel Power Corporation (on behalf of W. Kenneth Davis) to Michel T. Halbouty, 4 November 1980, Box 91, Richard Thomas Kennedy Papers, Hoover Institution Archives, Stanford, California (hereafter RTK-HIA)

2. Ibid.

3. Ibid.

4. Letter from F. M. Staszesky, Jr., to Michel T. Halbouty, 4 November 1980, Box 91, RTK-HIA.

5. Hendrick Smith, "President Concedes: Republican Gains Victories in All Areas and Vows to Act on Economy," *New York Times*, 5 November 1980, 2, 18.

6. Kevin Kruse and Julian E. Zelizer, *Fault Lines: A History of the United States Since 1974* (New York: W. W. Norton), Chapter 5: Turning Right; Kim Phillips-Fein, *Invisible Hands: The Businessmen's Crusade Against the New Deal* (New York: W. W. Norton, 2010), Chapter 11: The Market Triumphant.

7. On this transformation originating in the economic crisis of the 1970s, see Judith Stein, *Pivotal Decade: How the United States Traded Factories for Finance in the Seventies* (New Haven, CT: Yale University Press, 2010).

8. Jayita Sarkar, "The Economic Strategies of U.S. Nonproliferation Policy During the Nixon-Ford Years," *Journal of Global Security Studies* 6, no. 1 (March 2021) 1–6; see also "U.S. Reactor Makers' Recovery in Doubt After 4-Year Market Dip," *New York Times*, March 7, 1978, 47, 59.

9. The Nuclear Nonproliferation Act required recipient countries to accept full-scope IAEA safeguards on U.S. nuclear exports, which few foreign countries were keen to do, thereby hampering export prospects for the nuclear industry. See Public Law 95-242, Nuclear Nonproliferation Act, 10 March 1978, https://www.govinfo.gov/content/pkg/STATUTE-92/pdf/STATUTE-92-Pg120.pdf#page=1 (accessed 9 August 2021).

10. *Report of the President's Commission on the Accident at Three Mile Island: The Need for Change: The Legacy of TMI*, 30 October 1979.

11. Tomas Kellner, "Lights, Electricity, Action: When Ronald Reagan Hosted 'General Electric Theater,'" *GE Reports*, 17 February 2019, https://www.ge.com/reports/ronald-reagan-ge/ (accessed 9 August 2021).

12. Bob Spitz, *Reagan: An American Journey* (New York: Penguin, 2018), 291–293; Jacob Weisberg, "The Road to Reagandom," *Slate*, 8 January 2016, https://slate.com/news-and-politics/2016/01/ronald-reagans-conservative-conversion-as-spokesman-for-general-electric-during-the-1950s.html (accessed 9 August 2021).

13. William Greider, "The Boys from Bechtel: Will Ronald Reagan Reverse U.S. Policy on Nuclear Proliferation?," *Rolling Stone*, 2 September 1982; "Bechtel and the Reagan Cabinet," *CBS*

Evening News, 28 June 1982; Ward Sinclair, "Reagan's Special Mideast Envoy Is Consultant to Bechtel Group," *Washington Post*, 25 June 1982.

14. Charles A. Beard, *An Economic Interpretation of the Constitution of the United States* (New York: Macmillan, 1913); Charles A. Beard, *Economic origins of Jeffersonian Democracy* (New York: Macmillan, 1915). For major works of the Wisconsin School, see, among others, William Appleman Williams, *The Tragedy of American Diplomacy* (Cleveland, OH: World Publishing Company, 1959); Walter LaFeber, *The New Empire: An Interpretation of American Expansion, 1860–1898* (Ithaca, NY: Cornell University Press, 1963); Lloyd Gardner, *Economic Aspects of New Deal Diplomacy* (Madison: University of Wisconsin Press, 1964); William Appleman Williams, *Empire as a Way of Life: An Essay on the Causes and Character of America's Present Predicament along with a Few Words About an Alternative* (New York: Oxford University Press, 1980).

15. On this subject, see, for example, Francis J. Gavin, "Strategies of Inhibition: U.S. Grand Strategy, the Nuclear Revolution, and Nonproliferation," *International Security* 40, no. 1 (Summer 2015): 9–46. Gheorghe makes a commendable attempt to foreground the role of the market in nuclear proliferation but does not account for economic factors, actors, and processes, but instead assumes that market share is the equivalent of political power distribution (or "polarity," as she calls it). See Eliza Gheorghe, "Proliferation and the Logic of the Nuclear Market," *International Security* 43, no. 4 (Spring 2019): 88–127.

16. U.S. nonproliferation policy can be defined as unilateral, bilateral, and multilateral strategies to prevent other countries from developing their own nuclear weapons.

17. Emily Rosenberg, *Spreading the American Dream: American Economic and Cultural Expansion, 1890–1945* (New York: Hill and Wang, 1982); Phillips-Fein, *Invisible Hands*; Paul A. Kramer, "Embedding Capital: Political-Economic History, the United States, and the World," *Journal of the Gilded Age and Progressive Era* 15 (2016): 331–362.

18. "Convocation, 17 September 1978, John G. Kemeny," Papers of John G. Kemeny, MS-988, Box 1, Rauner Special Collections Library, Dartmouth College, Hanover, New Hampshire (hereafter JGK-DC).

19. B. Drummond Ayres, Jr., "Three Mile Island: Notes from a Nightmare," *New York Times*, 16 April 1979, 1–2.

20. Warren H. Donnelly and Donna S. Kramer, "Nuclear Power: The Three Mile Island and Its Investigation," Congressional Research Service Issue Brief IB79035, 3 May 1979, Box 2, JGK-DC.

21. Ibid.

22. Ibid; "Live Discussion with Richard Thornburgh: Governing a Nuclear Crisis," *Washington Post*, 29 March 1999.

23. Remarks of the President on Appointment of a Presidential Commission to Study Events at Three Mile Island, 11 April 1979, 4:30 PM EST, Office of the White House Press Secretary, Box 1, JGK-DC.

24. Summary for News Conference on Role of Utility and its Suppliers, Patrick Haggerty, Folder Apr.-Jul. 1979, Box 1, JGK-DC.

25. Ibid.

26. B. Drummond Ayres, Jr., "Engineers Warned Builder of Danger Year Before Three Mile Island Accident," *New York Times*, 19 July 1979.

27. Natasha Zaretsky, *Radiation Nation: Three Mile Island and the Political Transformation of the 1970s* (New York: Columbia University Press, 2018), 104.

28. David Burnham, "Death of Plutonium Worker Questioned by Union Official," *New York Times*, 19 November 1974, 28.

29. William K. Stevens, "Silkwood Heirs Win $10.5 Million in Setback to the Nuclear Industry," *New York Times*, 19 May 1979, 1.

30. Richard Jones, "The Price-Anderson Act," 2000, https://www.osti.gov/etdeweb/servlets/purl/20111062 (accessed 9 August 2021).

31. Report of the President's Commission on the Accident at Three Mile Island, The Need for Change: The Legacy of TMI, 30 October 1979, 34.

32. Ibid.

33. Jacob I. Fabrikant, "Health Effects of Low-Level Ionizing Radiation," presented before the Senate Committee on Human Resources, Subcommittee on Health and Scientific Research, chaired by Sen. Edward Kennedy, for inclusion in the official records of the hearings of April 4, 1979, Box 4, JGK-DC.

34. Jacob I. Fabrikant, "Health Effects of the Nuclear Accident at Three Mile Island," presented, as Invited Speaker, at the Conference on Environmental Regulation of the Nuclear Industry: A New Decade, Atomic Industrial Forum, San Francisco, CA, May 18-21, 1980, Box 4, JGK-DC.

35. Frank J. Prial, "Civil Trial on Blame for Accident at Three Mile Island Opens Today," *New York Times*, 1 November 1982, 17.

36. J. Samuel Walker, *Three Mile Island: A Nuclear Crisis in Historical Perspective* (Berkeley: University of California Press, 2004), 223.

37. Mara Drogan, "The Nuclear Imperative: Atoms for Peace and the Development of U.S. Policy on Exporting Nuclear Power, 1953-1955," *Diplomatic History* 40, no. 5 (2015): 948–974; John Krige, "Atoms for Peace, Scientific Internationalism, and Scientific Intelligence," *Osiris* 21, no. 1 (2006): 161–181; Jonathan E. Helmreich, "The United States and the Formation of the EURATOM," *Diplomatic History* 15, no. 3 (July 1991): 387–410.

38. The 1954 U.S. Atomic Energy Act was an amendment to the 1946 Atomic Energy Act that had retained in postwar years the wartime secrecy and censorship of all things nuclear that prevailed during the Manhattan Project. Before 1954, U.S. companies accessed nuclear know-how through government contracts but could not own the know-how, and hence could not trade in it, even though a good number of them, like DuPont, Union Carbide, and Westinghouse, participated in the Manhattan Project. See Alex Wellerstein, *Restricted Data: The History of Nuclear Secrecy in the United States* (Chicago: University of Chicago Press, 2021), chap. 6.

39. The Price-Anderson Act has been amended a number of times including most recently in 2005, when it was extended until 2025. The act authorizes the U.S. Nuclear Regulatory Commission to limit the liability of its reactor licensees for radioactive damages to the public. Mark Holt, "Price-Anderson Act: Nuclear Power Industry Liability Limits and Compensation to the Public After Radioactive Releases," Congressional Research Service, In Focus IF10821, February 5, 2018, https://crsreports.congress.gov/product/pdf/IF/IF10821/4 (accessed 9 August 2021).

40. Mark Hertsgaard, *Nuclear Inc.: The Men and Money Behind Nuclear Energy* (New York: Pantheon Books, 1983), 40–60.

41. William H. Becker and William M. McClenahan Jr., *The Market, the State and the Export-Import Bank of the United States, 1934–2000* (Cambridge, UK: Cambridge University Press, 2003), 3.

42. Letter from L. Manning Muntzing (of Doub and Muntzing, Chartered Attorneys at Law) to W. Kenneth Davis (of Reagan Energy Task Force at Bechtel Corporation), 16 October 1980, Box 91, RTK-HIA.

43. Letter from Norval E. Carey (vice-president of General Atomic Company) to Richard T. Kennedy (of NRC Transition Team) 17 December 1980, Box 91, RTK-HIA.

44. Ibid.

45. Subcommittee on Nuclear Power and Electric Utilities, Recommended Action Plan for the New Administration, 4 November 1980, Box 91, RTK-HIA.

46. "Ronald Reagan's Statement Announcing a Series of Policy Initiatives on Nuclear Energy," 8 October 1981, Ronald Reagan Presidential Library, https://www.reaganlibrary.gov/research/speeches/100881b (accessed 9 August 2021).

47. Ibid.

48. Mark Hertsgaard, "Nuclear Reaganomics," *New York Times*, 9 October 1981.

49. By 1983, both the House and the Senate voted to cut its funding for economic reasons. On Clinch River, see Michael Camp, "'Wandering in the Desert': The Clinch River Breeder Reactor Debate in the U.S. Congress, 1972–1983," *Technology and Culture* 59, no. 1 (Jan. 2018): 26–47.

50. On the history of the reactor accident, see Walker, *Three Mile Island*; Zaretsky, *Radiation Nation*.

51. Letter from Frank M. Staszesky (of Bechtel Corporation) to Richard T. Kennedy (of NRC Transition Team), 8 December 1980, Box 91, RTK-HIA.

52. Ibid.

53. White Paper on Nuclear Nonproliferation Policy (Civilian Power Aspects) by John W. Wydler (Ranking Minority Leader, House of Representatives), enclosed with Wydler's letter to Richard T. Kennedy (of NRC Transition Team), 9 December 1980, Box 91, RTK-HIA

54. Ibid.

55. Ibid.

56. Ibid.

57. Judith Miller, "Reagan Names Aide to Fight A-Arms Spread," *New York Times*, 15 September 1982, 13.

58. Michael Getler, "Ties with Bechtel Group Cause the Senator's Unease," *Washington Post*, 14 July 1982.

59. Victor McFarland, *Oil Powers: A History of U.S.-Saudi Alliance* (New York: Columbia University Press, 2020), 53–54.

60. Thomas C. Haynes, "Bechtel: A Reclusive Giant," *New York Times*, 8 July 1982.

61. Ibid; see also William Greider, "The Boys from Bechtel: Will Ronald Reagan Reverse U.S. Policy on Nuclear Proliferation?," *Rolling Stone*, 2 September 1982; on the controversial West Germany-Brazil nuclear cooperation see William Glenn Gray, "Commercial Liberties and Nuclear Anxieties," *International History Review* 34, no. 3 (2012): 449–474; Fabian Hilfrich, "Roots of Animosity: Bonn's Reaction to US Pressures in Nuclear Proliferation," *International History Review* 36, no. 2 (2014): 277–301.

62. Getler, "Ties with Bechtel Group."

63. National Security Study Directive 12-82, "U.S. Relations with China and Taiwan," 7 December 1982, Ronald Reagan Presidential Library, https://www.reaganlibrary.gov/public/digitallibrary/smof/nsc-asianaffairsdirectorate/laux/r22/40-315-12026384-R22-007-2019.pdf; National Security Decision Directive 76, "Peaceful Cooperation with China," 18 January 1983, Ronald Reagan Presidential Library, https://www.reaganlibrary.gov/public/archives/reference/scanned-nsdds/nsdd76.pdf (accessed 9 August 2021).

64. Bernard Weinraub, "Reagan and Mrs. Gandhi Resolve Dispute for Nuclear Fuel for India," *New York Times*, 30 July 1982.

65. Philip M. Boffey, "Experts Fear Argentina is Planning an A-Bomb," *New York Times*, 17 September 1983; Philip Taubman, "Shultz Tells India that U.S. Will Drop Reactor-Parts Ban," *New York Times*, 1 July 1983.

66. Zaretsky, *Radiation Nation*, 105–106.

67. The administration, however, walked out of the IAEA General Conference in September 1982 in protest against the international agency's attempt to suspend Israel for its counterproliferation strike on Iraq the previous year. Judith Miller, "U.S. Walks out as Atom Parley Bars the Israelis," *New York Times*, 25 September 1982.

68. National Security Decision Directive 6, "United States Nonproliferation and Peaceful Nuclear Cooperation Policy," 16 July 1981, https://www.reaganlibrary.gov/public/archives/reference/scanned-nsdds/nsdd6.pdf (accessed 9 August 2021).

69. See, for example, Or Rabinowitz and Nicholas L. Miller, "Keeping the Bombs in the Basement: U.S. Nonproliferation Policy Toward Israel, South Africa, and Pakistan," *International Security* 40, no. 1 (Summer 2015): 47–86; Rabia Akhtar, *The Blind Eye: U.S. Non-Proliferation Policy Towards Pakistan from Ford to Clinton* (Lahore: University of Lahore Press, 2018).

70. Or Rabinowitz, *Bargaining on Nuclear Tests: Washington and Its Cold War Deals* (Oxford, UK: Oxford University Press, 2014), chaps. 6–7; Giordana Pulcini and Or Rabinowitz, "An Ounce of Prevention, a Pound of Cure? The Reagan Administration's Non-Proliferation Policy and the Osirak Raid," *Journal of Cold War Studies* 23, no. 2 (2021), 4–40.

71. Zaretsky, *Radiation Nation*, 185.

72. INPO Responses to Questions by the Senate Committee on Energy and Natural Resources, 18 July 1986, Sent to Senator James A. McClure by Zack T. Pate, President of INPO (Washington, DC: U.S. Government Printing Office, 1986).

73. James Cook, "Nuclear Follies," *Forbes*, 11 February 1985, 100.

74. Ben A. Franklin, "U.S. Panel Votes to End Shutdown of a Reactor at Three Mile Island," *New York Times*, 30 May 1985, 1; Lindsey Gruson, "After 6 years, Undamaged Reactor at 3 Mile Island is Restarted," *New York Times*, 4 October 1985.

75. Thomas J. Lueck, "Charges Disputed on 3 Mile Island," *New York Times*, 1 December 1983.

76. "Three Mile Island Fined $64,000," *Chicago Tribune*, 6 March 1986.

LIST OF CONTRIBUTORS

Abou Bamba is an associate professor in history and Africana studies at Gettysburg College and the author of *African Miracle, African Mirage: Transnational Politics and the Paradox of Modernization in Ivory Coast* (Ohio University Press, 2016).

Giulia Crisanti received her Ph.D. from Fordham University and is a research fellow at the University of Gastronomic Sciences in Pollenzo, Italy. She is currently taking part in the PRIN project "Transatlantic Transfers: The Italian Presence in Post-War America."

Christopher R. W. Dietrich is an associate professor of history and the director of American Studies at Fordham University. He is author of *Oil Revolution* (Cambridge University Press, 2017) and editor of the multivolume *Blackwell Companion to the History of U.S. Foreign Relations, Colonial Era to the Present*. His articles have appeared in *Diplomatic History*, *Diplomacy & Statecraft*, and *International History Review*.

Max Paul Friedman is a professor of history and international relations at American University in Washington, D.C. He is the author of *Nazis and Good Neighbors: The United States Campaign Against the Germans of Latin America in World War II* (Cambridge University Press, 2003), which won the Herbert Hoover Prize in U.S. History and the A.B. Thomas Prize in Latin American Studies, and *Rethinking Anti-Americanism: The History of an Exceptional Concept in American Foreign Relations* (Cambridge University Press, 2012).

Joseph Fronczak is an associate research scholar and lecturer in the Department of History at Princeton University. He received his Ph.D. from Yale University and was a Mellon Mahindra Postdoctoral Fellow at Harvard

University. He is currently writing a book titled *Everything Is Possible: Antifascism and the Makings of a Global Left During the Great Depression.*

Alec Hickmott is a postdoctoral scholar in the History Department at the University of Chicago. He received his Ph.D. in history from the University of Virginia and is writing a book titled *Black Belt Capitalism: The Land Question and the Making of the African American Freedom Struggle.*

Jennifer M. Miller is an associate professor of history at Dartmouth College and the author of *Cold War Democracy: The United States and Japan* (Harvard University Press, 2019). Her articles have appeared in *Diplomatic History, Modern Intellectual History,* and the *Journal of Contemporary History,* among others.

Alanna O'Malley is chair of United Nations Studies in Peace and Justice at Leiden University in The Netherlands. She has a Ph.D. in history from the European University Institute and is author of *The Diplomacy of Decolonisation: America, Britain, and the United Nations During the Congo Crisis, 1960–64* (Manchester University Press, 2018).

Nicole Sackley is an associate professor of history and American studies at the University of Richmond. She has published in *Diplomatic History, History and Technology, Journal of Global History, Modern Intellectual History,* and *Agricultural History.* She is completing a book entitled *Co-op Capitalism: Cooperatives, International Development, and American Visions of Capitalism in the Twentieth Century.*

Jayita Sarkar is senior lecturer in economic and social history at the University of Glasgow and the founding director of the Global Decolonisation Initiative. Prior to joining Glasgow, she was a tenure-track faculty at Boston University. She is the author of *Ploughshares and Swords: India's Nuclear Program in the Global Cold War* (Cornell University Press, 2022).

Erum Khalid Sattar is a lecturer (core faculty), program director, and water diplomacy track leader in the Sustainable Water Management Program, Friedman School of Nutrition Science and Policy and the Tufts Institute of the Environment at Tufts University. Her articles have appeared in *Water Policy,* the *University of Michigan Journal of Law Reform,* and the *Journal of Food*

Law and Policy, among others. She has upcoming chapters in the *Research Handbook on Energy Law and Ethics* and the *Research Handbook on Political Economy and Law* and is completing a book titled *Water as Power: The Law and Politics of Federalism in the Indus Basin.*

Jason Scott Smith is a professor of history at the University of New Mexico. He is the author of *Building New Deal Liberalism: The Political Economy of Public Works, 1933-1956* and *A Concise History of the New Deal*, both published by Cambridge University Press.

INDEX

ACKNOWLEDGMENTS

This volume began as a three-day conference sponsored by the O'Connell Initiative for the History of Global Capitalism and by the History Department at Fordham University. Special thanks to David Hamlin, Asif Siddiqi, and Audra Furey-Croke for their support with the conference, as well as to Rosemary Wakeman for her early discussions about the shape of such an endeavor. Rosemary and Asif have been unfailingly thoughtful and kind as directors of the Initiative. Dave consistently exceeded his remit as Department Chair, and many discussions with him have helped shape my understanding of the how diplomacy and capitalism functioned in concert throughout history. In their tireless work, these historians are sterling examples of how warm collegiality and rigorous debate can help create new intellectual homes. A hearty thanks as well to Steven Stoll, Samantha Iyer, and Vanessa Ogle for their comments on individual papers. In addition to the authors of each chapter here, thanks to Jamie Martin and Christy Thornton for their papers and comments at the conference.

Finally, thank you to Bob O'Connell for his generous support of studies of capitalism in U.S. and world history through his initiative with the Fordham History Department. In addition to his financial support, we also had the invaluable fortune of his fellowship and participation in the conference. It is wonderful to have a donor so interested in creating a stimulating environment for intellectual exchange.

Working with Bob Lockhart and his team at the University of Pennsylvania Press has been both a constructive process and a joy. Thank you to Jon Dertien, Noreen O'Connor-Abel, and Zoe Kovacs for their close attention to detail. Thanks, too, to Alexander Trotter for his careful preparation of the book's index. Two anonymous peer reviewers made several terrific suggestions about improving individual chapters and the volume as a whole.

My deepest gratitude is to my family. Rick, Robin, and Nathanael Dietrich have provided support in ways big and small for just over four decades, as have Eduardo Jiménez Vega, Paula Vega Ventura, and Eduardo Jiménez Fragoso more recently. Finally, I could not have completed this project without the extraordinary love and patience of Verónica Jiménez Vega and Emiliano Dietrich-Jiménez. I love you both always.

CPSIA information can be obtained
at www.ICGtesting.com
Printed in the USA
JSHW050813140322
23837JS00003B/3

9 780812 225310